Missionaries and modernity

Manchester University Press

STUDIES IN IMPERIALISM

General editors: Andrew S. Thompson and Alan Lester
Founding editor: John M. MacKenzie

When the 'Studies in Imperialism' series was founded
by Professor John M. MacKenzie more than thirty years ago,
emphasis was laid upon the conviction that 'imperialism as
a cultural phenomenon had as significant an effect on the
dominant as on the subordinate societies'. With well over
a hundred titles now published, this remains the prime concern
of the series. Cross-disciplinary work has indeed appeared
covering the full spectrum of cultural phenomena, as well as
examining aspects of gender and sex, frontiers and law, science
and the environment, language and literature, migration and
patriotic societies, and much else. Moreover, the series has
always wished to present comparative work on European and
American imperialism, and particularly welcomes the
submission of books in these areas. The fascination with
imperialism, in all its aspects, shows no sign of abating, and
this series will continue to lead the way in encouraging the
widest possible range of studies in the field. 'Studies in
Imperialism' is fully organic in its development, always
seeking to be at the cutting edge, responding to the latest
interests of scholars and the needs of this ever-expanding
area of scholarship.

To buy or to find out more about the books currently available in
this series, please go to:
https://manchesteruniversitypress.co.uk/series/studies-in-imperialism/

Missionaries and modernity

Education in the British Empire, 1830–1910

Felicity Jensz

MANCHESTER UNIVERSITY PRESS

The right of Felicity Jensz to be identified as the author of this work has been asserted by them in accordance with the Copyright, Designs and Patents Act 1988.

Published by Manchester University Press
Oxford Road, Manchester M13 9PL
www.manchesteruniversitypress.co.uk

British Library Cataloguing-in-Publication Data is available

ISBN 978 1 5261 5297 8 hardback
ISBN 978 1 5261 7443 7 paperback

First published by Manchester University Press in hardback 2022

This edition published 2023

The publisher has no responsibility for the persistence or accuracy of URLs for any external or third-party internet websites referred to in this book, and does not guarantee that any content on such websites is, or will remain, accurate or appropriate.

Typeset by Sunrise Setting Ltd

Contents

Acknowledgements

This monograph was funded by the Deutsche Forschungsgemeinschaft (DFG, German Research Foundation) Excellence Strategy – EXC 2060 'Religion and Politics. Dynamics of Tradition and Innovation' – 390726036. In this Cluster of Excellence located at the Westfälische Wilhelms-Universität Münster, Germany, I am privileged to be part of a dynamic interdisciplinary academic community and have benefited greatly over the years from the discussions and ideas that have circulated between and with colleagues, and from the work of these those behind the scenes. These people include: Hanna Acke, Gerd Althoff, Liliya Berezhnaya, Heike Bungert, Pia Doering, Wolfram Drew, Frauke Drewes, Sait Duran, Dina El Omari, Iris Fleßenkämper, Christel Gärtner, Klaus Große Kracht, Judith Grubel, Regina Grundmann, Nils Jansen, Kirsten Kamphuis, Mareike König, Vít Kortus, Andrew Krause, André Krischer, Julia Lingens, Armin Owzar, Mrinal Pande, Ulrich Pfister, Detflef Pollack, Rüdiger Schmitt, Christina Schröer, Julia Simoleit, Barbara Stollberg-Rilinger, Julian Strube, Martina Wagner-Egelhaaf, Annette Wilke and Alexander Yendell. Funding from the Cluster has provided me with the opportunity to organise two international conferences to discuss themes which have been central for the completion of this monograph, one on missionary periodicals (with Hanna Acke in 2010) and one on non-European missionary teachers (in 2014). The ideas in this book were also sharpened through interactions with a broader academic community including workshops, guest lectures and conferences in Australia, Austria, Canada, Denmark, India, Ireland, Germany, South Africa, the United Kingdom and the United States. I particularly thank my mum, Ann Jensz, for flying alone from Australia to Germany and then together with me and my toddler from Germany to South Africa so that I could attend a conference, mostly undistracted. My thanks extend to Peter Kallaway and Rebecca Swartz for inviting me to that memorable conference at the University of Cape Town.

I wish to thank the staff at the research libraries I consulted in Australia, Canada, Germany, the UK and the United States. Not all of the research that I undertook for this monograph ended up in the printed form, and for this I am grateful to my editor, Emma Brennan at Manchester University Press, as well as the series editors and reviewers for helping me shape what I had into something different, but, hopefully much better, than I initially anticipated. Any shortcomings remain mine. My work was made lighter by a number of research assistants including Rahel Daams and Sarah Knorr. My sincere thanks also extends to the following non-exhaustive list of people, some with whom I discussed specific ideas within this monograph, and some with whom I discussed ideas that shaped the broader context of this monograph: Almut Schneider, Daniel Gerster, Geertje Mak, Hugh Morrison, Jan Hüsgen, Julia Hauser, Lanie Yaswinski, Lorraine Parsons, Matthew Fitzpatrick, Patricia Grimshaw, Paul Peucker, Rebekka Habermas, Richard Hölzl and Tim Allender.

The two most important people in my life are thanked last: thank you Mark and Ezra for filling my non-working moments with joy, laughter and bike rides.

Abbreviations

Aborigines Committee	Select Committee on the Treatment of Aborigines (British Settlements) of 1836–37
APS	Aborigines Protection Society
BFSS	British and Foreign School Society
BMS	Baptist Missionary Society
CMS	Church Missionary Society
CO	Colonial Office
HC Deb	House of Commons Debate
HC PP	House of Commons Parliamentary Papers
HL Deb	House of Lords Debate
LMS	London Missionary Society
LSA	London Secretaries Association
National Society	National Society for Promoting the Education of the Poor in the Principles of the Established Church throughout England and Wales
SFG	Brethren's Society for the Furtherance of the Gospel
SPCK	Society for Promoting Christian Knowledge
SPG	Society for the Propagation of the Gospel in Foreign Parts
TNA	The National Archives
WMMS	Wesleyan Methodist Missionary Society

Introduction: entangled histories of missionary education

In April 1834, Jabez Bunting, Secretary of the Wesleyan Methodist Missionary Society (WMMS), wrote to John Lefevre of the Colonial Office, London, England, in relation to a plan proposed by the British government to establish a system of education for the soon to be freed slaves in the British West Indies. His letter began with:

> Our long experience, as a Missionary Society, in various parts of the world, and especially among various tribes and classes of *heathen* and other *previously uninstructed* people, has fully convinced us, that any Education dissociated from religion, or not avowedly and habitually connected with *some* form of Christianity Profession and Discipline, is exceedingly inefficient, and will fail to accomplish, in any large or permanent degree, those objects even of civil amelioration and of social order and security, which must be supposed to be contemplated by the State, when it undertakes to afford pecuniary assistance to plans of this description. We respectfully state our earnest hope, that no alterations will be made in the plan for educating the Negro Youth, which would so far *generalize* the instruction to be given, as in fact to *neutralize* it also, as to its moral influence and public benefit. [emphasis in original][1]

Bunting's comments encapsulated the beliefs of many evangelical missionary societies in the nineteenth century that education without religion would fail to shape non-Europeans within the British Empire into good Christians and good subjects. Christian education was imperative, Bunting argued, to underscore governmental desires for 'civil amelioration [...] social order and security'.[2] Bunting's comments were specifically directed to the proposed Negro Education Grant, for which governments and missionary bodies cooperated to provide 'religious and moral education' for emancipated slaves.[3] His comments also reveal the growing expectations of evangelical missionary societies from the 1830s that they would collaborate with governments more generally as the providers of education to 'heathen' and 'uninstructed' peoples. In this logic, missionary societies were the most suited to provide schooling as they were the only ones with the ability to provide religious and moral instruction infused across all aspects of the curricula and thereby help colonised societies to fulfil their potential.

Western schooling was a tool used to transform people considered to be 'traditional' into people considered to be 'modern'. Along with infrastructure, such as railways, plantations and factories, colonial schools were visual markers of colonial modernity. Schooling had the potential to reorder societies through creating epistemic cleavages and provided other ways to view and connect to the broader world. Through schooling, European ideas of modernity were presented to, and at times indeed forced upon, non-European peoples. The technologies taught in schools, such as writing, were thought to 'modernise' peoples in oral cultures. Colonial schooling also provided local people with a means to engage with Western forms of knowledge, sometimes on their own terms. The ideologies, premises and assumptions that informed colonial education were themselves constantly in flux, responding to local specificities as well as to broader social and political changes. A constant in this flux was the belief held by evangelical Protestant missionary groups that they were best placed to provide education to non-Europeans in the colonies and with it access to missionary modernity. From the instigation of the Negro Education Grant in the 1830s, missionary schooling in the colonies was increasingly undertaken with the support of colonial governments, yet this relationship was not always easy. This book traces mission schooling from the 1830s, a period in which missionary education was central to humanitarian governance, to the disappointments of the early twentieth century when missionary schooling was perceived as not having reached its full potential due to the secularising influences of colonial modernity and of local and imperial governments.

Within the framework of the nineteenth century, there was a belief in progress, development and growth associated with the implementation of Western-style modernity. I make a distinction in this book between what David Scott has called 'colonial modernity' and what I term 'missionary modernity'.[4] Both colonial and missionary modernity recognised that the rate of modernisation might be different across different cultures and colonies dependent upon the institutions and peoples encountered, yet both forms rested on the assumption of Western superiority of politics or religion.[5] I argue that whereas colonial modernity was driven by aspects of colonial governmentality that shaped and categorised non-Europeans into political subjects through 'modern' political instruments such as voting, political participation and the census, the rationale driving missionary modernity was religious rather than political. Missionary modernity took on many of the liberal ideas of the age such as economic independence of individuals through the toils of their own labours, universal education and female emancipation from 'traditional' roles, including those associated with 'traditional' marriage. Missionary modernity focused on the rejection of 'heathen' superstition and 'traditional' religions and expected an embracing of Christian faith and morality. It used religious instruments such as church order and moral discipline to shape non-Europeans into religious subjects, and used modern forms of media, such as mass published tracts and periodicals, photographs and magic lantern shows, to raise awareness and support amongst potential donor communities to extend missionary reach in colonised lands. Schooling was an integral instrument of missionary modernity, even as the concept of missionary modernity shifted over time to respond to local and larger circumstances. Schooling was a consistent means used to instil Christian morality and to create strong ties to denominational identities. Although missionary modernity co-existed within a colonial system, it did not always do so easily, nor did all participants in mission schooling conform to various ideals of modernity. This monograph examines competing expectations held for the schooling of non-Europeans in the British Empire by evangelical missionary societies, various governments and non-European groups as a means to participate in or reject certain ideas about 'modernity' within the colonial context. The main argument developed within this book is that British missionary groups sought to combat their marginalisation in the nineteenth century during a period of secularisation by dynamically positioning themselves as the most apt providers of education to non-Europeans within the British colonies. In examining schooling as an aspect of missionary modernity, the book underscores the ways in which missionary groups proved and maintained their legitimacy in a modernising and secularising world amidst countervailing criticism from varied sources.

Across the British Empire, there were historical commonalities as well as disjuncture across varied temporal and spatial sites in the history of mission education. To chart these, I predominately follow the major and most important missionary groups in Britain in the nineteenth century, including the Baptist Missionary Society (BMS, 1792), the Church Missionary Society (CMS, 1799),[6] the London Missionary Society (LMS, 1795), the Moravian Church (under the auspice of the 'Brethren's Society for the Furtherance of the Gospel among the Heathens' from the 1760s) and the WMMS (1813).[7] These missionary bodies targeted various groups, and often had separate missions to target home, colonial and foreign (or 'heathen') groups. Here the focus is upon the latter: missions to non-Europeans, often initially referred to as 'heathen' missions. The main spaces examined in this book are British India, Ceylon (Sri Lanka), Southern Africa and the West Indies, with reference made to other colonial spaces, such as the settler colonies in Australia and Canada and the political entities that they became after federation and confederation respectively. In some of these spaces, such as Sri Lanka, the remnants of other European colonial powers affected the ways in which missionary schooling was conceived of and enacted. Across the broad geographical space of the British Empire there was no universal policy for schooling, nor was this ill-defined polity uniformly governed. Numerous political entities affected policies for the schooling of Indigenous and non-European children on mission stations, from community, local, missionary and colonial to imperial bodies. In the dynamic and constantly changing environments of colonial societies, missionaries were often the instigators of schooling, yet their work was contingent on both local as well as governmental engagement. In order to conceptualise and analyse such a seemingly disparate topic, I distinguish three overarching topics in transnational educational spaces: organisations and actors; ideologies and discourses; and spaces.[8] Here the organisations and actors are predominantly British evangelical missionary societies, their executives as well as individual missionaries. Ideologies surrounding the provision of education are predominantly examined through three frames of reference: government discussions on the role of missionaries in colonial education; at missionary conferences to which numerous missionaries from various societies attended; and in missionary periodicals that aimed to engage home audiences to support continuing missionary work. The reactions to these ideologies from local people are examined through their own words, particularly through the writings of prominent individuals and local workers. Both actors and discourses circulated throughout global as well as local religious networks, demonstrating that the boundaries of the British Empire were porous, with influences on schooling coming from beyond the British world. In examining actors, ideas and spaces this book offers a rich understanding of how the changing concepts of schooling affected the self-representation of missionary groups in their strivings to shape the 'rising generation' (a Biblical reference to Matthew 13:33) in the colonial world. These changes, in turn, reveal the tensions between missionary modernity and colonial modernity with its secularising effects.

By placing various Protestant missionary societies in the same frame, the book does not generalise missionary education, but rather provides insight into moments in which similarities in aims and methods were evident, and times when they diverged. It also does not assume that missionary societies and individuals cooperated unconditionally with one another, as there were many tensions and much competition between different missionary groups. Yet they did at times collaborate and openly communicate, such as at the 1860 Liverpool Missionary Conference and the 1910 World Missionary Conference in Edinburgh, both of which are examined in depth in this book. These conferences brought missionaries from various societies together to share their experiences with schooling and to make general recommendations on how best to facilitate the Christian education of non-Europeans against the backdrop of missionary modernity. Missionary groups were aware of the particulars of their situations and were themselves often careful to detail the specific historical, cultural and political influences that affected their work. Nevertheless, beyond these specificities was an unwavering belief that Christianity embodied the highest moral tone of all religions, with evangelical missionary education considered to be the most appropriate means to 'raise' the moral and religious tenor of all societies, particularly through the schooling of children and females. Thus, although the methods and circumstances of schooling may have been adapted to different local circumstances by various missionary bodies, an overarching belief was maintained that schooling without religion was no education at all.

The two terms – education and schooling – are intertwined and their interplay had ramifications beyond their singular implications. Education is conceived here in broad terms to connote attempts made to mould and change the character of the pupil within, but also beyond, the geographical confines of the school proper with the hope that epistemic change within an individual would influence broader societal notions of morality, character, respectability, religion and politics. Schooling is conceived here as a means to effect such changes within the structures and confines of the immediate geographical sites of schools through the normalisation of knowledge attained by the provision of specific curricula increasingly dictated by external actors over the time period examined here. It is acknowledged that the physical sites of schools were not homogeneous with schools taking place in the open, in churches, in other structures and in purpose-built structures. Missionary schooling was thus one of a variety of forms of missionary education, with preaching also a form of broader education for social change. In focusing upon schooling, the book examines how it was part of the concerted effort of missionaries to cultivate a person, with many of the lessons learnt in the classroom expected to be enacted in daily life and diffused throughout communities. Indeed, schooling was an important means through which social and moral change was expected to 'prepare' people for inclusion into British colonial contexts and a particular form of missionary modernity. Here the focus is upon schooling as a site in which non-Europeans were educated in terms of European expectations and to fulfil European needs and Christian norms. This is not to suggest that local parents had no influence on how schools were run, but rather that their ability to influence school curricula was limited compared to the influence of missionaries, and increasingly of governments.

During the nineteenth century, questions increasingly emerged in political and humanitarian circles as to the status of non-Europeans within the British Empire. Education, and schooling particularly, was seen as key to the 'civilising mission' of creating new colonial subjects who would be 'disciplined to be subject to others'.[9] Religious groups were the natural allies for governments to provide education, as schooling was an essential part of evangelical Protestant missionary work.[10] Education systems served to establish and maintain structures of social power, and education contributed to the discipline of a people through the production and reinforcement of norms.[11] Scholars have argued that education was 'vital to colonial work', yet it was never neutral or benign.[12] It was always connected to political power and often formed part of the epistemic violence inflicted on non-European peoples. Such epistemic violence contributed to the dispossessing of Indigenous peoples, it created injustices and it contributed to the 'operations of hegemonic social structures and systems of power'.[13] It also provided new opportunities and new technologies for non-Europeans to engage in a globalised world, and for local people to become involved in various structures of colonialism. Education and colonialism were entangled so tightly that scholars such as Sanjay Seth have argued that colonialism was 'an essentially *pedagogic* enterprise' [emphasis in original].[14] Schooling was not the only means of knowledge transmission, but its increasing formalisation and standardisation contributed to the normalisation of knowledge, often to the detriment of Indigenous epistemologies.

The practices of colonial education, as for colonialism more broadly, were too varied to generalise in absolute terms. Indeed, as many authors have noted, there was no one unified imperial policy for colonial education.[15] However, as I argue here, the ideology that non-Europeans were 'lacking' and needed 'raising' through (missionary) schooling was common across the British Empire. It was in the interests of various colonial governments to engender notions of civic inclusion through education, both to mitigate the likelihood of violent uprisings, and to assimilate and regulate potential labour forces. Government groups were also keen to instil Western morality in non-Europeans as a form of self-regulation, or, in Foucauldian terms, a form of governmentality which rested upon the pastoral care undertaken by various religious organisations as opposed to external discipline.[16] Beyond such aims was the desire to provide non-Europeans with skills that would facilitate their assimilation into the economic and political structures of colonial society. On an ideological level, schools, as well as universities, were able to instil a sense of group cohesion, whether based on social, religious or political common denominators.[17] Evangelical missionary bodies wished to be engaged in this process in order to maintain their own status as well as to fulfil their aims of converting people to Christianity and of raising the moral tone of society. Local elites were commonly the initial targets of education, and when they were not amenable missionaries turned to non-elite children, believing both that the minds of young people were easier to mould, and that the labour of older people was too economically important to engage them with 'bookish' learning. There was an expectation that children would informally impart knowledge that they had learnt in mission schools to family and other community members and would thus diffuse Christian teachings beyond the school.

Through providing schooling, missionaries exposed masses of non-Europeans to Western forms of (post) enlightenment thought. Schools were conceived of as 'nurseries of the church', and were spaces in which pupils were cultivated to be model Christians, moral subjects and loyal church members. Those were indeed the hopes; however, the realities were often more complicated, with missionary bodies at the start of the twentieth century disparaged for their lack of success in cultivating New Christians in non-European lands. In the complex, heterogeneous and messy spaces of colonial encounters with Indigenous and non-European peoples, missionary education was considered a means to 'civilise and Christianise', with the relative focus upon these two concepts often in flux. Debates pertaining to missionary education reverberated in the metropole, notably through addressing questions of moral authority, liberalism, religious equality and the appropriateness of religious groups receiving government funding. This book considers the ideologies behind the provision of schooling, the representations of schooling, the tensions surrounding government involvement and the global networks in which associated ideas and ideals were spread, shared, contested and discussed. While it acknowledges and alludes to moments in which colonised peoples adapted and resisted forms of missionary education, this book does not consider in depth the adaptation of ideas by colonised peoples, partly as this would require a different methodology that relied upon micro analysis and case studies rather than the focus upon the history of ideas and ideologies taken here. Moreover, the majority of the sources that this book draws on were written by men, an indication of the gendered structure of nineteenth-century missionary societies, as well as the silencing of women's voices through archival practices. Accordingly, the book considers the ideal of missionary schooling yet does not undertake in-depth examinations of pedagogical theory or practice, an area in which many women and non-Europeans were engaged.[18] But missionaries who are the broader subjects of this book also did not spend much time engaging with pedagogical theory. Teachers in mission schools were often untrained men and women who learnt in the field, or had some limited training before being sent overseas, or were seen to be capable pupils turned teachers of such schools. Generally speaking, nineteenth-century missionary teachers were not the educational experts that missionary bodies eventually cultivated by the start of the twentieth century.

Positioning of this book

The role of missionaries in Indigenous education was and is ambiguous and often contradictory, with contemporaneous observers as well as recent scholars often divided over how to evaluate the results of missionary education. Some scholars view missionary education as a humanitarian rather than imperialist act, while others focus upon the detrimental nature of missionary education in terms of cultural destruction and cultural hegemony.[19] In 2020, Kirsten Kamphuis and Elise van Nederveen Meerkerk characterised the literature on education under colonialism into four 'different strands'.[20] They distinguished one strand that has focused on the 'moral uplifting' and conversion of local people through missionary education. A second strand has focused on the introduction of primary education by colonial governments as an aspect of the 'civilising missions', and thereby has focused upon secular motives. A third strand has focused on statistical analysis of the level of colonial governmental investment into education, often in an attempt to find economic roots of educational disparity. The most recent developments they characterised under a fourth strand, which 'analyses colonial education through the lens of a less strict division between missionaries and state actors', bringing to light 'the complex dynamics between the mission, the state and indigenous actors that were at play beyond their often conflicting interests'.[21] They situate their own work in this last strand of historiographical tradition. In this book, I also follow this position of not focusing on a purely religious or secular position; rather, I place missionaries of different denominations, various levels of governments as well as various groups of local people in the same frame of analysis. This approach underscores the complexities, nuances, differences and similarities of the dynamical spaces of missionary education in the British colonial world.

This book is one of the first in a new wave of monographs engaging with the broader topic of education for non-Europeans across and within the British Empire, and addresses multiple state and non-government actors. Central to these studies is the idea that knowledge and ideologies circulated in imperial circuits, often outside and parallel to the metropole–periphery dichotomy, creating 'networks' and 'circuits of empire'.[22] Scholars such as Alan Lester and Fae Dussart, Catherine Hall and Tony Ballantyne use missionaries and humanitarians as lenses though which ideas and practices that did not necessarily originate from Britain were disseminated and morphed over the permeable boundaries of empire.[23] In the last few years, a number of book-length studies have appeared on the topic of education for Indigenous children, which take the British Empire, or a large section of it, into consideration and often focus upon the actions of missionary societies. Helen May, Baljit Kaur and Larry Pochner's 2014 study dealt specifically with infant schools, and examined them in the context of a broader imperial setting, examining schools in British India, Canada and New Zealand.[24] This present book extends their scope through encompassing various schools beyond those just for infants, and extends beyond their geographical locations, whilst following their approach of examining the way in which ideas about education circulated throughout the British Empire. In her 2019 monograph, Rebecca Swartz examined education, including schools for different aged pupils, as a means of bringing non-Europeans into labour markets within the British Empire.[25] However, she did not place mission schools or their ideologies as a central part of her focus, nor did she focus upon the tensions between secular and religious education. In contrast, this book argues that missionaries were central actors in providing and shaping colonial forms of schooling.

Missionary work in the colonies, including their educational work, has been deemed 'cultural imperialism', and often seen as an inextricable aspect of European empire building.[26] Secular historians have increasingly drawn upon missionary archives to determine the roles of individuals, institutions and denominations in colonialism.[27] Despite the ubiquitous nature of missionary schooling and the centrality of education for the formation of the 'other' into a colonial subject, mission schools have not received much sustained scholarly attention within colonial or imperial histories in terms of an empire-wide approach.[28] More commonly, histories of missionary schooling have been bounded spatially or denominationally.[29] The site of the most intense academic focuses on the role of missionaries in colonial education has been British India, where a number of studies have examined the role of missionary education in light of the secular educational landscape established by the British.[30] Outside the Indian context, missionary education has often been a topic confined to scholars of the history of education, with initial work focusing upon case studies. One of the first major studies was Brian Holmes' edited collection from 1967 on educational policy and mission schools which examined case studies from the British Empire. The reprinting of this book in 2007 demonstrates its ongoing relevance some forty years later.[31] Holmes postulated that there was a general sequence throughout the British Empire of the arrival of traders, the arrival of missionaries, the establishment of mission schools and the subsequent arrival of British officers, who 'gradually secularized the control of education'.[32] I demonstrate that this general sequence was more complex.

Secularisation did not always occur in all aspect of missionary schooling, and at times not always at the behest of governments, but sometimes also from communities where missionaries were active. More recent studies on missionary education in colonial spaces (often in edited collections) have moved towards examining the topic of mission schools through transnational and postcolonial perspectives.[33] Taken together, such studies demonstrate the dynamic nature of missionary education, noting that such work was not monolithic, but rather in practice played itself out differently as the various colonies and protectorates dynamically responded to local environments.[34]

When the study of Christian missions in the non-European world increasingly became a topic of interest for secular scholars from the 1990s, schooling was not initially a focus of investigation.[35] Moreover, secular historical studies were often bounded geographically, like those in the history of education.[36] The methodological approach of placing colonial education within a larger imperial framework has been increasingly taken up by scholars in the last few years. As proponents of such an approach, Peter Kallaway and Rebecca Swartz have argued that: 'Colonial educational history can only be satisfactorily explained if it is related to social, economic and political changes in the imperial heartlands *and* the specific circumstances of diverse colonial contexts' [emphasis in original].[37] The present study, whilst agreeing with the premises of Kallaway and Swartz, takes a slightly different approach by placing the dynamic ideologies of missionary education in the foreground. With this study, a particular focus is placed on how these ideologies were transferred, transformed and transmogrified across geographical, political, denominational and cultural frames over the long nineteenth century into a period of perceived increasing secularity. This approach highlights the ambiguous nature of missionary education, and complicates simple narratives of cultural imperialism. Although missionary societies argued that they were the most appropriate groups to provide education, by the start of the twentieth century, they themselves were ambivalent of the outcome, being aware that mission schools could both contribute to the creation of a moral social order as well as having the potential to foster moral crisis and anti-British sentiments.

Missionaries and governments: religion, modernity and secularisation

In the nineteenth century, education was generally seen as 'a characteristic feature of modern civilization'.[38] The provision of universal liberal education was considered to reduce crime, to improve the condition of the poor, to improve the 'moral character of man' and to unite people 'in one whole, or integral part of the nation [such that] they will be enabled, by the immense strength arising from their union, to obtain redress of their grievances by prudent, sober, and legal means'.[39] The welfare of the nation as well as the welfare of the individual were perceived to jointly benefit from universal liberal education. Colonial governments also had an interest in the creation of moral subjects; as Jabez Bunting's comments at the beginning of this introduction elucidate, religious people were considered to be necessary for the social order and security of a society. Religious education was thus considered indispensable for the creation of Christian subjects; however, questions were increasingly raised in government circles as to what else should be included in curricula.

It has been argued that the most important legacy of Christian missions was the introduction of secular education, which is seen by many to have modernised the non-Western world.[40] Yet, as this book argues, there was a belief amongst missionary groups that for non-Europeans to embrace 'modernity' efficiently, they needed a particular form of modernity – 'missionary modernity' – that included the Christian education of locals in schools. In the nineteenth century, the distinction between religious and secular education was not always clear, particularly as missionary groups were the predominant providers of schooling. The British Imperial government supported religious schools in its colonies (with India being somewhat of an exception), and debates surrounding schooling generally did not focus on whether religion ought to be taught but rather on who ought to supply schooling in general. This differed to the situation in the French colonies where a strict(er) separation between religion and politics was in place, often making the work of missionaries difficult.[41] However, as British Imperial and colonial governments took much more active roles over the century in schooling their subjects, missionaries were forced to reconsider how the religious content of schooling could still be delivered and how they could maintain their moral authority in light of governmental conditions applied to educational work in return for providing funding and implementing external examination.

Missionary methods were heterogeneous; however, as attested to by discussions at various missionary conferences, there were similarities in the ways in which schooling and education were thought best to be brought to non-European groups over three distinct stages of mission, even though *in situ* reactions differed widely. These stages of mission 'progress' are conceived of here as introductory, permanent and reproductive stages of mission. In the introductory stage, mission groups commonly taught in English and tried to gain adherents for the mission. In the second stage, the permanent stage, a shift of teaching to the vernacular often occurred with an increase in local teachers. In the third stage, the reproductive stage, local people took over more responsibilities as missions progressed towards becoming local churches. The stages did not occur in all places neatly. Missionaries also reacted to local conditions, and adapted through changes in target pupils or subject matter. Such adaptations were by no means one-way processes: Indigenous peoples also shifted their allegiances away from missionaries when schooling did not accord with their desires – for example, through changing denominations or confessions, often creating rivalries between religious groups, or even establishing their own schools with their own 'Native' teachers.[42] Mission schools were also ideological 'spaces' which, through their form and function, articulated notions of the 'rightful' place of non-Europeans in colonial societies, whether on mission stations, in broader colonial settings or as members of transnational churches, with 'ideology' itself referring to a set of normative beliefs held by a group that informs the group's actions.[43]

In agreeing to work within government systems, missionary groups opened themselves to a double secularisation in terms both of school curricula and of structural authority. Important here is the consideration of secularisation as a form of functional differentiation between church and state duties rather than as a weakening of private religious beliefs.[44] Not all missionary groups, or individual missionaries, agreed with government involvement in schooling, yet in many ways it was an inevitable consequence of the 'civilisation' of non-European countries through colonisation as governments increasingly tried to control the lives of their subjects. Missionaries advocated the modernisation of the societies in which they worked, as did British educational reformists, with both groups equating education with modern civilisation and the increased welfare of individuals and society at large.[45] Within the mission field, Western religious education was also assumed to liberate people from heathen superstitions, following a process of introducing Enlightenment-inspired ideas such as those summed up by Immanuel Kant's dictum: '*Sapere aude! Habe Mut, dich deines eigenen Verstandes zu bedienen!* (Dare to be wise. Have courage to make use of your own reason.)'[46] This dictum called for intellectual liberation through reason, and was consequently a call for individuals to release themselves from 'self-incurred tutelage'. 'Modern' Enlightenment ideals were indeed considered compatible with Christianity.[47] Yet, many missionary societies did not equate modernisation with secularisation; rather, missionary modernity rested on Christian morals being the foundation of mission schooling, which aimed to shape a pupil into a modern colonial subject.

The secularisation of missionary schooling was complex and although it did not necessarily prevent religion being taught in schools, it shifted the authority of schooling into the hands of governments rather than religious groups. Through government intervention in mission schools, religious bodies lost their privileged positions as the dominant providers of education to non-Europeans, and thereby also lost some of their moral relevance. The scope of schooling was broadened from the creation of religiously minded people bounded by moral governance to include the creation of colonial subjects to be assimilated, integrated and included or excluded from colonial structures. Secular subjects were considered to be important for the 'raising' of the so-called 'heathen' into the folds of 'civilisation', and were perceived to contribute to the transition from communities that were steeped in superstitions to groups of modern, civilised Christian individuals who were rational and enlightened. Christian education was seen by many to facilitate the modernisation of 'traditional', non-Western societies, and to produce people aware of their individual souls that could transcend the imminent.[48] This process was seen to be in opposition to traditional beliefs, and to allow converts to Christianity to detach themselves from traditional community structures and beliefs. As Martin Fuchs, Antje Linkenbach and Wolfgang Reinhard have argued, missionaries did not limit themselves to fostering the individualisation of non-Europeans; rather, they saw themselves as 'ambassadors of a materially and intellectually superior Western culture and thus set out along with colonial administrators to propagate the modernization of all areas of life'.[49] In other words, the modernisation of non-Europeans was expected to be a total endeavour. Yet, as I argue, the different logic of colonial and missionary modernity used the same tools, such as schooling, for different ends.

Although historical argument has drawn a continuum between the Enlightenment, modernisation and secularisation, such theses have been refuted on many levels and particularly in relation to missions and enlightenment thought.[50] Moreover, there is no one master narrative that can be applied to all situations when discussing processes of secularisation.[51] Peter van der Veer has described 'secularism as a project to remove religion from public life', and notes the difference between 'secularisation as a *project*' and 'secularisation as a *process*'.[52] Religion and religiosity can also be understood in various ways, with the processes of secularisation playing out differently depending upon what aspect of religion is under examination. Here the question is not whether personal religiosity was enhanced or diminished through attending mission schools, but rather to what extent mission schools were secularised in the interaction between religious societies and government bodies in the provision of (religious) schooling. And, as a follow-up question, how did missionary bodies respond to threatened or real processes of secularisation? In this light, Mark Chaves' term 'structural secularisation' is useful for understanding secularisation as 'the declining scope of religious authority', and not the decline of religion per se.[53] He defines 'a religious authority structure as a social structure that attempts to enforce its order and reach its ends by controlling the access of individuals to some desired goods, where the legitimation of that control includes some supernatural component, however weak'.[54] His definition does not question the religiosity of people themselves, but focuses upon the capacity for religious proponents to maintain authority in light of other ideological, material or political alternatives. Extrapolating from Chaves' argument, if 'knowledge' is the goods here at stake, then missionaries used schooling to control the access of individuals to knowledge through their inclusion or exclusion as determined by religious norms. The increased involvement of governments meant that missionary groups were not the only ones with control over who obtained knowledge, or, perhaps more importantly, what knowledge was disseminated. Through exerting control over mission schools, governments were not necessarily suggesting that their citizens turn away from their private adherence to denominational religion; rather, governments wished to realise their expectations projected onto the schooling of non-Europeans in the face of the influence that churches held over the content and structure of such schools. If the knowledge that missionaries proffered could be obtained without recourse or reference to the supernatural, then this could be considered as a form of secularisation in terms of declining religious authority.

Discussions as to the nature of secularisation and the role of state and church in terms of the moral reform and education of non-Europeans provide an important framework for this study. The concept of secular education could be imbued with various definitions. As Catherine Byrne has shown in the context of the introduction of secular education in Australia in the late nineteenth century, although the concept of secular education was meant to reduce the tension between denominations, it was interpreted differently in the various colonies in which it was introduced, resulting in ongoing confusion and division.[55] She argues that secularisation was understood in terms of two definitions in the late eighteenth century and into the nineteenth century. One form was characterised as being 'hard' in so far as it argued for a distinction between government and church,[56] while the 'soft' version of secularisation was characterised by the active involvement of the state in supporting religion in the public sphere.[57] Following both Chaves and Byrne, secularisation is seen here to express a decline in religious groups' legitimisation of authority, and, in the context of this book, a decline in (religious) authority over the education of Indigenous and non-European pupils.

The entwined nature of church and state in regard to education in mission schools represents an area in which clear boundaries were initially not drawn, and even when and where boundaries crystallised the moral codes upon which mission schools were established, they maintained their validity in more secular settings and structures. In his examination of differences in the ideal of the separation of state and church over the course of the nineteenth century, Hugh McLeod has demonstrated that in reality many states and churches remained intertwined, and suggests four main reasons as to why the ideal of the separation between state and church was secondary to the reality. First, 'Dominant elites' remained connected to religious structures, which consequently maintained a 'privileged position de facto'. Second, with the advent of confessional parties in the later nineteenth century, voters were able to elect representatives who would espouse a confessional voice in parliament. Third, the state often relied upon the work of religious societies in the fields of welfare and schooling (and other philanthropic services) and thus provided religious groups with funding (and legitimisation). Fourth, some states tried to undermine the authority of the churches rather than religion itself, leading to systematic secularisation, as epitomised in the relationship between communist states and churches from 1917.[58] McLeod's third reason, the supply of philanthropic services, is evident within the educational framework, with this study revealing a highly ambiguous involvement of government in the context of missionary education; missionary workers were needed to help establish and maintain systems, yet their influence could be limited by the state. In settler colonies such as Canada and Australia where missionaries were free to provide religious instruction and where conversions to Christianity were not uncommon, governments intervened in missionary schooling in order to control Indigenous peoples, with the secularisation of schools through curricula and examinations a by-product rather than an aim of government involvement. In India, where missionaries were limited in their abilities to proselytise and where numbers of converts were low, the governments of British India reacted to the perceived threat of local agitation by secularising schools and limiting missionaries' ability to provide religious teachings within government-funded schools, leaving missionaries struggling to maintain the religious primacy of their schools. Governments in the West Indies immediately after emancipation looked to Nonconformists to partner them in educational offerings as a means to limit costs. Government inspection was undertaken with a clear directive not to interfere in religious teaching, and missionaries competed to gain and maintain denominational adherents. In southern Africa, where missionaries controlled most of the educational landscape into the twentieth century and generally enjoyed government support, governments tolerated religious education, yet increasingly pushed missionaries to teach according to government curricula, consequently provoking tensions between missionaries, governments and the recipients of instruction. Through examining the various discourses and ideologies circulating in government, missionary and colonial settings, this book examines missionary reactions to the causes, processes and aims of the secularisation of mission schools, and how these affected the aims of colonial schooling. In focusing upon the ways in which missionary groups fashioned themselves within the framework of governmental legislation and colonial policy, this study contributes to our understanding of the role of religion in the British Empire against the backdrop of increasingly secular policies.

Moral progress and 'character'

In the nineteenth century, both 'religion' and 'moral' were profoundly ambiguous terms, and could thus be loaded with meaning as required or desired. At the 1860 Liverpool Missionary Conference, the theologian and Church of England minister, Rev. Dr Baylee, posited that 'nineteen out of twenty of any cultivated audience in England would be unaware of the meaning of' the word religion, equating it with 'godliness' or 'piety', despite there being no foundation for such an interpretation in the Bible.[59] Not only theologians, but also philosophers, were aware of the difficulty of defining both these terms. In pedagogical circles, the question of whether moral and religious education were synonymous was debated, with many people take on the discussions of the German philosopher Immanuel Kant, who created a division between religious and moral instruction at the end of the eighteenth century. Kant expected virtues to determine the worth of a person without regard to the person's faith, merely according to his or her good moral conduct. Yet, even in this configuration Kant deemed religious education as important.[60]

Over the nineteenth century, governments increasingly provided provisional funding to missionary groups with the expectation that explicit doctrinal teachings would be substituted with general moral instruction, partly in order not to cause division between denominations and confessions. The close entanglement between 'morality' and 'Christianity' ensured that a Christian morality was taught. Christianity, was deemed to be the 'true religion' with regulating function. It was considered not only to civilise people, but also tended to 'ensure social peace, to maintain durable order, to strengthen the authority of the law, so limited and impotent in themselves, to dispel anarchy and barbarism, and to instil and foster tranquillity, concord, contentment, beneficence, comfort and prosperity'.[61] Religion does not have a monopoly on morality, and even in the nineteenth century, morality could be conceived of outside of religion. However, as the turn-of-the-eighteenth-century theologian William Bennet's writings indicate, Christian morality was seen as superior to all other forms as it included the following four unique principles. The first was the authority of God, who was 'an all perfect Being', in contrast to Greek and Roman philosophers who, although moral, were human and thus fallible. Second, Christian morality operated upon faith, with faith itself 'originating in knowledge and in reason'.[62] Bennet created a dichotomy between 'true religion' 'established in love, and sustained by knowledge' and the non-Christian religions of non-European peoples, which were characterised by their foundation in fear and were 'nurtured by ignorance'.[63] Education was thus an integral aspect of converting peoples to Christianity through knowledge and reason, although Bennet himself did not explicitly state this. His third peculiar principle of Christian morality was a supreme love of God, with his fourth being the necessity of living to the glory of God.[64] For Bennet, the 'extent of Christian morality is holiness, a term which comprehends every virtue and excludes every vice'.[65] Bennet's text placed more emphasis on virtues such as 'humility, meekness, true charity, forgiveness of injuries, chastity of person, [and] purity of soul' than vices, which were only cursorily mentioned, but can be generally understood as the contrary positions of the virtues.[66] His ideas of Christian virtues are found throughout many other nineteenth-century publications, including many missionary texts for children.

Although Bennet was vague as to the exact nature of a vice, within the broader genre of religious writings, and religious educational texts in particular, other publications were more forthcoming. For example, an early eighteenth-century book on the methods for erecting Charity Schools explicitly listed the following as vices that teachers should discourage in their students: 'lying, swearing, cursing, stealing, taking God's name in vain, Prophaning the Lord's-Day, speaking evil of dignities, and in any Way irreverently or disrespectfully of the Powers'.[67] This list of vices was still current in the nineteenth century, when the ideals associated with Christian respectability included self-restraint and respect for authority. The fact that seventeenth-century tracts for the moral training of infants were still being reprinted in the nineteenth century is an indication of the historical continuance of these ideas and their relevance to contemporaneous pedagogy. In one such tract reprinting Johan Amos Comenius' work, it advised that children be instilled from an early age with virtues such as temperance, cleanliness and decorum, reverence for elders, obedience, truthfulness, benignity, justice, patience, restraint, civility, courteousness and modesty.[68] Comenius' morals and virtues, as with those of the Charity Schools, were embedded in Christian traditions with the basis for much of Christian morality being the Ten Commandments, the first three which state humans' obligations to God, and the other seven their obligations to other humans. Of course, Christian morality encompasses more than just the Ten Commandments with the Bible containing further laws both of prescriptive and proscriptive nature, as well as other directives, such as the Sermon on the Mount (Matthew 5–7).[69] Indeed, Bennet, in his musings about Christian morality, placed a greater focus on the Sermon on the Mount than on the Decalogue. In addition to the Biblical legitimisation for Christian morality there was also an aspect of contemporaneous social expectations, revealing the historically located and malleable nature of morality.

Many moral tenets remained static throughout the nineteenth century; however, the broader terms of 'morality' and 'morals' were slippery, not only amongst theologians, but also amongst other influential members of the public. For example, one of the most influential policy-makers in terms of British education policy for the poor was the inaugural Secretary of the Committee of Council on Education, Dr James Phillips Kay (later Kay-Shuttleworth), who imbued the term 'moral' with various meanings including using it as a synonym for 'culture' or to ascribe blame for those lacking 'morality'.[70] As historian Richard Johnson has suggested, such practices were not confined to Kay-Shuttleworth himself, but rather reflected a trend that 'might well be traced through the whole corpus of orthodox early nineteenth-century social comment'.[71] In relation to non-Europeans, not only were their morals found lacking due to the absence of Christianity, they were generally considered as a whole to be in a threatened moral state due to the negative aspects of Western civilisation. Such sentiments were exemplified in a 1870s German-language publication – although it could well have been published in any of the major English-language missionary periodicals of the day – in which it was stated that:

> the greatest hindrance to the spread of Christianity is not the heathen with their idols, priests, and sorcerers, nor is it the Mohammeds with their sword in one hand and the Koran in the other, rather, it is the Christians themselves. From whom did the Indians and the Niggers learn to drink firewater, when not from so-called Christians? Who teaches still today the Chinese and Japanese ragamuffins to swear and to blaspheme, when not the Christian merchants, seamen, and soldiers? Who in Australia and New Zealand, South Africa and North America has exterminated the natives, when not the brutal, unscrupulous, self-serving Christians?[72]

The fight against negative moral influences was thus a two-pronged one, against both those in 'heathen' societies as well as against the vices stemming from Western society in colonial settings. Missionary groups placed themselves as the most capable group to resist both fronts, particularly through moral training in schools and extracting people from the negative influences of colonial modernity. They established mission stations far from colonists where they could, and extracted children where possible from the perceived negative effects of local customs and morals, often placing these separated children in boarding and residential schools.[73] Within the morally regulating environments of a mission station, maintaining moral discipline was imperative with sanctions implemented for immoral behaviour.[74] Children were an important focus of the missionary endeavour as they were seen as the foundations upon which new societies might be built – and schools were the physical spaces where many children received prolonged exposure to Christian values, norms, morals and virtues in order to fulfil the evangelical, edificatory and leavening aims of missionary schooling.

Sources

The sources that this book draws on include printed material, and specifically missionary periodicals, government sources such as Hansards, Royal Commissions, Acts, parliamentary papers and departmental reports, as well as archival material drawn from missionary and governmental archives, including correspondence, reports, autobiographical notes, diaries and letters. Although published missionary writings were carefully edited to provide a particular image of missionary work designed to appeal to metropolitan supporters, and their use as sources must be treated cautiously, their almost *pro-forma* nature enables the extraction of common ideas about schooling and education to be drawn from examining a large body of missionary writings, revealing common tropes about, and images of, for example, the 'heathen other', the 'infidel' and the 'new convert'.[75] Many of these tropes related to the schooling of non-Europeans, and linked into broader tropes of the helplessness, perceived stupidity, unwillingness or moral laxness of non-Europeans, and thus served to justify their schooling by European missionaries and their connection with the colonial state through government funds. The focus on missionary periodicals is intended to reveal representations of schooling that were considered appropriate for a religious public, but not necessarily the realities. Government reports and select committee debates have been utilised to elicit government responses to missionary schooling, with reports on missionary conferences used to map discussions between missionary practitioners. Missionary archives have been used to draw out the local realities of ideologies shaped in global frameworks. It has been necessary to cast a wide net over the sources as the ubiquitous nature of schooling is paradoxically responsible for the widespread dearth of printed material reporting on the quotidian life of mission schools. We have many statistics about numbers of schools, pupils and attendance rates, but comparatively little in printed materials about what pupils or communities thought about Christian schooling. The assumed normality of the endeavour consigned local responses to Christian schooling as unremarkable – that is, not remarked upon. This is a similar finding for the lives of many of the local teachers in mission schools, who are also overshadowed in missionary literature by local elites, such as bishops or preachers, or by European teachers.[76] In some ways the more common something is, the less likely it is to be considered worthy of commenting on. To take school primers as an example, from as early as the seventeenth century, they were seen as pragmatic commodities not worthy of collecting or archiving in themselves, and thus were often destroyed. The book historian John Barnard has noted that from a print run of 84,000 school primers from 1676 to 1677, only one copy is in existence today.[77] Many primers are still in existence from the nineteenth century, yet this does not necessarily tell us how they were used or what people thought of them. Although references to schools pepper missionary texts such as periodicals, they are often vague or merely a description of school statistics, rendering them uninformative about the responses to individual schools by communities. However, as a corpus and in combination with texts that elucidate the ideology behind missionary schooling, such as from missionary conferences, a more differentiated view of the role of schools for missionaries, governments and locals can be extracted. The voices of local people, often elusive in printed material, can sometimes be found in unpublished letters and diaries in missionary and government archives. Drawing upon these sources provides more detailed analyses as to local people's reactions to missionary schooling, albeit often through responses from people who had been acculturated through conversion to Christianity into a normative Christian view. These latter sources can also reveal the complexity of missionary schooling and responses often missing in official reports. For example, in the diary of a missionary couple in Australia, the wife – Polly Hartmann – noted that there was much laughter in the classroom when she tried to collect Indigenous words from her pupils.[78] This instance of cross-cultural learning and mirth serves as a reminder that not all educational offerings by missionaries were one-way, nor were they all framed by discipline and the normalisation of knowledge. Education was a complex, multifaceted, dynamic process that could never be fully controlled, and could engender laughter and lightness in spite of its indubitably hegemonic nature.

Notes on nomenclature

In this book, the term 'Evangelical' is used often in relation to the missionary groups examined. The term follows the usage as described by David Bebbington with the four major characteristics being:

> *conversionism*, the belief that lives need to be changed; *activism*, the expression of the gospel in effort; *biblicism*, a particular regard for the Bible; and

what may be called *crucicentrism*, a stress on the sacrifice of Christ on the cross. Together they form a quadrilateral of priorities that is the basis of Evangelicalism.[79]

Although evangelical groups have changed over time, here they refer to the foreign missionary movements within Anglican, Protestant, Reformed, Nonconformist, Dissenting, Presbyterian and Free Churches in the nineteenth century. This nomenclature is used with full acknowledgement that many groups of Anglicans in the nineteenth century, especially those belonging to High Church groups such as the Society for the Propagation of the Gospel in Foreign Parts (SPG), would not have considered themselves Evangelical, but rather would have preferred to have called themselves Anglo-Catholics.[80] When religious denominations are important, groups are specifically identified. The discussion of Nonconformists (Protestants not conforming to the Church of England) as a group is made in full awareness of differences between groups in terms of dogma, and that differences of opinion within groups could at times be greater than differences of opinion between groups. At times the term 'Dissenters' is used interchangeably with 'Nonconformists'. Despite differences, there were nevertheless many similarities between Evangelical groups, including their beliefs in the evangelical, edificatory and leavening aims of mission.

This study also follows common practices within colonial historiography to capitalise the words 'Indigenous', 'Black', 'White' and 'Coloured', along with 'Aborigines', 'First Nations', 'Native American Indian' and 'Native', with this last term used as an adjective to denote particularly Indigenous and non-European church workers.[81] The term 'non-European' is often used here, as missionary groups not only provided schooling to Indigenous groups, but to emancipated slaves in British colonies, who had themselves been dislocated violently from their home lands in Africa through the slave trade. At times 'local' is used as a term for non-Europeans. Indigenous group names have been used where known or appropriate. Terms that follow contemporaneous usage have also been included in quotation marks with due acknowledgement that some such terms are seen in current usage to be pejorative. Western and European are used here as terms both for people born in Europe, particularly in Western Europe, and more specifically Britain, and for people of European descent living or born in spaces in the British Empire. When referring to people of European descent who were born in the colonies, then the term 'settler colonists' is used, or sometimes 'Whites'. Differentiation between 'native' born Europeans – that is, Europeans born in the colonies – and Europeans born in Europe is only made when the distinction is necessary. Although Martin Fuchs, Antje Linkenbach and Wolfgang Reinhard suggest that 'scholars should be discouraged from classifying the world into binary, mutually exclusive categories, such as Christian vs. heathen, converted vs. not converted, individual vs. collective, modern vs. traditional, Western vs. non-Western etc',[82] despite best intentions, it would be difficult to write a history of Western missionaries in non-European spaces that did not draw upon such classifications. The caveat here is that such binary divisions were in reality always messy and bi-directionally fluid. Multiple identities were possible, hybridity plausible, third spaces inevitable and categories not mutually exclusive.

Structure of this book

This study is temporally framed between the Negro Education Grant of 1835 and the 1910 World Missionary Conference in Edinburgh. Following this introduction, Chapter 1 presents a detailed examination of the Negro Education Grant of the 1830s, which provided 'religious and moral education' to the children of emancipated slaves. It analyses the educational landscape in Britain in order to contextualise the debates and discussions that led the instigation of the Negro Education Grant, particularly those debates that focused upon the term 'liberal and comprehensive'. By focusing upon this term and imbuing it with their own meanings, numerous secretaries of evangelical missionary societies bounded together to assert their position as important partners for the Imperial government to work with to provide schooling to emancipated peoples. Schooling was not the only means by which evangelical missionary groups spread their message; however, it was the most amenable means through which they could collaborate with governments and become part of the colonial structure. The provision of missionary schooling was considered necessary to address the moral vacuum that was perceived to be left when the system of slavery was abolished in British colonies. Through arguing that they were the most apt providers of religious and moral education, Anglicans and Nonconformists increased their own standing in religious circles in Britain as their work was legitimised through collaboration with governments. Tellingly, the debates surrounding the Negro Education Grant did not include voices from those to be instructed under this system, which reflected the broader biases evident with the educational offerings of early nineteenth-century missionary societies towards transposing British educational ideas rather than incorporating local people's expectations.

After the abolition of slavery in the British colonies, humanitarians in Britain turned their attention to the mistreatment of non-Europeans in British colonies, with a Select Committee on Aborigines (British Settlements) sitting from 1835 to 1837. This Committee, the focus of Chapter 2, was established during a time of intense debate on the morality of the British Empire, and on the fates of the millions of non-Europeans who were currently, and who would potentially come, under British rule. The Committee heard evidence from missionaries, including Dr John Philip, of the LMS, and from Jan Tzatzoe (also known as Dyani Tschatshu), who was a minor Xhosa chief and Christian worker. After contextualising the Select Committee, this chapter examines Tzatzoe's evidence, plus his correspondence with the LMS after returning home, and thereby sheds light on the desires of Christian locals for the provision of missionary schooling as a means to counter the negative effects of British colonisation. The Secretaries of the LMS, CMS and WMMS also gave evidence before the Select Committee as to the negative aspects of British settlements, thereby placing the morality of the Empire in question. These same men were also involved in the discussions surrounding the Negro Education Grant, and as such underscored the notion that Christianity was considered imperative to 'reform' locals, particularly through schooling. The report has been examined by other scholars in light of humanitarian claims on the moral integrity of the British Empire. Chapter 2 examines the Report in a different light through focusing upon missionary education and Indigenous engagement with schooling in the report. It also examines the role that missionary schooling was ascribed in the recommendations. Through examining the Select Committee in the context of the Negro Education Grant examined in Chapter 1, I argue that in the there was a significant yet subtle shift in emphasis from the term 'religious *and* moral education' [my emphasis] used in the debates surrounding the Negro Education Grant to 'religious instruction *and* education' [my emphasis] in the Select Committee. Missionary schooling was still considered essential to the 'improvement' of non-Europeans. However, the moral progress of non-Europeans was no longer the all-encompassing aim to be reached through Evangelical education; rather, religious education was seen to be one part of the schooling that non-Europeans required. These two chapters together demonstrate that government discussion in Britain to include Dissenting missionary groups as providers of school contributed to the legitimisation of missionary groups both in the colonies as well as in Britain. Such discussion set the tone at the start of the century for a working relationship of these groups in the provision of 'modernity' to non-European peoples, including those recently emancipated as well as those recently brought under the rule of British colonialism.

Chapter 3 shifts the attention from discussions around schooling led by governmental groups, to discussion of schooling held by missionary groups and individuals themselves, particularly at missionary conferences. The chapter examines one of the first significant interdenominational missionary conferences to be held in the mid-nineteenth century, the Liverpool 1860

Missionary Conference. The conference was held shortly after the Indian Uprising of 1857, which had prompted anxiety as to the stability of British rule in India as well as the role of religion there. Missionary groups were quick to point out that no Christian Indians had joined in the violence and to assert that this was an indication both of the morally regulating effect provided by Protestant Christianity, and of the need for Christian religion to be taught in schools. This chapter focuses upon the role of missionary schooling in the report. It argues that the missionary conferences of 1860 reflected contemporaneous missionary ideas that formal schooling of non-Europeans was an important means to impart religious training in order to facilitate the construction of morally upstanding members of the broader Christian community, who would be versed in elementary skills necessary for assimilation into broader colonial societies, and into 'missionary modernity'. As missions progressed through the initial, permanent and reproductive stages, the aims fluctuated between evangelistic, edificatory and leavening. The stages and aims were also changed to reflect the various obstructions that missionaries confronted when working with governments and with local peoples. At the Liverpool conference, the education of women was a major topic. Chapter 3 examines ideologies behind mission schooling for females in the third quarter of the nineteenth century through examining the writings by the Indian missionary Behari Lal Singh, who was the only non-European delegate at Liverpool. Singh was a strong advocate of female education, and after returning to India after the conference, he, with his wife, who was also a teacher, established female orphan schools. Through reading Singh's writings in the context of the Liverpool Missionary Conference and the broader role of women in missions of the period, the chapter particularly highlights the changing focus of some missionary groups to more explicitly include women in schooling, and in doing so demonstrates the central role which British and local women were ascribed in missionary modernity to facilitate the Christianisation of non-European societies.

Chapter 4 focuses upon the CMS in Sri Lanka, and by doing so explores the establishment of schools within this heterogeneous cultural, social and religious landscape. Through examining autobiographical writings of converts in Ceylon, I explore what role Christian schooling played in influencing their life choices. Sri Lanka under colonial rule was a complex site where religious identities, castes and political identities were in constant flux. The chapter argues that in the framework of missionary modernity, morality, rather than academic aptitude, was the foremost quality that missionaries desired in their teachers. Yet for local people, the reasons to become teachers were complex and not just an expression of faith. In a second section, the chapter contrasts the relationship between government and Christian schools in Sri Lanka with examples in India. It argues that even under a liberal religious equality model within a government system, as was practised in Sri Lanka, mission schools were progressively secularised over the century, partly due to the forces from outside and the demands of 'modernisation'. In doing so, the chapter provides a framework in which to conceptualise government funding and inspection as a form of secularisation of mission schools.

Chapter 5 examines the outcomes of the World Missionary Conference in Edinburgh in 1910. Commission III at Edinburgh, which was dedicated to examining 'Education in relation to the Christianisation of National Life', and which declared that the educational work of missionaries over the century had largely failed in its aims to create a new generation of Christians. As with the Liverpool conference, there was a specific focus upon women's education at Edinburgh including discussions on the need to provide women in African Protectorates with low-level manual training as a form of moral education. The appropriate levels of training for Africans were based on racial hierarchies circulating at Edinburgh that portrayed Africans as intellectually less capable than Europeans or indeed Indians. Africans were considered more suited to manual labour, particularly agricultural labour, than to 'bookish' learning. At Edinburgh, the onus on the 'dignity of labour' and the moral value of work was apparent through the shift to adaptive education. Such ideas were drawn from American ideas of schooling for African-Americans from the American commissioners of the report, with the inclusion of these ideas in the Edinburgh report demonstrating internationally transposable notions of race, class and morality. Commission III's report reveals that mission education was facing mounting pressures from various sides. The three major pressures perceived to affect mission schools were, in no particular order, the spread of Islam, the increasing instigation of national educational systems, which in turn sidelined missionary efforts, and, finally, the increase in nationalist sentiments often expressed through anti-Western, anti-missionary stances. Thus, Commission III encapsulated the growing anxiety that missionary bodies were unable to effectively compete against mounting religious, political and nationalist pressure. The chapter examines the recommendations given to ensure that missionary groups would be able to maintain their position as the self-appointed most appropriate providers of education to non-Europeans, even in the face of competing religious groups, increasing nationalisation of educational systems and the burgeoning nationalist sentiments evident in the colonial world of the new century. Through analyses of the discussions at Edinburgh, the chapter illustrates the ever-present struggle to reconcile missionary and government ideals, made all the more difficult by the necessity to compromise ideals on both sides in the face of local realities and demands.

In the conclusion, the book demonstrates the constant struggle to reconcile missionary and government ideals, made all the more difficult by the necessity for both to compromise such ideals in the face of unforeseeable local realities. It argues that missionary groups constantly reshaped missionary schooling as the solution to moral anxieties throughout the British colonies. Missionary schooling was framed as the solution for the moral anxiety surrounding structural change (Chapter 1), as the solution for the moral anxiety of settler colonial violence (Chapter 2), as the solution for the moral anxiety caused by colonial uprisings (Chapter 3) and as the solution for the 'moral depravity' of local cultures and secular government schooling (Chapters 4 and 5). By the time of the Edinburgh World Missionary Conference, 1910, the self-critical nature of the report on missionary education considered missionary schooling to have failed in creating a new generation of Christians, as it struggled against the forces of secular modernisation, nationalism and Islam. Missionary schooling was too entwined within government structures and too engrained in missionary ideology to contemplate relinquishing control of educational institutions or to transfer them to secular or non-Christian groups. Rather than considering Edinburgh as a break with the idea of missionary schooling, it was a moment of reinvention as missionary groups sought to professionalise and refashion themselves as educational experts, particularly in the context of adaptive education in Africa. Through providing advice to governmental committees, missionaries ensured that their concept of missionary modernity, including ongoing investment in educational enterprises and the moral (re)formation of local groups, was secured into the twentieth century.

Notes

1   The National Archives, UK (TNA), Colonial Office (CO) 318 Colonial Office and Predecessors: West Indies Original Correspondence/118 West India Miscellaneous 1834, vol. 1, Public Office, Jabez Bunting (Wesleyan Mission House) to John Lefevre (Colonial Office), 16 April 1834, p. 406.
2   TNA, CO 318/118, Bunting to Lefevre, 16 April 1834, p. 406.
3   House of Lords Debates, UK (HL Deb), 20 June 1833, vol. 18, cc1014–1015, 'Ministerial Plan for the Abolition of Slavery'.
4   David Scott, 'Colonial governmentality', *Social Text*, 43 (1995), 191–220; Nira Wickramasinghe, 'Colonial governmentality: Critical notes from a perspective of South Asian Studies', *Comparativ: Zeitschrift für Globalgeschichte und vergleichende Gesellschaftsforschung*, 21:1 (2011), 32–40.
5   From the mid-twentieth century, there would be critical debates about the normative elements of universal theories of modernisation stemming from the West. One of the assumptions of this model was that in the process of

modernisation societies would become secularised and formalised religions would lose public standing. Empirical evidence did not support this aspect of the theory, leading sociologists such as Shmuel N. Eisenstadt to propose alternative concepts such as 'multiple modernities'. Within other fields such as critical social theory, a modernity/colonialist school emerged which also critiqued the normative elements of universal theories of modernisation, informing the field of postcolonial theory. The concept of 'missionary modernity/modernities' is informed by these debates.

6　The Church Missionary Society changed its name to Church Mission Society in 1995. The former name will be used in this book to reflect the contemporaneous usage.

7　For an overview of these societies and their missionary work see: Jeffrey Cox, *The British missionary enterprise since 1700* (New York and London: Routledge, 2008).

8　Esther Möller and Johannes Wischmeyer, 'Transnationale Bildungsräume – Koordinaten eines Forschungskonzepts', in Esther Möller and Johannes Wischmeyer (eds), *Transnationale Bildungsräume: Wissenstransfers im Schnittfeld von Kultur, Politik und Religion* (Göttingen: Vandenhoeck & Ruprecht, 2013), pp. 7–20.

9　Catherine Hall, 'Making colonial subjects: Education in the age of empire', *History of Education*, 37:6 (2008), 774, doi: 10.1080/00467600802106206.

10　Norman Etherington, 'Education and medicine', in Norman Etherington (ed.), *Missions and empire* (Oxford: Oxford University Press, 2005), p. 261.

11　Michel Foucault, *Discipline and punish: The birth of the prison*, trans. Alan Sheridan (London: Penguin Books, 1977); Graham Burchell, Colin Gordon and Peter Miller (eds), *The Foucault effect: Studies in governmentality with two lectures by and an interview with Michel Foucault* (Chicago: University of Chicago Press, 1991). See also: Sarah de Leeuw and Margo Greenwood, 'Foreword. History lessons: What *Empire, education, and indigenous childhoods* teaches us', in Helen May, Baljit Kaur and Larry Pochner (eds), *Empire, education, and indigenous childhoods: Nineteenth-century missionary infant schools in three British colonies* (Farnham: Ashgate, 2014), pp. xv–xxii.

12　de Leeuw and Greenwood, 'Foreword', p. xvi.

13　Ibid.

14　Sanjay Seth, *Subject lessons: The Western education of colonial India* (Durham, NC: Duke University Press, 2007), p. 2.

15　Clive Whitehead, 'The historiography of British Imperial education policy, Part II: Africa and the rest of the colonial empire', *History of Education*, 34:4 (2005), 441–454, doi: 10.1080/00467600500138147; Rebecca Swartz, *Education and empire: Children, race and humanitarianism in the British settler colonies, 1833–1880* (Cham: Palgrave Macmillan, 2019).

16　Michel Foucault, 'Governmentality', in Graham Burchell, Colin Gordon and Peter Miller (eds), *The Foucault effect: Studies in governmentality with two lectures by and an interview with Michel Foucault* (Chicago: University of Chicago Press, 1991), pp. 87–104. See also: Alan Hunt, *Governing morals:*

A social history of moral regulation (Cambridge: Cambridge University Press, 1999), pp. 1–3.

17 Benedict Anderson notes that the colonial school-systems played a unique role in promoting colonial nationalism. See: Benedict Anderson, *Imagined communities: Reflections on the origin and spread of nationalism* (London and New York: Verso, 1991), pp. 119–122.

18 In focusing on ideals, rather than on the effects of missionary policies on colonised peoples, this monograph follows the methodology of Catherine Hall in her article on colonial education. See: Hall, 'Making colonial subjects', p. 774.

19 For a brief overview on the humanitarian versus imperial agent debate in the Australian context see: Anne O'Brien, 'Creating the Aboriginal pauper: Missionary ideas in early 19th century Australia', *Social Sciences & Missions*, 21:1 (2008), 6–30, doi: 10.1163/187489408x308019. See also: Francis B. Nyamnjoh, '"Potted plants in greenhouses": A critical reflection on the resilience of colonial education in Africa', *Journal of Asian and African Studies*, 47:2 (2012), 129–154, doi: 10.1177/0021909611417240.

20 Kirsten Kamphuis and Elise van Nederveen Meerkerk, 'Education, labour, and discipline: New perspectives on imperial practices and Indigenous children in colonial Asia', *International Review of Social History*, 65:1 (2020), 1–14, doi: 10.1017/S0020859019000750.

21 Ibid., 3.

22 Tony Ballantyne, 'Review: Religion, difference, and the limits of British imperial history', *Victorian Studies*, 47:3 (2005), 428. See also: Tony Ballantyne, *Webs of empire: Locating New Zealand's colonial past* (Vancouver and Toronto: UBC Press, 2012); Penelope Edmonds, 'Travelling "under concern": Quakers James Backhouse and George Washington Walker tour the antipodean colonies, 1832–41', *The Journal of Imperial and Commonwealth History*, 40:5 (2012), 769–788, doi: 10.1080/03086534.2012.730830.

23 Alan Lester and Fae Dussart, *Colonization and the origins of humanitarian governance: Protecting Aborigines across the nineteeth-century British Empire* (Cambridge: Cambridge University Press, 2014); Catherine Hall, *Civilising subjects: Metropole and colony in the English imagination 1830–1867* (Cambridge: Polity, 2002); Tony Ballantyne, *Entanglements of empire: Missionaries, Maori, and the question of the body* (Auckland: Auckland University Press, 2015); See also: Tony Ballantyne and Antoinette Burton, *Moving subjects: Gender, mobility, and intimacy in an age of global empire* (Urbana and Chicago: University of Illinois Press, 2009).

24 Helen May, Baljit Kaur and Larry Pochner, *Empire, education, and Indigenous childhoods: Nineteenth-century missionary infant schools in three British colonies* (Farnham: Ashgate, 2014). See also their article: Larry Prochner, Helen May and Baljit Kaur, '"The blessings of civilisation": Nineteenth-century missionary infant schools for young native children in three colonial settings – India, Canada and New Zealand 1820s–1840s', *Paedagogica Historica*, 45:1/2 (2009), 83–102, doi: 10.1080/00309230902746495.

25 Swartz, *Education and empire*.

26 For an overview see: Ian Copland, 'Christianity as an arm of empire: The ambiguous case of India under the Company, c. 1813–1858', *The Historical Journal*, 49:4 (2006), 1025–1054, doi: 10.1017/S0018246X06005723.

27 The increased focus upon missionaries has led some people to suggest a 'boom' in secular scholarship on missionary work. Patrick Harries advocated the study of missionaries as a means of examining global history and transnational history. See: Christine Egger and Martina Gugglberger, 'Doing mission history. Ein Gespräch mit Rebekka Habermas, Patrick Harries and David Maxwell', *Österreichische Zeitschrift für Geschichtswissenschaften*, 24:2 (2013), 162. For an overview of the historiography of missionary history see, for example, Patricia Grimshaw and Andrew May, 'Reappraisals of mission history: An introduction', in Patricia Grimshaw and Andrew May (eds), *Missionaries, Indigenous peoples and cultural exchange* (Brighton, Portland and Toronto: Sussex Academic Press, 2010), pp. 1–9. Important here is also the work of Johan and Jean Comaroff, whose work encouraged others to examine missionary archives. See: Jean and John Comaroff, *Of revelation and revolution: Christianity, colonialism, and consciousness in South Africa*, vol. 1 (Chicago and London: University of Chicago Press, 1991); John Comaroff and Jean Comaroff, *Of revelation and revolution: The dialectics of modernity on a South African frontier* (Chicago: University of Chicago Press, 1997).

28 In large overviews of the British Empire, such as the multi-volume series published by Oxford at the end of the 1990s, no single chapter was devoted to education and empire, although chapters were devoted to exploration and empire, art and empire, and architecture and empire. This oversight was rectified in a 2005 chapter in the Oxford History of the British Empire Companion Series volume on Missions and Empire, which bucked the usual trend of focusing upon discrete locations, missionary societies or audiences. See: Etherington, 'Education and medicine'. See also: Hall, 'Making colonial subjects'; Antonio Novoa, 'Empires overseas and empires at home', *Paedagogica Historica*, 45:6 (2009), 817–821, doi: 10.1080/00309230903370972; Heather J. Sharkey (ed.), *Cultural conversions: Unexpected consequences of Christian missionary encounters in the Middle East, Africa, and South Asia* (Syracuse, NY: Syracuse University Press, 2013), p. 3.

29 Etherington, 'Education and medicine', pp. 261–284; Kamphuis and van Nederveen Meerkerk, 'Education, labour, and discipline'.

30 See, for example, Tim Allender, *Learning femininity in colonial India, 1820–1932* (Manchester: Manchester University Press, 2016); Tim Allender, *Ruling through education: The politics of schooling in the colonial Punjab* (New Delhi: New Dawn Press, 2006); Seth, *Subject lessons*; Hayden J.A. Bellenoit, *Missionary education and empire in late colonial India, 1860–1920* (London: Pickering & Chatto, 2007).

31 Brian Holmes (ed.), *Educational policy and the mission schools: Case studies from the British Empire* (London: Routledge & Kegan Paul, 1967, reprinted 2007).

32 Ibid., p. 7.

33 See, for example, the articles in the special section 'Imperial, global and local in histories of colonial education', edited by Rebecca Swartz and Peter Kallaway in *History of Education*, 47:3 (2018), 362–431. See also: Joyce Goodman, Gary McCulloch and William Richardson, '"Empires overseas" and "Empires at home": Postcolonial and transnational perspectives on social change in the history of education', *Paedagogica Historica*, 45:6 (2009), 695–706, doi: 10.1080/00309230903384619.

34 See, for example, Amanda Barry, 'Broken promises: Aboriginal education in South-eastern Australia, 1837–1937' (PhD thesis, University of Melbourne, Melbourne, 2008); May, Kaur and Pochner, *Empire, education, and Indigenous childhoods*; Rebecca Swartz and Johan Wasserman, '"Britishness", Colonial governance and education: St Helenian children in Colonial Natal in the 1870s', *Journal of Imperial and Commonwealth History*, 44:6 (2016), 881–899, doi: 10.1080/03086534.2016.1227032; Felicity Jensz, 'Missionaries and Indigenous education in the 19th-century British Empire. Part I: Church–state relations and Indigenous actions and reactions', *History Compass*, 10:4 (2012), 294–305, doi: 10.1111/j.1478-0542.2012.00839.x; Felicity Jensz, 'Missionaries and Indigenous education in the 19th-century British Empire. Part II: Race, class, and gender', *History Compass*, 10:4 (2012), 306–317, doi: 10.1111/j.1478-0542.2012.00838.x.

35 Seminal works include: Andrew Porter, *Religion versus empire? British Protestant missionaries and overseas expansion, 1700–1914* (Manchester: Manchester University Press, 2004); Brian Stanley, *The Bible and the flag. Protestant missions and British imperialism in the nineteenth and twentieth centuries* (Leicester: Apollos, 1992). Clive Whitehead has also contributed substantially to the discussion on government policy and missionary education. See, for example, Clive Whitehead, 'The historiography of British imperial education policy, Part I: India', *History of Education*, 34:3 (2005), 315–329, doi: 10.1080/00467600500065340; Whitehead, 'The historiography of British imperial education policy, Part II'; Clive Whitehead, 'The contribution of the Christian missions to British colonial education', *Paedagogica Historica*, 35, sup 1 (1999), 321–337, doi: 10.1080/00309230.1999.11434947.

36 To cite just a few examples since 2010 see: Sharkey (ed.), *Cultural conversions*; Martin Fuchs, Antje Linkenbach and Wolfgang Reinhard (eds), *Individualisierung durch Christliche Mission?* (Wiesbaden: Harrossowitz, 2015); Rebekka Habermas and Richard Hölzl (eds), *Mission global: Eine Verflechtungsgeschichte seit dem 19. Jahrhundert* (Köln, Weimar and Wien: Böhlau, 2014); Ulrich van der Heyden and Andreas Feldtkeller (eds), *Missionsgeschichte als Geschichte der Globalisierung von Wissen* (Stuttgart: Franz Steiner Verlag, 2012).

37 Peter Kallaway and Rebecca Swartz (eds), *Empire and education in Africa: The shaping of a comparative perspective* (New York: Peter Lang, 2016), p. 2.

38 'Education among the poorer classes of society', *The Quarterly Journal of Education*, 5 (1833), 233.

39 Ibid.

40 Jessie G. Lutz, 'Education – religious, theological', in Jonathan J. Bonk (ed.), *The Routledge encyclopaedia of missions and missionaries* (New York and London: Routledge, 2007), p. 132.

41 For an overview of such debates see: Möller and Wischmeyer, 'Transnationale Bildungsräume', p. 15.

42 See, for example, Stephen J. Ball, 'Imperialism, social control and the colonial curriculum in Africa', *Journal of Curriculum Studies*, 15:3 (1983), 237–263, doi: 10.1080/0022027830150302; Edward H. Berman, 'African responses to Christian mission education', *African Studies Review*, 17:3 (1974), 527–540, doi: 10.2307/523799; Brian Garvey, 'Colonial schooling and missionary evangelism: The case of Roman Catholic educational initiatives in North-Eastern Zambia, 1895–1953', *History of Education*, 23:2 (1994), 195–206, doi: 10.1080/0046760940230204; Terence Ranger, 'African attempts to control education in East and Central Africa 1900–1939', *Past & Present*, 32 (1965), 57–85, doi: 10.1093/past/32.1.57.

43 For the conceptualisation of mission school as spaces see: Felicity Jensz, 'The cultural, didactic, and physical spaces of mission schools in the nineteenth century', *Österreichische Zeitschrift für Geschichtswissenschaften*, 24:2 (2013), 71–92.

44 The sociologist José Casanova provides three distinctions: 'secularization as differentiation of the secular spheres from religious institutions and norms, secularization as decline of religious beliefs and practices, and secularization as marginalization of religion to a privatized sphere'. Casanova as cited in: J.C.D. Clark, 'Secularization and modernization: The failure of a "grand narrative"', *The Historical Journal*, 55:1 (2012), 161–194, doi: 10.2307/41349650.

45 'Education among the poorer classes of society', p. 233.

46 Immanuel Kant, 'Beantwortung der Frage: Was ist Aufklärung?', *Berlinische Monatsschrift*, 12 (1784), 481–494.

47 Mark Chaves, 'Secularization as declining religious authority', *Social Forces*, 72:3 (1994), 749–774, doi: 10.2307/2579779; for an overview see: Brian Stanley, 'Christian missions and the enlightenment: A re-evaluation', in Brian Stanley (ed.), *Christian missions and the enlightenment* (Grand Rapids, MI: William B. Eerdmans Publishing Company, 2001), pp. 1–21.

48 See, for example, Martin Fuchs, Antje Linkenbach and Wolfgang Reinhard, 'Introduction' in Martin Fuchs, Antje Linkenbach and Wolfgang Reinhard (eds), *Individualisierung durch christliche Mission?* (Wiesbaden: Harrossowitz, 2015), pp. 38–63.

49 Ibid, p. 40.

50 See, for example, the contributions in Stanley (ed.), *Christian missions and the enlightenment*.

51 This present study is informed by Shmuel Eisenstadt's theory of multiple-modernities, which references the multiplicities of cultural, historical, social or political differences in modern(ising) societies. See: S.N. Eisenstadt, 'Multiple modernities', *Daedalus*, 129:1 (2000), 1–29.

52   Peter van der Veer, 'Religion and education in a secular age: A comparative perspective', *Extrême-Orient Extrême-Occident*, 33 (2011), 235, 236.

53   Chaves, 'Secularization as declining religious authority', 750.

54   Ibid., 755–756.

55   Catherine Byrne, '"Free, compulsory and (not) secular": The failed idea in Australian education', *Journal of Religious History*, 37:1 (2013), 20–38, doi: 10.1111/j.1467–9809.2011.01163.x.

56   This is akin to Niklas Luhmann's functional differentiation, or Casanova's differentiation thesis on the macro level. See: Philip S. Gorski, 'Was the confessional era a secular age?', in Karl Gabriel, Christel Gärtner and Detlef Pollack (eds), *Umstrittene Säkularisierung. Soziologische und historische Analysen zur Differenzierung von Religion und Politik* (Hemsbach: Berlin University Press, 2012), pp. 189–224.

57   Byrne, '"Free, compulsory and (not) secular"', 23. This soft version could be seen as the anti-thesis of Charles Taylor's secularity 1 thesis. See: Gorski, 'Was the confessional era a secular age?', pp. 191–192.

58   Hugh McLeod, 'Separation of church and state: An elusive (illusive?) ideal', in Karl Gabriel, Christel Gärtner and Detlef Pollack (eds), *Umstrittene Säkularisierung: Soziologische und Historische Analysen zur Differenzierung von Religion und Politik*, 2nd edition (Berlin: Berlin University Press, 2014), pp. 460–480.

59   Secretaries (eds), *Conference on missions held in 1860 at Liverpool: Including the papers read, the deliberations, and the conclusions reached; with a comprehensive index shewing the various matters brought under review* (London: Strangeways & Walden, 1860), pp. 132–133.

60   W. Rein, *Encyklopaedisches Handbuch der Pädagogik. Band VII Prinzenerziehung – Schulberichte*, 2nd edition (Langensalza: Beyer, 1908), p. 923.

61   William Bennet, *The excellence of Christian morality: A sermon, preached before the Society in Scotland for Propagating Christian Knowledge, at the anniversary meeting, Thursday, 6th June 1799* (Edinburgh: J. Richie, 1800), p. 70.

62   Ibid., p. 16.

63   Ibid., p. 7.

64   Ibid., pp. 23–28.

65   Ibid., p. 28.

66   Ibid., p. 29.

67   Anon., *The methods used for erecting Charity-Schools, with the rules and orders by which they are governed. A particular account of the London Charity-Schools: With a list of those erected elsewhere in Great Britain & Ireland: To which is added, a particular account of such schools as are reported to be set up since last year. And an appendix, containing forms, &c. relating to the Charity-Schools*, 15th edition (London: printed and sold by Joseph Downing in Bartholomew-Close near West-Smithfield, 1716), p. 9.

68 Will S. Monroe, *Comenius' school of infancy. An essay on the education of youth during the first six years* (Boston, New York and Chicago: D.C. Heath & Co., 1896), pp. 18–19.

69 For more detail see: John Hare, 'Religion and morality', in Edward N. Zalta (ed.), *The Stanford encyclopaedia of philosophy* (Winter 2010 edition), http://plato.stanford.edu/archives/win2010/entries/religion-morality/ [last accessed 12 October 2020].

70 Richard Johnson, 'Educational policy and social control in early Victorian England', *Past & Present*, 49:1 (1970), 96–119, doi: 10.1093/past/49.1.96.

71 Ibid., 103.

72 'Ein schwarzer Fleck im schwarzen Erdteil', *Evangelisches Missions Magazine*, 20 (1877), 129 [my translation].

73 Geertje Mak, Marit Monteiro and Elisabeth Wesseling, 'Child separation: (Post)colonial policies and practices in the Netherlands and Belgium', *BMGN-Low Countries Historical Review*, 135:3–4 (2020), 4–28, doi: 10.18352/bmgn-lchr.10871. There is a growing literature on the legacies of boarding and residential schools for Indigenous peoples, acknowledged through governmental inquiries in some places such as Canada. See, for example, Anne Haebich, *Broken Circles: Fragmenting Indigenous families 1800–2000* (Fremantle: Fremantle Press, 2000); James R. Miller, *Shingwauk's vision: A history of native residential schools* (Toronto: University of Toronto Press, 2009); David Wallace Adams, *Education for extinction: American Indians and the boarding school experience, 1875–1928* (Lawrence: University Press of Kansas, 1995); Jacqueline Fear-Segal, 'Nineteenth-century Indian education: Universalism versus evolutionism', *Journal of American Studies*, 33:2 (1999), 323–341.

74 See, for example, Natasha Erlank, 'Sexual misconduct and church power on Scottish mission stations in Xhosaland, South Africa, in the 1840s', *Gender & History*, 15:1 (2003), 69–84, doi: 10.1111/1468-0424.00290.

75 See, for example, Robert A. Bickers and Rosemary Seton (eds), *Missionary encounters: Sources and issues* (Richmond: Curzon Press, 1996); Felicity Jensz, 'Firewood, fakirs and flags: The construction of the non-Western "other" in a nineteenth century transnational children's missionary periodical', *Schweizerische Zeitschrift für Religions- und Kulturgeschichte*, 105 (2011), 167–191; Anna Johnston, *Missionary writing and empire, 1800–1860* (Cambridge: Cambridge University Press, 2003).

76 Felicity Jensz, 'Non-European teachers in mission schools', *Itinerario*, 40:3 (2016), 389–465.

77 John Barnard, 'The survival and loss rates of psalms, ABCs, psalters and primers from the stationers stock, 1660–1700', *The Library*, s6–21:2 (1999), 148–150, 10.1093/library/s6-21.2.148.

78 Moravian Archives Bethlehem, PA, USA (MAB), Personal Papers (PP) Hartman, John Adolphus Hieronymus (HJAH), 9 Diary written by Adolf [and Polly] Hartmann (1863–1873), 8 June 1865.

79 D.W. Bebbington, *Evangelicalism in modern Britain: A history from the 1730s to the 1980s* (London: Unwin Hyman, 1989), p. 3.
80 Brian Stanley, *The World Missionary Conference, Edinburgh 1910* (Grand Rapids, MI: William B. Eerdmans Publishing Company, 2009), pp. 9–10. For a discussion of the term see also: Stuart Piggin and Robert D. Linder, *Fountain of public prosperity: Evangelical Christians in Australian history* (Clayton: Monash University Publishing, 2018), particularly the Introduction.
81 Julie Evans, Patricia Grimshaw, David Phillips and Shurlee Swaine, *Equal subjects, unequal rights: Indigenous peoples in British settler colonies, 1830–1910* (Manchester: Manchester University Press, 2003), p. 11.
82 Fuchs, Linkenbach and Reinhard, 'Introduction', p. 41.

1

'Liberal and comprehensive' education: the Negro Education Grant and Nonconforming missionary societies in the 1830s

In his 1838 report to the House of Commons, London, on his inspection tour of schools funded by the Negro Education Grant in the West Indies, Charles Joseph Latrobe was clear as to his position that: 'I have never forgotten that the special object aimed at by the measures adopted by Her Majesty's Government was the moral and religious improvement of the Negro population, and that provided that was obtained, the precise manner was of secondary importance.'[1] Latrobe had written his report just two years after the Negro Education Grant had been established in the West Indies. This grant was an experiment within the British Empire as it provided funding to both Anglican and Nonconformist missionary societies to partner with the government to supply schooling as a means of ameliorating the situation of the freed slaves and their children in the wake of emancipation. There was much concern and moral anxiety as to what would become of the West Indies in the wake of emancipation, with recent slave rebellions and uprisings in the region being a warning sign that unless a morally regulatory system was in place at emancipation then turmoil would ensue. As such, an Apprenticeship System was put in place for four years after slavery was abolished as a means of transitioning into freedom. In this chapter, the focus is on the religious and moral education that was provided. Within British government and humanitarian circles, religious and moral education was perceived to be the remedy to the morally reprehensible system of slavery. Missionary groups wished to be the providers of such education. 'Moral and religious improvement' implied the development of traits such as diligence, obedience, chastity and Christian morals. The educational offerings provided by evangelical missionaries in the West Indies before emancipation were not as extensive as in other places in the British Empire such as Canada, Ceylon (Sri Lanka) or India. The Revised Slave Code of 1823 had limited the educational offering allowed in the West Indies. Emancipation offered missionary societies the opportunity to throw themselves into schooling in a more concrete and wide-ranging way. Yet it was not self-evident that Nonconformist missionary groups would be allowed to be part of any system of education provided for emancipated slaves. Of particular importance for their potential role in providing education through the Negro Education Grant were the discussions surrounding the fifth resolution of the Ministerial Plan put forward in June 1833 in the House of Lords in London in relation to emancipation. It read:

> That his Majesty be enabled to defray any such expense as he may incur in establishing an efficient stipendiary Magistracy in the colonies, and in aiding the Local Legislatures in providing, upon liberal and comprehensive principles, for the religious and moral education of the negro population to be emancipated.[2]

The term 'liberal and comprehensive principles' was discussed in various forums at length, with these discussions encapsulated in the anxieties of government and missionaries as to the role of non-Anglican religious societies in government funding educational schemes. Not all missionary bodies were willing to work with the government, with some groups in the lead-up to the establishment of the Negro Education Grant questioning the appropriateness of collaborating with government as this could potentially limit religious freedom. In cooperating with government, missionary societies pushed for religious liberty as per their own denominational needs, yet they also bounded together as a unified front. When the Negro Education Grant was finally introduced in September 1835, initially for the building of school houses, it was extended to Anglican and non-Anglican societies, yet excluded Catholic missionary societies. By obtaining government grants, Dissenting missionary groups in Britain obtained government legitimacy for their work, and they used this to solidify their support base in Britain. This chapter examines some of the debates around the introduction of the Negro Education Grant as well as the broader British educational context in which it was introduced. Voices from parents or pupils to be taught under this system are absent, reflecting an early nineteenth-century tendency by missionary groups and colonial officials alike to speak for people, rather than to allow them to speak for themselves, especially when the people under discussion were perceived to be on a 'lower' level of 'civilisation'.

The Negro Education Grant was an opportunity for missionary societies to collaborate on the matter of schooling and to provide a common argument towards the Colonial Office as to their intrinsic role in providing the right kind of 'civilisation' to people under British colonial rule. This 'right kind' of 'civilisation' was intrinsic to the idea of missionary modernity, which took on many of the liberal ideas of the age such as economic independence of individuals through their own labours, universal education and female emancipation from 'traditional' roles; however, in contrast to 'colonial modernity', the rationale driving missionary modernity was religious rather than political. Schooling was only one method in the attempt to Christianise a population, yet, as I argue, it was the one most amenable to being incorporated into formalised government structures. Even when missionary schooling operated alongside colonial government school systems it reflected, mirrored and was in dialogue with colonial structures. This chapter examines a consolidating moment of missionary education within a government system. Through analysing the discussions and ideas which informed the introduction of the Negro education, this chapter elucidates a foundational example of missionary societies' attempts and abilities to respond to changing colonial and global circumstances, using their arguments for education as a means to prove their legitimacy and worth in the broader imperial endeavour of civilising and converting non-Europeans.

From religious offering to state duty: the beginnings of government involvement in schools

The discussions around the provision of education in the West Indies was part of a broader discussion in the 1830s as to the intrinsic value of popular schooling. In this decade, there was a movement within parliament towards a 'universal and national' British educational system that would be on par with Prussia, France and New York State in the USA,[3] with a radical movement suggesting that universal education should be run by the state and be free, compulsory and secular.[4] Such international comparisons were based upon the threat of commercial competition in countries with compulsory education, with Prussia's compulsory education seen as the basis of its military victories.[5] Universal education in Britain in the 1830s did not find the support of both political parties; rather, the parties opposed it fiercely, not at least due to the strain that such provision would place upon government coffers as well as structures.[6] The government had not contributed extensively to popular education prior to the 1830s, as before this date, and particularly throughout the eighteenth and into the nineteenth centuries, education was predominantly in the hands of voluntary societies.[7] Societies such as the Society for Promoting Christian Knowledge (SPCK, established in 1698) and the SPG (established in 1701), Sunday Schools, Charity Schools, the British and Foreign School Society (BFSS, established 1808) and the National Society for Promoting the Education of the Poor in the Principles of the Established Church throughout England and Wales (National Society) all provided formalised instruction for children of the poorer classes in various parts of Britain, and in the colonies.[8] These voluntary societies were closely connected to evangelical religious organisations of various denominations, and, characteristically, these forms of schools placed an emphasis upon the imparting of Christian morals. Charity Schools, for example, were closely connected with the SPCK, with the 'chief business' of teachers within such institutions being to 'instruct the Children in the *Principles* of the Christian Religion' [emphasis in original], those being prescribed by the Church of England.[9] Whereas education for adults was directed towards self-improvement with a religious angle, education of children was focused primarily on creating a morally upstanding element of society. The benefits of a religious education for Charity School pupils, noted the Lord Bishop of Lincoln in a SPCK sermon of 1715, was to render a pupil 'more fit for civil society'.[10] One hundred years later the SPCK was still engaged in this activity, with part of the goal being to make a pupil fit to be a future diligent employee. Similarly the ideology behind Sunday Schools was to instil working-class children with religious and secular values that advanced ideals such as Christian morality, respectability, diligence and self-improvement, as well as to strengthen the national character and to underscore British nationalism.[11] The religious and moral benefits of such education were unquestionably held to be part of the overall improvement of society to the mutual benefit of Church and State.

The idea that Christianity 'improved' people was adhered to by evangelical missionary groups into the British colonies and other parts of the non-European world. Based upon the dual concept of 'civilising and Christianising' non-European peoples, there was much discussion, and little agreement, as to which aim should be undertaken first.[12] Many missionary organisations saw preaching as the primary means to spread the Christian word, with teaching a secondary means, reaching children and women.[13] Teaching encompassed a range of activities from formalised frontal teaching in a purpose-built classroom to informal gatherings outside where basic literacy and numeracy were taught. Evangelical Christian education was founded upon the teachings of the Gospel with one important aim being 'religious and moral' improvement.[14] Ideas of religious and moral improvement and progress, civilisation and education were so tightly entwined that, as Hayden Bellenoit has noted in the context of India, missionaries 'often blurred the distinction between "moral improvement", "civilisation" and "Christianity"'.[15] For many missionary groups, Christianity and morality were so entwined that a Christian convert following Christian norms was a morally upstanding person. Or, in the words of the Moravian missionary in mid-century Jamaica, J. Buchner: 'no people can be religious and immoral at the same time'.[16] Such statements point to the broader nineteenth-century missionary belief that Christianity embodied the highest moral codes, with all other religions being inferior, and that schooling without religion was no education at all.

Schools were seen in general by missionaries to be 'nurseries of the Church' in which 'good soldiers of Jesus Christ' were shaped.[17] Evangelical missionary groups focused upon teaching the very young, as children were seen to be not as polluted by 'heathendom' as adults. Contemporary thought believed the minds of infants to be blank canvases upon which the best influences of society could be impressed, with missionaries initially treating Indigenous children as being no different in this regard.[18] The Infant schools of the LMS, for example, were opened to children from as young as one year to the age of six.[19] The focus upon infants and children was seen by many Evangelicals to be of potential benefit for the instilling of Christian love and principles at the youngest practicable age. It was also seen as an effective method of gaining 'the hearts even of heathen parents' as they observed the 'faithful care bestowed upon the children' by missionaries.[20] Children and youth were the main targets of missionary schooling, with missionary groups hoping to convert young people to Christianity, to make them life-long loyal supporters of a particular denomination and to gain access to these children's parents, their siblings and ultimately to also convert other family members to Christianity. Through the broader effects of schooling, missionary groups hoped to reach all members of a society and usher them into a missionary modernity. There was, nevertheless, also a pragmatic aspect to focusing on children as subjects of schooling, since young children were often not so entrenched within a labour force as to make their absence economically discernible.

Global discourses and knowledge transfer

Schooling was seen as an important avenue for the moral and social advancements of all children regardless of race, and as such, there were many commonalties between missionary education in the colonies to 'heathen' and 'primitive' people, and education for the poor and working classes in Britain. In both sites schooling was aimed at disciplining the young in order to enhance their subsequent social, moral and financial status, which ultimately was a means of ensuring social order through reform rather than coercion and punishment. Education through schooling was seen as a way to control and contain Indigenous and non-European peoples in the face of anxiety amongst many parts of colonial society – missionaries included – that people brought into contact with Westerners would not have the moral capacity to refrain from engaging in European vices. Or, being brought into a Western economic system, they would not be able to cope with this new wealth, but rather would squander their money in immoral ways. Schools were idealised spaces in which the pupil was safe from both Western vices and the negative influence of the 'heathen' parent and broader society. Similar ideas about the need to 'save' people from themselves through education were circulating in relation to the poor in Britain.[21] In the majority of the British Empire, race and class were intertwined concepts, as demonstrated by the use of the urban poor of London as training grounds for outgoing missionaries of the LMS.[22] These intertwined concepts were not, however, treated analogously, particularly in terms of schooling. Missionary groups used schooling as an important means of converting 'heathen' children to Christianity, and through this engaging in edificatory and leavening aims. Conversion was not the defining feature of British education (or the education of British children in the colonies); rather, British education assumed that children were already Christian with schooling deemed an important means to raise the moral tone of society. Indeed, a contemporaneous belief considered moral education to reduce crime.[23] Ideas of discipline, education and lower incidence of crime filtered to the colonies, with Canadian Dominion reports in the late nineteenth century explicitly drawing parallels between illiteracy and crime, and advocating for compulsory schooling in order to reduce numbers of prison and reform house inmates.[24] Missionary groups dwelt on similar parallels between irreligion and vice. The moral and mental improvement of non-Europeans facilitated through missionary education dovetailed well with colonial governments' desires to assimilate non-Europeans into colonial societies as labourers.[25] Yet, as this book argues, the logic of missionary modernity was foregrounded in Christian conversion rather than the creation of secular workers. Schooling was a tool used for the moral reformation of British and by extension colonial society, with schools traditionally seen to be in the service of the social bonds of the state, the church and the family.[26] However, the inclusion of Dissenters into this relationship in the colonies caused anxiety about the role of the Church of England, about religious and national loyalties, as well as about uprisings and rebellions of colonised peoples against their British colonisers.

In England, much of the rhetoric surrounding the education of the poor in the early part of the century was inherently religious and moral due to the fact that many of the bodies that provided education beyond private individual enterprise were religious. Yet even when there was a 'reassignment of administrative and charitable activities (in education, health, crime) from churches to civil agencies' throughout the nineteenth century, it should not be seen as a decline in religious commitment, but rather as a contemporaneous means to break the 'perceived monopolies' of the Church of England.[27] Schooling of the poor was strongly connected to a Victorian belief in progress. Humanitarian concern for the poor also acknowledged that moral instruction and the associated social control and discipline were constructive for national interests, including imperialism. Such sentiments were expressed in the Minutes of the Committee of Council on Education of 1846, in which schooling of the poor was seen as a means to 'promote the growth of a truly Christian civilization'.[28] Children of the urban poor were seen to be devoid of the ability to obtain an honest livelihood and to be so ignorant of Christian teachings that they were 'practically heathen'. The solution to their salvation, both physically and morally, was seen to be industrial training with religious instruction. A trade was seen to provide the children with an opportunity to escape 'from the misery of a life of crime and privation', and Christian instruction was hoped to save such children from 'ruin'.[29] As the century progressed, industrial schools were increasingly advocated by governments in current and former British colonies as a means of creating skilled labourers able to support local economies. In the aims behind the provision of industrial schools a difference between race and class can be extracted. Industrial schools were intended to save the lower classes from a life of crime and thus class could be constituted as having an essential criminal element. Race, on the other hand, was more connected to moral inferiority, but not necessarily legal transgression. For both categories of class and race, religious schooling was deemed the most effective way of regulating children and youth, and protecting them from the evils of their environments.

Pedagogical ideas as well as practices circulated in the British Empire. One of the most prominent practices was the monitorial system established simultaneously, but independently, by the Scottish Episcopalian Andrew Bell (1753–1832), who had been a chaplain in Madras, India, at the end of the eighteenth century, and the Quaker Joseph Lancaster.[30] The monitorial system relied upon the use of able children to help the teacher to impart the lessons to other, less advanced, pupils. Such a system was very attractive for schools that often struggled to find funds as well as teachers, for it obviated the need to employ more than a skeleton staff of teachers given that the students instructed each other. This system had its origins in the British colonies; indeed, early twentieth-century Indian texts explicitly state that the system of 'mutual tuition' was embedded in traditional Indian teaching practices, mitigating any British claims to having devised the system.[31] The importation of the system back into Britain demonstrated that the colonies had the potential to greatly affect the political, pedagogical and religious landscape of Britain. Its use also highlights denominational boundaries, with Bell's system being used by the Church of England from 1811, in all schools of the National Society for the Education of the Poor (National Society), a society which was closely tied to the Church of England. The Madras system – as Bell's system was alternatively known – was also used overseas by the CMS, the evangelical missionary society of the Church of England, with the Bishop of London recommending its use in 1808 for 'Negro children' to all governors of the British West Indies.[32] Lancaster's methods, rather than Bell's, were favoured by parliament and supported in the Poor Laws in 1807, and received royal support from King George III.[33] As Lancaster was a Quaker, his methods were non-sectarian, which led to him initially finding support amongst Nonconformist and secular aspects of society, including the BFSS.[34] Missionary societies, themselves often stretched financially, found use for both Bell's and Lancaster's methods, with their use depending sometimes upon denominational allegiances. The monitorial system was not without its critics, with contemporaries often criticising the system due to the rote nature of learning and stagnation of many pupil-monitors themselves due to the paucity of attention they received from the teachers. Yet with the backing of influential figures such as William Wilberforce, the system had important supporters in evangelical circles.[35] The monitorial system was seen to instil such traits as order, discipline and industry, which were traits that missionary societies valued, and hoped to instil in the people they worked amongst.[36] Moreover, Lancaster himself saw his method as a way to teach children of the laboring poor to be 'more useful and intelligent, without elevating them above their station in life for which they may be designed'.[37] It was deemed important throughout to maintain the perceived social order that was transferred through missionary schooling for non-Europeans in the colonies.

Education in Britain

From modest expenditures on schooling in the 1830s, state grants increasingly grew over the course of the nineteenth century to become, together with prisons and the funding attached to the Poor Law, the most significant sites of non-military government spending.[38] From the early 1830s, the British government granted funds for the building of schools in England. Such grants demonstrated the government's financial commitment to education, yet also the limitations of religious involvement. The first amount of £20,000 was provided through Henry Brougham's 1833 Education Grant,[39] with ensuing grants only provided to schools connected to the Church of England or to the BFSS, effectively excluding Nonconformists.[40] Furthermore, the grants stipulated that a proportion of the funds needed to be raised locally, and funding was to be dependent upon both student results and the grades of teachers employed, thus effectively preventing impoverished areas from being eligible for grants.

The British government used various methods to both include and exclude various religious bodies from providing religious education. In Ireland, a former colony of England, and part of the Union of Great Britain from 1801, schools had been subjected to British forms of education from 1816, as a means of political socialisation into English ideology, particularly through the use of ideological texts.[41] Religious education was a point of contention within the Irish education system, with the Roman Catholic Church and the Church of Ireland both holding varied opinions as to what constituted religious education and what means were needed to provide it. The discussion on Irish education in the British parliament as well as in religious and public spheres reflected the entangled nature of educational debates in the early nineteenth century and the competing voices that came from various political, religious and secular sectors for the education of the disenfranchised poor.[42] Problems of religious difference not only played out in inter-confessional debates, but rather were also manifest between denominations. For example, in contemplating the establishment of universal education in England during the 1830s there was also a question as to the provision of religious education to Nonconformist children within schools that were predominately Anglican. One touted solution was the separation of religion from secular subjects, as per the Irish National System, established in 1831. This was not, however, a viable solution for many staunch believers amongst the Anglicans and Nonconformists, as religion was seen not to be able to be extracted as a subject in its own right, infused as it was in all that children should learn.[43] A differentiation between religious and secular systems in terms of distinctions between school subjects was thus inconceivable for these religious actors. The fear of denominationalism was pervasive, both at home and in the colonies, as it had the power to upset the status of the Church of England.

Church leaders, members of voluntary societies and parliamentarians all spent much time discussing the need for education and how this might best be instigated, with historian Richard Johnson positing that education, and particularly that of the poor, was 'one of the strongest Victorian obsessions'.[44] As religious groups had traditionally been the major supporters of education they were suspicious of government interference in popular education, not least due to the question of how much religious education should be allowed in government schools.[45] By the 1840s, there were four clear positions in relation to religious education and models of universal education in Britain and in the colonies. Dr James Phillips Kay (later Kay-Shuttleworth), one of the most influential policy-makers in terms of British education policy for the poor and inaugural Secretary of the Committee of Council on Education, categorised them: the Established Church which saw it as their divine responsibility to provide education; Dissenters and politicians who saw the government to be the 'legitimate arbiter of civil rights' and thus lobbied for a system based upon religious equality; politicians who saw education to be a civil institution to be solely in the hands of government and thus secular; and those who could separate the secular and religious instruction and saw it to be the government's duty to support and facilitate the former and religious bodies the latter.[46] These four models can be generalised and categorised in order of church influence as follows: a pure Church of England model; a liberal religious equality model within a government system; a primarily government model with additional religious components; and a purely secular government model. Both the second and third models could theoretically be non-denominational, or even include Catholics, depending upon how religion was incorporated and taught. For Dissenters, both the first and last models were incomprehensible. Such discussions were not centred upon Britain, but rather, as in the case of the Negro Education Grant, spread into the British colonies and to the education of non-Europeans.

As missionary groups provided personnel and funds, governments were keen to profit from their support in offering educational services, working together in various regions to provide education. However, the difference of opinion on the matter of the quality and quantity of religious education remained one of the major difficulties in instigating a universal educational system during the mid-nineteenth century. People questioned when, and how much, religious instruction should be provided, or even whether religious instruction was imperative for public morality, or whether this could be taught through purely secular knowledge, as per the Enlightenment thinker Immanuel Kant's ideas. Kay-Shuttleworth himself noted: 'the whole question of the authority of the State and of the Church, of civil rights and religious immunities, and of combined and separate education, necessarily became subjects of controversy'.[47] Such controversies were commonly carried into the colonies, and reverberated back into Britain as the following section on the Negro Education Grant exemplifies.

The Negro Education Grant

The 'moral and religious improvement of the Negro' through the Negro Education Grant was one colonial moment in which ideas about religious and moral education reverberated throughout the Empire. It was also a moment in which Dissenting missionary groups in London banded together to provide a common voice to the Colonial Office as to their ability to provide education to emancipated slaves and their children. The Colonial Office of the period was not a cohesive well-oiled machine, but an understaffed and sometimes chaotic office where individuals, rather than policies, were influential in the decision-making process.[48] In the establishment of the Grant, educational functionality was more important than religious homogeneity, and economic pragmatism trumped religious ideology – all to the benefit of the Nonconformists. In the years before emancipation some missionary societies, such as the BMS, the CMS, the LMS, the Moravians and the WMMS were already working amongst the approximately 770,000 slaves in the British West Indies, the Cape of Good Hope and Mauritius.[49] Dissenting missionary groups, as well as the CMS as the evangelical missionary group of the Anglican Church, had gained members amongst slave populations often to the disapproval of plantation owners who considered religious education dangerous as it had the potential to make slaves aware of the discrepancy between religious and slave codes, and provided them with a reason to revolt. The limited access to religious education was lamented by the newly appointed Secretary of State for War and the Colonies, Edward Geoffrey Smith Stanley, 14th Earl of Derby, in a ministerial debate on the proposition for the emancipation of slaves in the British colonies in the House of Commons on 14 May 1833, viz:

> The slaves have no education, and you deny them any; for, as slaves, they can have none. They have hitherto been treated as chattels attached to the soil-do you think they can be made fit for freedom, till freedom has exercised its influence upon their minds and upon their moral character? The treatment of the West-India negroes is a stain upon a Christian age, and upon a country professing itself Christian. If the slaves be made acquainted with religion, they must learn that slavery is inconsistent with the Christian religion; and will you shut out religion, in order that you may maintain slavery?[50]

For Stanley, education and religion were compatible with slavery. Slavery was, according to him and many of his contemporaries, a blemish on the liberal Christian age, which upheld the pursuit of moral progress. Pertinently, it was incomprehensible to him that anyone should be denied Christianity. Stanley's anti-slavery stance was one that proliferated throughout the House of Commons, building upon over half a century of anti-slavery campaigning from such prominent figures as Hannah More, William Wilberforce, Thomas Clarkson and Thomas Fowell Buxton. Many of these campaigners were closely connected to the Church of England. For example, Wilberforce was a devout member of the Church of England, was associated with the formation of the CMS, the *Christian Observer* and the British and Foreign Bible Society (BFBS) – some of the most influential religious organisations and organs of the missionary movement. His passion for abolition and emancipation reflected his interest in morality and justice for slaves as well as British society in general – he was very concerned about the general lack of piety and virtue in British society. For him, religion was a key component in a moral society as it dignified 'the conduct of multitudes of our labouring classes' in England.[51] Buxton too was a Church of England member, and also associated himself with the Quakers (Society of Friends). Both men wrote prolifically about social concerns, and the ameliorating nature of religion. This was also the case with their work on abolition. Wilberforce reiterated his belief in the regenerative nature of religion in one of his last publications, an 1823 tract entitled *An appeal to the religion, justice, and humanity of the inhabitants of the British Empire, in behalf of the Negro Slaves in the West Indies*. For him, one of the most serious of all the vices of the West Indian system was 'the almost universal destitution of religious and moral instruction among the slaves'.[52] Christianity, he adamantly believed, taught a person self-control and allowed a person to 'sustain with patience the sufferings of their actual lot', while at the same time preparing for the next life.[53] Wilberforce did not provide a plan in his *Appeal* for how instruction should take place, yet it is obvious that he believed that it should be grounded in Christian religion.

Emancipation was a social experiment insofar as a new social order needed to be created in order to fill the vacuum of power that was assumed to occur once slavery had been abolished. It was a chance to modernise society in the British West Indies, with missionary societies wishing to play a leading part in this experiment. The momentum of the abolition movement caused fundamental change, with the implementation of the Negro Education Grant an 'afterthought' rather than an aim of the movement.[54] Eventually funds for building schools would be provided through a ten-year grant, which initially provided £25,000 annually. Over the period the annual sum was reduced, with the belief that the system would not need any further support from the Imperial government after this period.[55] The debates and discussions that surrounded the establishment of the Negro Education Grant were not only centred on creating more diligent workers through Christian teaching, as Rebecca Swartz has argued, but were also debates in which the centrality of Christian teaching as the moral basis of any society were discussed.[56] That is, education was seen not just as a form of social control used to create industrious workers to support the local economy, but also as a form of self-control through the instilling of Christian moral principles that were to guide a person through this life into the next. Education was instilled with various attributes from the various ideological standpoints of missionaries in the colonies, religious societies in Britain, the Colonial Office, both Houses of Parliament as well as the agents of the West Indian plantation owners, who all had various interests and conflicting as well as at times complementary views as to the value of education. As with so many other schemes which were devised to 'protect', 'support' and 'raise' colonised peoples, there is no evidence to suggest that the soon to be emancipated slaves were involved in decisions about how to establish an educational system for them and their children.

The establishment of the Negro Education Grant was a protracted affair, involving many actors over a lead-up period of several years. One of the leading figures in facilitating the inclusion of the term 'liberal and comprehensive principles' was Buxton. One motivation of the present analysis is to demonstrate the importance of this term for missionary groups vying to be involved. Historical analyses of the Grant have focused on some of the religious issues surrounding the Grant, with papers written in the 1970s and 1980s focusing mostly upon the situation in the West Indies, without considering the ramifications for schooling on a broader imperial level. Patricia Rook's work, for example, focused upon the tensions between missionary groups and the economic obstacles surrounding the introduction.[57] Rebecca Swartz, who recently examined aspects of the Grant in a global context, focused on ideas of labour and race and did not examine the religious component of the Grant.[58] Yet it is this focus upon 'religious *and* moral education' [my emphasis] which set the expectations for collaborations between missionary and government groups in subsequent periods in the British Imperial world. Through a focus on the religious aspects of the Negro Education Grant and how missionary societies were engaged in crafting the plan, it becomes evident how Nonconformists pushed to be involved and what were the consequences of their inclusion for missionary education beyond the West Indies. Of those historians who have examined the debates surrounding the establishment of the Negro Education Grant, only Carl Campbell has cursorily examined what was understood by 'liberal and comprehensive' religious and moral education. His work from the 1960s focused on what the term meant for the inclusion or exclusion of Catholics from the terms of the Grant, coming to the conclusion that he was unsure of what was meant by the term.[59] Here a more detailed and encompassing analysis of 'liberal and comprehensive' is undertaken, examining how different groups filled the term with various meaning. The discussion demonstrates that definitions and understanding were fluid and dynamic with contesting groups vying for their interpretations of the terms and their religious legitimacy.

The term 'religious and moral education' was part of the fifth resolution put forward to the House of Commons in London in June 1833 in relation to emancipation of slaves in the majority of the British Empire. Of the five resolutions of June 1833, the first proposed the 'entire abolition of slavery throughout the colonies'; the second declared all children under the age of six free at the time of abolition; a third proposed a system of apprenticeships for four years; and a fourth provided £20,000,000 for the compensation of the slave owners. Resolution five rested upon the perception that on their way to emancipation, former slaves needed to have external and internal regulating systems to ensure the maintenance of the new social order. The system of slavery had operated upon a presumption that people were motivated by fear to conform to the system. Once slavery had been abolished and fear was no longer the driving factor, other incentives needed to be provided so that people would conform to the post-emancipation system. A system of magistrates would ensure that the planters adhered to the external regulating system provided by the new law. A system of schools, by means of a religious system that taught people to internalise Christian moral codes, would prevent them from engaging in morally questionable activities in the first place, and thus would offer an internal regulating system. Resolution five provided regulatory functions for both the planters and the slaves and at the same time opened possibilities for a governmentally supported education system for ex-slaves and their children based 'upon liberal and comprehensive principles, for the religious and moral education of the negro population to be emancipated'.[60]

In the heated and lengthy discussions in the House of Commons surrounding the five resolutions in June 1833, only the fifth was passed with little debate.[61] This was in contrast to the lengthy debates that resolution five would engender in the ensuring debates in the House of Lords discussed below, which were centred on the three major questions of who should teach; what should be taught; and what such a system might cost. One aspect that was not questioned in either House in any debate was the ability of education to Christianise previously heathen peoples, to humanise the slaves, to civilise them in preparation of entering civil society as freed people or to socialise them within the new society to be formed following emancipation. These points were all accepted, and such there was no doubt that the education of the ex-slaves and their children should be religious in nature.[62] Instead the debates raged about the religiously liberal nature of the Grant, and the role of Nonconformists. The term 'liberal and comprehensive principles' had been added at a late point of the proceedings in the House of Common debates of June 1833. After over six hours of discussing the fourth resolution on compensation for slave owners, which had been hotly contended, the fifth resolution was tacked onto the discussion. This decision was made, despite the lateness of the hour, in order that the packets of correspondence destined for the colonies might be sent off with the decisions of the House of Commons. The demands of time led to there being only two responses to the fifth proposal. The first was from the Tory Alexander Baring, who had spoken out against the rash distribution of £20,000,000 as compensation. His was the sole voice that expressed objection to the additional expenses the resolution would create; however, no discussion resulted from his comment. The second response was from the anti-slavery campaigner Buxton, who, in an extremely brief comment, proposed the addition of the words 'upon liberal and comprehensive principles'. The Secretary of State for the Colonies, Mr Stanley, took the response on board and replied that 'it was not the wish of Government that any exclusive system of religious education should be adopted'.[63] The amended proposal was agreed to in the House of Commons.

Through including the term 'liberal and comprehensive principles', Buxton was connecting the debates around education in the slave colonies to the state of Nonconformists in Britain, as well as to broader debates around the two principles of religious liberty and religious equality. From the context of the discussion it is clear that 'liberal' did not refer exclusively to liberal education. The term 'liberal education' itself was as much as an ideal as a practice. In the eighteenth century, liberal education was connected to the notions of 'character formation, as preparation for life, as the acquisition of Taste or particular kinds of knowledge'.[64] By the mid-nineteenth century the drive behind liberal education was not so much to improve relations between elites, but rather to educate leaders of society in order to effectively 'direct the course of the community'.[65] In the context of British schooling, liberal education included such subject matter as modern languages, literature, grammar, history and geography, and occasionally arithmetic and science.[66] In this sense, 'liberal education' was mostly confined to universities, reflecting educational thought of the times which believed in stratified education for the various classes of society. However, 'liberal' did not refer only to the content of education; it was also understood to refer to choice in the education provided. Furthermore, religious liberty was promoted by Nonconformists as the freedom that one had to choose where she or he worshipped without political involvement. This stood in contrast to religious equality, which was the movement extending civil rights to all religious groups within Britain and other European countries.[67] Comprehensive principles, although less well defined, could be understood as including all Anglican and Nonconformist religious societies.[68] This interpretation of the wording as referring not to the system of education but to the funding of various groups to provide education was reiterated in contemporaneous reports as an indication of their religious right to provide it.[69]

The second reading of the bill in the House of Lords

When the Bill was read a second time in the House of Lords in late June 1833, a number of points pertaining to the fifth resolution were expressed.

The Duke of Wellington, Sir Arthur Wellesley, an Anglo-Irish Church of Ireland member who was in the Tory party, was against the phrase 'on [*sic*] liberal and comprehensive principles'.[70] Although he agreed in principle with the notion that freed slaves should be able to choose their own religious denomination, and thus infused the term 'liberal' with the notion of religious liberty and individual consciousness as per Catholic emancipation debates,[71] he insinuated that Nonconformist missionaries had been responsible in inciting slaves to rebel against their owners. This was a common belief, particularly in relation to the Slave Rebellion in Jamaica of 1831–1832, which was also known as the Baptist War for many of the instigators were connected to this church.[72] With this event in recent memory, Wellesley dismissively complained that the wording of the resolution 'evidently contemplated the sending out a new band of missionaries to the West Indies', which was assumed would create further tensions.[73] The Whig Lord Suffield (Edward Harbord) took Wellesley to task on this point. Suffield saw no veracity in Wellesley's claims that Nonconformist missionaries were to blame for rebellions such as the Jamaican Slave Rebellion of 1831–32. Planters had accused missionaries of inciting the slaves, which led to some missionaries being charged for crimes associated with the rebellion. Suffield further argued that the Christian public attached great importance to the phrase 'liberal and comprehensive principles' and would not be satisfied with the resolution if these words were omitted.[74]

Suffield's comments can be seen in light of metropolitan debates about religious liberty, evident in the repeal of the Test and Corporation Acts through the Sacramental Test Act of 1828 (9 Geo. IV, c.17). The seventeenth century Test and Corporation Acts had prevented non-Anglicans from attending university, holding seats in parliament or holding public office. With their repeal, many Tories thought that the ties between state and church would be irreparably loosened, although the liberal faction of the Tory Party were aware of the need for reform to ensure that greater political change was avoided.[75] Moreover, the Reform Act of 1832 (2 & 3 Will. IV c.45) increased the number of eligible voters through a reform of the House of Commons' representational spectrum.[76] A pragmatic response to the increase in eligible voters and eligible candidates for parliamentary representation was an increase in the provision of education in Britain, with potential voters wishing for choice in religious educational offerings. The term 'liberal and comprehensive principles' was also attached to the petitions and debates surrounding the emancipation of Roman Catholics in Britain, particularly Irish Catholics, in the early nineteenth century. For example, in March 1805, a petition was presented to the House of Lords from the Roman Catholics of Ireland who expressed their dissatisfaction with British laws. These laws were seen to be in their 'manifold incapacities, restraints, and privations, [...] absolutely repugnant to the liberal and comprehensive principles recognized by their most gracious sovereign and the parliament of Ireland'.[77] Within this petition, the Catholics of Ireland wished for 'full participation of all the rights and privileges of the other subjects' of the crown. However, as Lord Auckland noted, if the petition of the Roman Catholics in Ireland was conceded as they wished, there would be ramifications for the relationship between state and church, as well as questions of allegiance.[78] The petition received much criticism from Dissenters in Britain and it was not until 1829 that the Catholic Relief Act (10 Geo IV, c. 7) was finally passed, at a time when there was a threat of rebellion in Ireland.[79] Despite the passing of the Bill, distrust of Catholics still remained present within both the popular press as well as amongst Protestant and Anglican groups. Nevertheless, the Act can be seen as part of a broader movement in which Catholics and Nonconformists were receiving more legal rights within Britain, in the midst of greater parliamentary reform. Through such acts, Britain was providing more religious liberty and more religious equality, with many staunch supporters of the Established Church resenting this trend, as reflecting in the debates surrounding emancipation.

Wellesley's staunch opposition to the phrase 'liberal and comprehensive' reflected his own ambiguous and changing stance towards non-Anglican groups, who he was willing to compromise with if this maintained peace and prevented democratic revolution.[80] His stance was political, rather than religious, and reflected his concern for the tensions that would arise if the educational field was to be opened to all potential providers. The political nature of his stance was evident in his second point of concern, which was a reiteration of his earlier argument in the debates, that the phrase would create ill feelings and act as an irritant in the West Indian societies. There was already distrust of Nonconformist missionaries and he assumed that the phrase would be read as an invitation for further Nonconformist missionaries to work in the colonies. And, finally, according to Wellesley, any such ill feelings would be counterproductive to the first resolution, because the abolition of slavery should combine the welfare of the freed with that of the proprietors.[81] Nonconformist missionaries could make the fragile social situation between planters and soon to be ex-slaves even more precarious, and thus were explicitly not desired. In this reading, Wellesley's opposition to 'liberal and comprehensive' was both to the 'who' could teach as well as to the 'what' would be taught. Although his motion was defeated, the discussions surrounding it provide insight into how the phrase was understood by contemporaneous politicians. Buxton himself was 'amused' at Wellesley's protests, writing in his *Memoirs* that 'it did us real service, giving fifty-fold emphasis to the terms, and preventing the possibility of their being forgotten'.[82] For Buxton the terms were important to ensure that the system of instruction would not be 'exclusive' or 'intolerant'. In his *Memoirs* he wrote:

> I am the more anxious on this point, as I know, on the one hand, the extreme animosity of the colonists to all religious teachers of their slaves except those of the Church of England, while on the other, I know the vast benefits which the dissenting missionaries have imparted, and are likely to impart, to the negro population. I think a system of perfect and unbounded toleration ought to prevail in the West Indies as in England.[83]

Buxton was thinking about the English situation when he proposed the words 'liberal and comprehensive', believing that English religious toleration could be transposed onto the West Indies. However, his phrase was open to interpretation and debate, both within and beyond parliamentary circles, and the addition of these words had far-reaching consequences for the inclusion of Nonconformists in the resulting Negro Education Grant. The inclusion of the term 'liberal and comprehensive principles' in the fifth resolution led to the establishment of a religiously heterogeneous educational system funded by government or, to use the terminology inspired by Kay-Shuttleworth, a liberal religious equality model within a government system.

'Liberal and comprehensive' and the question of Dissenters

In his analysis of the Negro Education Grant, Carl Campbell noted that it was not initially clear what meaning should be given to the term 'liberal and comprehensive' within the parliamentary resolution.[84] He came to the conclusion that the terms were broad enough to allow the British government to support Protestant schools on 'Protestant' British West Indian islands (and in doing so provided Nonconformists in the colonies 'fuller reign' than in 'Protestant England') and narrow enough so that the non-denominationalism of the Irish national school system could be applied to the predominantly Catholic West Indian islands.[85] He admitted, however, to being unsure of the meaning.[86] I argue that the phrase 'liberal and comprehensive' pertained to both the provision of education by Nonconformists as well as to the content of education that could include sectarian principles. Campbell's references to the Catholic islands are also important given the lack of attention to them within the parliamentary debates in lieu of the attention given to Nonconformists. It is obvious within governmental communications that Nonconformists along with Anglicans were assumed to be the receivers of the Grant, rather than Catholics, even on previously Catholic-influenced islands, as the Catholics were assumed not to be able to supply the required funds or personnel.[87] In both government and religious circles, engaging Noncon-formist groups was preferable to engaging Catholics.

It was unclear from the outset whether Dissenters would be allowed to apply for the Grant with one of the sticking points being payment for Dissenting teachers. The Church of England could not provide all the teach-ers required, noted the Earl of Ripon, also known as 1st Viscount Goderich, Frederick Robinson, in the House of Lords. He in doing so pointed to an aspect of the plan that had not yet been clarified: whether the funds were to be used to employ Dissenters. He was evidently ill when passionately debat-ing the pro-emancipation cause and needed to rest a number of times. When discussing education, he only focused upon religious education, noting that the crown had gone to considerable expense to establish the Church of England in the colonies, and as such religious education for the African population was assumed to be clearly established in the West Indies. In describing Nonconformist groups he stated that:

> Although it was not proposed to pay dissenting teachers, yet it was thought necessary to make some alteration in the law on the subject. It was doubted whether such persons had at present full scope for the exercise of their zeal and talents, and it was considered necessary to remove all difficulties and obstacles out of their way, and leave the religious instruction of the negroes fairly open to the exertions of any individuals who should endeavour to extend to their fellow-creatures in the colonies the benefit of the consolations of that religion which they thought it their bounden duty to diffuse.[88]

As such, although Nonconformist missionaries might work as teachers they were not expected to be on the crown's payroll. In the immediate period following the passing of the Act, the Nonconformist missionaries were placed in a peculiar situation. Pragmatically they were needed, yet there remained an ideological rift between them and the state. Historically the state preferred to support the Established Church in the provision of education whilst being opposed to using state funds to disseminate Dissenting religious voices. This quandary was circumvented through initially providing funding for the building of schools and not for the employment of Noncon-formists with the Negro Education Grant. At the passing of the Bill, which resulted in the Abolition of Slavery Act (3 & 4 Will. IV c.73) effective of 1 August 1834, there was no clear plan as to how Resolution Five would be enacted in terms of education. The resulting grant was modelled on Henry Brougham's 1833 Education Grant in Britain.[89] As the 'liberal and comprehensive' principles of resolution five had foreseen the engagement of Dissenters, they were drawn into conceptualising the Negro Education Grant, with the Imperial government seeking the advice of, and information from, both religious societies as well as government officers, drawing upon a diverse group of government and non-government actors both locally and in the colonies.

The Church of England was generally unimpressed about the inclusion of Dissenters in the educational scheme. The Bishop of London was very critical of the idea of non-Anglican schooling, being incensed that anyone other than Church of England members should be entrusted to provide religious education. He thought that inclusion of Dissenters would undermine the religious authority of the Church of England.[90] In the West Indies, the Bishop of Barbados and the Leeward Islands drew up his own educational plan in late 1833, in which Catholics and Dissenters were left out and it was assumed that planters would be willing to provide suitable buildings on their land for the education of parents and children.[91] The Archbishop of Canterbury was sceptical of Catholic engagement; however, he stated that: 'Though I cannot approve of the principle of what I believe is called general religious education, I cannot go as far as to exclude it, where no other is to be had'.[92] The Secretary of the CMS, Dandeson Coates was initially very clear on his stance in a letter to Buxton discussing the matter at the end of 1832, doubting whether either Catholics or 'a union of Voluntary Societies' would be able to provide emancipated slaves the religious education needed for in the transition from slavery to freedom.[93] However, pragmatics won over ideology as the government needed the support of the numerous Nonconformist missionary societies in order to establish a system quickly. Mission societies in London were also willing to cooperate if they would be permitted to supply religious education without government interference in terms of content or personnel. Such liberties for Nonconformists groups were perceived by the Established Church to undermine its religious dominance.

The 1834 draft version of 'Heads of a Plan'

In April 1834, a draft version of a 'Heads of Plan for Promoting the Education of Youth in the British West Indies [Education Plan]' was circulated to missionary societies in London through the Colonial Under-Secretary, John Shaw-Lefevre.[94] This plan included the principles of 'instruction in the Doctrines and Precepts of Christianity' as the basis of education, of 'liberal and comprehensive principles' and also of funding non-Anglican groups – that is, religious liberty – all ideas which had been previously discussed in some length.[95] The plan circumvented any major role by the West Indian legislature, which was not a natural partner for the Imperial government to supply education due to its dominance by people who had no commercial interest in providing education to ex-slaves. The plan proposed school districts and collaboration between these and missionary bodies and the Colonial Office.[96] Providing funding to the legislature to establish a school system was also considered not practical for three reasons. The first was because this was supposed to lead to a secular educational system for children which would be separated from the denominationally specific religious education and environments that adults may engage in. Separating children from the religious teachings of their parents through a pure secular government system was undesirable given the need to create a totally encompassing moral environment. Second, providing the local colonial government with funding was seen to necessitate the founding of a Public Department and probably also a Board of Commissioners to run a secular school system. This was deemed to be too much of a burden for many of the colonial governments who were not equipped to deal with the structural needs such a grant would require. Third, it was argued that if the money was to be given to the colonial governments, then religious societies would likely withdraw their funding, with this funding simply disappearing from the system as neither the Colonial nor Imperial government would cover the deficit.[97] There seemed to be no choice but to work within the ad hoc system that had developed mostly due to the donations and support of the English public even in spite of the antagonism and tensions that this had caused with certain colonial governments. As the West Indian assemblies had been lackadaisical in improving the education of slaves, they had not provided a comprehensive plan for the religious and moral education of the emancipated slaves, and it was therefore understandable that the material for the report was predominately collected through the secretaries of religious societies in London.

The initial response by many Dissenting missionary societies on reviewing the plan was a sense of gratitude that they had been consulted. As some of the missionary societies had only a tenuous footing in the colonies – indeed many missionaries had been imprisoned for their roles in recent uprisings in the British West Indies – the change in tune of the government to see them as 'the best benefactors of the human race'[98] was an indication that they had gained much-needed official recognition for their work, particularly in the areas of education and moral and religious improvement. However, they were critical of many points in the plan and expressed their desire for the plan to be modified, particularly in terms of religious involvement.[99] A number of societies criticised aspects of the plan that might lead to religious tensions, particularly those that would leave teachers from minority religious groups working in schools that did not follow their own religious principles.[100] The Baptists criticised the establishment of school districts, and drew attention to the need for parents of pupils to be asked what denominational schools they would like in their districts, rather than leave such decisions up to government officials.[101] However, the plan was also praised for its focus upon both religious education and 'liberal and comprehensive principles'.[102] Jabez Bunting of the WMMS particularly commended the Colonial Office on this principle. Moreover, he applauded the government's focus on religion as the basis of education, underscoring the aptitude of the WMMS to provide such education through its lengthy and extensive experience around the globe in religious education, thus placing the Negro Education Grant in a global context of 'civil amelioration and [...] social order and security'.[103]

The plan was disseminated just before the summer break of the London Secretaries Association (LSA). It also coincided with a time of disruptions in government. The LSA, established in 1819 by the executive secretaries of the CMS, LMS, WMMS and the BMS, thought the issue so important that they called a special session to discuss 'a plan for promoting the Christian Education and Instruction of the Negroes recently emancipated in the West Indies, by a well-regarded system of schools'.[104] So important was this special session that Peter Latrobe (also written La Trobe) of the missionary arm of the Moravian Church (the Brethren's Society for the Furtherance of the Gospel (SFG)), and brother of Charles Joseph Latrobe, was invited to attend, a rare honour, since it took another decade for him to be invited to be a permanent member of the LSA. A week after this special session, a second meeting on the topic was held. As meetings were normally held monthly, the second meeting within a month demonstrates the importance of the matter at hand. At this meeting, at which Latrobe was not in attendance, the secretaries 'brought into form [the plan] to be submitted to the respective committees of the several societies' for further discussion.[105] By December 1834, Coates of the CMS sent copies of the amended 'Heads of a Plan for Promoting the Education of Youth in the British West Indies' to the four other societies, which was based on the Lefevre's version. Although the secretaries of the LSA had discussed the plan amongst themselves on several occasions and were in agreement on many points, once it went to their own boards they came up against boundaries.

Coates as the Secretary of the Anglican CMS had been the main gatherer of support from the BMS, the Moravians and the WMMS in relation to the plan. He was looking for support to extend the work of the CMS, and once the CMS in London had become aware of the Imperial government's desire to extend educational work in the British West Indies, Coates had proactively addressed Stanley, as Secretary of State for the Colonies, as well as the religious authorities of the Archbishop of Canterbury and the Lord Bishop of London. The CMS was advised by the Archbishop to address the Bishops of Jamaica and Barbados, which it did, albeit not directly, rather than through the mediation of the Archbishop.[106] The results of the communications with the Bishop of Jamaica were disappointing. The CMS had referenced church law that allowed them to be appointed to plantations in the West Indies in order to teach to the slaves; however, the Bishop had mostly restricted their teaching work to the enfranchised population. In a veiled criticism of the limitations that the Diocese placed on their work, the CMS published a claim in their magazine that 'the arrangement does not afford all the advantages, for the attainment of that object, which the Committee could desire'.[107] The communications with the Bishop of Barbados, although somewhat more extensive, did not provide any encouragement for extension into that Diocese and thus the CMS focused its attention upon expanding into Jamaica.[108]

In December 1834, Coates, as the spokesperson for the LSA to government on the issue, wrote to Buxton, noting the lacklustre governmental response to the individual missionary societies' comments and critiques of the plan.[109] The LSA was concerned about the equability of the distribution of funds and equally concerned that schools would not be doubled up or be established in 'inconvenient situations'.[110] It proposed that: 'the Government should possess a veto on a proposal for the establishment of a school subject, in case of refusal, to an appeal to the Colonial Secretary'.[111] This effectively gave government the power to limit or curtail denominational rivalry. As this initiative came from the LSA, and not from the government, it demonstrates that missionary bodies in London themselves were aware of potential conflict and worked towards finding ways to avoid religious rivalry. This letter puts a different slant on Campbell's claim that one of the biggest faults of the plan was that it assumed religious unanimity, and on Rooke's focus upon interdenominational rivalry, and not on interdenominational collaborations.[112] Yet there were also particular concerns from various missionary groups. The Baptists agreed with the plan, but wanted an additional clause referring to the '*liberty of conscience* to the parents as to the attendance on public workshop, & the use of religious formularies' [emphasis in original].[113] The Moravians were willing to be part of the plan; however, they were concerned that the Imperial government's focus upon the establishment and maintenance of new schools, and the exclusion of established schools from the Grant, would disadvantage them as they already had established schools.[114] The CMS and the WMMS also generally agreed with the plan; however, the latter objected to the 'introduction of a system analogous to that adopted in Ireland under the Education Board', in which both Catholics and Protestants provided education.[115] This system had been criticised by the Methodists, Roman Catholics and Anglicans, and as such the Methodists' opposition to the proposed system in the colonies was consistent with their opposition to the same system in Britain. The LMS found it unnecessary to consider the plan or to connect themselves with the missionary collaboration formed by Coates, as they were waiting to hear of the Imperial government's intentions.[116] At the same time, British supporters of the LMS were displeased with the Board's decision to participate in government grants as it went against the policy of voluntarism. Despite the consensus between four of the five missionary societies, it was acknowledged that no progress on the matter would be made before the replies to a questionnaire sent out by Thomas Spring Rice, of the Colonial Office, in November 1834 came back from the West Indies with more statistical data and information from the colonies.

One major point of the plan that the religious societies disagreed on was school fees. This point was, according to Coates, 'one of the principal reasons which rendered the Plan originally proposed by the Government unacceptable to the Societies by whom it was to be worked'.[117] There was unanimous agreement amongst missionary societies that local people needed to contribute to the costs of the school through fees, with the rationale being that the 'co-operation and exertions of the people themselves, in promoting their moral and religious improvement' were 'most effectual not to say the only course by which that end can be fully attained'.[118] The religious societies objected to the Imperial government setting the terms, wishing themselves to have more room for 'discretion', and to gradually raise school fees as situations warranted.[119] Missionaries needed to convince pupils, both actual and potential, along with their associated communities of the value of missionary schooling, and during the initial stage of missions fees often impeded rather than encouraged education. The issue of fees was not limited to the West Indies; rather, it was an issue that missionary bodies struggled with throughout the century, and one which was also circulating in Britain in relation to poverty. Kay-Shuttleworth drew the conclusion that the poor of England did not value education, as they were not willing to pay school fees or forgo the income their children earned to send them to school.[120] The payment of fees was thus itself considered to be a didactic means of instilling an appreciation of the worth of schooling or, in contemporaneous terms, 'to prevent their undervaluing that which they can have for nothing'.[121] The sentiment was expressed succinctly by a Moravian missionary in Barbados from 1856, viz: 'unless our people have to pay for a thing, they do not value it'.[122] Thus, the question of fees was not merely one of economics, but one of moral value.

Unsurprisingly, the term 'liberal and comprehensive principles' was taken up with enthusiasm by missionary organisations. In their correspondence with the Colonial Office in March 1835 the CMS and the WMMS both underlined this phrase, demonstrating its importance amongst Dissenting and some Church of England societies, despite the indifference of Church of England bishops in Britain and the West Indies.[123] This phase was also extensively used in the publications of the societies when they were raising public awareness for the Grant and the need for funds from home supporters.[124] Yet 'liberal and comprehensive principles' ultimately included only Anglo-Protestant groups, and not Catholics. The LSA itself provided a list of societies that it thought should be included as recipients of the Grant, including the BMS, CMS, LMS, WMMS and the Moravians, along with the Slave Conversion Society (with predominantly Church of England members) and the Scottish Missionary Society.[125] The inclusion of the Slave Conversion Society was in the eyes of some Nonconformists an indication that the Established Church had no grounds for complaint as to their participation in the scheme.[126] The voices amongst the Nonconformists saw the necessity to be liberal in their inclusion of both Established and Dissenting bodies. Bunting of the WMMS fervently insisted that 'liberal' should not be interpreted as a term that would 'generalize the instruction as in fact [to] neutralize it', but rather that it should be rendered to mean that all groups eligible to be assisted by the plan would be.[127] Yet, these liberal views did not stretch to Catholics, who were omitted by the missionary societies consulted about the plan. They were not, however, overlooked by all. In his commissioned report of May 1835 to the Colonial Office on the state of education in the West Indies, the Rev. John Sterling considered in depth the role of Catholics. His report helped inform the government's recommendations to the Treasury for the Negro Education Grant, and thus had the potential to infuse the term 'liberal and comprehensive' with further meanings. Sterling was suited to the task through his practical experience in the West Indies, having owned slaves and worked as an Anglican minister in St Kitts, as well as his knowledge of the recent developments in educational policies in Britain and on the continent.[128] Sterling's own prejudices towards various religious societies were evident within his report. In addition to being dismissive of Nonconformists, he was decidedly off-hand concerning the efforts in schooling that the Roman Catholics had undertaken in the West Indies,[129] reflecting the confessional conflicts that continued to be played out in Britain, particularly amongst evangelical Protestants.[130] He also maintained a distinction between the Established Church and Dissenters, raising the question at one point as to whether the Church of England alone should be responsible for education. For him, the primary maxim of Protestantism was a 'personal and individual reception of certain moral & religious principles', a maxim that Catholicism did not share, being as it was a religion through which adherence to the Holy See was incompatible with the Protestant notion that a person was an 'upright & progressive moral agent'.[131] Despite this prejudice against Roman Catholics, Sterling posed the rhetorical question whether 'liberal & comprehensive principles' might extend also to the Catholics, or whether they should be limited only to the 'Protestant

sects that have Missionaries in the W. Indies?'[132] He decided for the inclusion
of the Roman Catholics in the Grant as this followed the religious liberty
principles essential to the proposed plan.[133] However, if Roman Catholics
were to apply for the Grant they should be required to follow similar conditions put in place by the Education Board in Ireland, including the use of
Irish textbooks. In Ireland, the Catholics had criticised the Imperial government for the Irish National Education scheme, and within the colonies Sterling did not provide them with any concessions beyond those they had
received in Britain. Yet by acknowledging their educational work he provided a more positive view of Catholics than most other reports of the time
on the question.[134] Ultimately, no Catholic bodies would be invited to apply
for the Grant.

In addition to Sterling's May 1835 report, the Secretary of State for War
and the Colonies, Lord Glenelg, had at his disposal the reports and letters
of William Gladstone, who had written a detailed plan for the 'Negro
Education Grant' to his superior Lord Aberdeen in March 1835 in his
capacity as Under-Secretary of State for War and the Colonies.[135] As a
staunch Anglican and supporter of West Indian commercial interests,
Gladstone was against the inclusion of Nonconformists as recipients of
government funding for education.[136] Both Gladstone and Sterling wished
to engage only the Church of England in educating the emancipated slaves
and their children; however, Sterling knew that this was an unreasonable
wish and conceded that Nonconformists would have to be involved in any
educational plan for purely pragmatic reasons of funding.[137] Sterling's
concept of education was broad, including as it did preaching, public worship, role models, laws, public opinion and formal teaching within schools.
As such, he suggested that more Christian ministers should be employed
which would be a 'most efficient means of moral & religious improvement' – knowing full well that such a suggestion was outside the scope of
the resolution.[138] Like Gladstone, the staunch opponent of concurrent
endowment, Sterling knew that it would not be possible to exclude Dissenters, particularly as the wording of the fifth resolution opened the way
for Dissenters to be involved in any proposed educational plan.[139] Gladstone argued in a similar vein in a letter to the Secretary of the Colonial
Office, the Earl of Aberdeen, aiming to increase the influence of the Church
of England, providing a detailed plan as to how Church funds could be
rearranged to employ more clergymen and catechists.[140] As the number of
the Church of England clergy was only marginally greater than the combined number of Nonconformist ministers, such a suggestion would have
the potential to increase numbers of Established Church clergy without
placing a strain on the Imperial government's coffers. Both men found
ways to advocate the work of the Established Church, despite the swing

away from a religious monopoly towards greater religious equality. Ultimately the Church of England would obtain the majority of the funds, but through the SPG rather than the CMS.

Sterling's report included some general suggestions such as that schools should be for children as young as possible; that fees should be paid; that there should be more schools rather than larger class sizes, with some of these suggestions following European trends in educational reform.[141] One of his most controversial recommendations, and one which was implemented, was that each school funded by the Grant should be subjected to frequent inspections. These recommendations followed British and European best practice in which inspections were seen as a means of improving quality of schooling. They also reflected Focaultian notions of governmentality and discipline through examination and inspection.[142] Many missionary bodies were opposed to inspection as they feared that their religious instruction might be curtailed, leading to a forced non-denominationalism. In order to allay these fears Sterling recommended that any inspector of schools should not be an ordained minister of any denomination, thereby reducing the chance of sectarian conflict. This recommendation was taken up in the final Grant; however, it still caused concern amongst religious bodies that inspections were to be undertaken by officers appointed by the government. In order to mitigate such concerns, schools were to be given religious freedom, with the only inspections those that were deemed necessary to 'ascertain that they really conduce to the moral and religious education and improvement of the negro population, and thus answer the end for which the public money has been advanced'.[143] Thus, public accountability was desired, but not at the expense of religious freedom; the secular aspects of the Grant were in terms of regular external inspection rather than restrictive internal regulation. These strictly non-interfering inspections were subsequently carried out by Charles Joseph Latrobe, who would later become the Governor of the Colony of Victoria.[144]

Despite the newly created legal possibility for providing funding to Dissenters as civil functionaries to fulfil duties as schoolmasters under the abolition of the Test and Corporation Acts and the introduction of the Roman Catholic Relief Act, the social situation was still such that Sterling's opposition was based upon historical prejudices rather than legal realities. Sterling argued that it was the system of slavery itself that created such an awkward situation in which the Church of England ministers in the West Indies were themselves reliant upon the funds provided to them through the legislature, with circumstances necessitating that these ministers be antagonistic towards Nonconformist ministers. As Shirley Gordon has argued, Sterling's choice lay between providing the West Indian legislature with funding or subsidising religious groups to provide funding. Sterling preferred the latter option due to the continuity it afforded as well as the lower costs when compared to introducing a new system.[145] The question was not quite so straightforward for it touched upon the separation of state and church in England. Indeed, Sterling broadened his argument to include the example of the French system in which virtually all ministers were paid by the state regardless of confession. Conversely, in Britain there was a structural and functional differentiation between Church of England ministers, paid by the state as civil functionaries to fulfil religious duties, and Nonconformist ministers, who were protected by law, but not necessary remunerated by government.

In contemplating how a mixed religious system might be undertaken, Sterling raised two major issues: first, whether the Dissenters would become employees of the state if the religious societies accepted the Grant; and, second, what the property rights of these religious societies would be if their buildings were predominately built with government money. The first issue was bound up in the fundamental differences between the Established Church and Dissenters in relation to moral and religious purposes and principles. The Church of England was established on the religious principle of the duty of a clergyman to work amongst all people to enlighten their 'intellectual powers, their consciences, & higher affections' with this duty to be undertaken on a governmental stipend, as thus the state supported the moral progress of its citizens through paying members of the Established Church. Sectarian principles were seen to be in opposition to the relationship between state and religion, as people ought to be allowed themselves to decide which religious groups they contributed to and took advantage of.[146] Thus, Sterling drew a distinction between schooling provided by the Established Church, which was seen to provide education to all, and that of a liberal, or user-pays, model in which no person was obliged to pay for what he or she would not necessarily benefit from (a model that he described as peculiar to voluntary or sectarian principles, of which he was critical).[147] Deciding for one model would be a choice against the other, for according to Sterling, both could not exist simultaneously. As the plan was connected to funding the question also was 'who shall be the agents of the State?'[148] Other debates over education in Britain prior to the Negro Education Grant had circumvented these fundamental questions of moral and religious purpose because the grants had only been disseminated amongst national schools, which were, by definition, connected to the Church of England. In all of the discussions surrounding the establishment of the Grant, one aspect that remained vague was the actual curriculum. This is not surprising given the focus upon the agents involved, rather than on the receivers of education. Generally, two contrasting images of Africans were held amongst the residents on the islands: a negative description of their moral characteristics and mental capacities posited by planters

and supporters of slavery; and the optimistic description of moral and intellectual progression put forward by religious teachers from the various
denominations active in the colonies.[149] Swartz notes that education provided by the Negro Education Grant focused on 'reading, writing and religion' rather than practical skills.[150] As in other places in which the labour of
local people was central to the economics of the colony, too much 'bookish'
education without moral content or practical skills was deemed dangerous to
the colonial order.[151] In the logic of missionary groups, the modernising of a
society could not be successfully undertaken without Christian religion. As
the debates around the introduction of the Negro Education Grant eluci-
dated, Dissenting missionary groups did not want to upset the colonial order,
but rather to actively engage in creating religious and moral order in the West
Indies through their educational work with the children of emancipated
slaves. Exactly who was deemed capable of providing the 'right type' of
schooling was an issue of discussion the raised concerns of threats to the
religious and moral order of the colony.

After emancipation: funding the Grant

On 1 August 1834 slavery was abolished in the majority of British colonies. To celebrate this momentous achievement the BFBS send thousands
of copies of the New Testament with the Psalms annexed to the British
West Indies, with the admiralty allowing the packet to be sent free of
charge to the colonies. Each slave that could read at liberation was to
receive a free copy of the text, with the distribution of the texts contingent
on the recommendation of a Minister, Teacher or Employer.[152] Missionary
groups in the West Indies claimed that the distribution of Bibles had
'excited both among children and adults an earnest desire to learn to read'
with 'application for admission into the established school, far beyond the
possibility of being complied with', and with plans being made to open
more schools.[153] That is, missionary groups reported an increase in the
active participation in schooling and placed the causality on the distribution of edifying texts, rather than secular uses for reading. After emancipation, opportunities were opened up for emancipated slaves and their
children to learn to read through the establishment of more schools, many
of which were funded through the Negro Education Grant. The grant was
first enacted in September 1835, over a year after emancipation.[154] Ultimately, ten missionary societies and religious organisations were invited to
apply for the funds: the CMS, LMS, WMMS, BMS, the Moravians, the
Slave Conversion Society, the Scottish Missionary Society (also known as
Scotch Missionary Society), the Church of England's SPG, the Ladies'

Negro Education Society and the BFSS.[155] The SPG was the largest bene-
factor of the Negro Education Grant receiving the lion's share of the
Grant in its first year of operation, with 52 SPG schools receiving over a
third of the total Grant.[156] Despite their initial reservations the LMS
enthusiastically threw themselves into the venture, expanding their work
into agricultural apprenticeships, which was a new venture for them.[157]
Less than two years later, the LMS were less inclined to extend themselves
in the West Indies; rather, they had shifted their focus to establishing
schools in the colonies of South Africa.[158] The Wesleyans too had decided
to shift their attention from the West Indies to the mission field of
Australia,[159] demonstrating that although the Imperial government was
willing to fund religious societies, these societies often followed their own
agendas.

To obtain funding under the Grant, missionary societies had to raise a
third of the price of erecting a school house, either from Britain or within
the colonies. This idea had been put forth by Coates, with the acknowledgement that the government would not pay for the full costs of the
schools, and, more pointedly, 'because placing the arrangement on this
footing is calculated to stimulate the exertions of the different societies in
raising funds, and to give them a powerful plea with the public in their
appeals for that purpose'.[160] In those colonies in which not enough private
funding could be raised (a veiled reference to the lack of Protestant capacities within the 'Catholic' colonies), the system was to reflect either that of
the BFSS or of the National Board of Education in Ireland.[161] In this way
the influence of Catholics was also restricted. For the building of a number
of Normal, or Training, schools an additional annual grant of £5,000 was
needed beyond the £20,000 of the Grant. Thus, all in all, £25,000 was
earmarked for distribution in 1835 – less than half the funds that Sterling
had calculated, and slightly less than the funds distributed to English
schools of the same year. In 1837, the annual grant was raised to £30,000
with some of these funds allowed to go towards the payment of teacher's
salaries, causing another round of contemplation amongst Dissenters
whether this compromised their religious liberty.[162] From 1842, funds
were decreased yearly. The Grant was never meant to continue in perpetu-
ity, but rather to aid local legislatures in establishing and maintaining a
system of education for the moral progress of freed slaves.

The discussions around the Negro Education Grant engaged Nonconformist missionary societies in public debate on British imperialism. As a
result, Nonconformist and Anglican missionary societies obtained governmental support for their religious and educational work. This in turn
provided non-Anglican missionary societies with important government
legitimacy within British colonies – a legitimacy that reverberated within

missionary networks in Britain. Through government funding as well as grants of land, missionary organisations became financially, materially and ideologically tied to governmental plans for the education of Indigenous and non-European peoples in British colonies – ties with which not all sections of the religious public agreed. Government funding did not prevent missionary criticism of British Imperial rule, and missionaries could be both collaborators and opponents of government institutions. Moreover, as government funding only partly covered the costs of educational work, missionary societies needed ongoing funding from a variety of other sources including local colonial groups, home groups and the parents of pupils in order to augment their educational work. In order to engage their supporters, missionary groups used various and innovative ways to raise funds. Many fund raising techniques involved disseminating information about the state of the missions through missionary propaganda, such as through tours, meetings, periodicals, annual reports and special collection funds, such as those of Sunday School children within Britain.

In his comments, Sterling astutely noted that the religious societies currently working in the West Indies had large support groups in Britain that provided financial assistance for missionaries in the colonies. Yet for some groups, such as the LMS, the decision to accept government funding through the Negro Education Grant was met with protest in Britain, particularly amongst supporters outside London.[163] Thus, although the Grant opened up the possibility of the LMS directing their attention to education, it also complicated the relationship between church and state, or, more pertinently, between religion and politics. Indeed, true to Sterling's fears, supporters of the LMS threatened to withhold funding if the society accepted government grants.[164] Moreover, missionaries in the West Indies argued that any potential funding from the government towards their salaries would be against the Dissenting spirit and their refusal to 'serve two masters' – a somewhat ironic comment given that these Biblical words were used as an anti-slavery slogan in Jamaica prior to emancipation.[165] Moreover, as historian Michael Rutz rightly notes in regard to the LMS involvement, colonial politics and policies contributed to metropolitan discussion on the role of state and church, and to the 'reform of metropolitan society and politics'.[166] Issues relating to church–state relations remained much discussed in the pages of the LMS's periodicals. It was also in the pages of the missionary periodicals and tracts that a new self-awareness of Nonconformist missionary education, now legitimised through government funding, was evident. Appeals highlighted the importance of education and the reliance on supporters in Britain in order to fulfil the stipulations of the Grant.[167] The *Wesleyan-Methodist Magazine* argued that 'the provision of means for ['apprenticed negros'] religious instruction and Christian education appeared to be strickly a debt of justice to that long-injured race'.[168] The *Quarterly Papers* of the BMS spoke of the 'the strong attachment felt for their school, by the little negroes', drawing on emotive images evident in transnational missionary funding networks.[169] The British readership of the Moravian *Periodical Accounts* was asked to provide funding so that the West Indian population could receive 'the blessings of a sound Christian education'.[170] Such appeals were focused upon financial need and the assumption of Christian charity, rather than the inclusion of children's testimonies as a means to raise awareness (this tactic would be used in later decades). These appeals in British periodicals were directed towards a British public drawing upon notions of Christian duty to help maintain the educational work already begun by missionary societies in the West Indies.

Periodicals were one of many means of raising awareness and funds, including printed and visual means such as tracts, annual reports, bulletins, monographs, sketches, lithographs and, later in the century, photography.[171] Such textual and visual material were circulated around the colonies through missionary, government and humanitarian networks, raising interest in the fates of colonised peoples, and contributing to an comparative understanding of imperial problems. Within Britain, supporters of missionary societies were able to attend auxiliary and specific meetings both in London and the outside of the metropole where reports were given on the progress of various missions and where specific pleas for funding were made.[172] At missionary meetings at Exeter Hall, a renowned place for evangelical gatherings, prominent speakers appealed to packed audiences to donate generously for particular purposes. Thomas Fowell Buxton frequently spoke, and on one occasion in 1834, just before the introduction of the Negro Education Grant, he addressed the WMMS meeting to express the need for a hundred missionaries, and many schoolmasters as well as funds to support them in the post-emancipation West Indies.[173] An even more authoritative and personalised account of the mission field came from missionaries on furlough who provided face-to-face information through speaking tours of Britain. This was the tactic used by the WMMS to raise funds for the erection of school houses in the West Indies.[174] In 1837, it invited the former slave, the Rev. Edward Fraser of Antigua, to spend a year in England 'in order to make such collections at once efficient and interesting to our friends'.[175] Fraser's tour, like those of the LMS converts Jan Tzatzoe and Andries Stoffels from Southern Africa who we will encounter in the next chapter, demonstrated that the medium of public speaking was not limited to White missionaries. Fraser's talks were both informative and a spectacle as the speaking tours of Christianised non-Europeans were still quite a novelty. He was already familiar with the European circuit, having attended the

Wesleyan-Methodist Conference in Ireland in 1835 (where he spoke on religious education of the emancipated slaves).[176] Along with Charles Knight of Sierra Leone, Fraser was one of the few non-Europeans ordained by the Methodist Church in the nineteenth century. Such a unique man contributed significantly to the fund raising if the amounts collected are an indication. Alone in 1837, the year in which Fraser toured, a third of the total for the Special West Indies Fund was collected.[177] Secular newspapers of the day reported on his lectures and listed funds raised at these events, demonstrating the broader appeal of his tour beyond the confines of the Methodist publications, or indeed religious publications.[178] However, these funds from British supporters were not enough for the maintenance of the established schools in the West Indies, given the general inability of local parents to afford school fees and the lacklustre local government support.[179] Throughout the life of the Negro Education Grant, missionary groups underscored the promising nature of religious and moral education to a British audience through texts and tours, informing them of their continued moral obligation to provide for the for the rising generation in the British colonies.

Conclusion

Reflecting the fervour that many missionary societies applied to the task, some scholars have dismissed the religious bodies that partook in the Grant as having been 'more zealous than competent',[180] with criticism being raised that schools were duplicated in various areas as many denominations used the grant system to further their potential congregations over those of rival denominations. This duplication, which was foreseen and countered in the suggestions put forward by the LSA, can however also be understood when we keep in mind that missionary societies saw schools as 'nurseries of the Church', and through schooling were vying for their own part of the religious market within a system that had previously limited the participation of slaves in terms of both education and public religion. Patricia Rooke has described 'the bitter inter-denominational wrangling over spheres of influence and the petty rivalries between missionaries of the same denomination'.[181] Such interdenominational rivalries may have been based upon jealousies in success rates.[182] Numbers of pupils in mission schools in the West Indies often exceeded church numbers, which indicates a desire on behalf of West Indians for knowledge for their children that was not necessarily attached to church membership.[183] The fact that former slaves sought out education as well as religious services was an indication for some scholars to suggest that emancipation had not been a total failure.[184]

The anti-slavery campaign involved changing concepts of emotions, sin and philosophy against a backdrop of political turmoil facilitating the re-conceptualisation of slavery and Britain's moral responsibility. It was the system, not the slaves themselves, that was seen as immoral. However, once slavery had been abolished it was the ex-slaves who were categorised as in need of moral education in order to participate in the 'modernising' post-emancipation society. The British public's attention failed to be maintained in the West Indies; it was drawn to other campaigns, including the state of Indigenous peoples in other British colonies and settlements, who were often seen to be more in need of protection and conversion than emancipated slaves, as explored in the following chapter. The emotional tide that had turned the system of slavery had also led to the introduction of a pragmatic scheme for the moral advancement of emancipated slaves and their children at the hands of religious societies and government officials whose correspondence lacked the emotive power of the anti-slavery campaigners. Indeed, almost all correspondence and public discussion prompted by the Grant pertained to its structure rather than its actual content. Given that the government needed to provide liberal religious ideals in order to encourage missionary bodies to participate in the scheme, the concept of 'moral and religious' education needed to be diffuse enough that all Dissenters felt included, yet exclusive enough that Roman Catholics and more extreme Dissenters would not apply for funding. The resultant development of a system in which imperial and colonial governments, the Established Church and Nonconformists could work together was more important than educational content itself. Metropolitan demands thus dictated the way in which structures for moral progress were organised, yet not how moral improvement was to be transmitted to the rising generation.

More broadly, the Negro Education Grant shaped Dissenting groups engagement with governments in schooling non-Europeans in the colonies for the next century, as it provided a means for the official collaborating of religious groups, including Dissenting groups, and governments in educating non-Europeans. Within this collaboration, missionary groups placed schooling that was infused with religion and morals as the means for modernising a society. The Negro Education Grant was one of the first major events in the schooling of non-Europeans in the colonies in which missionary groups had the opportunity and ability to respond to changing colonial and global circumstances. Missionary groups placed themselves as the most appropriate people to provide schooling, using such arguments to prove and maintain their legitimacy and worth in a modernising and secularising world, both in the British West Indies, but also back in Britain. The ripples of this newly formed relationship was seen in Britain in the Select Committee on the Treatment of Aborigines (British Settlements) of 1836–1837 examined in the next chapter.

Notes

1 House of Commons Parlimentary Papers (HC PP) 1837–1838 (113) 'Negro education, Jamaica', p. 7.

2 HL Deb, 20 June 1833, vol. 18, cc1014–1015, 'Ministerial plan for the abolition of slavery'.

3 James Murphy, *Church, state and schools in Britain, 1800–1970* (London and New York: Routledge, 2007), p. 16.

4 W.B. Stephens, *Education in Britain 1750–1914* (Basingstoke and London: Macmillan Press, 1998), p. 17.

5 Stephens, *Education in Britain*, p. 78. See also: Sylia Schütze, 'Das preußische Regulativ für den Seminarunterricht von 1854 – Standards für die Lehrerbildung?', *Die Deutsche Schule*, 106:4 (2014), 324–343.

6 Murphy, *Church, state and schools in Britain, 1800–1970*, p. 16.

7 As Nonconformist missionary societies were voluntary societies they need to obtain the bulk of their funding from private rather than government funds. There were differences in how these voluntary societies were organised and governed. See: Jeffrey Cox, *The British missionary enterprise since 1700* (New York and London: Routledge, 2008), p. 100.

8 Donald H. Akenson, *The Irish education experiment. The national system of education in the nineteenth century* (London and Toronto: Routledge & Kegan Paul and University of Toronto Press, 1970), pp. 6–7.

9 Anon, *The methods used for erecting charity-schools, with the rules and orders by which they are governed. A particular account of the London charity-schools: with a list of those erected elsewhere in Great Britain & Ireland: To which is added, A Particular Account of such Schools as are Reported to be set up since last Year. And An Appendix, containing Forms, &c. relating to the Charity-Schools.* The fifteenth edition, with additions (London: printed and sold by Joseph Downing in Bartholomew-Close near West-Smithfield, 1716), p. 8.

10 University of Cambridge Archives (UCA), Society for Promoting Christian Knowledge (SPCK), Manuscript (MS) B1, Society's Reports, 1704–1714. Lord Bishop of Lincoln, *The excellency, and benefits, of a religious education ...* (London: J. Downing, 1715), p. 22.

11 On morality and Sunday Schools see: Trygve R. Tholfsen, 'Moral education in the Victorian Sunday school', *History of Education Quarterly*, 20:1 (1980), 77–99, doi: 10.2307/367891; Anne M. Boylan, 'Sunday schools and changing evangelical views of children in the 1820s', *Church History*, 48:3 (1979), 320–333, doi: 10.2307/3163986.

12 Andrew Porter, *Religion versus empire? British Protestant missionaries and overseas expansion, 1700–1914* (Manchester: Manchester University Press, 2004), pp. 91–115.

13 The Secretaries to the Conference, *Conference on missions held in 1860 at Liverpool: Including the papers read, the deliberations, and the conclusions reached; with a comprehensive index shewing the various matters brought under review* (London: Strangeways & Walden, 1860), p. 111.

14 Ibid., p. 115.

15 Hayden J.A. Bellenoit, 'Missionary education, religion and knowledge in India, c. 1880–1915', *Modern Asian Studies*, 41:2 (2007), 369, doi: 10.1017/S0026749X05002143.

16 J.H. Buchner, *The Moravians in Jamaica: History of the mission of the United Brethren's Church to the Negroes in the island of Jamaica, from the year 1754 to 1854* (London: Longman, Brown & Co., 1854), p. 167.

17 'Antigua', *Periodical Accounts*, 15 (1839), 227.

18 Anne O'Brien, 'Creating the Aboriginal pauper: Missionary ideas in early 19th century Australia', *Social Sciences & Missions*, 21:1 (2008), 16, doi: 10.1163/187489408x308019.

19 'South Africa', *Missionary Register* (January 1842), 37. For the connection between humanitarianism an infant schools see: Helen May, Baljit Kaur and Larry Pochner, *Empire, education, and Indigenous childhoods: Nineteenth-century missionary infant schools in three British colonies* (Farnham: Ashgate, 2014).

20 August Gottlieb Spangenberg, *Instructions for missionaries of the Church of the Unitas Fratrum, or United Brethren*, trans. from the German, 2nd (Revised and Enlarged) edition (London: Brethren's Society for the Furtherance of the Gospel among the Heathens, 1840), p. 47.

21 James Kay-Shuttleworth, *The school, in its relations to the state, the church and the congregation, being an explanation of the minutes of the Committee of Council on Education, in August and December, 1846* (London: John Murray, 1849).

22 See, for example, Thomas O. Beidelman, 'Contradictions between the sacred and the secular life: The Church Missionary Society in Ukaguru, Tanzania, East Africa, 1876–1914', *Comparative Studies in Society and History*, 23:1 (1981), 79; Patricia T. Rooke, 'Missionaries as pedagogues: A reconsideration of the significance of education for slaves and apprentices in the British West Indies, 1800–1838', *History of Education*, 9:1 (1980), 69, doi: 10.1080/0046760800090106; May, Kaur and Pochner, *Empire, education, and Indigenous childhoods*, esp. chapter 2. Amanda Barry, '"Equal to children of European origin": Educability and the civilising mission in early colonial Australia', *History Australia*, 5:2 (2008), 41.1–41.16, doi: 10.2104/ha080041.

23 James Kay-Shuttleworth, *Recent measures for the promotion of education in England* (London: Ridgeway, 1839), pp. 1–19. See also: Kay-Shuttleworth, *The school*, pp. 17–19.

24 Geo. W. Ross, *Report on compulsory education in Canada, Great Britain, Germany and the United States. Printed by order of the legislative assembly* (Toronto: Warwick & Sons, 1891), p. 92; for similar concerns in Britain see: Stephens, 'Education in Britain', p. 78.

25 See, for example, Jacqueline Fear-Segal, 'Nineteenth-century Indian education: Universalism versus evolutionism', *Journal of American Studies*, 33:2 (1999), 323; Julie Evans et al. (eds), *Equal subjects, unequal rights: Indigenous peoples in British settler colonies, 1830–1910* (Manchester: Manchester University Press, 2003), esp. chapter 3; Rebecca Swartz, *Education and empire: Children,*

race and humanitarianism in the British settler colonies, 1833–1880 (Cham: Palgrave Macmillan, 2019).

26 W. Rein, *Encyclopaedisches Handbuch der Pädagogik. Band VII Prinzenerziehung – Schulberichte*, 2nd edition (Langensalza: Beyer, 1907), p. 425.

27 J.C.D. Clark, 'Secularization and modernization: The failure of a "grand narrative"', *The Historical Journal*, 55:1 (2012), 177, doi: 10.2307/41349650.

28 Kay-Shuttleworth, *The school*, p. 57.

29 Ibid., pp. 55–56.

30 For studies on Lancaster see, for example, David Hogan, 'The market revolution and disciplinary power: Joseph Lancaster and the psychology of the early classroom system', *History of Education Quarterly*, 29:3 (1989), 381–417, doi: 10.2307/368910; for an overview of the differences between the two groups see: Robert E. Luster, *The amelioration of the slaves in the British Empire, 1790–1833* (New York: Peter Lang, 1995), pp. 103–110; for Bell see: Andrew Bell, *An experiment in education, made at the male asylum at Egmore, near Madras: Suggesting a system by which a school or family may teach itself under the superintendence of the master or parent* (London: Cadell and Davies, 1797).

31 B.D. Basu, *History of education in India under the rule of the East India Company* (Calcutta: The Modern Review Office, n.d.). See also: Jana Tschurenev, 'Diffusing useful knowledge: The monitorial system of education in Madras, London and Bengal, 1789–1840', *Paedagogica Historica*, 44:3 (2008), 245–264, doi: 10.1080/00309230802041526.

32 'Miscellaneous. The Bishop of London's letter', *The Methodist Magazine*, 31 (November 1808), 518–520.

33 G.F. Bartle, 'Lancaster, Joseph (1778–1838)', *Oxford dictionary of national biography* (Oxford: Oxford University Press, 2004; online Jan 2008), doi: 10.1093/ref:odnb/15963 [last accessed 12 October 2020]; Jane Blackie, 'Bell, Andrew (1753–1832)', *Oxford dictionary of national biography* (Oxford University Press, 2004; online Jan 2008), doi: 10.1093/ref:odnb/1995 [last accessed 12 October 2020]. The Poor Laws themselves were a response to the number of soldiers returning from the Napoleonic Wars, and tied into broader discourses of charity, respectability and right to assistance. See: O'Brien, 'Creating the Aboriginal pauper'.

34 Bartle, 'Lancaster, Joseph (1778–1838)'; Paul Sedra, 'Exposure to the eyes of God: Monitorial schools and Evangelicals in early nineteenth-century England', *Paedagogica Historica*, 47:3 (2011), 263–281, doi: 10.1080/00309231003625562.

35 Mary Clare Martin, 'Church, school and locality: Revisiting the historiography of "state" and "religious" educational infrastructures in England and Wales, 1780–1870', *Paedagogica Historica*, 49:1 (2013), 77, doi: 10.1080/00309230.2012.744070.

36 Sedra, 'Exposure to the eyes of God', p. 274.

37 As quoted in: Hogan, 'The market revolution and disciplinary power', p. 383.

38 Stephen Colclough and David Vincent, 'Reading', in David McKitterick (ed.), *The Cambridge history of the book in Britain* (Cambridge and New York: Cambridge University Press, 2009), p. 292.

39 Michael A. Rutz, 'The problems of church and state: Dissenting politics and the London Missionary Society in 1830s Britain', *Church and State*, 48 (2006), 385.

40 Murphy, *Church, state and schools in Britain, 1800–1970*, pp. 16–17; Kay-Shuttleworth, *The school*, pp. 31–33.

41 John Coolahan, 'The Irish and others in Irish nineteenth century textbooks', in J.A. Mangan (ed.), *The Imperial curriculum: Racial images and education in the British colonial experience* (London and New York: Routledge, 1993), pp. 54–55.

42 For more on the Irish system see: John Coolahan, 'Imperialism and the Irish national school system', in J.A. Mangan (ed.), *'Benefits bestowed'? Education and British imperialism* (Manchester: Manchester University Press, 1988), pp. 76–93.

43 Murphy, *Church, state and schools in Britain, 1800–1970*, p. 12.

44 Richard Johnson, 'Educational policy and social control in early Victorian England', *Past & Present*, 49:1 (1970), 98, doi: 10.1093/past/49.1.96.

45 Kay-Shuttleworth, *The school*, p. 60.

46 Ibid., pp. 10–11.

47 Kay-Shuttleworth, *The school*, p. 12.

48 Elizabeth Elbourne, *Blood ground: Colonialism, missions, and the contest for Christianity in the Cape Colony and Britain, 1799–1853* (Montreal and Ontrio: McGill-Queen's University Press, 2002), p. 286. Zoë Laidlaw, *Colonial connections 1815–1845: Patronage, the information revolution and colonial government* (Manchester: Manchester University Press, 2005).

49 Trevor Burnard, 'British West Indies and Bermuda', in Robert L. Paquette and Mark M. Smith (eds), *The Oxford handbook of slavery in the Americas* (Oxford: Oxford University Press, 2010), pp. 134–153.

50 House of Commons Debates, UK (HC Deb), 9, 14 May 1833, vol. 17, cc1193–1262, 1217, 'Ministerial proposition for the emancipation of slaves'.

51 William Wilberforce, *An appeal to the religion, justice, and humanity of the inhabitants of the British Empire, in behalf of the Negro slaves in the West Indies* (London: J. Hatchard and Son, 1823), p. 34.

52 Ibid., p. 19.

53 Ibid., p. 53.

54 Patricia T. Rooke, 'The Christianization and education of slaves and apprentices in the British West Indies: The impact of evangelical missionaries (1800–1838)' (PhD thesis, University of Alberta, 1977).

55 For the impact of the system see: Patricia T. Rooke, 'A scramble for souls: The impact of the Negro Education Grant on evangelical missionaries in the British West Indies', *History of Education Quarterly*, 21:4 (1981), 429–447; M. Kazim Bacchus, *Education as and for legitimacy: Developments in West Indian education between 1846–1895* (Waterloo, Ontario: Wilfrid Laurier University Press, 1994).

56 Swartz, *Education and empire*.

57 Rooke, 'A scramble for souls'; Patricia T. Rooke, 'Evangelical missionary rivalry in the British West Indies. A study in religious altruism and economic reality', *The Baptist Quarterly*, 29:8 (1982), 341–355; Rooke, 'The Christianization and education of slaves'; Rooke, 'Missionaries as pedagogues'.

58 Swartz, *Education and empire*.

59 Carl Campbell, 'Towards an imperial policy for the education of Negroes in the West Indies after emancipation' (University of the West Indies, Department of History, n.d.) [held at the University of Leiden]; Carl Campbell, 'Social and economic obstacles to the development of popular education in post-emancipation Jamaica, 1834–1865' (University of the West Indies, Department of History, n.d.) [held at the University of Leiden]; Carl Campbell, 'Towards an imperial policy for the education of Negroes in the West Indies after emancipation', *The Jamaican Historical Review*, 7 (1967), 76; Carl Campbell, 'Denominationalism and the Mico Charity schools in Jamaica, 1835–1842', *Caribbean Studies*, 10:4 (1971), 152–172.

60 HL Deb, 20 June 1833, vol. 18, cc1014–1015, 'Ministerial plan for the abolition of slavery'.

61 HC Deb, 11 June 1833, vol. 18, cc573–598, 597–598, 'Ministerial plan for the abolition of slavery'. For discussion on the influence of the West Indian planters in the parliamentary debates and discussion on the resolutions, albeit with no discussion on the education provisions, see: Izhak Gross, 'The abolition of negro slavery and British parliamentary politics 1832–33', *The Historical Journal*, 23:1 (1980), 63–85; Paula Elizabeth Sophia Dumas, 'Defending the slave trade and slavery in Britain in the era of abolition, 1783–1833' (PhD thesis, School of History, Classics, and Archaeology, University of Edinburgh, 2012). See also: William Green, *British slave emancipation: The sugar colonies and the great experiment, 1830–1865* (Oxford: Clarendon Press, 1976).

62 See, for example, Olwyn Mary Blouet, 'Slavery and freedom in the British West Indies, 1823–33: The role of education', *History of Education Quarterly*, 30:4 (1990), 627, doi: 10.2307/368950.

63 HC Deb, 11 June 1833, vol. 18, cc573–598, 597–598, 'Ministerial plan for the abolition of slavery'.

64 Sheldon Rothblatt, *Tradition and change in English liberal education: An essay in history and culture* (London: Faber and Faber, 1976), p. 195.

65 William Whewell, *Of a liberal education in general; and with particular reference to the leading studies of the University of Cambridge* (London: John W. Parker, West Strand, 1845), p. 2. For a history of the term 'liberal education' within eighteenth- and nineteenth-century thought see: Rothblatt, *Tradition and change in English liberal education*.

66 Stephens, *Education in Britain*, p. 45.

67 R.G. Cowherd, 'The politics of English dissent, 1832–1848', *Church History*, 23:2 (1954), 136–143, doi: 10.2307/3161486; Todd Thompson, 'The Evangelical Alliance, religious liberty, and the evangelical conscience in nineteenth-century Britain', *Journal of Religious History*, 33:1 (2009), 49–65, doi: 10.1111/j.1467-9809.2009.00746.x.

68 Cowherd, 'The politics of English dissent', 136.

69 'Negro schools', *Evangelical Magazine and Missionary Chronicle*, 15 (1837), 130.

70 HL Deb, 25 June 1833, vol. 18, cc1163–1229, 1193–1194, 'Ministerial plan for the abolition of slavery'.

71 On Catholic debates and the notion of liberal see: HL Deb, 13 May 1805, vol. 4, cc743–843, 786, 'Roman Catholic petition'.

72 John Stauffer, 'Abolition and antislavery', in Robert L. Paquette and Mark M. Smith (eds), *The Oxford handbook of slavery in the Americas* (Oxford: Oxford University Press, 2010), pp. 556–577. For the Baptist entanglements between Jamaica and Britain see: Catherine Hall, *Civilising subjects: Metropole and colony in the English imagination 1830–1867* (Cambridge: Polity, 2002).

73 HL Deb, 25 June 1833, vol. 18, cc1163–1229, 1193–1194, 'Ministerial plan for the abolition of slavery'.

74 HL Deb, 25 June 1833, vol. 18, cc1163–1229, 1197–1198, 'Ministerial plan for the abolition of slavery'; for more on the 'rebellion' see: Mary Turner, *Slaves and missionaries: The disintegration of Jamaican slave society, 1787–1834* (Urbana, Chicago and London: University of Illinois Press, 1982), Chapter 6.

75 Kenneth Morgan, *Slavery and the British Empire: From Africa to America* (Oxford: Oxford University Press, 2007), p. 185.

76 Ivor Morrish, *Education since 1800*, First published 1970 (London and New York: Routledge, 2007), p. 12.

77 HL Deb, 25 March 1805, vol. 4, cc97–105, 101, 'Roman Catholic petition'.

78 Ibid.

79 See, for example, Thomas Le Mesurier, *A serious examination of the Roman Catholic claims, as set forth in the petition now pending before parliament* [first published in 1805], 2nd edition (London: T.C. Hansard, 1812), 9; HC Deb, 5 April 1805, vol. 4, cc215–217, 'Petition from London respecting petition of the Catholics of Ireland'; HC Deb, 5 April 1805, vol. 4, cc217–218, 'Petition from Oxfordshire respecting petition of the Catholics of Ireland'. See also: G.I.T. Machin, 'Resistance to repeal of the Test and Corporation Acts, 1828', *The Historical Journal*, 22:1 (1979), 115–137; Denis Paz, *Popular anti-Catholicism in mid-Victorian England* (Stanford, CA: Stanford University Press, 1992).

80 G.I.T. Machin, 'The Duke of Wellington and Catholic emancipation', *The Journal of Ecclesiastical History*, 14:2 (1963), 190–208, doi: 10.1017/S0022046900064940. See also: HL Deb, 21 July 1851, vol. 118, cc1063–1143, 1113–1117, 'Ecclesiastical Titles Assumption Bill'.

81 HL Deb, 25 June 1833, vol. 18, cc1163–1229, 1228–1229, 'Ministerial plan for the abolition of slavery'.

82 Thomas Fowell Buxton, *Memoirs of Sir Thomas Fowell Buxton, Baronet*, ed. Charles Buxton (London: John Murray, 1848), p. 326.

83 Ibid.

84 Campbell, 'Towards an imperial policy', 72.

85 Ibid., 72.

86 Ibid., 76.

87 TNA, CO 318/122, G. Grey to Treasury, 21 July 1835, 559–560, 559.

88 HL Deb, 25 June 1833, vol. 18, cc1163–1229, 1178–1179, 'Ministerial plan for the abolition of slavery'.

89 Rooke, 'A scramble for souls', p. 430; Rutz, 'The problems of church and state', p. 385.

90 Campbell, 'Towards an imperial policy', p. 80. See also: Rooke, 'A scramble for souls', p. 431.

91 TNA, CO 318/115, C.J. London to E.G. Stanley M.P. (London), 13 December 1833; TNA, CO 318/115, Copy of a letter from the Lord Bishop of Barbadoes and the Leeward Islands to the Secretary of the Incorporated Society for the Conversion &c of the Negro Slave, 1 November1833.

92 TNA, CO 318/122, W. Howley (Archbishop of Canterbury) to Lord Stanley, 20 July 1835, p. 533.

93 University of Birmingham (UB), Cadbury Research Library Special Collections (Cadbury), Church Mission Society Archive (CMS), General Secretary's Department (G), Administration, Correspondence (AC), 19/1, Dandeson Coates' correspondence, 16 September 1824–26, February 1835, Extent 1 volume, D. Coates to T. Buxton, 1 December 1832, marked 'PRIVATE', p. 49.

94 TNA, CO 318/122, D. Coates to T. Buxton, 3 December 1834, pp. 82–85.

95 TNA, CO 318/122, 'Heads of a plan for promoting the education of youth in the British West Indies', pp. 467–471.

96 Shirley C. Gordon, 'Documents which have guided educational policy in the West Indies – I: Rev. John Sterling's Report, May, 1835', *Caribbean Quarterly*, 8:3 (1962), 145–153; Campbell, 'Towards an imperial policy', 81.

97 TNA, CO 318/122, John Sterling's Report, May 1835 (Sterling's Report), pp. 476–477.

98 'The Missionary Magazine and chronicle. Valedictory service of the London Missionary Society', *The Evangelical Magazine and Missionary Chronicle*, 14 (1837), 546.

99 See, for example, TNA, CO 318/118, 12 April 1834, Jabez Bunting (Wesleyan Mission House) to John Lefevre (Colonial Office), pp. 403–405; TNA, CO 318/118, 8 April 1834, John Dyer (Secretary, Baptist Missionary Society) to Johan Lefevre, Esq. Under Secretary of State to the Colonies, pp. 399–402.

100 See, for example, TNA, CO 318/118, 19 April 1834, D. Coates to Johan Le Fevre [*sic*], PRIVATE, pp. 418–420.

101 TNA, CO 318/118, 8 April 1834, J. Dyer to J. Lefevre, pp. 399–400.

102 TNA, CO 318/118, 16 April 1834, J. Bunting to J. Lefevre, pp. 407–408.

103 TNA, CO 318/118, 16 April 1834, J. Bunting to J. Lefevre, pp. 406–408.

104 University of London (UL), School of Oriental and African Studies (SOAS), Microfilm (MF) M6293, *The London Secretaries' Association minutes, 1819–48*, M6293 (Reel 1), 6 November 1834 and 13 November 1834.

105 UL, SOAS, MF M6293 (Reel 1), 13 November 1834.

106 'Home proceedings', *Church Missionary Records*, 12 (1834), 14.

107 Ibid., 280.

108 TNA, CO 318/122, D. Coates to G. Gladstone, 25 March 1835, p. 93; TNA, CO 318/122, D. Coates to Lord Glenelg, 8 August 1835, 101–104; 'Home proceedings', *Church Missionary Records*, 5:12 (1834), 280.

109 TNA, CO 318/122, D. Coates to T. Buxton, 3 December 1834, pp. 82–85.

110 Ibid., p. 83.

111 Ibid.

112 Campbell, 'Towards an imperial policy', 79; Rooke, 'Evangelical missionary rivalry'.

113 TNA, CO 318/122, J. Dyer to D. Coates, 6 January 1835, p. 87.

114 TNA, CO 318/122, P. Latrobe to D. Coates, 22 December 1834, pp. 86–87.

115 TNA, CO 318/122, CO Note, 9 March 1835, 144; HL Deb, 19 March 1833, vol. 16, cc778–826, 779, 'Education (Ireland)'.

116 TNA, CO 318/122, J. Arandell (LMS) to D. Coates, 3 December 1834, p. 87.

117 TNA, CO 318/122, D. Coates to T. Buxton, 3 December 1834, p. 84.

118 Ibid., pp. 82–85.

119 Ibid.

120 Kay-Shuttleworth, *The school*, pp. 53–54.

121 'Education among the poorer classes of society', *The Quarterly Journal of Education*, 5 (1833), 222–234, 229–230.

122 'Barbadoes', *Periodical Accounts*, 22 (1856), 135.

123 TNA, CO 318/122, Wesleyan Missionary Society, 'Heads of a plan...', received by CO 9 March 1835, pp. 140–142, 144; TNA, CO 318/122, Church Missionary Society, 'Heads of a plan for promoting the education of youth in the British West Indies', received by Colonial Office 10 March 1835, pp. 81–85; Cox, *The British missionary enterprise since 1700*, p. 85.

124 'West Indian Missions', *The Wesleyan-Methodist Magazine* (May, 1834), 395.

125 TNA, CO 318/122, D. Coates to T. Fowell Buxton, 3 December 1834, p. 82.

126 TNA, CO 318/122, P. Latrobe to D. Coates, 22 December 1834, p. 86.

127 TNA, CO 318/118, J. Bunting to J. Lefevre, 16 April 1834, p. 407. Also cited in: Rooke, 'A scramble for souls', p. 432.

128 For more on Sterling see: Campbell, 'Towards an imperial policy', pp. 93–97; Gordon, 'Documents', p. 145. Shirley C. Gordon, 'The Negro Education Grant 1835–1845: Its application in Jamaica', *British Journal of Educational Studies*, 6:2 (1958), 143, Swartz, *Education and empire*, esp. chapter 2.

129 TNA, CO 318/122, Sterling's Report, p. 413.

130 John Wolffe, 'Anti-Catholicism and evangelical identity in Britain and the United States, 1830–1860', in Mark A. Noll, David W. Bebbington and George A. Rawlyk (eds), *Evangelicalism: comparative studies of popular Protestantism in North America, the British Isles, and beyond, 1700–1990* (New York and Oxford: Oxford University Press, 1994), pp. 179–197.

131 TNA, CO 318/122, Sterling's Report, p. 480.

132 Ibid., pp. 478–479.

133 Ibid., pp. 479–480.

134 Ibid., p. 481; see also: Campbell, 'Towards an imperial policy', p. 86.

135 TNA, CO 318/122, W.E. Gladstone, 'West Indian education, Mch. 1835' (received by CO on 21 April 1835) (Gladstone's Report), pp. 521–535. See also: Campbell, 'Towards an imperial policy', p. 91.

136 Matthew, H. C. G., 'Gladstone, William Ewart (1809–1898)', in *Oxford dictionary of national biography* (Oxford University Press, 2004 online ed., May 2011), www.oxforddnb.com/view/article/10787 [last accessed October 2020].

137 Campbell, 'Towards an imperial policy', p. 90.

138 TNA, CO 318/122, Sterling's Report, p. 387.

139 TNA, CO 318/122, Sterling's Report, p. 465; TNA, CO 318/122, Gladstone's Report, p. 524.

140 TNA, CO 318/122, Gladstone's Report, p. 515.

141 TNA, CO 318/122, Sterling's Report; May, Kaur and Pochner, *Empire, education and Indigenous childhoods*.

142 Michel Foucault, *Discipline and punish: The birth of the prison*, trans. Alan Sheridan (London: Penguin Books, 1977); Graham Burchell, Colin Gordon and Peter Miller (eds), *The Foucault effect: Studies in governmentality with two lectures by and an interview with Michel Foucault* (Chicago: University of Chicago Press, 1991).

143 HC PP 1836 (211) 'Negro education', p. 4.

144 HC PP 1837–1838 (520) 'Negro education, Windward and Leeward Islands. Report from C. J. Latrobe, Esquire, to Lord Glenelg, on negro education in the Windward and Leeward Islands, &c'; HC PP 1839 (35) 'Negro education, British Guiana and Trinidad. Copy of a report from C. J. Latrobe, Esq. on negro education in British Guiana and Trinidad' (London, 1839); On Latrobe's employment as inspector see: Dianne Reilly, 'The creation of a civil servant: La Trobe in the West Indies', *The La Trobe Journal*, 71 (2003), 67–84.

145 Gordon, 'Documents', p. 145.

146 TNA, CO 318/122, Sterling's Report, p. 466.

147 Ibid., pp. 466–467.

148 Ibid., p. 468.

149 Ibid., pp. 397 and 438.

150 Swartz, *Education and empire*, p. 52.

151 World Missionary Conference, 1910, *Report of Commission III. Education in relation to the Christianisation of national life* (Edinburgh and London: Oliphant, Anderson & Ferrier, 1910), p. 191.

152 TNA, CO 318/118, A. Brandran & G. Browne (Secretaries of the *British and Foreign Bible Society) to T. Spring Rice (Secretary of the State for the Colonies), 21 June 1834, pp. 383–385*.

153 Anon, *The eighteenth report of the Committee of the London Association in aid of the Mission of the United Brethren, commonly known as Moravians, for the Year 1835* (London: Jaques and Co: 1836), p. 19.

154 HC PP 1836 (211) 'Negro education', pp. 3–4; TNA, CO 318/122, Sterling's Report, pp. 503–504; TNA, CO 318/122, G. Grey to Treasury, 21 July 1835, pp. 560–561.

155 HC PP 1836 (211) 'Negro education', p. 3.

156 Ibid.

157 TNA, CO 318/122, W. Ellis to Lord Glenelg, 29 April 1835, pp. 148–150; TNA, CO 318/122, W. Ellis to G. Grey, 1 December 1835, pp. 197–198; TNA, CO 318/122, W. Ellis to G. Grey, 3 December 1835, pp. 199–200. See also: Rooke, 'Evangelical missionary rivalry'.

158 TNA, CO 318/131, W. Ellis to G. Grey, 4 March 1837, pp. 170–172.

159 TNA, CO 318/131, J. Beecham to G. Grey, 12 May 1837, p. 141.

160 TNA, CO 318/122, D. Coates to T. Buxton, 3 December 1834, p. 84.

161 TNA, CO 318/122, G. Grey to Treasury, 21 July 1835, pp. 560–561.

162 'Education in the West Indies, to the editor of the Evangelical Magazine', *Evangelical Magazine and Missionary Chronicle*, 15 (1837), 23–26.

163 Rutz, 'The problems of church and state'.

164 Ibid.

165 Ibid., 389–390; Mary Reckord, 'The Jamaica slave rebellion of 1831', *Past & Present*, 40 (1968), 115.

166 Rutz, 'The problems of church and state', p. 379.

167 'Negro schools in the British West Indies', *Periodical Accounts*, 14 (1836), 252–254, 463–464.

168 'Negro education', *The Wesleyan-Methodist Magazine*, 15 (March 1836), 233–234.

169 TNA, CO 318/131 *Quarterly papers, for the use of the weekly and monthly contributors to the Baptist Missionary Society*, 62 (April, 1837), 229.

170 'Negro schools in the British West Indies', *Periodical Accounts*, 14 (1836), 252–254.

171 Felicity Jensz and Hanna Acke, 'The form and function of nineteenth-century missionary periodicals: Introduction', *Church History: Studies in Christianity and Culture*, 82:2 (2013), 368–373, doi: 10.1017/S0009640713000036.

172 Hall, *Civilising subjects*; Steven Maughan, '"Mighty England do good": The major English denominations for the support of foreign missions in the nineteenth century', in Robert A. Bickers and Rosemary Seton (eds), *Missionary encounters: Sources and issues* (Richmond: Curzon Press, 1996), pp. 11–37.

173 'Religious intelligence. Wesleyan Missionary Society', *Evangelical Magazine and Missionary Chronicle*, 12 (1834), 236–237.

174 'Wesleyan Missionary Society', *Evangelical Magazine and Missionary Chronicle*, 15 (1837), 266–267.

175 'Negro school-houses in the West Indies', *The Wesleyan-Methodist Magazine*, 16 (1837), 386.

176 'Religious intelligence: The Wesleyan-Methodist Conference in Ireland', *The Wesleyan-Methodist Magazine*, 14 (1835), 701–705.

177 G.G. Findlay and W.W. Holdsworth, *The history of the Wesleyan Methodist Missionary Society*, in five volumes, vol. 2 (London: The Epworth Press, 1921), pp. 321–322.

178 'Advertisements', *The Manchester Times and Gazette*, 8:448 (Saturday 3 June 1837), front page; 'Derry Benevolent Society monthly report', *The Derby Mercury* (Wednesday 14 June 1837), 3; 'Advertisements & notices', *The Bristol Mercury*, Issue 2515 (Saturday 5 May 1838), 3.

179 Findlay and Holdsworth, *The history of the Wesleyan Methodist Missionary Society*, vol. 2, 322–323.

180 Kenneth Ramchand, *The West Indian novel and its background* (Kingston: Ian Randle Publishers, 2004), p. 4.

181 Rooke, 'A scramble for souls', p. 440.

182 Patricia T. Rooke, 'Evangelical missionaries, apprentices, and freedmen: The psycho-sociological shifts of racial attitudes in the British West Indies', *Caribbean Quarterly*, 25:1/2 (1979), 1–14, 7–8.

183 Rooke, 'A scramble for souls', p. 442.

184 Zoe Laidlaw, 'Heathens, slaves and Aborigines: Thomas Hodgkin's critique of missions and anti-slavery', *History Workshop Journal*, 64:1 (2007), 133–161, doi: 10.1093/hwj/dbm034.

2

'The blessings of civilization':[1]
the Select Committee on Aborigines
(British Settlements)

With the introduction of the Negro Education Grant in the West Indies, the Imperial government demonstrated its commitment to the 'moral, intellectual, and religious improvement'[2] of its non-European denizens through collaborative work with the Established and Nonconformist Churches. It was in the metropole that the anti-slavery campaigners drew the most support for their cause; however, once slavery had been abolished the British public's attention was diverted from raising funds for the establishment and maintenance of schools in the West Indies to a new humanitarian cause, the protection of the Indigenous inhabitants of the British Empire. Riding high on his success in the anti-slavery campaign, Thomas Fowell Buxton, who was mentioned in the last chapter, moved a motion on 1 July 1834 in the House of Commons for an inquiry into the state and condition of the Indigenous populations of Britain's colonies. His motion, brought forward a month before the Emancipation Act came into effect, was tacked onto the sitting of the third reading of the Poor-Law's Amendment, reflecting the humanitarian slant of parliament at that time, as well as the acknowledgement that the state had a moral obligation to intervene in the lives of those subjects perceived of as in need of help or protection.[3]

Buxton contended that colonialism had injured rather than benefited Indigenous peoples in every place that the British had presided. Brandy and gunpowder had made their indelible mark on Indigenous populations, with southern African colonists considering it a 'most meritorious action' to 'shoot the natives'.[4] Rather than putting forward a motion to request a parliamentary inquiry, Buxton moved that an address be presented to the King asking him to start an inquiry. The Secretary for the Colonies, Thomas Spring Rice, seconded the motion, which was then passed. The King was addressed by the House the following day with his directive being that Indigenous rights should be protected, justice maintained and civilisation spread amongst Indigenous peoples and means undertaken to 'lead them to the peaceful and voluntary reception of the Christian Religion'.[5] Spring Rice dutifully sent a circular to the Governors of the British Colonies shortly thereafter, repeating this directive as well as acknowledging that similar instructions had been disseminated in the past. Buxton's motion was, however, badly timed, as parliamentary disputes over the Irish Coercion Act led to the resignation of the Prime Minister, Lord Charles Grey, and the dissolution of parliament by the end of the year.[6] With the disruption to parliament as well as the delay in the report on the situation in the Cape of Good Hope, which would have provided more information on relationships between settlers and Indigenous peoples there, it took until the next year for Buxton to move a motion in the House of Commons for a Select Committee into the treatment of Indigenous peoples in the British Colonies.[7]

The Select Committee on the Treatment of Aborigines (British Settlements) of 1836–37 (hereafter 'Aborigines Committee') reflected contemporaneous views of government, humanitarians, philanthropists and settlers in relation to the educational work of missionaries for the 'Native Inhabitants of Countries where British Settlements are made' in the first half of the nineteenth century.[8] Although the Aborigines Committee ultimately had limited long-term effects, it nevertheless has traditionally be seen by historians as the high point of the collaboration between British humanitarians and missionaries. In the wake of this report these groups no longer collaborated as intensely and humanitarians further lost their influence in parliament.[9] Generally, historically analysis has focused upon the humanitarian aspects of the Aborigines Committee Report. Elizabeth Elbourne, for example, has analysed the prominent opposition by settler colonists to humanitarian actions.[10] Alan Lester has argued that the broader 'humanist political principles' found in the suggestions of the 1836–37 reports, such as the introduction of Protectors, were seen to threaten the interests of settler colonists throughout the British Empire, thereby elucidating the tension between colonial realities and humanitarian ideologies in the metropole.[11] Such tensions were enhanced through missionaries portraying the behaviour of settlers as immoral. In response, settler discourse in the colonies sought to 'defend settler colonial practices from a critique elaborated by British humanitarians'.[12] Lester has further argued that this discourse was trans-imperial in nature and contributed to separate colonial, yet entangled imperial identities, which contested the nature of Britishness itself. Zoë Laidlaw's work concurs with Lester's in concluding that the committee's report contributed to a British understanding of an imperial and colonially connected world, in which trans-colonial categories, such as 'Aborigine', underscored the Brits' own notions of Britishness.[13] Together with Penelope Edmonds, Zoë Laidlaw has argued that the two versions of the report were published after the Select Committee's conclusion for two different strands of humanitarian networks.[14] Yet such a focus upon the tensions between humanitarians and settlers, or between various groups of humanitarians, often overlooked the necessity assumed within the report of missionary work to provide 'civilisation and Christianisation' to Indigenous peoples, especially establishing schools for religious and Christian instruction throughout the British colonies for the perceived benefit of Indigenous peoples. The majority of studies of the report have focused upon humanitarian lobbying groups in London and on the nature of the networks between influential people in the colonies and in London. Analyses have considered how the report engendered a sense of an imperially connected colonial world, as well as how the moral anxieties of the British population influenced government responses. More focus has been placed upon the political challenges that missionaries and humanitarians together posed for British settler colonialism, through their combining forces against immoral practices, rather than examining missionary practices per se. An exception is the recent work of Tim Keegan on the LMS's Dr John Philip,[15] who, as we shall read below, was an important actor in the Aborigines Committee.

Building upon the previous chapter, this chapter argues that in the logic of missionary modernity, modernising 'progress' was equated with the moral and religious 'improvement' of non-European populations in the British colonies. However, as the previous chapter has demonstrated, discussions as to the practicalities of missionary work were often excluded from debates on the ideological importance of education. The first section of this chapter digresses slightly from missionary education to explore the porous boundaries between groups of missionaries and humanitarians, in order to understand the complementary as well as the conflicting aims and objectives of both groups. A second, longer, section examines the discussions surrounding the 1836–37 Aborigines Committee in relation to missionary involvement and potential for missionary education. Rather than just focusing upon missionary writings, the chapter examines government and settler perceptions of missionary education for non-Europeans through the lens of parliamentary debates, reports from Select Committees and settler responses. This report, as in the debates surrounding the implementation of the Negro Education Grant, reflects missionary societies' attempts and abilities to respond to changing colonial and global circumstances, using their arguments for education as a means to prove and maintain their legitimacy and worth in a modernising and secularising world. Missionaries were instrumental in providing evidence of the negative aspects of British settlements for the Report, thereby placing the morality of the Empire in question. Yet even their statements were compromised to suit political ends such that the Aborigines Committee proposed that 'religious instruction and education' should be supplied to Indigenous inhabitants as compensation for their loss of land. I argue that this was a much less liberal phrase than the 'religious and moral education' debated in relation to the Negro Education Grant.

Differentiating religious instruction from education was a subtle yet significant shift that indicated the moral progress of non-Europeans was no longer the all-encompassing aim of education, but rather that the term 'education' could be infused with skills that would be useful to current and future British settlements in the colonial world. Missionaries, although still needed in the endeavour of schooling the 'rising generation', were set on a different path to the humanitarians involved in metropolitan societies such as the Aborigines Protection Society (APS), which focused on changing the system rather than saving individual souls. The Aborigines Committee thus brought to the fore the conflicting tensions between missionary, humanitarian, settler and governmental interests and competing notions of colonial and missionary modernity.

The Evangelical movement and British humanitarianism

In the 2010s, there was a rise in scholarly interest in humanitarianism, with a notable focus upon twentieth-century forms, and particularly upon emergency humanitarianism.[16] Emergency (or intervention) humanitarianism aims to 'provide relief only in times of particular crisis'.[17] This form of humanitarians sits in contrast to a nineteenth-century form, being 'progressive' (or alchemical) humanitarianism that 'focused upon removing the causes of suffering'.[18] Progressive humanitarianism often rested upon the perceived need to free peoples from forms of suffering brought on by the system of imperialism itself, such as slavery, which, through causing suffering, was deemed immoral and thus needed to be removed. Michael Barnett posits a further categorisation, Imperial Humanitarianism (1800–1945), which was informed by the forces of compassion that 'encouraged individuals to widen their horizons and to imagine new kinds of obligations to one another', including bringing Christianity and Western civilisation to non-Western peoples.[19] Zoë Laidlaw argues that even in the seemingly benevolent nineteenth-century humanitarian movement, there was much self-interest as well as a blurring of the lines between moral and political reform, with humanitarians often noting that equality for non-White imperial subjects was good for British trade and governance.[20] Her comments reflect a broader argument that humanitarians were interested in more than just the welfare of others. In a similar line of thought scholars have argued that the Aborigines Committee of 1836–37 allowed for the construction of a British understanding of an imperial and colonially connected world, in which trans-colonial categories, such as 'Aborigine', underscored British peoples' own notions of Britishness, and indeed moral superiority.[21] Although there were many nineteenth-century missionaries, philanthropists and parliamentarians who were aware of their obligations to non-Europeans, they did not necessarily refer to themselves as humanitarians.[22] Many of the members of the Aborigines Committee have been termed 'humanitarians'; however, they themselves would have used other terms, such as 'abolitionists' or 'philanthropists', or terms more apposite to religious world-views, such as 'Christians', 'evangelicals' or 'missionaries'.[23] The term 'humanitarian' has been described as anachronistic by some historians, with others noting its contemporaneous negative connotations.[24] Despite its anachronism, the term 'humanitarian' is nevertheless of some use, especially in trying to draw a distinction between humanitarian and philanthropic aims. In his study of early Victorian social conscience, David Roberts has argued that: 'At the center of humanitarianism was a simple, direct, nearly spontaneous compassion for all who suffered unmerited pain; at the center of philanthropy lay a desire to reform morals, to improve people, and to save souls.'[25] In his categorisation, humanitarians were interested in saving individuals from harmful external influences and often sought to shape legislation in order to improve the material conditions of people, whereas philanthropists focused upon reforming the individual through religious and moral improvement. Although both of Roberts' definitions could be applied to missionary organisations, missionaries are perhaps more accurately described as philanthropic because of their primary focus on moral reformation. The distinction between the two terms is porous so that Roberts' definition is unsustainable in absolute terms, especially in describing the overlapping interests of philanthropists and humanitarians in the nineteenth century.[26] It is, nevertheless, important that an awareness of the difference between focusing more on changing structures and systems (humanitarians) and the focus on individual change (philanthropists) be maintained in order that any assumptions about the intention and driving factors behind both groups do not become conflated.

Missionaries, as philanthropists, aimed to facilitate moral reform, particularly through school-based education. In contrast, humanitarians sought to mitigate the negative effects of the broader systems under which individuals lived, through, for example, government inquiries as a means to reshape the early nineteenth-century British Empire, particularly in ways that were deemed to reform rather than revolutionise.[27] Humanitarians were on occasion harsh critics of missionaries, whom they believed placed too much emphasis upon saving souls to the detriment of immanent material needs. This privileging of the reform of self over systems also led to missionary groups, such as the Moravians, not to initially challenge the system of slavery, for it was the reform of the self and not of the system that they privileged. This is not to say that missionaries could not be humanitarian in their aims, nor that humanitarians were not interested in the improvement of individuals. Indeed, the Aborigines Committee deemed missionaries necessary partners with the Colonial state both to protect Indigenous people – a form of humanitarianism manifest through external control – as well as to promote the moral and social improvement of them – a form of philanthropy manifest through internal control. The evangelistic, edificatory and leavening aims of the nineteenth-century missionary endeavour were both humanitarian and philanthropic, with these two aspects entangled within religious expectations and norms.

In perceiving themselves as the moral arm of the British Empire, missionaries provided *in situ* information to British Christian philanthropists and humanitarians which was used to affect change and movement within the British public and governmental spheres. Missionaries and missionary societies also had their own networks separate to those that fed into humanitarian networks, and had the ears of parliamentarians without always needing the mediation of non-governmental humanitarians or philanthropists. The Select Committee of 1836–37, was one such demonstration of how these networks came together to discuss the situation of non-Europeans in the colonies and to suggest some ways in which to mitigate the negative effects of colonialism. It is also an example of two contrasting contemporaneous views of Empire: Empire as a God-given right with reciprocal moral responsibilities, or a belief in the liberties of colonists. The first view, often called 'liberal imperialist', held that empire facilitated moral improvement, with missionaries and humanitarians readily fitting into the broad framework.[28] The British Empire was seen to be a divine gift connected to the human duty to convert heathens and guide them on a path of moral progress. The second view, reflected in a particular strand of historiography, focused more upon the rights of colonists and their belief that the British parliament should be limited in its ability to meddle in settlers' liberties.[29] Exemplary in this regard are mid-nineteenth-century politicians such as the Whig John Russell, who described the purpose of colonies as, first, to settle the globe with British citizens and thus spread the 'freedom and the institutions of the mother country', and, second, to 'maintain strict commercial monopoly' and thus increase domestic profit.[30] For British people within the colonies, such ideas were connected to ideas of self-representation through the cultural spread of British institutions, as well as self-profit through the commercial monopolisation of colonial products.

Within Britain itself influential periodicals such as the *London and Westminster Review*, exclaimed in 1836 that 'it is proverbial how little England knows of her colonies', reflecting the British public's generally lacklustre engagement in colonial affairs.[31] The conflicting interests of settlers and politicians along with an uninterested general public meant that concern for Indigenous peoples within British colonies was often confined to missionary and humanitarian networks. Given the efforts that colonial governments had undertaken to protect and expand British influence, what was to be done for the Indigenous peoples of the British settlements, for those who lay beyond the reach of British institutions, and for those who had not been protected nor provided with a chance to be 'improved' through Western forms of justice and education, nor to engage fully in British commercial networks? It was with such questions in mind that the Aborigines Committee was established in 1835.

Establishing a Select Committee on Aborigines (British Settlements)

A year after first bringing his motion to the House of Commons, Buxton's motion to report on the treatment of Indigenous peoples in British settlements was once again before the House. George Grey questioned Buxton as to why a Select Committee should be formed when a year before a motion was put forward that the King should be addressed on this topic. Buxton had meant to put the motion for an inquiry to the House in May; however, he had postponed it in lieu of proceeding with a separate motion to curtail the international slave trade, that aimed to search out, capture and destroy all slave ships.[32] Buxton had been proactive in the abolition fight, yet it was not because this was higher on his list of priorities; rather, he was awaiting further 'highly important' papers from the Cape Colony before he proceeded.[33]

In the Cape Colony the Sixth Frontier War had just broken out. The Frontier Wars, also known as the Xhosa Wars, had been going since the late eighteenth century. This war, however, was different as it gained the attention of liberal humanitarians in England in ways the other wars had not done, due in part to the information provided by missionaries. By March 1835, reports of the atrocities that the 'Caffre nation' [Xhosa] had carried out against the colonists were published in newspapers and read in parliament, creating an image of Indigenous brutality and concern for further bloody violence against settlers and their property.[34] In that month, Buxton sympathised with the horrors presented in parliament and responded with the hope that 'our treatment of the natives in that Colony would undergo strict revision, for sure he was, that our treatment of them had been such as to make every honest man blush'.[35] It was this conflict of interests over Indigenous rights on the eastern Cape frontier that had raised Buxton's concern over the state of Aboriginal people in the colonies, having as he did a source of intelligence about the atrocities in the colony in the form the superintendent of the LMS at the Cape, Dr John Philip, who he referred to as 'my chief informant and adviser'.[36]

Buxton and many of his like-minded colleagues relied upon networks of correspondences in the colonies, including missionaries such as Philip, for information on the plight of non-Europeans.[37] Philip himself would be a major witness at the Aborigines Committee and provided Buxton beforehand with much material about the situation in southern Africa, of which a large amount had been collected from other missionaries of the LMS and of the Glasgow Missionary Society.[38] Philip's letters to Buxton provided an alternative and brutal description of colonialism that uncovered a truth not present in official dispatches and correspondences, and which placed British colonialism in a negative light compared to the colonial practices of other European empires.[39]

At the time of the Aborigines Committee in the mid-1830s, the British government was reflecting upon colonial legislation, and the colonial system in general. British settlements had preceded British colonies in places such as New Zealand and some South Sea (Pacific) Islands, which were not yet under formal British control, with there being various options touted as how best to undertake the colonisation of these territories, if at all.[40] The merits of the colonising of an area in South Australia had also been discussed at the same time, with the South Australia Colonisation Bill being read a second time in the House of Commons in July 1834, the month in which Buxton first called for an inquiry.[41] The desire for land in the colonies was a matter that was often raised in parliament. It played a role in the Aborigines Committee as this scramble for land was associated both with negative consequences for Indigenous peoples, and with the duty of the British to compensate for Indigenous losses.[42] The scramble for land and the potential opportunities that this brought to many aspiring British colonists had in the past been associated with violence towards Indigenous peoples. There was concern that an unwanted class of emigrants would be lured to the colonies with the promise of uncolonised land. Many British emigrants were seen as the 'dregs' of society, being negatively affected by the processes of modernisation in Britain.[43] The creation of further colonies was seen as a means to alleviate pressures upon resources and jobs in Britain and to create wealth across the Empire.[44] Yet there were concerns within parts of British governmental and especially humanitarian circles that colonisation was Machiavellian in nature, and needed to be rectified with the morally uplifting influences of both humanitarians and missionaries. In this light, the focus upon regulation and protection of Aboriginal peoples from the vices of European civilisation is to be read as the desire to order and systematise colonial regulations.

The House of Commons supports a Select Committee on Aborigines (British Settlements)

Prior to the Aborigines Committee there had been various dispatches and collated reports on the general mistreatment of non-Europeans in British colonies, which shed a poor light on British colonisation.[45] Such reports demonstrated that there was no general approach or policy in the Imperial government's dealings with Indigenous peoples in various spaces in which British settlements had been established, despite the general acknowledgement that moral progress was desirable. Moreover, the violent behaviour of settlers against non-Europeans was an indication that British civilisation 'instead of proving a blessing, had proved a curse to the Aborigines of the different countries, into which we had carried what we called the blessings of civilization'.[46] Once proposed, the House of Commons quickly agreed to the motion for a Select Committee on the state and treatment of Aborigines in British Settlements. The historian Elizabeth Elbourne has argued that this was not because of a necessary willingness for parliament to champion the cause, but because Buxton had moved a motion some three days earlier which, although defeated, threatened to reopen the debates on slavery in light of the reports of abuse against emancipated slaves by former masters.[47] Given the broader concern for the welfare of Indigenous peoples within all British settlements, beyond that just of the Cape Colony, as well as the momentum that humanitarians had raised in parliamentary circles, the setting was ripe for the House of Commons to agree with the motion to appoint a Select Committee.[48] As Alan Lester has argued, what was up for discussion in the Aborigines Committee was the 'morality of British colonization per se'.[49] Although not the first time that the morality of British colonisation had been put to question,[50] what made this time different was the encompassing nature of the resulting Select Committee, which brought masses of information into one report that attested to the atrocities being committed, and one which laid down general recommendations as to how British colonialism should realign itself to become more humane.

In bringing the motion to establish the Aborigines Committee before the House of Commons in July 1835, Buxton focused upon the material causes for the demise of Indigenous peoples, including them being deprived of their land. Coercion, Buxton stressed, should be replaced by kindness, for this was the safer, cheaper and more profitable option.[51] He utilised the example of the Cape Colony, where war had once again broken out between settlers and the Xhosa, to demonstrate the potential dire consequences of British colonisation. His objection was not, however, to individual colonists, but rather to the system itself, which he deemed 'wholly unworthy of this great nation'.[52] In contrast, he extolled missionaries as individuals capable of negotiating between 'the colonist and the hostile barbarians', with missionaries being exemplary of what 'proper behaviour' on behalf of Europeans could affect amongst 'the part of the black population'.[53] Despite the current danger that missionaries were in within the Cape Colonies, no missionary had been attacked, which Buxton took as a sign that their moral and religious conduct had protected them from the turmoil and violence between the settlers and Xhosa.

Sir George Grey, Under-Secretary of State for War and the Colonies, was supportive of Buxton's 1835 motion for a Select Committee although he acknowledged that the current parliamentary sitting would not be long enough for evidence to be collected and a report to be completed, and thus suggested that the inquiry also be conducted in 1836, with a few key witnesses to be interviewed immediately before they left the country to return to the colonies.[54] Grey was not as pessimistic in his opinion of colonial government and not as quick as Buxton to blame the British colonial system for the demise of the Indigenous inhabitants. In his view the colonial government 'had not been of a character to reflect discredit upon the country'. Indeed he believed that 'the greatest blessings had, in many instances, flowed from it',[55] although what exactly he meant by this was not recorded in the Hansard.

Debates in the House of Common questioned what aspects of the British colonial presence were the cause of the demise of Indigenous peoples. Were individuals to blame? Was the system itself to blame? And if neither, who or what was to blame? Indigenous peoples and their inability to resist European vices? Or settlers who provided them with fire-water and guns? Or the processes used to 'modernise' people? When Buxton first put forward his motion for an Address to his Majesty in 1834, Thomas Spring Rice had supported him; however, he differed in opinion to the notion of expelling all evil from the colonies. In a slightly more pragmatic approach to mitigating the cause of Indigenous moral decline he noted that: 'There must be evils to a certain extent, consequent on the introduction of civilisation into a savage country, and these evils, though he could not hope that they could be done away with altogether, he would use every exertion to reduce.'[56] In the context of the religiously socialised British parliament, it can be assumed that 'evil' was interpreted in both transcendental and immanent terms. Although parliament was only able to regulate against the evils and vices that colonists brought with them into the colonies, the inclusion of so many missionaries and their supporters in the evidence of the Aborigines Committee ensured that a religious voice prevailed throughout the evidence from 1836 to 1837, as well as the resulting report.

The evidence and the report

The Aborigines Committee collected evidence in two sessions. During the first, 43 sittings were held from July 1835 to August 1836, of which 14 were with missionaries or secretaries of missionary societies. A second session was held from February to May 1837 with 9 sittings. A total of 46 witnesses providing evidence over the two sittings, with some 800 pages of testimony giving weight to the importance of the issues at stake.[57] With over a quarter of the witnesses being connected to missionary societies, and with Buxton and other committee members being supportive of missionary work, the end report had a decidedly pro-missionary slant. Some of the witnesses who had travelled to Britain especially for the Aborigines Committee took the opportunity to undertake speaking tours when not testifying, thus rousing support for the state of Indigenous peoples amongst a public, rather than political, audience.[58]

One missionary to give evidence was the aforementioned Dr John Philip of the LMS. Philip had arrived in the Cape in 1818, and by 1828 had demonstrated his public engagement with Indigenous issues through his two-volume book entitled *Researches in South Africa* in which he addressed an 'Appeal to British Justice and Humanity' to deliver the 'Hottentots' (Khoikhoi[59]) from the inhumane treatment that they were under in South Africa. The book, as the subtitle suggested, provided information on 'the progress of the Christian missions, exhibiting the influence of Christianity in promoting civilization'.[60] Fitting into the LMS's series of missionary monographs, it functioned both as a rousing narrative for the evangelical public and evidence of the transformative powers of Christianity. Drawing upon the economic theories of Adam Smith and David Ricardo it was a call for labour without race classifications. It also had a political role to play. The book was influential in Buxton's endeavour in 1828 to get the House of Commons to ratify that the Khoikhoi of South Africa were a free people, and to provide instructions to the government of the Cape to protect Khoikhoi freedom. The book was written at the behest of Buxton and others as an instrument to sway public opinion and to serve as a weapon against Tory impassiveness to the plight of the Khoikhoi.[61] Such motions reflected humanitarian concerns within parliament, and gave the White settlers of the Cape Colony another reason to be critical of the interference of British-based humanitarians in the laws of the colony. Settlers were of the opinion that the freedom that the Khoikhoi received under the passing of the laws 'ruined' them. They had preferred to keep the Khoikhoi under their control as it was thought to be both in the public's and in the Khoikhoi's best interest.[62] These entwined notions of control over Indigenous (and non-European) peoples and public interest were not confined to settler colonists, but were prevalent within missionary and humanitarian discourses of the nineteenth century. They were already evident in the discussions around slave emancipation, and became even more conspicuous in the latter half of the century when religious paternalism became more prominent.

Buxton was keen on obtaining Philip as a witness for the Aborigines Committee and found funding for his travel back to England. Accompanying him, at the request of the LMS, were the African Christians: Jan Tzatzoe (also known as Dyani, Jan Tshatshu or John Tzatzoe), who was a minor Xhosa chief, and Christian worker Andries Stoffels, a Khoi mission worker, and James Read junior, a man of mixed racial parentage and former teacher at the LMS Kat River settlement.[63] As Elizabeth Elbourne has noted, the African men were 'generally presented as tangible incarnations of the remade Africans', paraded as evidence of the transformative power of religion on the 'savage' man.[64] Philip had specifically targeted Tzatzoe for the role over men of higher standing, as the former was deemed a presentable, humble Christian convert, who had sided with the colonial forces in the most recent war.[65] Once in England the men were presented to English audiences through images of them in evangelical magazines and through missionary meetings, where they spoke to large audiences.[66] Tzatzoe also spoke at the famed centre of the evangelical movement in London, Exeter Hall.[67] A common appeal in their speeches was for the English to supply more schoolteachers and missionaries to 'elevate' their people.[68] Tzatzoe was not only involved in the Select Committee and evangelical meeting (being interpreted through James Read), he also sat in on a session of parliament and attended the Annual Meeting of the LMS in 1837, in which year South Africa was the third largest mission field (although it was only a tenth of the size of the East Indies in terms of stations and native assistants[69]). Tzatzoe was therefore versed in local as well as broader colonial politics and religious networks, using his voice to demonstrate his loyalty to the British as well as to his own people.

Philip's party dined personally with Buxton, yet were not invited to the Colonial Office, for Philip's aggressive complaints about the governor of the Cape, Benjamin D'Urban, were seen to be too antagonistic for the Colonial Office to publicly meet with him.[70] The Office was, nevertheless, in possession of many of Philip's correspondences and used these in their own reports.[71] In their handling of Philip, the Colonial Office demonstrated its ambiguous relationship with missionaries. It relied upon them for supplying information and undertaking schooling and welfare work for them in the colonies, yet distanced itself from when missionary criticism became too politically sensitive. Philip's evidence before the Select Committee was a harsh criticism of the way in which the British had disposed the 'Caffre'

[Xhosa] of their land. His claims were refuted by other witnesses who accused him of exaggerations and misstatements.[72] Such claims and counterclaims were common throughout the Empire as missionaries had detractors in many places, particularly amongst people whose commercial or political interests could be put under scrutiny from missionary intelligence. In this light, the Aborigines Committee provided missionary societies a chance to present themselves as friends rather than foes of colonisation, albeit their preferred type, infused with evangelic missionary principles and institutions.

The Secretaries of the CMS (Dandeson Coates), the LMS (William Ellis) and the WMMS (John Beecham) were also key witnesses, and often appeared together. They made the general claim that the influences of the Gospel led to the first steps in civilisation: the introduction of clothing, then the promotion of a sedentary lifestyle, then industry, with education 'naturally' following as a step of civilisation.[73] In their idea of modernisation, Christian values prevailed. The admission of the three secretaries as witnesses was not surprising given the close correspondence they had had with the Colonial Office in relation to the Negro Education Grant, and their continued communications with the Colonial Office throughout the 1830s.[74] Coates even offered his opinion to Buxton on a draft report of the Select Committee, indicating his willingness to provide government with suggestions as how missionaries could improve the civil and religious conditions of colonised peoples, as governments had not always 'done its part', particularly in relation to 'improving the civil and religious conditions of Africans'.[75] The Select Committee was a further stage on which they could voice their religious concerns for non-Europeans under British colonial rule, and simultaneously reiterate their arguments for religious education of non-Europeans as a means to ingrain and legitimise missionary work within the British Empire.

Liberal humanitarianism and the 'right' type of colonisation

In his function as chairman of the Aborigines Committee Buxton often raised questions of territoriality, ownership of land, treaties, justice and the moral states of Indigenous peoples both prior and subsequent to the advent of British colonialism.[76] Buxton pushed for the 'right' type of colonisation, infused with liberal humanitarianism, which was at odds with many aspects of settler colonialism. The 16-member committee included Buxton as chair as well as men who were active in the anti-slave movement and other humanitarian causes, such as Andrew Johnston, Charles Lushington, Sir George Grey, Joseph Pease and Edward Baines. Also included in the committee was William Gladstone, who had pushed the interests of the Established Church over those of Nonconformist missionary societies in relation to the Negro Education Grant. Gladstone, a conservative Tory, would be a thorn in Buxton's side.[77] Although Buxton's name is intimately connected to both the proposal for the Aborigines Committee as well as the final report itself, women in Buxton's family played an important role in both the collation of material for the 1836 report of 853 pages printed with the minutes of evidence, appendix and index, as well as the drafting of the 1837 final report of some 300 pages. Two women of particular importance were Buxton's cousin Anna Gurney, who wrote much of the final report, and Buxton's daughter Priscilla, who inspired the establishment of the Aborigines Committee.[78] Such examples serve as a reminder of the pivotal, yet hidden, role that women played in the shaping of policy in the British Empire. Philip too was also heavily involved in writing the final report; however, he was careful to keep his contributions secret lest it affect the judgements of other committee members, not all of whom shared the same humanitarian convictions as Buxton.[79]

According to Buxton's memoirs, his focus in the report was on the 'evils of the system hitherto pursued towards the native tribes, and of the remedies to be applied'.[80] The report was intended as a 'manual for the future treatment of aboriginal nations in connection with [British] colonies'.[81] The resultant polemic report was skewed from the outset, with the objective being to prove: 'first, the destructive cruelty to which the native tribes had generally been subjected; and, second, that, wherever they had received equitable and humane treatment, they had increased in numbers, acquired the arts of civilized life, and accepted the blessings of religion'.[82] The report was thus written from the premises that a boundary existed between 'good' and 'bad' civilisation. Missionaries in their role as civilisers and bringers of Protestant Christianity (the 'right' form of religion), were on the side of good. The pivotal role of religion was evident in the establishment of the Aborigines Committee in order to:

> consider what Measures ought to be adopted with respect to the Native Inhabitants of Countries where British Settlements are made, and to the Neighbouring Tribes, in order to secure to them the due observance of Justice and the protection of their Rights; to promote the spread of Civilization among them, and to lead them to the peaceful and voluntary reception of the Christian Religion.[83]

The Committee focused upon the Indigenous inhabitants of existing colonies, as well as Indigenous inhabitants in areas that bordered upon British colonies, possibly with an expansionist view of potentially incorporating these people into British settlements at a later period or engaging them in economic activities such as trade. The foci of the report were to be upon justice, protection of Indigenous rights, civilisation and Christianisation. These foci point to the fact that the committee was not intent upon upholding aspects of Indigenous society, but rather that British law, society and religion were to be the fundamental components of new social systems for Indigenous peoples within British colonies. The Report was explicit in its damnation of low moral character of previous British settlement in the colonies, and was emphatic that a break should be made between past misdemeanours and future practice.[84] As chair of the Aborigines Committee, Buxton questioned how European contact had affected Indigenous peoples, particularly in terms of morality. To that end, he often enquired about the establishment of missions and whether any improvements in Indigenous peoples could be noted since the coming of missionaries.[85] He also frequently questioned witnesses on the effects of European civilisation on the moral character of Indigenous peoples, with the general conclusions being that where European civilisation met with Indigenous cultures it was only the positive influence of Christianity that had countered the negative vices that traders, merchants, settler colonists and other Europeans took with them into the colonies.[86]

Evidence relating to schooling in the report

Many of the witnesses for the Aborigines Committee spoke of a great desire amongst Indigenous peoples to receive religious instruction and Western forms of schooling. From New Zealand, the Rev. W. Yate spoke of the establishment of schools run by Maori youth in their own villages which were visited by missionaries once a month.[87] Witnesses from the Cape Colony spoke of a great desire amongst the 'Hottentots' (Khoikhoi) for schools and Western instruction, with those who could spell sought out by others to teach them, and children eager to learn.[88] Yet his broader complaint was that the Khoikhoi had been deprived of their woods, water and land by the Europeans, with the only the missionaries protecting them from further violence. As redress for these injustices he wished for missionary schools to be reinstated and children to be taught.[89] Tzatzoe's evidence also mentioned Philip's recurring suggestion to chiefs to send their children to school, which was often considered difficult with the threat of colonial violence.[90] More broadly, the provision of moral and religious education was seen as a great experiment, given that many Indigenous peoples of the British colonies had no written language of their own. Although children were educated through traditional ways and means, it was an open question whether children from other cultures could be taught as British children were, or, more pertinently, whether British forms of schooling would change and 'improve' Indigenous people. There were enough examples in the Empire of Indigenous people having actively sought out Western forms of education for ends that were not necessarily aligned with those of missionaries. For example, amongst the Griquas (known under the broad term of 'Coloured' in apartheid South Africa), writing became a necessary skill for a man to succeed to a chieftainship, demonstrating how the acquisition of Western knowledge and skills contributed to symbolic social status.[91] Indeed, the promise of increased status, rather than access to Christianity, was a pragmatic reason for non-Europeans to attend missionary schools. Both colonial governments and missionaries saw the willingness of Indigenous people to engage in Western forms of instruction as an indicator of potential engagement and assimilation into settler colonial society, including eventual absorption into colonial labour markets, and thus willingness to learn was often equated with willingness to assimilate.

Along with willingness, an ability to learn was also important. Within the 1836 report there was a pervasive belief amongst missionary and other religious educators that Indigenous peoples were able to be trained, and were not inherently stupid. Such a belief contrasted to the views of many settlers. In his testimony, James Read (of Philip's party), stated that the children of the Kat River settlement showed aptitude in religious and general education and were 'inferior to none', with education.[92] Yet in his testimony, Archdeacon Broughton of New South Wales noted that the advent of Europeans had had detrimental effects upon the moral and physical state of Aborigines. According to Broughton, these were not unintelligent people; rather, 'their intellect, when it is exercised, is very acute upon subjects that they choose to apply it to'.[93] That is, it was not the intellect that was seen to be wanting, but the will. This was an important point, for in the intellectual enlightenment milieu the ability to reason was seen as an essential human component, and in a period when many settlers questioned the humanity of Indigenous peoples, the ability to reason and the capacity to be instructed were seen as two aspects of human behaviour that Indigenous peoples needed to prove in order to be seen as members of the human race. Missionaries were more willing than many other settlers to ascribe intellect to Indigenous people. For example, the 1837 Aborigines Committee Report noted that amongst settlers in South Africa there was a general feeling that Africans were 'incapable of benefiting by instruction', with settlers 'of the Cape ... considered to have been averse to their [the Africans] receiving moral or religious instruction of any kind'.[94] In this colony the work of missionaries was touted as ineffectual, and humanitarians in the metropole were labelled as meddling.

In Australia, many settlers at the end of the 1830s believed that Indigenous Australians were incapable of being instructed, which led colonists to

> arrive at the natural conclusion that [...] the Blacks being but a part and parcel of the brute creation, being deficient of intellect, there can be no responsibility attached to their destruction, more than there is to the extirpation of any other animal whose presence is obnoxious to the possessor of the soil.[95]

Thus, colonists could justify killing Indigenous people purely because they were not considered to be on the same intellectual level as Europeans. A different view had been taken in the 1836 Aborigines Committee Report, where evidence of Indigenous peoples wishing for instruction, and of the ability of Indigenous peoples to learn, indicated to both missionaries and humanitarians that Indigenous peoples deserved the 'blessings of civilization'. Moreover, that they should be provided with religious instruction and education to be instructed in moral codes and knowledge of civil expectations to render them useful members of the 'modernising' colonial society. However, the Report of 1836 also noted the disappointment that missionaries in Australia had faced as Aboriginal people were uninterested in Christian instruction. Uncommitted and dismissive responses were not limited to the Australian experience: they were common from New Zealand through to South Africa and Canada.[96] The disinterest in the Christian message by Australian Aborigines led Broughton to agree to Buxton's claim that the majority of Aborigines were 'entirely abandoned to that ignorance and degradation'.[97] Other witnesses suggested that Australian Aborigines were not lacking in ability to be taught; rather, there was a deficiency in the methods used and the zeal of the teachers.[98]

The 1836 Aborigines Committee Report expected good to come of religious education, as part of a broader focus upon justice, and moral and civil improvement. Given the ubiquity of frontier violence and injustices towards Indigenous peoples, the writers of the report made a connection between the domestication and control of Indigenous peoples. Activities such as agriculture, village life and schooling were all intended to encourage sedentary habits, while justice towards (and for) Indigenous peoples was seen to be played out through British institutions such as courts, and not on the battle field. Tzatzoe himself stated so much at the Select Committee, answering in the affirmative to Buxton's question 'If your people were all made Christians, and instructed in agriculture and the arts, which Europeans have introduced amongst them, would not that be a recompense for the wrongs which your people have sustained?'[99] Yet to a previous question of whether Christian instruction alone would be a '[recompense] for all the injuries which Europeans have done to the natives of Africa' he replied: 'That is not my part to say; I come here to complain.'[100] His comments suggest that Christian teaching was considered only useful to counter the ravages of colonisation when embedded within a broader European episteme.

The 1837 final report

In July 1837 the final report of over 300 pages was printed for communication with the House of Lords.[101] Almost a year had lapsed since the publication of the 1836 report on the Aborigines Committee, which contained transcripts of the interviews between the witnesses and the committee without comment. As the final report was at the printers Buxton was forced to stop its publication due to pressure to include further evidence. George Grey, in the company of Buxton, went through the report with a red pen, crossing out material that was deemed too politically sensitive. In particular, many of the passages that Philip had helped to inform and craft were struck out, as they were too damming of the involvement of colonial officers in the atrocities of the latest Frontier war.[102] Missionary intelligence was excluded to appease political pressure. The final report was thus less politically charged than initially intended.

The 1837 Final Report to the House of Lords on the Aborigines Committee gave an overview of the general state of Indigenous peoples in British settlements before moving on to a more detailed overview of each of the colonies as well as places such as New Zealand and some South Sea (Pacific) Islands, which were not yet under formal British control, and thus seen as 'settlements'.[103] It also contained a 30-page section entitled 'Effects of Fair Dealing, combined with Christian Instruction, on Aborigines', a two and a half page brief conclusion, nine general suggestions and further geographically specific suggestions for each of the colonies and settlements. Attached to this report were the minutes of evidence recorded in the 1837 sessions as well as an appendix containing assorted papers and extracts from letters and dispatches.

Religious ideals dominated the final report, with both the introductory paragraphs and conclusion of the 1837 report being unapologetically Christian. The blessings of Providence were evoked to draw notice to the Christian obligations that the British held towards the Indigenous inhabitants of the lands they had colonised.[104] Within this world-view, missionaries were seen as the moral counterweights to certain forms of settler colonialism And indeed, the conclusions and suggestions from the report advocated a collaboration between religious and government groups, with missionaries deemed 'invaluable agents' in the provision of 'moral and religious improvement [together with] well-matured schemes for advancing the social and political improvement of the tribes'.[105] Such suggestions were reminiscent of the language used in relation to the West Indies, where the moral improvement in the character of slaves was deemed necessary in order to prepare them 'for a participation in those civil rights and privileges which are enjoyed by other classes of His Majesty's subjects'.[106] That is, moral and civil improvement were seen to be complementary, indeed, inextricably entwined. Moreover, Indigenous peoples were expected to conform and embrace ideals such as duties, obligations, responsibilities and privileges bestowed upon them as British subjects. In the section on South Africa, James Read's evidence was used as an indication of the willingness of Africans to receive education. He was quoted as saying: 'The Caffres [Xhosa] begin to see that they have not the same intelligence (I mean as far as regards books and knowledge) as the Hottentots [Khoikhoi], and they have often wished to have missionaries, like the Hottentots, to instruct them and their children.'[107] The competition amongst Africans for schooling was presented as the willingness of Africans to embrace missionaries as friends and protectors.

Evident throughout the report was a religious world-view, one that was particularly informed by the views of the evangelical Christians on the Aborigines Committee, and of the broader religious milieu that Buxton and his family came from. Already on the first page of the 1837 report the moral obligations of an 'enlightened and Christian people' towards 'uncivilized' peoples in lands that the British settled were raised – thus setting a tone of 'imperial theology' within the report.[108] Such a tone was further evident in the 30-page section of the report entitled 'Effects of Fair Dealing, combined with Christian Instruction, on Aborigines'. Comprising one third of the actual report (not including the evidence), this section described the benefits that European civilisation could bring to Indigenous peoples in British Settlements. Not only was it seen as a Christian obligation to provide Indigenous peoples with Christian instruction, it was deemed 'for our advantage to have dealings with civilized men rather than with barbarians', because 'Savages are dangerous neighbours and unprofitable customers, and if they remain as degraded denizens of our colonies, they become a burthen [*sic*] upon the State'.[109] As the 1836 report had detailed, 'Christianity and civilisation advance *pari passu*' with it generally being agreed that Christianity was the primary force without which no 'true' civilisation could occur.[110] Yet there were differences of opinion. Archdeacon Broughton was of the opinion that Aborigines should be Christianised before civilised, as they should be given a 'knowledge of religion, and make that the groundwork of better habits of life',[111] sentiments that were widely shared within evangelical Christian circles. Yet others, such as the influential Quaker and member of the APS and the Anti-Slavery Society Thomas Hodgkin, held a deep sense of the embedded nature of religion within Western civilisation. For Hodgkin, the conversion of people to Christianity without the provision of education and other 'civilising' agents, was bound to be temporary only, and thus, 'civilisation' and 'Christianisation' could not be separated.[112] This sentiment not only reflected the perceived benefits for Indigenous peoples but also the missionary conviction that only religiously zealous people would leave the comforts of civilisation to bring Christianity to Indigenous peoples.[113] The question of whether non-Europeans should first be introduced to 'civilisation' or Christianisation was of great importance to the Aborigines Committee. It recommended that missionaries should be encouraged, and in doing so placed missionaries as the moral counterweights to empire, counterweights who themselves were also to balance religious and practical teaching.

The conclusions of the 1837 report

The two-and-a-half page conclusion of the 1837 report began with the reprinting of the evidence provided by the three missionary secretaries, Dandeson Coates (CMS), John Beecham (WMMS) and William Ellis (LMS). All three unsurprisingly agreed with Buxton's statement that European settlers introduced vices to Indigenous peoples and hindered the spread of 'civilization, education, commerce and Christianity'.[114] They further agreed with Buxton's leading question that European contact 'tends [...] to deteriorate the morals of the natives', except in the places where missions had been established.[115] In proposing a solution to future scenarios in which Indigenous peoples were engaged in violence towards British colonists two options were presented: either military control or 'a line of temperate conduct and of justice towards our neighbours'.[116] This second option saw Christian instruction as pacifying the violent retaliations of Indigenous peoples. As the conclusions had been read and approved by Grey (in his function as Under-Secretary of State for the Colonies) before being printed, it can be surmised that the movement away from military to missionary control was one that was approved of in both evangelical and governmental circles.[117] Yet 'temperate conduct' was also conceived of in terms conducive to 'trade, commerce, peace and civilization'.[118] The moral concern which was infused throughout the report was not only for the welfare of Indigenous people. There was concern that if the current system was to continue then many peoples would be exterminated, which would put a bad stain on Britain. After having atoned for the evils of slavery, it was seen as imperative for Britain to combat any evils that colonisation may bring with it. This was, however, not only for religious reasons, but also in the hope of increased economic growth. There was also concern expressed that negative aspects of colonisation might either diminish trade with Indigenous peoples or increase the costs of wars in the colonies.

The expression of such economic incentives have led some scholars to argue that the humanitarian ideology within the report was overshadowed by economic motives to the detriment of Indigenous concerns.[119] However, it could also be argued that the protectionist suggestions of the report indicate the centrality of its progressive humanitarianism. Some of the suggestions, had they been enacted, would have curtailed the economic growth of settlers through, for example, making void some purchases of land.[120] The conclusions of the report made clear that the blame for much of the mistreatment of Indigenous peoples within British colonies lay with settlers and the 'system of dealing with the rights of the natives',[121] thereby absolving representatives of government either in the colonies or in Britain from blame. Particular blame was placed upon the 'dregs' of British civilisation sent to the colonies, especially to the colonies of Australia.[122] These 'dregs' included convicts, people that had immigrated to the colonies in the hope of raising their economic chances, traders and sailors. Rather than embodying Christian morals, such people were often seen as spreading the vices of European culture. Given that the penal system was still in place to fulfil 'the national necessity of finding some outlet for the superabundant population of Great Britain and Ireland', many colonies, especially those in Australia, were to continue to receive the 'dregs' of British society, and although this practice would be stopped in the near future, the effects of such a population continued to incur upon the 'rights of those who have not the means of advocating their interests or exciting sympathy for their sufferings'.[123] The greatness of the British Empire was, according to the conclusion, a blessing of Providence, with it being the moral obligation and reciprocal duty to bring the blessings of civilisation and Christian faith to Indigenous peoples in British settlements, who were themselves seen as helpless and in need of paternalistic protection.

Suggestion VI: 'Religious instruction and education to be provided'

The 1837 Aborigines Committee report included nine suggestions. Some were general and others specific in nature reflecting the perceived variance in moral and physical condition of Indigenous peoples in various parts of the British Empire. The focus of the suggestions reflected the report's primary aims to 'fix the rules of our conduct towards them',[124] and were accordingly of a legislative, regulative and secular nature, aiming to save people through changing the external system in which they were enmeshed – a form of progressive humanitarianism. Reflective of this were suggestions that focused upon the protection of Indigenous peoples through governmental means (Suggestion I – Protection of Natives to devolve on the Executive) or one which recommended the abolishment of certain laws and regulations that impinged upon the ability of Indigenous peoples to freely offer their labour for the best price (Suggestion II – Contract for Service to be limited). Further suggestions included: Sale of ardent Spirits to be prevented (Suggestion III); Regulations as to Lands within British Dominions (Suggestion IV); New Territories not to be acquired without Sanction of Home Government (Suggestion V); Punishment of Crimes (Suggestion VII); and, Treaties with Natives inexpedient (Suggestion VIII). Only two suggestions explicitly focused upon philanthropic work: Religious Instruction and Education to be provided (Suggestion VI) and Missionaries to be encouraged (Suggestion IX).

Suggestion VI deemed the provision of religious instruction and education to be a moral responsibility of the British as compensation for the land that had been taken from its original inhabitants. In the eyes of the British, uncultivated land was 'rude and barren', yet even in this state it was 'worth a large amount of money', from which the Indigenous inhabitants had mostly not benefited.[125] Buxton had stated prior to the Aborigines Committee that religious instruction and education was a British duty to compensate for land loss in the colonies, and thus it is no surprise that this suggestion appeared in the report.[126] Yet unlike the Negro Education Grant, which received funds from the British government, the colonies themselves were to carry the cost of supplying religious education through charging a Land Revenue upon lands which the Crown sold within the colonies. The funds from crown land sales were also to be put aside for the 'protection of the survivors of the tribes' both current and future under British rule.[127] Many of the examples cited in the Aboriginal Committee report of 1837 came from Australia, a land which was considered waiting to be 'developed'. In cultivating the land for agriculture the British believed that they had 'improved' it, with uncultivated land being another indication for the British that Indigenous peoples did not deserve the land as they did not know the value of it in its uncultivated state.[128] In lieu of land, Indigenous people were to receive 'instruction of the adults, the education of their youth, and the protection of them all'.[129] Compared to the discussions centred on emancipation, which focused upon the freed slaves – mostly children aged under six and those apprentices who could be spared from their work – this was broadening of the aims of education, in which adults were specifically targeted for 'instruction'.

As we read in the previous chapter, Buxton had been responsible for the inclusion of the phrase 'liberal and comprehensive' in the fifth resolution pertaining to emancipation, with these words causing some confusion and much debate. However, these terms did not appear in the Aborigines Committee report or the suggestions at all, raising the question as to which missionaries Buxton and his fellow commissioners had in mind to provide 'religious instruction and education' to the denizens of the British colonies. And what if the phrase opened up a space for non-denominational teaching, or for the division of secular from religious subjects (as per the Irish system), or even for secular schools? Nineteenth-century missionaries and British colonial governments were commonly unified in their desire to provide schooling to non-European peoples; however, whereas the focus for missionaries was primarily upon the religious aspects of education to make good Christians out of Indigenous peoples in order that they could be good citizens, the British government's objectives were to educate a section of colonial society to become good subjects of that society who were also good (Protestant) Christians. These differences, I argue, highlight the variance between missionary and colonial modernity. Within Recommendation VI the Aborigines Committee did not explicitly state that it should be missionaries who provided religious instruction and education to 'the survivors of the tribes to which the lands comprised in that Colony formerly belonged',[130] a phrase which in and of itself reflected a fatalist belief for the future state of Indigenous peoples following British contact.

The wording of the Aborigines Committee's recommendation VI hinted at government involvement in what should be taught, expanding beyond just moral and religious education to include 'religious instruction *and* education' [my emphasis]. This was a subtle, yet significant departure from earlier recommendations promoting the 'religious *and* moral education' [my emphasis] of Indigenous peoples, as it suggested that religious instruction could be separated from secular instruction.[131] It was also a departure from the wording of the fifth resolution pertaining to emancipation that called for 'liberal and comprehensive principles, for the religious and moral education of the negro population to be emancipated'.[132] The terms had been expanded beyond reference to moral progress to place more focus upon the usefulness of instruction for social, political and economic ends of all members of the 'tribes' under the benevolence of the British Empire.

Suggestion IX: 'Missionaries to be encouraged'

Suggestion IX explicitly encouraged missionaries and their plans for moral, religious, social and political improvement. This reflected the effective monopoly that missionaries had upon schools for Indigenous peoples, partly due to their close relationships with Indigenous peoples. As discussed in the previous chapter, the Negro Education Grant created similar situations in which missionaries had full control of the curricula of their schools, despite an initial suggestion from Buxton in 1832 that they only be responsible for religious instruction and that 'school masters & houses will, we hope, be provided from another quarter'.[133] As we read above, suggestion VI in the 1837 report pushed for a certain curricular to be provided, one that encouraged instruction beyond that of just a religious nature.

The suggestion was vague as to which missionary groups were to be encouraged. What, for example, did the suggestions mean for Catholics? Although denominational or confessional allegiances of missionaries were not addressed in the 1837 report, there is nevertheless a sense that a united Protestant front was more important than denominational factions. Thomas Hodgkin, for example, desired that missionary work would be non-sectarian, in order to 'avoid misleading and confusing potential converts'.[134] However, in specific instances, such as in the suggestions for the colonies of Australia limits were placed upon the nationality of missionaries. For these colonies it was recommended that 'the choice of [the missionaries], and the direction of their labours, should be confined to the missionary societies in this kingdom'.[135] It is not immediately clear within the report why nationalistic restrictions should be placed upon missionaries. The suggestion did, however, follow in the wake of the Negro Education Grant, which only invited British-based organisations with a presence in the West Indies to apply for funding, and thus effectively excluded Catholic groups. In regard to the Australian colonies and British missionaries, Archdeacon Broughton's evidence brought before the 1836 Aborigines Committee advocated that as the Church of England was 'endowed with pre-eminent advantages here, she should justify the distinction by leading the way as a missionary, and by becoming the mother of missionaries who should attempt the recovery of this unhappy generation'.[136] Such comments reflected a desire to maintain the dominance of the Established Church, even if this was undertaken through the disesteemed CMS.

The exclusion of non-British missionaries is particularly interesting given the close relations that German and British missionary societies had maintained since the eighteenth century, as well as the work that the German-based groups such as the Moravian Church, the Danish-Halle-English Mission or the Gossner Mission had undertaken in various British colonies since the eighteenth century. The work of German missionaries was so venerated that by the late 1830s religious leaders in Australia were actively seeking out Germans to work amongst Australian Aborigines, as they were considered to be particularly apt for the task as their linguistic and cultural background made them unsuitable to accept calls to English-speaking congregations of settlers in towns.[137] At the time of the Aborigines Committee there were a number of incipient Australian colonies. The Colony of South Australia, for which much land had been sold, was about to be established. Hope was expressed that better conditions would prevail for Aborigines than had in other Australian colonies.[138] German missionaries would make some of the first efforts in this colony,[139] which went against the suggestions of the Aborigines Committee.

Within Suggestion IX, the general suggestion to encourage missionaries, the report encroached upon religious liberties in suggesting that missionaries needed to be more than just zealous and pious to be effective. A responsible missionary society, the report posited, would send out missionaries that would attend to more than just the souls of Indigenous peoples. There were limits to what the 'providence of a Parliamentary Committee' could suggest as necessary attributes and qualities of such missionaries.[140] Yet an ideal missionary would advance the social and political welfare of the people he or she worked amongst. Indeed, the suggestion did not place moral progress and concern for moral order as the defining impetus; rather, the 'plans of religious and moral improvement should be combined [with] well-matured schemes for advancing the social and political improvement of the tribes, and for the prevention of any sudden changes which might be injurious to the health and physical constitution of the new converts'.[141]

The focus upon 'advancing the social and political improvement of the tribes' was a step beyond the mere 'religious and moral education' of the Negro Education Grant, and called for a more varied approach to education than just the provision of Bibles. The change in phrase also reveals a perceived need to train non-Europeans in skills rather than just fill them with teachings as a course for moral progress. That is, education within the terms of the 1837 Aborigines Committee report was tied to broader notions of commerce within a certain form of humanitarian imperialism. Alan Lester has argued that this fitted into evangelical missionary notions of Christianisation and civilisation within settler colonies.[142] Education (and also instruction) was linked to commerce in terms that were more progressively humanitarian than purely economic. Helped along by events such as David Livingstone's mid-nineteenth-century explorations across Africa, the popular missionary slogan 'Commerce and Christianity' would increasingly find resonance within missionary circles throughout the century.[143] Although missionary groups initially distanced themselves from secular affairs such as commerce, increasingly throughout the century they themselves needed to engage in commerce in order to fund their missions.[144]

Prior to that time, however, many of the missionary groups involved in the British colonies in the 1830s were more concerned with the spiritual welfare of their converts and protecting them from the evil vices of civilisation than with economic improvement. The section on the 'Effects of Fair

Dealing, combined with Christian Instruction, on Aborigines' in the 1837 report presented the propagation of Christianity as the only means of 'imparting the blessings of civilization' and the only way to mitigate the evils that civilisation entailed.[145] Various extracts were reprinted from the 1836 report to underscore this point, with editorial comments further emphasising the connection between Christianity and civilisation. As with the discussions at the Liverpool Missionary Conference some twenty years later (discussed in depth in the next chapter), secular education alone was not deemed suitable for non-Europeans. Education without religion (or indeed civilisation without religion) was considered not enough to improve the social and civil condition of Indigenous peoples.[146] Yet, missionaries did not only introduce moral and religious instruction, but also trained Indigenous peoples in 'useful trades',[147] thereby preparing them to become serviceable members of British settler society in their capacity as labourers.[148] The general argument was that Christianity was the means through which Indigenous peoples could become beneficiaries of 'true' civilisation, with industrial training contributing to their absorption into colonial labour markets and economies. Religious groups would more generally use this argument across the nineteenth century to legitimise their educational work in the British colonies.

In general, the report considered converted people as being better British subjects as they adhered to civil and moral codes, greatly enabling the administration of colonial spaces (beyond any personal and religious aspects of conversion). It was thus deemed the government's duty to encourage missionaries, who themselves would be instrumental in bringing the 'right' type of civilisation to Indigenous peoples. Although the suggestions of the report desired missionaries to advance 'the social and political improvement of the tribes',[149] missionaries themselves were not to be political beings. In his evidence to the Aborigines Committee Sir Rufane Donkin, the former Governor of the Cape of Good Hope from 1820 to 1821, exemplified this sentiment. He was of the opinion that missionaries were the best means of introducing Christianity to Indigenous people for missionaries would 'zealously and religiously devote themselves to that good work without intermeddling with the politics either internal or external to the colony'.[150] For him, politically oriented missionaries were unfit for religious work, with the connection between religious and civil duties seen as undesirable. Despite numerous missionary societies insisting that their missionaries not meddle in political affairs, enforcement was often not practical or desirable. In order to gain the trust of Indigenous groups, missionaries at times worked against colonial commands, which led other witnesses at the Aborigines Committee to suggest that missionaries in southern Africa had stirred up trouble between the colonial officers and the Indigenous people, and that 'on several occasions the missionaries persuaded them that they were much greater men than the officers who are sent out to be with them'.[151] In further denigrating missionaries, Captain Robert Scott Aitchison, an officer in the Cape Mounted Riflemen in the Cape Colony, criticised them for living off the funds and material goods they received from supporters and not from their own industry, with the missionary presence not improving the state of the 'Caffres' at all.[152] Missionaries therefore were working in a difficult nexus between settlers, colonial officials and Indigenous needs and wants, with these difficulties remaining throughout the rest of the century and into the next.

The provision of 'religious instruction and education' and the encouragement of missionaries went hand-in-hand in the 1837 recommendations; however, this was not always the case in subsequent government commissions and discussions. In 1846, James Kay-Shuttleworth was asked to prepare a memorandum on industrial education as to be applied to the colonies. His recommendations were not ever completely implemented and it has been suggested that the impact of the memorandum has been overstated by historians.[153] Kay-Shuttleworth's recommendations mark a different trajectory of government policy, promoting as they did the principles of Christianity without explicit mention of the role of missionaries.[154] He did not request information from missionary groups as to industrial training, but relied upon 'official' reports and communications from governments. Thus, from being the major suppliers of 'religious and moral instructions' in the early 1830s, missionaries were increasingly omitted from government discussions on education. By the end of the century, parallel systems of government and missionary educational conferences had been established demonstrating the disentanglement of religion and politics in schooling in many of the (former) British colonies.[155] Such omission of missionaries from government discussions on Indigenous education did not, however, prevent missionaries from positioning themselves as experts on Indigenous education. As the Select Committee Report demonstrates, missionary groups were involved in the report writing and the final recommendations; however, their role was limited in comparison to the Negro Education Act, with this diminished role particularly apparent in places where land, not labour, was the focus of colonisation.

After the Aborigines Committee report

Within Britain and throughout the colonies, edited versions of the report, as well as the original, were made available to different groups. The secretaries of the CMS, WMMS and the LMS reprinted some of the evidence that they and others had provided to the Aborigines Committee in a book entitled *Christianity the Means of Civilization* in 1837 to underscore the importance of missionaries.[156] The title of the book reflected contemporaneous debates as to whether Christianity or civilisation should be given priority within missionary circles. By 1837, Samuel Marsden's theory that civilisation should precede Christianisation had lost currency within missionary circles, reflected in the fact that all three secretaries responded in their evidence that civilisation should never precede Christianity, although the two could go hand-in-hand. The secretaries' report was, as with many missionary publications, carefully edited to omit descriptions deemed too explicit for general consumption.[157] Through the republication of excepts from the report the missionary societies portrayed themselves as necessary and acknowledged helpers for the higher cause of protecting Aboriginal peoples within British colonies. They used such government legitimation in their further self-promotion, and in particular used tangible objects such as schools to rally support for their work in the colonies. The Society of Friends, also known as Quakers, produced their own edited version of the report in order to inspire the Quakers to be actively involved in the protection of Indigenous peoples in the colonies. Recently, scholars have argued that in the Quakers version of the report, reference to missionaries as a solution to Indigenous degradation was jettisoned; however, this claim is exaggerated as all of the titles of the suggestions are presented, albeit without the explanatory text of the 1837 government report.[158]

Another version was published by the APS, which itself was founded in 1837 in response to the Aborigines Committee.[159] The society, of which Buxton was the inaugural president, aimed both to use the momentum of the evangelical movement to raise public concern within Britain of the need to improve the situation of Indigenous peoples in the colonies as well as to provide a mouthpiece by which humanitarian concerns might reach official circles.[160] The rationale behind the APS republishing a shorter version was that the society could focus on the evident and recommendations that mirrored the aims of the society, with Philip joining with them to ensure that some of the more political material which had been jettisoned from the 1837 report reach the British public.[161] A significant aim of publishing the report was to shake the British public out of their indifference to the fate of Indigenous peoples. It was, according to the APS, only through the work of missionaries that information on the deplorable state of Indigenous peoples in British colonies could be made available to the British public. The APS commended missionaries as it was through them that the 'truth' of the situation had been revealed, or in the words of the report: 'Amid persecution and scorn, obloquy, ridicule, and contempt, they have steadily persevered in their work of faith and labour of love, until to them, in an especial degree, belongs the honour of having first exposed the evil workings of our colonial policy.'[162]

With the 'truth' exposed, it was up to both the British public to be alert to the situation, and the APS and similar organisations to maintain pressure upon the government to change legislation. To this end, the Society requested the lawyer Standish Motte, a member of the committee, to draw up an outline of a legal code that might best serve Indigenous peoples.[163] The resultant book entitled, *Outline of a system of legislation, for securing protection to the Aboriginal inhabitants of all countries colonized by Great Britain*, was sold for a shilling, and also disseminated amongst the legislature of Great Britain and to the Colonial Minister.[164] The main text in the tract was introduced with a statement taken from the 1837 report which depicted the British as 'an enlightened and Christian people' that had moral obligations over those peoples that had been colonised,[165] a concept that by the end of the century would be immortalised through Rudyard Kipling's poem 'The White Man's Burden'. The events which occurred in the antipodes under the name of British colonisation were deemed to be commonly associated with atrocities, cruelties, injustices, suffering and death for Aboriginal peoples, and were seen to have slighted the political and commercial interests of Britain, whilst tarnishing the national honour. Motte's report focused upon the need for 'an efficient system of legislation', which would control the colonisers and thereby render any Indigenous rebellion or continued barbarism needless. Mirroring the language of missionary reports, he placed blame on the Aboriginal population themselves for being easily influenced by the bad vices of colonisers due to their lack of those virtues admired by British Victorians such as moral restraint, education, knowledge and self-control.[166] Nevertheless, his focus on the structural requirements of protecting the Aborigines relegated missionaries as subordinate to the educational agent of the Local Board of Protection for the Aborigines, not as agents in their own right. In relation to schooling he suggested that that Native schooling with 'native teachers' be provided for moral and religious instruction as well as secular subjects, and not European teachers. Hodgkin was also convinced that the most appropriate way to provide education was through Native teachers instructing pupils in the vernacular.[167] However, in order for this to occur, these people themselves needed to be instructed in Western forms of education. This took time. To ensure that the Native teachers of such schools were embedded within the values of Great Britain, Motte suggested that a number of

> youths be selected from the aborigines of each colony and sent to England, to be educated under the direction of the aborigines commissioners in such useful arts and sciences, and in such knowledge as may best conduce, on their return to their native country, to the improvement and civilization of their brethren.[168]

Missionary organisations had themselves used this method, which was often unsuccessful as many of the youths died in the unfamiliar climate of England.[169] Indeed, this was the fate of Andries Stoffels, one of Philip's envoy, who did not make the journey home, dying of tuberculosis in Portsmouth harbour.[170] Jan Tzatzoe did return. Back in South Africa in September 1838, he wrote to the 'very honoured Fathers' of the LMS, informing them of his safe arrival in southern Africa after some two years absence. There he continued his work as a politician and chief. In Philipstown, he spend some days talking to chiefs about his time in England, the generosity of the Christian public and how the concerns of 'natives' around the Empire were heard, no doubt a reference to the Select Committee. He also relayed a message from Lord Glenelg, that 'they must maintain peace with the colony' and that the colonial government would protect them if they took their complaints about settler brutalities to the Governor.[171] This was a message that he been relaying since before he left for England. From 1833, the Xhosa had not been able to communicate with the colonial authorities directly as they were forbidden to enter the Cape Colony due to various ordinates. The only means of communication had been through missionaries.[172] The way to the heart of government was, as Tzatzoe and other chiefs had found, through missionary organisations.[173] Missionary organisations had provided the Xhosa with education, which provided opportunities for the Xhosa to model themselves on the British, whilst at the same time the British were ensuring the traditional way of Xhosa life was being destroyed. On his return to his family and people, Tzatzoe was meet with a barrage of questions as to his time across the 'great water'. His experiences and descriptions were conceived by some as evidence of the benevolence of the English, despite the local realities of the colonial situation. Tzatzoe himself expressed his hope in the letter to the LMS that more of his people would convert to Christianity, and many more missionaries would be sent out to establish more stations. As evidence of the willingness of his people to engage in Christianity, he underscored the importance of education, writing:

> We have their schools. 1 infant school a Sunday school and another day school kept by a Caffre who began the school of his own accord. I hope we shall be able to establish some more schools if we can get other Hottentot or Caffre youth to become teachers. I am quite sure that the gospel will not be treated with great confidently till natives become teachers and go away where to preach the gospel.[174]

Tzatzoe's comments reflected the assumption that Christianity was best disseminated through local people, both preachers and teachers. Yet there was concern expressed by European missionaries, for example at the missionary conference in Liverpool in 1860 – the subject of the next chapter – whether Indigenous peoples would be able to undertake missionary work without the supervision of European missionaries. Tzatzoe knew from experience how important local people were in disseminating Christian knowledge, with one of his daughters being a teacher to some 100 children.[175] Indeed, some two decades before Tzatzoe's statement, a LMS missionary at Bethelsdorp – where Tzatzoe had been raised – noted that women at that mission station attributed their spiritual awakening to Christianity not to White missionaries but rather to the preaching of their own people.[176] Although local people were needed, their recruitment and training, as we shall read in Chapter 4, was complex and difficult to realise due to funding, time and broader competing expectations of Christian schooling. These competing expectations at times were present in local families such as Tzatzoe's. In a second letter to the LMS in 1845, Tzatzoe beseeched them to provide funding so that he could help cover the costs arising from sending his daughters to a good Christian school. He began the letter by stating: 'I have always been deeply concerned about the education of my children, but never more so than at the present time.'[177] Two of his sons had not followed his Christian path; rather, they had 'adopted the customs of our heathen ancestry which while it deeply grieves me has done great injury to the cause of God'.[178] His hope was that the LMS would provide funding to offset some of the costs of sending his daughters to a Christian school, so that they would be beyond the influences that had affected his two sons. For him, the Christian education of his daughters was not a means to gratify his hopes as a parent, but would contribute to the broader aim of the Christianisation of Africa. His words resonate with the ideas that would spread more broadly around the British Empire in the following decades; that the education of local women was imperative to the Christianisation of local communities due to their perceived roles as moral cornerstone of new Christian families.

Tzatzoe perceived missionary education as a useful means to strengthen alliances and to gain European knowledge that could benefit his people in the changing political, social and epistemic landscape of colonial southern Africa. Yet, by the time he died in 1868 the changes had become devastating both to his people, and to him individually. He had regained his land, which the government had taken from him, and which had been a reason for his complaints in England before the Select Committee, only to be removed from this land for a final time in 1847. He had been loyal to the colonists in the 1830s, yet in the following decade he had fought on the side of the Xhosa in the 1848 uprising against the colonists, and again in 1851. He had been abandoned by the LMS, yet continued to support missionaries – for example, in 1857, when he spoke against false prophets to other chiefs. He resisted the new colonial order yet remained a Christian. In the decades after the Aborigines Committee, the missionaries, who had once been his allies, themselves were losing influence over colonial politics.[179] Yet the influence of missionary education as an entry into transnational political and religious networks continued in the lives of Tzatzoe and his family. One of his sons, Boy Henry Duke Tschatshu, like many other African boys from elite families, attended Zonnebloem College boarding school in Cape Town, and then continued his education at a boarding school in England in the 1860s.[180] Some of these boys would return as ordained ministers, becoming African leaders and cultural intermediaries, just as a future generation of Xhosa, epitomised by Nelson Mandela, would attend missionary schooling in their progression to political leadership.

Conclusion

The Aborigines Committee of 1836–37 has been seen by many historians as the highpoint of humanitarian concern for Indigenous peoples in British settlements. This chapter has focused on an overlooked aspect of the report, the provision of education as tool of 'modernising' and 'civilising' non-Europeans, and as compensation for British settler imperialism. The role that missionaries were subscribed to this report, reflected broader notions of modernity, morality and justice. The report was filled with references to Indigenous peoples' desires to receive Western education and to be 'raised' in Western forms of civilisation, creating an image of willing participants in British colonial expansion given the right conditions and access to Christianity. In suggesting that Indigenous peoples in the colonies should be protected from the negative effects of civilisation, the report privileged the benevolent efforts of Christian missionaries, who were to provide religious instruction and education embedded with Christian norms and morals. Despite the encouragement of missionaries being only one of nine suggestions, historians such as Andrew Porter have argued that this recommendation was seen as a 'triumph for the missionary movement' as missionaries were to be conduits between Indigenous peoples and the British settlers.[181] Another form of conduit between Indigenous peoples and European civilisation enabled by the 1836–37 report were Protectors, with the Committee suggesting their introduction in places such as Australia and British Guiana. The roles of Protectors and missionaries overlapped, with Protectors expected to cultivate 'a personal knowledge of the natives', to learn the local languages, to supply Aborigines with employment and to protect Aborigines from violence towards them.[182] Their roles were thus more aligned with regulation as well as policy formation than those of missionaries. Within southern Australia both settler resentment and Indigenous resistance left the

Protectorate system untenable by 1849, just a decade after being introduced.[183] In other colonial spaces, the Protectorate system was ultimately
downgraded so that the needs of Europeans were put ahead of Aborigines.[184] In contrast, missionary stations took deeper root in colonial spaces
and continued to spread throughout the nineteenth century.

Over the years and decades following the tabling of the report, events
such as the Indian Uprising, the failure of emancipation in the West Indies
and Indigenous disinterest in Christianity contributed to a feeling of disappointment in missionary circles. These events contributed to increased
racialist attitudes towards Indigenous peoples after the mid-nineteenth
century, with Indigenous peoples progressively believed not to deserve the
privileges and responsibilities of British subject-hood, as they were seen not
to fulfil the duties and responsibilities demanded by Western civilisation.
Simultaneously, a hardening of racial lines and ideas of racial determinism
and 'innatist discourses' arose in broader colonial and metropole discourses
(even if not necessarily prominent in humanitarian circles).[185] Such discourses
questioned assumptions of universal human improvement and development,
which, historians argue, had been a main driving force of humanitarians.[186]
At the time of the Aborigines Committee of 1836–37, universal human
improvement was a lofty and desired aim. The report, written as it was by
Christian philanthropists and humanitarians, desired for missionaries to be
the interface of Western civilisation. Yet in the years following its publication,
pressure groups that had championed the cases of the non-Europeans,
including the parliamentary evangelicals, were themselves becoming more
conservative and less unified, placing their attention more on domestic
rather than colonial affairs.[187] Many politicians who had championed the
humanitarian cause lost their seats in the 1837 elections, Buxton included,
reducing support to put the ideals of the Aborigines Committee into
legislative practice. Not only did parliamentary groups lose interest in the
state of Indigenous peoples, but by the 1850s, their plight was also waning
in the British public conscience.[188]

The Aborigines Committee Report portrayed a slight, yet significant
change in the role of missionaries as bringing more than just religious and
moral education to the 'tribes' under British rule. Missionary bodies
themselves had worked hard to be seen as legitimate focuses of civilisation
and Christianisation within the British Empire, with the social reformist,
humanitarian and philanthropic aims of missionary societies being
increasingly the same as those of colonial rulers and administrators, who
progressively justified imperial rule in terms of social and moral reform,
Christianity and 'progress'.[189] In such a configuration, the transcendental
aspects of religion became less relevant to the secular state than how
Christian values and attributes could be used to strengthen government and

civil society. Although close relationships were maintained between missionary societies and colonial and Imperial governments throughout the century, missionaries and humanitarians were never again as tightly aligned as they were during the time of the Aborigines Committee.

Through providing a global snapshot of the moral state of empire the report encouraged missionaries to engage in the civilising mission, not just in the Christianising mission. The Aborigines Committee would be the last time that missionary work around the globe would be discussed in any British Parliamentary Select Committee in such depth and breadth. The global reach of missionary work nevertheless remained a topic that was engaged with by governments, while missionary groups took up this global challenge through international meetings, such as those at Liverpool in 1860 (Chapter 3) and Edinburgh in 1910 (Chapter 5). These conferences provided overviews of missionary work and governmental collaborations in terms of the value of missionary education in relation to both the perceived value to non-Europeans as well as the value of schooling as a tangible outcome of missionary work. The 'success' of missionary schooling and the legitimation of missionary work through the collaborations with government and official backing through government Select Committees such as the Aborigines Committee 1836–1837 was used to encourage supporters to donate and thus solidify missionaries as the most capable providers of schooling in the colonies.

Notes

1 HC Deb, 1 July 1834, vol. 24, cc1061–1063, 1062, 'Colonies – Aboriginal tribes'.
2 This is a quote from Thomas Fowell Buxton's tract on the abolishment of the slavery in Africa, demonstrating that the rhetoric pertaining to 'raising' of non-Europeans was the same despite the various geographical contexts. See: Thomas Fowell Buxton, *The African slave trade and its remedy* (London: John Murray, 1840), p. 459.
3 HC Deb, 1 July 1834, vol. 24, cc1061–1063, 'Colonies – Aboriginal tribes'. Michael Barnett, *Empire of humanity: A history of humanitarianism* (Ithaca, NY: Cornell University Press, 2011), p. 63.
4 HC Deb, 1 July 1834, vol. 24, cc1061–1063, 'Colonies – Aboriginal tribes'.
5 HC PP 1835 (49) 'Colonies. Circular letter to the governors of His Majesty's colonial possessions, Downing-Street, 19 July 1834 [Colonies]'.
6 Grey resigned in lack of support received for the 'Suppression of Disturbances (Ireland) Bill'. See: HL Deb, 9 July 1834, vol. 24, cc1305–1335, 'Resignation of Earl Grey'. See also: HC Deb, 9 July 1834, vol. 24, cc1336–1142, 'Dissolution of the Ministry – Explanations of the Ministers'.

7 HC Deb, 14 July 1835, vol. 29, cc549–553, 'Treatment of Aborigines in British Settlements'.

8 The Select Committee took evidence from 1835; however, as the final reports were printed in 1836–1837, it is referred to by these dates.

9 Andrew Porter, *Religion versus empire? British Protestant missionaries and overseas expansion, 1700–1914* (Manchester: Manchester University Press, 2004), pp. 151–152, p. 307; Elizabeth Elbourne, *Blood ground: Colonialism, missions, and the contest for Christianity in the Cape Colony and Britain, 1799–1853* (Montreal and Ontario: McGill-Queen's University Press, 2002), p. 291.

10 Elizabeth Elbourne, 'The Sin of the settler: The 1835–1836 Select Committee on Aborigines and debates over virtue and conquest in the early nineteenth-century British white settler empire', *Journal of Colonialism and Colonial History*, 4:3 (2003), https://muse.jhu.edu/article/50777 [last accessed October 2020].

11 Alan Lester, 'Humanism, race and the colonial frontier', *Transactions of the Institute of British Geographers*, 37:1 (2011), 132–148, doi: 10.1111/j.1475-5661.2011.00450.x.

12 Alan Lester, 'British settler discourse and the circuits of empire', *History Workshop Journal*, 54 (2002), 25, doi: 10.1093/hwj/54.1.24.

13 Zoë Laidlaw, 'Integrating metropolitan, colonial and imperial histories – the Aborigines Select Committee of 1835–37', in Tracey Banivanua Mar and Julie Evans (eds), *Writing colonial Histories: Comparative perspectives* (Carlton: University of Melbourne, Department of History, 2002), p. 91.

14 Penelope Edmonds and Zoë Laidlaw, '"The British government is now awaking" How humanitarian Quakers repackaged and circulated the 1837 Select Committee Report on Aborigines', in Samuel Furphy and Amanda Nettelbeck (eds), *Aboriginal protection and its intermediaries in Britain's antipodean colonies* (New York: Routledge, 2020), pp. 38–57.

15 Tim Keegan, *Dr Philip's empire: One man's struggle for justice in nineteenth-century South Africa* (Cape Town: Zebra Press, 2016).

16 The interest in the topic is exemplified by two special issues of journals on the topic of humanitarianism. Both special issues, as the titles of both indicate, are embedded in newer scholarship on the global turn. See, for example, *Journal of Modern European History*, Special Issue Transnational Humanitarianism, 12:2 (2014); *Journal of Imperial and Commonwealth History*, Special issue Empire and Humanitarianism, 10:5 (2012).

17 Rob Skinner and Alan Lester, 'Humanitarianism and empire: New research agendas', *The Journal of Imperial and Commonwealth History*, 40:5 (2012), 730, doi: 10.1080/03086534.2012.730828.

18 Ibid.

19 Barnett, *Empire of humanity*, p. 30.

20 Zoë Laidlaw, 'Investigating empire: Humanitarians, reform and the Commission of Eastern Inquiry', *The Journal of Imperial and Commonwealth History*, 40:5 (2012), 749–768, doi: 10.1080/03086534.2012.730829.

21 Laidlaw, 'Integrating metropolitan, colonial and imperial histories', p. 91.

22 Barnett, *Empire of humanity*, p. 5.

23 Laidlaw, 'Investigating empire', p. 750.

24 Skinner and Lester, 'Humanitarianism and empire', 733. Some historians have argued that, in the context of Australian history, the use of the term 'humanitarian' was retrofitted to nineteenth-century Christian philanthropists in order to further the moral purpose of twentieth-century historians. Claire McLisky, '"Due observance of justice, and the protection of their rights": Philanthropy, humanitarianism and moral purpose in the Aborigines Protection Society circa 1837 and its portrayal in Australian historiography, 1833–2003', *Limina: A Journal of Historical and Cultural Studies*, 11 (2005), 57–66.

25 F. David Roberts, *The social conscience of the early Victorians* (Stanford, CA: Stanford University Press, 2002), p. 4.

26 An example is the work of the Quakers, or Society of Friends. See, for example, Penelope Edmonds, 'Travelling "under concern": Quakers James Backhouse and George Washington Walker tour the antipodean colonies, 1832–41', *The Journal of Imperial and Commonwealth History*, 40:5 (2012), 769–788, doi: 10.1080/03086534.2012.730830.

27 Laidlaw, 'Investigating empire', p. 761.

28 C.A. Bayly, 'The second British Empire', in Robin Winks (ed.), *The Oxford history of the British Empire*, vol. 5, *Historiography* (Oxford: Oxford University Press, 1999), p. 54.

29 Bayly, 'The second British Empire', p. 55.

30 HC Deb, 8 February 1850, vol. 108, cc535–567, 538, 'Colonial policy'.

31 'Art. IV. Hottentots and Caffres', *London and Westminster Review*, 4:1 (October 1836), 93.

32 HC Deb, 19 May 1835, vol. 27, cc1233–1236, 1233, 'The slave trade'.

33 HC Deb, 14 July 1835, vol. 29, cc549–553, 549, 'Treatment of Aborigines in British settlements'.

34 HC Deb, 9 March 1835, vol. 26, cc725–730, 726–729, 'Cape of Good Hope: The Caffres'; see also: 'Art. IV, Hottentots and Caffres', *London and Westminster Review*, 4:1 (October 1836), 93.

35 HC Deb, 9 March 1835, vol. 26, cc725–730, 729, 'Cape of Good Hope. The Caffres'.

36 Lester, 'British settler discourse and the circuits of empire', 26; Thomas Fowell Buxton, *Memoirs of Sir Thomas Fowell Buxton, Baronet*, ed. Charles Buxton (London: John Murray, 1848), p. 364.

37 Alan Lester and Fae Dussart, *Colonization and the origins of humanitarian governance: Protecting Aborigines across the nineteenth-century British Empire* (Cambridge: Cambridge University Press, 2014), pp. 78–86.

38 Alan Lester, 'Humanitarians and white settlers in the nineteenth century', in Norman Etherington (ed.), *Missions and empire* (Oxford: Oxford University Press, 2005), p. 68.

39 Keegan, *Dr Philip's empire*, pp. 191–192.

40 HC PP 1836 (538) 'Report from the Select Committee on Aborigines (British Settlements) Together with the minutes of evidence, appendix and index', iii;

'The Aborigines Protection Society, New Zealand', *The New Zealand Journal*, Saturday 2 May 1840, p. 75.

41 HC Deb, 23 July 1834, vol. 25, cc428–432, 'South Australian colonization'; this resulted in The South Australia Colonisation Act 1834 (4 & 5 Will. IV c. 95). See also: 'The new Colony of South Australia, and the penal colonies', *Tait's Edinburgh Magazine*, 5:60 (December 1838), 776–789.

42 See: 'Article IV. British colonization', *The British and Foreign Review: or, European Quarterly Journal*, 6:12 (April 1838), 472–505.

43 For a discussion on the 'dregs' of British society see: James Heartfield, *The Aborigines' Protection Society: Humanitarian imperialism in Australia, New Zealand, Fiji, Canada, South Africa, and the Congo, 1836–1909* (London: Hurst & Company, 2011), pp. 19–20.

44 'Art. VI. Book review. 1. *The condition and capabilities of van Diemen's Land, as a place of emigration.* By John Dixon. London: Smith and Elder. 1839, 2. *Twelve month's residence in New Zealand.* By John Walton. Glasgow: McPhun. 1839; *The Monthly Review*, 4:4 (December 1839), 521–537.

45 HC PP 1834 (617) 'Aboriginal tribes (North America, New South Wales, Van Diemen's Land and British Guiana). Return to several addresses to His Majesty, dated 19 March 1834; for, papers relating to the present state of the aboriginal tribes resident in His Majesty's dominions; the conduct pursued by the government in improving the condition of the aborigines, through the medium of the annual presents; account of all monies expended in or appropriated towards the religious instruction or education of such aboriginal inhabitants', p. 148, p. 151.

46 HC Deb, 1 July 1834, vol. 24, 1061–1063, 1062, 'Colonies – Aboriginal tribes'.

47 Elbourne, *Blood ground*, p. 284.

48 HC Deb, 14 July 1835, vol. 29, cc549–553, 'Treatment of Aborigines in British Settlements'.

49 Lester, 'Humanitarians and white settlers', p. 69.

50 Barnett, *Empire of humanity*, pp. 61–63.

51 HC Deb, 14 July 1835, vol. 29, cc549–553, 549, 'Treatment of Aborigines in British settlements'.

52 Ibid., 552.

53 Ibid.

54 Ibid., 553.

55 Ibid.

56 HC Deb, 1 July 1834, vol. 24, 1061–1063, 1062, 'Colonies – Aboriginal tribes'.

57 This figure comes from Andrew Porter. See: Porter, *Religion versus empire?*, p. 141.

58 Elbourne, *Blood ground*, p. 288.

59 For a detailed discussion as to the debates and historical nuances behind this terminology see: Elbourne, *Blood ground*, pp. 71–78.

60 John Philip, *Researches in South Africa, volume 1: Illustrating the civil, moral, and religious condition of the Native tribes: Including journals of the author's travels in the interior, together with detailed accounts of the progress of the Christian missions, exhibiting the influence of Christianity in promoting civilization* (London: James Duncan, 1838).

61 For a detailed examination of the scope of Philip's book see: Elbourne, *Blood ground*, pp. 246–254.

62 Lester, 'Humanitarians and white settlers', p. 67.

63 Keegan, *Dr Philip's empire*, pp. 201–202. For more on Jan Tzatzoe as an intermediary see: Roger S. Levine, 'Cultural innovation and translation in the Eastern Cape: Jan Tzatzoe, Xhosa intellectual and the making of an African gospel, 1817–1833', *African Historical Review*, 42:2 (2010), 84–101, doi: 10.1080/17532523.2010.517401; Roger S. Levine, *A living man from Africa: Jan Tzatzoe, Xhosa chief and missionary, and the making of nineteenth-century South Africa* (New Haven, CT: Yale University Press, 2000). For more on Andries Stoffels see: Elizabeth Elbourne, 'Sara Baartman and Andries Stoffels: Violence, law and the politics of spectacle in London and the Eastern Cape, 1809–1836', *Canadian Journal of African Studies/Revue Canadienne des Études Africaines*, 45:3 (2011), 524–564, doi: 10.1080/00083968.2011. 10541067.

64 Elbourne, *Blood ground*, p. 288

65 Keegan, *Dr Philip's empire*, p. 201.

66 Ibid., pp. 207–213.

67 Levine, *A living man from Africa*, p. 133.

68 Roger Saul Levine, 'Sable son of Africa: The many worlds of an African cultural intermediary on the eastern Cape frontier of South Africa, 1800–1848' (Doctor of Philosophy, Yale University, 2004), p. 268.

69 'The London Missionary Society', *The Wesleyan-Methodist Magazine*, 16 (June 1837), 445–450.

70 Buxton, *Memoirs*, pp. 369–371; Elbourne, *Blood ground*, pp. 288–289; Keegan, *Dr Philip's empire*, pp. 205, 209–210, 212–214, 219.

71 Keegan, *Dr Philip's empire*, p. 205.

72 HC PP 1836 (538) 'Report', Major William B. Dundas, 26 August 1835 [1273], 141.

73 HC PP 1836 (538) 'Report', Coates, Beecham and Ellis, 11 June 1836 [4411], 538–539.

74 TNA, CO 318/122 West India Miscellaneous 1835, vol. 3, Negro Education, J. Arandell (LMS) to Dandeson Coates, 3 December 1834, 87; TNA, CO 318/122, William Ellis to George Grey, 24 November 1835, 185; TNA, CO 318/122, William Ellis to George Grey, 1 December 1835, 197–198.

75 University of Birmingham (UB), Cadbury Research Library Special Collections (Cadbury), Church Missionary Society Archive (CMS), General Secretary's Department (G), Administration, Correspondence (AC), 19/2, Dandeson Coates to Thomas Fowell Buxton, 15 April 1837, p. 136.

76 See: HC PP 1836 (538) 'Report', Buxton (chair) questioning Captain R.A. Aitchison, 31 July 1835, 1–13.

77 Keegan, *Dr Philip's empire*, p. 194.

78 Elbourne, *Blood ground*, p. 283. Zoë Laidlaw, '"Aunt Anna's report": The Buxton women and the Aborigines Select Committee, 1835–37', *The Journal of*

Imperial and Commonwealth History, 32:2 (2004), 4–5, doi: 10.1080/030865 30410001700381.

79 Keegan, *Dr Philip's empire*, p. 216.

80 Buxton, *Memoirs*, p. 366.

81 Ibid., p. 415.

82 Ibid.

83 HC PP 1836 (538) 'Report', p. iii.

84 Ibid.

85 For example, Buxton enquired of Captain Aitchison of the Cape Colony if there had been any improvement in the state of the Tambookies (a tribe of Xhosa, disparagingly known in contemporaneous terms as 'Caffres') since the Moravians had established a mission. See: HC PP 1836 (538) 'Report', Captain R.S. Aitchison, 31 July 1835, p. 12.

86 For example, in relation to Australian Aborigines, contact with European civilisation was deemed to push them into a state of decay that led to extinction. Their moral character was compromised by Europeans, and, as to the effects of Europeans upon their religious state Broughton could not attest to as he believed that Aborigines had no religious state prior to the advent of Europeans. See: HC PP 1836 (538) 'Report', Archdeacon Broughton, 3 August 1835, p. 19.

87 HC PP 1836 (538) 'Report', The Rev. W. Yate, 13 February 1836 [1778], p. 200.

88 HC PP 1836 (538) 'Report', Captain A. Stockenstrom, 28 August 1835 [1387], p. 154; Captain C. Bradford, 28 August 1835 [1496–1498], p. 171; Andrew Stoffel, 27 June 1836 [5069], p. 588; see also: Elbourne, *Blood ground*, p. 288. Elbourne calls Andrew Stoffel Andries Stoffels.

89 HC PP 1836 (538) 'Report', Andrew Stoffel, 27 June 1836 [5069], p. 588.

90 HC PP 1836 (538) 'Report', John Tzatzoe, 22 June 1836 [4650, 4655, 4658], pp. 570–571.

91 HC PP 1837 (425) 'Report from the Select Committee on Aborigines (British Settlements); with the minutes of evidence, appendix and index', p. 69.

92 HC PP 1836 (538) 'Report', James Read, 29 June 1836 [5100], p. 590.

93 HC PP 1836 (538) 'Report', Archdeacon Broughton, 3 August 1835 [237], p. 17.

94 HC PP 1837 (425) 'Report', p. 60.

95 L.E. Threlkeld, *The annual report of the mission to the Aborigines, Lake Macquarie, 1838 and letter accompanying it sent to George Washington Walker, April 1841* (University of Tasmania Library Special and Rare Materials Collection, Australia: Unpublished, online version) http://eprints.utas.edu.au/1862/ [last accessed 4 March 2014].

96 HC PP 1837 (425) 'Report', p. 45; Thor Wagstrom, 'Broken tongues and foreign hearts: The religious frontier in early nineteenth-century South Africa and New Zealand', in Peggy Brock (ed.), *Indigenous peoples and religious change* (Leiden: Brill, 2005), pp. 51–77.

97 HC PP 1836 (538) 'Report', Archdeacon Broughton, 3 August 1835, p. 14.

98 HC PP 1836 (538) 'Report', Rev. John Williams, 29 July 1836 [5709], p. 675.

99 HC PP 1836 (538) 'Report', Johan Tzatzoe, 27 June 1836 [4857], p. 579.

100 Ibid.
101 HC PP 1837 (425) 'Report from the Select Committee on Aborigines (British settlements); with the minutes of evidence, appendix and index'.
102 Keegan, *Dr Philip's empire*, pp. 217–221.
103 HC PP 1836 (538) 'Report', p. iii.
104 HC PP 1837 (425) 'Report', p. 76. See also: Elbourne, *Blood ground*, p. 288.
105 HC PP 1837 (425) 'Report', pp. 80–81.
106 TNA, CO 318/117, Mr Canning's resolutions & Lord Bathurst's instructions, 15 May 1832, p. 325.
107 HC PP 1837 (425) 'Report', p. 73.
108 HC PP 1837 (425) 'Report', ii; Rowan Strong, 'A vision of an Anglican imperialism: The annual sermons of the Society for the Propagation of the Gospel in Foreign Parts 1701–1714', *Journal of Religious History*, 30 (2006), 175–198, doi: 10.1111/j.1467–9809.2006.00447.x.
109 HC PP 1836 (538) 'Report', p. 45.
110 HC PP 1836 (538) 'Report', Dandison Coates, John Beecham and William Ellis, 8 June 1836 [4385], p. 525; see also: HC PP 1836 (538) 'Report', The Rev. W. Yate (CMS), 13 February 1836 [1783], p. 200; D. Coates, J. Beecham and W. Ellis, 11 June 1836 [4401], p. 532.
111 HC PP 1836 (538) 'Report', Archdeacon Broughton, 3 August 1835, pp. 17–18.
112 Zoë Laidlaw, 'Heathens, slaves and Aborigines: Thomas Hodgkin's critique of missions and anti-slavery', *History Workshop Journal*, 64:1 (2007), 140, doi: 10.1093/hwj/dbm034.
113 HC PP 1836 (538) 'Report', D. Coates, J. Beecham and W. Ellis, 8 June 1836 [4387], p. 525.
114 HC PP 1837 (425) 'Report', p. 74.
115 Ibid.
116 Ibid., p. 75.
117 Heartfield, *The Aborigines' Protection Society*, p. 15.
118 HC PP 1837 (425) 'Report', p. 75.
119 See: Michael Blackstock, 'The Aborigines Report (1837): A case study in the slow change of colonial social relations', *The Canadian Journal of Native Studies*, XX:1 (2000), 67–94; Elbourne, 'The sin of the settler'.
120 Heartfield, *The Aborigines' Protection Society*, p. 21.
121 HC PP 1837 (425) 'Report', p. 75.
122 Ibid., p. 10.
123 Ibid., p. 75.
124 Ibid., p. 3.
125 Ibid., p. 79.
126 Buxton, *Memoirs*, pp. 369–370.
127 HC PP 1837 (425) 'Report', p. 79.
128 Merete Borch, 'Rethinking the origins of Terra Nullius', *Australian Historical Studies*, 32:117 (2001), 238, doi: 10.1080/10314610108596162.
129 HC PP 1837 (425) 'Report', p. 79.
130 Ibid.

131 HL Deb, 20 June 1833, vol. 18, cc1014–1015, 'Ministerial plan for the abolition of slavery'. See also: HC PP 1831 (261) 'New South Wales, Copies of instructions given by His Majesty's Secretary of State for the Colonies, for promoting the moral and religious instruction of the aboriginal inhabitants of New Holland or Van Diemen's Land'.

132 HL Deb, 20 June 1833, vol. 18, cc1014–1015, 'Ministerial plan for the abolition of slavery'.

133 Thomas Fowell Buxton, 'Circular to the Secretaries of the Mission Societies', 28 November 1832, as cited in: Rebecca Swartz, *Education and empire: Children, race and humanitarianism in the British settler colonies, 1833–1880* (Cham: Palgrave Macmillan, 2019), p. 44.

134 Laidlaw, 'Heathens, slaves and Aborigines', p. 141.

135 HC PP 1837 (425) 'Report', p. 83.

136 HC PP 1836 (538) 'Report', Archdeacon Broughton, 3 August 1835 [228], p. 676.

137 Felicity Jensz, *German Moravian missionaries in the British Colony of Victoria, Australia, 1848–1908: Influential strangers* (Leiden: Brill, 2010), p. 49.

138 HC PP 1837 (425) 'Report', p. 12.

139 John Harris, *One blood: 200 years of Aboriginal encounter with Christianity: A story of hope* (Sutherland: Albatross, 1990).

140 HC PP 1837 (425) 'Report', p. 80.

141 Ibid., pp. 80–81.

142 Lester, 'Humanitarians and white settlers'.

143 Brian Stanley, '"Commerce and Christianity": Providence theory, the Missionary Movement, and the imperialism of free trade, 1842–1860', *The Historical Journal*, 26:1 (1983), 71–94.

144 Andrew Porter, '"Commerce and Christianity": The rise and fall of a nineteenth-century missionary slogan', *The Historical Journal*, 28:3 (1985), 597–621.

145 HC PP 1837 (425) 'Report', p. 45.

146 Ibid., p. 49.

147 Ibid., p. 56.

148 Swartz, *Education and empire*.

149 HC PP 1837 (425) 'Report', p. 81.

150 HC PP 1836 (538) 'Report', Sir Rufane Donkin, 27 July 1836 [5455], p. 648.

151 HC PP 1836 (538) 'Report', Captain R.S. Aitchison, 31 July 1835, p. 10.

152 Ibid., pp. 11–12.

153 See, for example, Stephen J. Ball, 'Imperialism, social control and the colonial curriculum in Africa', *Journal of Curriculum Studies*, 15:3 (1983), 242–243, doi: 10.1080/0022027830150302.

154 The principle objectives of Industrial education in the colonies are cited in ibid., 243.

155 See: Peter Kallaway, 'Conference litmus: The development of a conference and policy culture in the interwar period with special reference to the New Education Fellowship and British colonial education in Southern Africa', in K. Tolley (ed.),

Transformations in schooling: Historical and comparative perspectives (New York: Palgrave Macmillan, 2007), pp. 123–149. An exception is Canada, where missionary groups and governments worked together to provide schooling, including residential schooling, for First Nation people. See: James R. Miller, *Shingwauk's vision: A history of Native residential schools* (Toronto: University of Toronto Press, 2009).

156 Dandeson Coates, John Beecham and William Ellis, *Christianity and the means of civilization: Shown in the evidence given before a Committee of the House of Commons, on Aborigines, by D. Coates, Esq., Rev. John Beecham, and Rev. William Ellis. Secretaries of the Church Missionary Society, the Wesleyan Missionary Society, and London Missionary Society. To which is added selections from the evidence of other witnesses bearing on the same subject* (London: R.B. Seeley and W. Burnside, L. and G. Seeley, and T. Mason, 1837), p. iii.

157 Ibid., p. 20. For the omitted text – for example, a description of the infanticide of children who were the result of illicit sex between Indigenous women and European men – see: HC PP 1836 (538) 'Report' [4280–4288], pp. 486–490.

158 Edmonds and Laidlaw, '"The British Government is now awaking"', p. 45.

159 For an overview of the society see: Heartfield, *The Aborigines' Protection Society*.

160 Raymond M. Cooke, 'British Evangelicals and the issue of colonial self-government', *Pacific Historical Review*, 34:2 (1965), 131, doi: 10.2307/3636989.

161 Aborigines Protection Society (APS), *Report of the Parliamentary Select Committee on Aboriginal Tribes (British Settlements). Reprinted, with comments, by the 'Aborigines Protection Society'* (London: William Ball, Aldine Chambers, Paternoster Row, and Hatchard & Son, Piccadilly, 1837), pp. 117–121; Keegan, *Dr Philip's Empire* pp. 220–221.

162 APS, *Report of the Parliamentary Select Committee on Aboriginal Tribes*, p. viii.

163 Frances Thiele, 'Superintendent La Trobe and the amenability of Aboriginal peoples to British law 1839–1846', *Provenance: The Journal of the Public Record Office Victoria*, 8 (2009), 7–8.

164 Standish Motte, *Outline of a system of legislation, for securing protection to the Aboriginal inhabitants of all countries colonized by Great Britain; extending to them political and social rights, ameliorating their condition, and promoting their civilization. Drawn up at the request of the committee of 'The Aborigines Protection Society,' for the purposes of being laid before the Government* (London: John Murray, Albermarle Street; Saunders and Otley, Conduit Street; Hatchard and Son, Piccadilly; Smith, Elder, and co, Cornhill, G. Fry, Bishopgate Street, Without; and W. Houlston, 35, High Holborn, 1840), p. 3.

165 Ibid., p. 5.

166 Ibid., pp. 6–7.

167 Ronald Rainger, 'Philanthropy and science in the 1830's: The British and Foreign Aborigines' Protection Society', *Man*, 15:4 (1980), 704.

168 Motte, *Outline of a system of legislation*, pp. 21–22.

169 For example, two youths that the LMS sent back to England to be trained at a Moravian institute died being able to return home as cultural and knowledge

brokers. See: William Thorp et al., *Four sermons, at the tenth General Meeting of the London Missionary Society, May 9, 10,11, 1804 etc etc* (London: T. Williams, 1804), p. 5.

170 Elbourne, *Blood ground*, p. 292

171 University of London (UL), School of Orient and Asian Studies Library Archives (SOAS), Council for World Mission Archive (CWMA), London Missionary Society (LMS)/South Africa incoming correspondence/Box 16A/1838/Folder 2/ Jacket Letter A/Item 29/To the Secretaries of the London Missionary Society from Jan Tzatzoe, King Williams Town, 1 September 1838.

172 Elbourne, *Blood ground*, p. 281.

173 Ibid., pp. 282, 298–299.

174 UL, SOAS, CWMA, LMS/South Africa incoming correspondence/Box 16A/ 1838/Folder 2/Jacket Letter A/Item 29/To the Secretaries of the London Missionary Society from Jan Tzatzoe, King Williams Town, 1 September 1838.

175 HC PP 1836 (538) 'Report', Johan Tzatzoe, 22 June 1836 [4688], p. 573.

176 Elbourne, *Blood ground*, p. 175.

177 UL, SOAS, CWMA, LMS/South Africa incoming correspondence/Box 21/1845/ Folder 3/Jacket B/Item 57/To the LMS from Jan Tsatzao, Caffreland, 8 October 1845.

178 Ibid.

179 Elbourne, *Blood ground*; Keegan, *Dr Philip's empire*; Levine, *A living man from Africa*.

180 Levine, *A living man from Africa*, p. 190, pp. 261–262.

181 Porter, *Religion versus empire?*, p. 144.

182 HC PP 1837 (425) 'Report', pp. 83–84; see also: Lester, 'Humanitarians and white settlers', p. 76.

183 See, for example, Lester, 'Humanism, race and the colonial frontier'; Michael Cannon, *Aborigines and protectors 1838–1839*, vol. 2B, *Historical Records of Victoria* (Melbourne: Victorian Government Printing Office, 1983).

184 Heartfield, *The Aborigines' Protection Society*, esp. chapter 8.

185 Lester, 'Humanism, race and the colonial frontier'; Henry Reynolds, 'Aborigines and European social hierarchy', *Aboriginal History*, 7 (1983), 124–133.

186 Lester and Dussart, *Colonization and the origins of humanitarian governance*, p. 227.

187 Elbourne, *Blood ground*, p. 291.

188 Heartfield, *The Aborigines' Protection Society*, p. 227.

189 Brian Stanley, *The Bible and the flag: Protestant missions and British imperialism in the nineteenth and twentieth centuries* (Leicester: Apollos, 1992), p. 49.

Female education and the Liverpool Missionary Conference of 1860

In 1859, Behari Lal Singh, a licensed Free Church of Scotland preacher in Calcutta (now Kolkata) in his late 30s, suffered poor health 'if not caused, certainly aggravated, by over-exertion'.[1] He had been working for the Free Church of Scotland in Calcutta since 1844 – just a year after the church had been established after a schism in the Church of Scotland – proselytising to Jews, Hindus and Muslims in the city, and teaching at a small seminary. Born in 1821 into a Rajpoot (Rajput) family in the North West Provinces, he was taken by his father to Calcutta as a young boy for an English education in Dr Alexander Duff's Native Institution, which had opened in 1830. After he had finished his education and moved to a teaching position in Central India, he converted from Hinduism to Christianity, as he was stirred by the example of Christian men in the Free Church of Scotland.[2] In order that this remarkable man could recuperate and be of further missionary service, he was sent to Britain for two years. Whilst there, he studied theology in London and Glasgow, and was ordained in Edinburgh in 1861. Following the footsteps of Jan Tzatzoe and other evangelical missionaries of the time, Singh spoke at Exeter Hall, giving a lecture at the fifty-sixth anniversary of the British and Foreign Bible Society.[3] He was seen to be a true Christian as he reduced his income to serve the Mission and was praised by many who came in contact with him for his Christian attributes.[4] His time in Britain also coincided with the 1860 Liverpool Missionary Conference, one of the biggest interdenominational missionary conferences to be held thus far. Over four days in March 1860, 126 delegates from over 25 Protestant missionary societies both in Britain and abroad congregated in Liverpool to discuss the state of modern missions to the 'heathen' in non-European spaces. Singh was the only non-European delegate. He spoke from a position of authority, having worked as a missionary for some sixteen years, effectively voicing his opinions against denominationalism, the need for advanced theological instruction and was vocal in the issue of salaries for local Christian agents.[5] Education in general and female education in particular were important topics of debate and discussion at Edinburgh, demonstrating the shift in missionary priorities to reach and shape non-European females through schooling. Already before he first went to England, Singh had a keen interest in female education, compiling a book on the topic from various sources in 1855 (reprinted in 1856 and 1874). The book was reviewed favourably by Alexander Duff, with Duff praising Singh for being 'exceedingly faithful and impartial' in his recording of the history of female education in Calcutta.[6] The book was expected to make a large impression upon the British Christian public. Many of Singh's own ideas of female education were reiterated in the speeches held at the Liverpool conference, where a whole session was devoted to education along with an evening soirée with the address on female education in the east. This chapter will examine the debates and issues surrounding missionary education discussed at Liverpool against the background of Singh's own experiences and Bengali Hindu social reform movements of the time. Through examining Singh's work in female education in Bengal in the mid-century, the chapter will demonstrate how various ideas about female Christian education were essential for the morality of a colonised society, but were not expected to facilitate radical social reform. This focus on women was a further extension of the ideas of missionary modernity, in that women should be taught to dismiss 'superstitions' and replace them with Christian morality and 'rationality' in order to help 'raise' the new generation of Christian subjects in colonial spaces.

At the time of the Liverpool conference, many missionary groups were frustrated at the lack of progress in achieving long-term goals, such as the establishment of Native churches run by Indigenous or local people which would facilitate the retreat of Europeans from missionary work. Singh provided a different perspective at Liverpool, remonstrating with his fellow delegates that they had 'not yet fully appreciated the value of that native agency'.[7] His physical presence at the conference also demonstrated the 'success' that Christian missions had in converting as well as retaining non-Europeans for work in the 'heathen' mission. The Liverpool Missionary Conference itself was understood by delegates to be of a different calibre than previous interdenominational meetings. At Liverpool, the Rev. Joseph Mullens, an LMS missionary in India, claimed in his overview of previous conferences on missions that the discussions at Liverpool were 'of far greater value than those of its predecessors in London [October 1854] and New York [May 1854]', which were seen as having been focused upon descriptive detail or upon general principles. For Mullens, the uniqueness of the Liverpool conference was that it went 'more deeply into plans' – that is, into the practicalities of missionary work, rather than just speculating on how missions should be run.[8] Topics discussed over the four days included: European Missionaries Abroad; the best Means of exciting and maintaining a missionary Spirit; Missionary Education; Native Agency in Foreign Missions; Candidates for Missionary Work; and Indian Converts in the recent Indian Uprising of 1857.[9] In addition to the seven sessions spread over the four days, there were also nightly missionary soirées on topics such as medical missions as well as a general public meeting for the subscribing friends of the missionary societies.[10] With a wide variety of missionary societies and topics, the Liverpool conference provided an exemplary lens of missionary views in the mid-nineteenth century, during the period before high imperialism, and at a time which historian Andrew Porter has characterised as a 'hiatus if not stagnation in important areas of missionary activity'.[11] The four days of the Liverpool conference provided a means by which the common goals of the movement were enthused anew. For historians it is an informative snap-shot of the attitudes that individual missionaries held towards the very important activity of education within various mission fields.

From the mid-nineteenth century, missionary conferences increasingly became a significant means for missionary groups to network and to exchange ideas. The types of conferences varied from small local conferences that included only the missionaries of one society in a particular geographic location to larger interdenominational meetings, such as the the 'Local Consultative Groups' formed in India from the 1820s or the more formalised conferences such as the 1858 Missionary Conference held at the hill station of Ootacamund (Ooty, also Udagamandalam, in Tamil Nadu) in India.[12] Liverpool was a larger interdenominational conference that encompassed missionary views from an even broader geographical area. Interdenominational missionary conferences of the long nineteenth century fostered networks that facilitated knowledge of pedagogical methods and ideas on global scales, albeit often predominantly only through White, male networks. Education was a constant topic of discussion at such conferences, indicating the centrality of education as a tool for missions in the conversion to Christianity. Knowledge was exchanged about the state of Christian education in the non-Christian world, and thoughts were aired for improving pedagogical methods and educational structures. They provided platforms in which ideas on the educability of women were contrasted with various political, social and moral settings, familiarising a select group of religious educationalists with local differences but at the same time reinforcing the belief in Western Christianity's moral superiority as the only tool which could effectively counter the negative aspects of modernisation affecting non-Europeans. As such, they provide important reference points to examine the shift in debates within missionary societies as to the goals and methods of Christian education for non-European females over the course of the second half of the long nineteenth century.

In his analysis of over five decades of missionary conferences, William Hogg notes the fundamental problems faced by missionaries were:

> education in all phases, the place and training of women, the development of effective literature in the vernacular, Bible translations, medical work, the evangelization of unoccupied areas, the relations between missionaries and the Christians among whom they laboured, especially between missionaries and their national co-workers, the growth of the church, its self-support and self-government, and comity and cooperation on the field.[13]

The reports from missionary conferences thus provide an insight into moments in which individuals – as was the case at Liverpool – willingly shared information about schooling and contributed to a network of knowledge in which concepts of morality and the position of non-Europeans were embedded. From 1900, the structure of missionary conferences changed, becoming more formalised with missionary associations commonly appointing official delegates and commissions formed to discuss issues before the presentation of a report at the conference.[14] The attendance of individuals, not societies, at pre-1900 meetings made it difficult for the early meetings to be effective in terms of the implementation of ideas, whereas the sheer size of later meetings where societies sent delegates made it also difficult for resolutions to be universally implemented.[15] The discussions held at such meetings provide insight into how missionaries were grappling with the realities on the ground, and what they thought might be the best solutions to some of the most pressing questions they faced both individually and as a collective group.

As the discussions at Liverpool demonstrated, missionary societies were aware of the importance of remaining attentive to the varied needs of different peoples within different locations and spheres of missionary work. This was also the case for schooling. There was much diversity in what missionaries taught and to whom, with the practicalities of education – including aspects of the curriculum, the language of instruction, the location of the physical school, as well as the economics of these schools – varying throughout the British Empire. Such a heterogeneous landscape made a universal plan for schooling across colonies never an obtainable reality. There were, nevertheless, generalities in the aims and means that missionary societies used and aspired to in their teaching of Indigenous and non-European pupils, particularly in the education of youth. Many of these ideas were crafted in Britain in relation to the education of the poor, or in the tensions between various confessions in the provision of education in Ireland at the beginning of the century. In all of these debates the respective roles of religion and politics were contested and played out in various ways that would shape the debates surrounding the education of Indigenous and non-European peoples throughout the rest of the century. In this light, the 1860 Liverpool Missionary Conference was particularly important, being held just after the Indian Uprising of 1857, in a period where the foundation of British rule in India was placed in question. As this chapter argues, Protestant missionaries saw themselves as best placed to provide schooling in India as an entrance to a missionary modernity that had, according to missionaries, the highest moral code. The education of women placed an important role in this vision of a modernising India.

The topic of education at the 1860 Liverpool Missionary Conference

The 1860 Liverpool Missionary Conference was arranged by the London Secretaries Association (LSA, established in 1819), an association of the executive secretaries of London missionary societies. The conference was funded at the expense of an anonymous 'Christian gentleman', who had also funded the printing of the proceedings, copies of which were purportedly sent to all the mission stations of the participating missionary organisations around the globe.[16] In Britain, copies of the 450-page proceedings were reputedly sent to 'every clergyman whose address could be found' as well as to study, school and public libraries, with over 20,000 gratis copies given away and more on sale for a subsidised rate, with at least 29,000 copies being printed in 1860.[17] The dissemination of the proceedings to such geographically dispersed audiences ensured that all – even those in the field – could benefit from this unique assemblage of interdenominational ideas and practical plans for the deepening and broadening of missionary goals. It was also an impressive propaganda campaign for the missionary endeavour. According to a contemporaneous report, of the 126 delegates, forty-three were Presbyterians, thirty-three were Church of England, ten were not able to be identified and the remaining forty 'included some of a great variety of sects – Baptists, Independents, Wesleyans, and Moravians'.[18] The predominance of Presbyterians was an indication to the author that 'the Presbyterians – who hitherto have engaged least in missions to the heathen', were 'ready to furnish eloquent or fluent speakers for home purposes' and other groups funds and personnel for the mission abroad, for – as the author suggested – it was the role of the conference to bring missionaries together to divide up the work to be done.[19] The self-congratulatory ecumenical mood of the conference was apparent in the introductory remarks to the morning session on the first day, with representatives of missionary societies heartily commending each other for the unity that led to such a conference. The first subject for discussion was that of European missionaries in non-European lands and the necessity of learning Indigenous and local languages. This session also focused upon the role that missionaries had as cultural mediators, including the necessity of establishing and maintaining an intimate relationship with all aspects of the lives of the people they worked amongst. The afternoon session was dedicated to raising the missionary spirit in the home country. One of the most important means suggested for this was the dissemination of information that portrayed an honest view of missionary work that included both positive and negative aspects. Information on missions was to be spread from pulpits, from pastors, in prayer meetings, through speeches given by missionaries at public meetings, through the religious press, through juvenile associations and systematically in theological colleges.[20] This multi-media dissemination tactic was directed at various levels and membership groups of the general church population from the young to the old, from the lay to those who were training to become religious professionals. Interestingly, no explicit mention was made of gendered groups within the church.

The main topic of the morning session of the second day was education, with missionary education conceived of as Christian schooling for non-Europeans in the missionary field. Three papers were delivered, all by men who had experience with education in India, which led one delegate to grumble that the session 'seemed rather like a committee on Indian affairs than anything else'.[21] The focus upon India was reflected in the make-up of members of the conference, with the chairman being Major General Alexander of Her Majesty's Indian Army, and with a handful of members of the Indian army being in attendance along with missionaries active in India. The Charter Act of 1833 had allowed Christian missionaries unrestricted entry to British India, with many missionary societies eagerly establishing themselves in the territory and willing to share their experiences at Liverpool. Conversely, there were few representatives from the West Indies at the 1860 missionary meeting, an interesting situation given, as we read in Chapter 1, the importance that missionary work gained through educational work in the post-emancipation era.[22] By the 1860s, the initial enthusiasm for educational work in the West Indies had been dampened, with funding cut and the interests of the local legislatures in education decidedly less than that of the imperial government. A further reason for the focus upon India at Liverpool was that at the time the evangelical Protestant missionary advance into Africa had not yet gained much of a footing, and missionary work in China was rather modest prior to the formation of the China Inland Mission in 1865.

Thus, given the timing of the Conference on Missions held in 1860 in Liverpool, it is not surprising that India was the focal point of discussion, particularly in relation to education. Many Protestant missionaries and societies considered the Indian Uprising of 1857 as a challenge to Christianity itself.[23] It was for many missionaries if not a turning point in their views on government aims of education then a solidification that their opposition to secular education – and as an extension secular modernity – had been correct all along. Alexander Duff had already in the 1830s noted that to provide an English education without religion to elite Indians would was the 'greatest blunder, politically speaking, that ever was committed'. He believed that this would create a group of infidels, who would become 'discontented, restless agitators, – ambitious of power and official distinction, and possessed of the most disloyal sentiments towards that government which, in their eye, has usurped all the authority that rightfully belonged to themselves'.[24] Charles Benjamin Leupolt, a German missionary who worked for the CMS for over two decades in Benares in India, was more succinct in his criticism of the British colonial government in India providing young men in India with secular education purporting that this 'nourish[ed] vipers in their bosom'.[25] He asserted that the resentment that Indian Muslims had of their colonial rulers was only exacerbated by secular education. More broadly, the events of the Indian Uprising in 1857 had shaken British confidence in their Empire and facilitated a reorientation of British policy and attitudes towards India. The historian Tim Allender has argued that the Indian Uprising also affected the perception of female education in India, as officials turned to earlier stereotypes of Indian women which had been 'developed by European missionaries about supposed Indian cultural backwardness and reluctance of the Indian women to learn'.[26]

In India, missionary education had gained missionary, public and government attention and support from the renewal of the charter of the British East Indian Company (EIC) in 1793 and the arrival of the Baptist missionary William Carey in the same year.[27] In the debates surrounding the renewal of the EIC charter it was proposed that a clause be added which would promote the 'religious and moral improvement' of the 'inhabitants of the British Dominions in India' through the work of ministers, schoolteachers and other religious workers.[28] Known as the Pious Clauses, these proposals were only accepted under the conditions of the 1813 charter, with their acceptance being a great part due to the lobbying of William Wilberforce and the petitioning of the BMS and the LMS.[29] Some military chaplains had missionised to locals prior to the 1813 charter.[30] Yet, even through the charter's outcome was limited in terms of the means available for 'religious and moral improvement', the events demonstrated that missionary petitioning in the metropole could affect missionary and educational work in the colonies and that government and missionary collaborated to provide schooling for Indians. The Charter Act of 1833 opened up India to Christian missionaries. Once the disruptions of the 1857 Uprising had subsided, Sir Charles Wood's Despatch of 1854 in relation to public education was able to be fully implemented. Wood, as president of the Board of Control of the East India Company, supported the establishment of universities in Bombay, Calcutta and Madras. The dispatch also provided the model for grants-in-aid for teaching a government-set curriculum, which consequently led to the establishment of more schools, both government and missionary. The Despatch also allowed for the established Departments of Public Instruction. Wood's despatch pushed European knowledge over Indian and English over the vernacular where demand for English existed. It also set the scene for secular education, or rather education devoid of dogmatic religious instruction. Although religion was not to be taught in Indian schools, moral training was still considered important in the context of India for improving character despite there being no paragraph in the 1854 Despatch specifically on this point.[31] The role of religion in Indian schools and colleges would continue to be a debated topic, as noted at Liverpool in relation to the Indian Uprising of 1857. One of the difficulties that educationalists faced in India was on what constituted a religion, and on what aspects of religion contained moral precepts deemed universally acceptable. The less divisive path was to exclude religion from the curriculum all together.

The Indian Uprising grabbed the attention of Protestant British, American and continental missionary societies, and more missions were established in British India after this time. Missionaries were convinced that Christianity had had a beneficial effect on the morals of society, for, as it was stated at the Liverpool conference, not one person educated in a missionary institution had joined the 'rebels'.[32] Christianity was considered to make loyal subjects of Indians. This was a sentiment that Singh embodied, stating at a soirée at the Liverpool conference, that although he was 'sorry to say that I belong to the rebel race of North-West India; still if you convert the rebels they will fight for you. [...] They will become your loyal subjects; they will defend your lives', to which the audience broke into applause.[33] The progressive effects of missionary education in India were described as an 'elevation and social change' in Indian society.[34] The logical conclusion for many missionary groups was that they needed to extend their work in India to convert more Indians to Christianity and thus 'raise' the moral tone of society through the introduction and maintenance of Christian morals. From the middle of the century, there was an increased awareness that females were the locus of societies' morals, and thus more missionary attention was placed upon educating women and girls. Christian education was expected to have a leavening function through permeating non-Christian societies with Christian thoughts and principles.[35] These sentiments were expressed by Singh himself a couple of years later as such: 'Knowledge without religion is a dangerous [...] but knowledge with the humbling and purifying spirit and influences of Christianity is a mighty, and indeed the only effectual instrument for bringing [non-Christians] into light and liberty.'[36] For Christianity to be spread in India, more missionaries, both European as well as local teachers, were sought. The latter were assumed to have a greater influence over locals, and were significantly more cost effective than the training, transportation and maintenance of European missionaries in foreign lands. As Leupolt touted at the Liverpool Missionary Conference, local teachers were needed for: 'until we have such, our efforts will be limited, and our success small'.[37] In the following chapter, the heterogeneous reasons behind some local people's engagement as teachers in mission schools will be examined.

The three main papers in the session devoted to education were focused upon the broader geographical area of British India. Despite the heterogeneous nature of the various missionary groups whose delegates spoke on India, there was consensus that mission schools were essential, if subordinate to preaching, in the broader aim of evangelising. The first paper came from the Rev. Charles Benjamin Leupolt of the CMS stationed in Benares; a man Behari Lal Singh called 'my friend'.[38] Leupolt was of the opinion that preaching was more important than teaching in bringing the Gospel to non-Christian groups.[39] The primary aim of missionary schools for Leupolt was to convert children to Christianity with a secondary aim of imparting of 'an amount of secular knowledge as will qualify [children] to become useful members of society'.[40] The Rev. Thomas Smith of the Free Church of Scotland in Calcutta was of a different opinion, noting in his paper that other people had conferred equal status on both as they were but different forms of bringing the gospel to non-Christian peoples,[41] however, he himself believed that the efforts put into educational work should not exceed that of other missionary work, and particularly preaching.[42] The third paper, presented by the Rev. J.H. Titcome of the Vernacular Education Society for India, provided a categorisation of the three stages of mission (introductory, permanent and reproductive stages) with schooling an essential feature of all stages, yet in each stage the form and role of schooling was to be adapted to best facilitate the 'progressive advancement of the mission'.[43] In all three papers, schooling was deemed an important, yet never the only, means of missionary work.

At the 1860 Liverpool conference, the Rev. Thomas Smith of the Free Church of Scotland defined education as 'of at once storing the mind with instruction, and cultivating all its faculties and powers'.[44] Education was considered a means to dispel superstitions as well as a means to train and mould children so that they would become the foundations of a new society with Western values, norms and knowledge, and which would reject cultural practices perceived of as 'abhorrent' or 'distasteful' to missionary sensibilities. Through missionary schooling it was assumed that an upcoming generation could be 'raised', or, in other terms, 'ameliorated' from their perceived low spiritual, cultural and mental states by being provided with the tools needed to engage in Western societies. One means to achieve these goals was assumed to be through religious and moral instruction inside the classroom. Schooling was deemed not only a form of 'civilising' Indigenous peoples, it was also seen from a European perspective as a sign of a civilised and modernising people. For all the discussion held at the Liverpool conference on the aims of missionary education, not much was said about the practicalities nor the ideology behind it. Indeed, the heterogeneous nature of missionary schooling, from informal schools for less than a couple of hours a week, to the highly systematised and regimented schools established within literate societies, made it difficult, if not impossible, to suggest anything other than broad ideals and aims of mission schooling. Mission schooling was seen to ameliorate the general population through providing moral instruction as well as contributing to the civilisation of non-Europeans. Similar comments were expressed at other missionary conferences, with missionaries at Calcutta in 1868 collectively arguing for the spread of Christian vernacular education as a necessity for the shaping of civil and religious subjects. At the Calcutta conference, religious education was deemed imperative to raise morals, as well as to 'protect people from [the] oppression' of unscrupulous traders and corrupt officials. Thus, schooling embedded with Christian religion was deemed useful for the process of modernising people, whilst at the same time providing these same people the skills to resist aspects of a 'modern' society. Christian schooling was furthermore deemed necessary for 'political reasons' in order that people could use reason to judge for themselves the veracity of 'absurd reports'.[45] Such comments reflected Enlightenment ideals of intellectual liberation through reason.[46] These ideas were not confined to European missionary discussion, but were also evident in Hindu reform movements of the period, including the Young Bengal as well as the Brahmo Sabha (later called Brahmo Samaj) in Bengal, where Singh later worked, and which will be discussed below.[47]

All three of the main addresses given at Liverpool on missionary education provided structural and conceptual understandings of what a mission school should achieve. There was, however, little concrete material given as to how exactly these structures and concepts should be put in place, despite Mullens' introductory comments to the contrary. Questions such as how much secular material was to be taught within schools were raised, but not dealt with in any depth. There was no sustained discussion as to the amount of time to be dedicated to schooling per day or the duration of schooling.

Nor was there any indication of what system of missionary work might be best placed to facilitate missionary education. Education was thus universally acknowledged as being important at Liverpool; however, the situation was so heterogeneous that no universal rules, measures or systems could be advocated. One delegate noted that educational work was 'not suitable to all localities', suggesting that despite the importance of schooling it could not be undertaken in some missionary fields due to the limited abilities or willingness of local peoples.[48] Leupolt saw a particular need for schooling to reach youth and females, groups that were hard to reach through preaching alone. His comments reiterated the notion that teaching, with its focus upon children, youth and women, was deemed subordinate to preaching, reflecting broader gender and social norms that privileged the male public sphere. He put forward a more concrete plan than his colleagues as to how universal education, in the sense of schools being open to all pupils regards of religious backgrounds, should be achieved. Each missionary district should, he thought, encompass a circle of schools in which all schools had a common curriculum and were overseen by a general inspector. He also noted the need to adapt the curricula to suit the abilities and needs of the various groups of scholars.[49] His comments reflected broader nineteenth-century desires for assessment and standardisation that would increasingly become important within missionary schools, especially those funded and supported by colonial governments via grants-in-aid schemes. In his analysis of the ways in which 'modern' societies can discipline individuals, Michael Foucault has highlighted the uses of time, space, examinations and hierarchies, all of which were evident in the increasingly formalised space of mission schools in the nineteenth century.[50] In this century, commonality and standardisation were as important in the later stages of missionary schooling as adaptation and individualisation were in the earlier stages.

What constituted a mission school in the various phases of mission?

One fundamental question circulating in missionary circles was what exactly constituted a mission school. This question was of broader importance in questioning what a school was. In some places where missionaries worked there were formal institutes for schooling, such as the *Madāris* in Islamic communities, or Buddhist schools in many parts of South-East Asia, such as the monastic colleges called *Pirivena* in Sri Lanka. Such schools were seen by many missionaries as both a hindrance and competitor to their desire to spread the Christian message, as well as an indication that Indigenous peoples were 'sophisticated' enough to appreciate formal Western education.[51]

Non-institutionalised forms of education were sometimes harder for missionaries to detect as this often relied upon oral transmission of knowledge, something that missionaries could only appreciate if they themselves had access to the local language.[52] The concept of school and schooling shifted over time and in various places, with a commonality being the missionary belief in the superiority of their form of knowledge transmission. In the context of India, The Rev. Thomas Smith of the Free Church of Scotland in Calcutta, argued at the 1860 Liverpool Missionary Conference that the essential difference between English schools and missionary schools was to be found in the 'ends and the views' of the teachers.[53] Although Smith did not elaborate on his point, his deliberations suggest that the essential difference between the two was that the aim of the missionary teacher was to convert children to Christianity. He placed emphasis upon the abilities and zeal of the provider of education rather than on the expectations of the consumers of education. He argued that the 'ends and aims' of English or Hindu parents were not essentially different, as neither group sent their children to school for conversion: the English parents did not need to entertain this wish as their children were already Christians, and the Hindu parents had no wish for their children to convert. Smith's address mirrored contemporary belief held that non-European 'heathens' were lazy and dull, particularly in regard to European forms of work, with this trope itself feeding into the European justification for colonial expansion and settlements. His comments imbued the teacher with the transformative power of turning inherently lazy pupils of missionary schools into good Christians through zealousness, and despite the wishes of their parents. Indeed, the zeal of missionary teachers was a trait lauded in missionary as well as government circles throughout the nineteenth century, with Smith's focus upon the centrality of Christian teachers in achieving the evangelistic, edificatory and leavening aims of mission schools reiterated in various forms throughout the century. These terms referred respectively to the spreading of the gospel amongst both children and their communities; the training and supply of Native leaders for Native churches; and the dissemination of Christian morals and teachings throughout Native communities, without focusing upon conversion per se – an aim that Brian Stanley has classified as a 'diffusionist view'.[54]

In the mid-century, the Rev. J.H. Titcomb, Secretary to the Vernacular Education Society for India, articulated the concept of three phases of mission and emphasised the need for education to be adapted to local situations in each of the three stages of mission: the introductory, permanent and reproductive. In the 'Introductory Stage', the period when a mission was first established in a new geopolitical location, schools would be established for the 'heathen' in which English 'must be taught'.[55] His four arguments for the teaching of English in this stage were: '(1) the missionaries are most familiar with it themselves; (2) they have no printed books in the vernacular; (3) it is sure to attract the natives; (4) it opens to them all our own stores of sacred literature'.[56] His deliberations on the use of English as the main conduit of instruction over Indigenous languages reflected the Anglicist train of thought in the contemporaneous Orientalist–Anglicist debate. Not all missionary societies followed Titcomb's stages, with some such as the LMS generally utilising local languages both in their mission work and in schools. This led to problems as the missionaries needed to be conversant in those languages or at least have Native helpers who were conversant in English or German (or another common European language) to be able to teach the local pupils. Titcomb's comments on the introductory stage of schools also suggest that schooling was improvised with whatever one had on hand, and aimed to convince pupils and their communities of the value of the mission school. As Titcomb's nomenclature for the first stage (introductory) was not universal, the term 'initial' is preferred within the following pages. The initial stage is characterised by a variety in the use of language, and by the absence of a sufficient body of converted Indigenous or non-European peoples who might be seen to be sufficiently instructed in Christian knowledge to be of direct use to the mission.

At Liverpool in 1860, the connections between the Indian Uprising and the need for vernacular education were mentioned, indicating the resonance of the uprising beyond geographical specificities. The Presidencies of Madras and Bombay, where the vernacular was learnt by civil and military British officers, were contrasted with that of Bengal, where the government provided education in 'a strange and foreign language', that was, in English.[57] The Rev. William Campbell, formerly of Bangalore, placed the blame for the disturbances squarely on the government for preventing Christian mission- ary work, lamenting that: 'if the Government [in Bengal] had given to the people the Bible and the worship of the living God, they would have coun- teracted these evils, which created this rebellion, and which have rendered Bengal the Ireland of India'.[58] In equating Bengal with Ireland, Campbell referenced an older discourse which saw it as the duty of England to raise the position of the Irish, and thus drew upon broader discourses of the unfair, and indeed sometimes nefarious, system of British colonial rule.[59] It also touched on the anxieties of the British in Bengal as the political, com- mercial and intellectual centre of India, and thus a site of power struggles. More generally, the disturbances in India and the question of missionary involvement rendered India a hot topic of debate at the time of the Liver- pool Missionary Conference, with Campbell's reference to Ireland reflecting the internal British political difficulties that were also based on religious inequities.

Throughout the nineteenth century, the question of vernacular or English language teaching had occupied missionaries. The question of whether mission schools should be conducted in the vernacular or English was indeed not just a question of language, but was connected to concepts of culture and morals and access to 'modern' ways of thinking and acting. Lord Macaulay, President of the Committee of Public Instruction in Calcutta from December 1834, published his influential minute on education in early 1835, in which he advocated that a class of 'Brown Englishmen' be educated in English to be cultural mediators to their fellow Indians. This minute contributed to the creation of colonial subjects, who would be a link between the ruling class of British and the colonised Indians. It also added to the Orientalist–Anglicist controversy, in which missionaries were heavily involved.[60] The provision of English (Anglicist position) rather than vernacular instruction (Orientalist position) was perceived to have contributed to the Indian Mutiny of 1857, with it providing fodder for anxieties about the use of English in other colonies, particularly those in Africa.[61] Later commentators would suggest that Macaulay's 'Root-and-Branch' method was a mistake, that his belief that English 'modern' concepts would replace the uprooted Indian ones was misguided.[62] Yet as other early nineteenth-century commentators have argued, in Bengal the promotion of English in schools over local languages was not only important, for English became almost a global prerequisite for employment within the Indian civil service, but English simultaneously was promoted as the language of trade and public business with similar trajectories experienced in other parts of India.[63] Singh also stated as much in 1863 when he noted the need to establish an English language school in Rajshahi, stating that: 'If we do not give them English education, they will go to other schools, and knowledge without the purifying and humbling influences of Christianity is a dangerous gift for young Rajshahee.'[64] Although English education was considered potentially dangerous as it could open up the minds of youth to infidel literature, it was considered more dangerous to not have any influence at all over Indian youth in the initial stages of missionary schooling.

For Titcomb, once the first stage of mission had been achieved 'beyond the need of mere pioneering and civilising process',[65] a new stage of missionary advancement began; the 'Permanent stage'. This stage was characterised by a number of people converted to Christianity along with a need to replace English with the vernacular, for this was the language in which 'Native Agents' – mostly new Christians with positions of responsibility in the mission – could be more effective in evangelising to a large proportion of the 'heathen' population. This was not to say that there was not still a need for English schools. Rather, the largest proportion of the population would benefit from being taught in their own language. The third, and final, stage of mission advancement was seen to be the 'Reproductive stage', in which the capacities of the new Christians were used and in which schools aimed to 'develope [*sic*] the internal resources of a mission, and become nurseries for native teachers and pastors'.[66] In this third phase – which was also referred to as the phase of 'Native churches' – Native Christians were expected to take responsibility of the religious work from their Western colleagues. The CMS secretary, Henry Venn, had characterised this phase as the phase of self-supporting, self-governing, self-extending Native churches, known also as the 'three-selves' ideal.[67] Titcomb's address thus reflected missionary thought of the day with its focus upon progression and advancement, and with educational means adapted for each stage of development. It also reflected more broadly the nineteenth-century notion, which Dipesh Chakrabarty has referred to as a particular form of historicism, in which non-Europeans were told that they were 'not-yet' ready to be included into European notions of development and civilisation, for the expectations keep changing.[68] Titcomb's three stages were defined by his time in India and are not applicable to all missionary societies, as some groups conducted mission schools from the introductory phases in the vernacular. Nevertheless, the broader idea of the three stages is an apt frame of reference, and thus will be used further here with the caveat that the introductory stage (Titcomb's 'initial stage') was not necessarily one that was conducted in English but one that preceded the large-scale conversion of locals. The permanent stage is to be understood as one in which new Christians increasingly took a leading role in the mission, including roles as teachers with the schools, regardless of what language was used. And the third phase, the reproductive stage, is to be understood as per Titcomb. And, as per Chakrabarty, it was this stage in which Europeans were expected to relinquish control, that was the most contested in the missionary movement of the nineteenth century and in which the idea of 'not yet' was the most evident.

Need for different types of mission schools

Delegates at the 1860 Liverpool Missionary Conference acknowledged the need for various types of missionary schooling, extending beyond categories of schooling extant in Britain at the time. The school system in Britain was largely built upon voluntary schools and typically included charity/industrial schools, public/voluntary schools, dame schools and grammar schools.[69] Missionary schooling included special schools for infants, to raise the moral tone from childhood and to affect the attitudes and behaviours of parents. Infant schooling was considered not only to reach the children, but also the mothers. At Liverpool, Leupolt, in advocating for infant schools, suggested that 'whilst they elevate the minds of the children and raise the moral tone from childhood, they affect the mothers at home, and prove a source of blessing to the congregation at large'.[70] The Christian schooling of children was expected to penetrate beyond the individual pupil into the intimate sphere of the family. Through their children, mothers in particular were hoped to be affected, providing them with contact to the Christian world-view which they may not necessarily have had in their own daily activities. It was thus expected that mothers would want to become good Christian role models for their children, with mothers being assumed to be the bastions of Christian morality. This fitted to broader Western norms of women as the carriers and cultivators of civilisation, and the belief, to quote a missionary in nineteenth-century Canada that, 'if we get the girls, we get the race'.[71] Missionaries were not the only people to use children to reach parents; rather, as the historian Donald Wilson has argued, this was a common assimilative device used by the nation-state of Canada in relation to First Nations peoples throughout the nineteenth century.[72] Indeed, throughout the nineteenth century, schooling was seen by governments to be the most important avenue for indoctrinating the next generation in both Britain as well as the colonies, for European as well as Indigenous children. Another type of missionary schooling was exclusively for Christian children, who were to be taught separately from 'heathen' pupils. These schools were seen as an extension of infant schools with instruction to be undertaken in the permanent stage of mission and in the vernacular, ensuring the relevance of such schools for the majority of the population. Although English was used as the language of instruction in the introductory stage of mission, by the permanent stage English language schools, especially in places such as India, were deemed important only in moderation and only for a small elite minority.[73]

A third type of mission school was schools for orphaned children. Like infant schools, pupils were to start young to 'escape contamination from their countrymen'.[74] Unlike in infant schools, however, these children were to be under the total control of missionaries day and night, and in this sense were analogous to the residential schools for Indigenous peoples that were increasingly established in settler colonial societies from the late 1860s in cooperation with churches and the state. Within historical analysis of these residential schools in settler colonial societies such as Canada, the United States and Australia, the rationale behind residential boarding schools was to create total epistemic rifts between community and child, in order to immerse the child in a settler colonial society, engendering cultural genocide.[75] In India, the role of boarding schools was slightly different as children were to be integrated back into Indian society. Thus, orphan schools were seen to be of particular importance in India through providing a space in which orphans were segregated from the 'heathen' population and formed 'one great family with the missionary'.[76] These schools enforced total segregation from the local society, and it was from such schools in particular that missionaries in India derived most of their converts.[77] This is not surprising given that children who attended orphan schools were socialised wholly within a missionary environment. Indeed, around the time of the Liverpool conference most of the few Christian converts that missionary societies had gained were either orphans or children of orphans,[78] demonstrating both the success of the orphan schools and the ability of missionary institutions such as orphanages to provide secure places of residency for people who may have had no next of kin, and at the same time engendering cultural and social dislocation for these people within their own societies.

A further type of mission school considered important were training institutions, also known as 'Normal' schools, in which non-Europeans were trained to become teachers as well as evangelists to promote the edificatory aim of missions. The discussions on how best to train Christian teachers at the missionary conference in Ootacamund, India in 1858 recommended that a system of Boarding Schools be established where 'boys are received at a tender age, and their minds cultivated by European supervision and instruction'.[79] 'Heathendom' was considered polluting and it was only by extracting young boys from their environments and surrounding them with Christian role models and close supervision that they had a chance to be raised as good Christians. However, even boarding schools could not affect everyone in ways which missionaries desired with it being warned in Ootacamund that: 'No doubt, many of these lads will eventually prove unfit for the work of Christian teachers, and we must prepare ourselves for much disappointment on this score.'[80] The pessimism attached to the aptitude of local people to become Christian teachers, or Christian helpers, was a manifest part of essentialist missionary beliefs which increased over the century, and according to which missionaries blamed local people for failing to live up to their expectations. Tellingly neither Ootacamund nor the remainder of the nineteenth century yielded any better suggestion for the training of teachers than within such closely supervised environments.

The different types of mission schools described at Liverpool reflected some of the school types being established in India by the British. From the 1860s, the British government maintained some six types of schools in India: '(1.) Village or Vernacular Schools; (2.) District Schools, where English is taught in the higher classes; (3.) Colleges, where the education is conducted in English; (4.) two Presidency Colleges, each with a faculty of arts and law; (5.) the Engineering and Medical Colleges; (6.) the Normal Schools.'[81]

Mission schools were in competition for pupils with government schools as well as with Hindu and Muslim schools which could also apply for grants-in-aid.[82] Indeed, the missionary school system was only one of a number of parallel systems in many places for educating youth, and in the following chapter we will examine some tensions that arose because of this competition. Religious instruction was not funded under the grants-in-aid scheme, as government officials were anxious not to arouse religious agitations through the work of Christian missionaries. Yet missionary schools benefited from this scheme as they could receive funding from the government if they fulfilled certain criteria, and, although in theory the schools were to be secular, in practice there was room for religious teaching.

The focus on female education

In summarising missionary education, the Liverpool conference provided a six-point minute which was considered to inform the most appropriate mission schools in a variety of situations, with experience being advocated as the best means of advice for the establishment of future mission schools.[83] The first point was that the language of instruction at missionary schools should be the vernacular, notwithstanding the possibility that some societies advocated the use of English in the initial stage of missions. The second point allowed for the establishment of English-language schools if the local people themselves expressed their desire for them. Parents were thus able to articulate their wishes and future desires for their children in terms of language acquisition and knowledge transfer. A third point was that orphan schools, built upon the principal of exclusion from the perceived morally polluted heathen environment, were advantageous for the conversion of pupils. The fourth point pertained to the necessity of female education, particularly as women were often excluded from the influence of preaching and indeed from much of the public sphere. The fifth point arising from Liverpool in relation to education was the importance of establishing training institutions for Indigenous and non-European peoples. Given the costs of employing Europeans and the large numbers of children yet to be educated in missionary schools, it was a prudent decision to engage local people, which in and of itself drew upon Venn's 'three-self' ideal in which Native churches were a major practical aim of missionary work. The sixth and final point was that more vernacular Christian literature was necessary in order that the correct views of religion and morality might be disseminated amongst new Christians. With the singing of the Doxology the morning session finished and with it the session on missionary education. The conference offered an idealised version of missionary schooling, one

that overlooked some of the more pressing concerns, including the relationship between government funding and missionary schooling. This was a
topic that would become more important within many missionary fields as
governments towards the end of the century became more involved in
national school systems within colonies and dominions.

As many at Liverpool spoke from their experiences in India, they noted a
general lack of support for schools for females, as well as in the inability of
male missionaries to attend to these schools.[84] Female teachers were needed,
yet, as other scholars have stated, there were cultural sanctions that did not
allow unmarried Hindu women to teach, with married women rarely
receiving the permission of their husbands to teach.[85] Such issue necessitated
the encouragement of European female missionaries for India, providing a
legitimate means for European women to engage in professional work.
Many European women took up the call to become missionaries, with the
majority of missionaries around the end of the nineteenth century being
female and the mission fields of China and India being particularly favoured
by women.[86] It was hoped that converted female Christians would work as
unpaid evangelists amongst their own families and further amongst their
countrywomen. The non- or low remuneration of females reflected
their lower position in Protestant missionaries' understandings of a reformed
society as well as strategies of missionary groups to keep personnel costs as
low as possible. By the time of Liverpool, missionary organisations were
aware of the expense of supporting paid European missionaries and
expressed a need to curtail costs through employing locals. However, undue
haste in employing locals had resulted in the employment of people who
were not as godly as desired, leading to caution being expressed in regard to
their ongoing employment. The need for remunerated female European missionaries was frequently mentioned at Liverpool as a means of reaching
local Indian women,[87] yet no mention was made of the possibility that they,
as professionals, might be role models to which Indian women might aspire.

The focus on female education at Liverpool departed from the traditional
missionary focus on elite males. From the 1820s, the education of females
had been a key strategy for many missionary groups in India.[88] Leupolt
noted at Liverpool that 'the necessity of girls' schools is thank God! Felt by
all'.[89] In some of his later writings, Leupolt noted that there had been a
tradition in India for Hindu women to have had 'experienced better treatment, and of their having been persons of some education'; however, he
noted that at the time of the conference this was not the presiding belief.[90]
Elementary schools were presented in Liverpool as the only way that female
Indians could be 'got at',[91] for cultural restrictions were seen to prevent
them from frequenting bazars or other public places where missionaries
proselytised.[92] Singh himself reiterated these remarks in his later writings

suggesting that the more respectable the family was the more likely they were to seclude their daughters.[93] Thus, neither females nor the young were considered reachable by public preaching. Moreover, the work in zenanas – the spaces within Hindu or Muslim houses reserved exclusively for females – was modest before 1860. In the 1860s until more Anglo-missionaries were engaged in this work, mission schools were thought the only way in which the gospel could be spread amongst these two groups. So, by the time of Liverpool in 1860, a tradition of evangelical Protestant missionary schooling amongst non-Europeans had become well established, and its importance for all genders and levels of society was unquestioned, if somewhat more ideological than practically implemented.[94] Had the male missionaries at Liverpool allowed their wives to speak, they would have had an insight into the daily running of schools for girls. Mrs Mullens, the wife of the Rev. Mullens present at Liverpool, for example, had established two zenana schools before she accompanied her husband to England in 1858. Returning after Liverpool in December 1860 she took up the work again.[95] Indeed, teaching in female missionary schools was often a family business, and not only for European missionaries. Singh's daughter, known as Miss Singh, and his son Herra Lal Singh worked in the mission's orphanage, and at the Cape, Jan Tzatzoe's daughter taught at the mission school.[96] Similar to their European counterparts, the educational work of local wives and daughters was less visible than similar work of local preachers and teachers; however, due to their different cultural backgrounds local women are even harder to find in the colonial records.[97]

Christian schooling for Indian females around the mid-century was primarily aimed at educating them to be moral beings rather than potential employees outside of missionary enterprises. Unlike English-language schools for elite males in India, mission schools for Indian females were not designed as stepping-stones into positions as clerks in colonial administrations, although they could potentially lead to positions as teachers. Missionary schools, of varying quality and duration for different groups of females in society, had the purpose of instilling females with Christian moral codes in which they, in their roles as mothers and wives, were expected to provide a moral influence upon the whole of Indian society. In the words of Leupolt: 'If all the mothers of India were imbued with gospel truth, what a different aspect India would exhibit as to the moral character of her sons! We can, therefore, never overrate female education.'[98] In his later writings, Singh also espoused similar sentiments stating that females needed to be educated to fulfil the broader scheme on 'the evangelization and civilization [...] for with minds strengthened with cultivation, and character refined and exalted with the benign influence of the Gospel, they would be able to train a better generation of men'.[99] Singh's and Leupolt's comments reflected broader ideas circulating in society that a non-Christian country could only be converted to Christianity if females were first converted, for women could change the hearts of men. Closely connected was the idea that Christianity held the highest moral codes, against which all other religions were compared and found wanting. In their roles as (potential) mothers, Indian women were rendered part of a universal womanhood bestowed with virtues such as nurturing, child-care and purity, all of which underscored the general Victorian ideal of femininity and the belief of universal female moral superiority.[100] The ideals of women as the source of family morality were not confined to India of the nineteenth century; they had circulated for centuries in various places in and outside of Europe, underscoring patriarchal attempts to confine women's sexuality to domestic settings that agreed with Protestant Christian norms of monogamous marriage and female respectability.[101] As with any ideal, the ideal of a domesticated femininity was not always willingly ascribed to by all members of Indian society.

In order to facilitate the schooling of female Indians, appeals were made in Britain to notions of global 'sisterhood' and the role that British women could play in 'raising up' their benighted Indian 'sisters'. Examples include Alexander Duff's 1837 lecture at the Scottish Ladies' Association, which was subsequently published under the title *Female Education in India*, or Priscilla Chapman's 1839 *Hindoo Female Education*, as well as Krishna Mohun Banerjea's 1840 prize essay on 'Native Female Education'.[102] Singh was aware of these publications, being a former pupil of Duff, referencing Banerjea's pamphlet and quoting from Chapman's book in his own publication on the history of female education in Calcutta. Within the movement for female education in India there was an assumption that a common gender allowed for insights that transcended national and racial boundaries. Antoinette Burton has convincingly argued that modern British feminism drew upon notions of 'a helpless Indian womanhood on whom their own emancipation in the imperial nation state ultimately relied'.[103] British women such as Mary Carpenter, a Unitarian with connections to the Bengali Hindu social reform movement Brahmo Samaj, had publicly highlighted the issue of social and female reform through education in India through her publications and speeches from the 1860s.[104] This reflected also a British public desire to facilitate social reform in India through female education. For example, the *London Review* of 1861 declared:

> That female education is essential to the improvement of any country, and that, until we have raised up a race of instructed Christian wives and mothers [in India], it is vain to imagine that its teeming millions will be leavened by the influence of Christianity, are points which no one controverts.[105]

However, as Clare Midgley notes, British women had been actively involved in providing 'help' to Indian women through supplying them with education since the 1830s, although less academic attention has been given to them.[106] The trope of Indian women held in a state of 'disgusting degradation' by the Hindu religion was used as a means to appeal to the charity of Christian 'sisters' in Britain for support in the concrete aim of building schools and supplying teachers.[107] The London (Ladies') Society for Promoting Female Education in China, India, and the East (Female Education Society), founded in 1834, was just one example of British women working for the cause of Indian women's education towards an emancipation from 'tradition', Indian gendered ideas towards Western 'modern' ideals, and, as I argue, a component of missionary modernity. The society selected and trained women to establish schools, predominantly in China and India. After fifty-eight years of work, the society closed in 1899, as it did not wish to stand in competition with the 'Female Branches of the larger Societies'.[108] Within these larger missionary societies, committees which focused upon female education increasingly not only asked for financial contributions, but, similar to the Female Education Society, trained women to be missionaries, particularly educational and medical missionaries.[109] So successful was the drive for female missionaries, that by the end of the century, female missionaries outnumbered males.[110]

The call to sisterhood was also made by male missionaries at the Liverpool Missionary Conference, with The Rev. J. Fordyce of the Free Church in Calcutta arousing the sympathies of the attendees at the third soirée in which he was invited to provide information upon the subject of female education in the 'East'. He offered a common judgement for the fate of all Indian women in stating: 'She was unwelcomed at her birth, untaught in her childhood, enslaved when married, accursed as a widow, and often unlamented at her death.'[111] Such emotive descriptions were common throughout missionary writings. According to Judith Rowbotham, missionary texts were edited to 'strike the hearts, not the heads' of the female readership to entice them to support the work amongst female Indians.[112] Fordyce expressed his hope that the appeal to educate the women of India 'should reach the ears of our beloved Queen, and prompt efforts to redress the wrongs of the suffering sisterhood'.[113] Through evoking the Queen as the head of the Church of England as well as the head of State, he drew upon female legitimacy of the highest spiritual and political kind. Indeed, her reign over India was itself seen to be a reflection of divine purpose and will, as well as embodying the idea of a women as a nurturing influence over India.[114] Through the Queen's and public support, it was hoped that: 'A host of Florence Nightingales would arise, and go forth to save millions, not from the diseases of the body merely, but from the more destructive maladies of the soul.'[115] Here missionary discourses privileged morality over corporality and the soul over the body.

Although the discussions of missionary education at Liverpool had drawn exclusively from Indian examples, the 'Minute on Missionary Education', a form of summary and recommendations, was more inclusive. The conference considered female education 'not only desirable, but necessary in every mission' and worthy of extension, with the implicit notion that non-European women were responsible for the moral state of their communities.[116] Explicitly, female New Christians were expected to convert their country-women, particularly because male European missionaries, who often concentrated upon preaching and reaching males in the public sphere, had few opportunities to engage in prolonged conversations with non-Christian females, and numbers of female European missionaries were still modest.[117]

At the time of Liverpool, discussions on education centred on India and the need for moral education of female Indians in order to raise the moral tone of the whole of Indian society. Beyond missionary circles, the social movements around the time of Liverpool included a growth in women's movements to support female education of Indian women both through portraying them as being in need and through empowering British women as capable of providing that help. Through their campaigning against Indian customs such as *Sati* (Suttee), child marriage and female infanticide, missionary groups, women's groups and other reformers had depicted Indian women as deserving and innocent victims of their own cultural and religious environments in need of the moral, physical and spiritual protection of British Christians, and had thus legitimised the British right to colonise.[118] Not only in female missionary circles, but also in British feminist circles, Indian women were increasingly looked towards as foils against which British morality, femininity, respectability and emancipation could be gauged.[119] Evident in many of these debates was the trope that non-Christian religions degraded women. Christian schooling was presented as an avenue for her natural intelligence to be regained so that she could facilitate the spread of the Gospel in her domestic role as mother and wife. The Indian Uprising was a moment in which discussion of secular education and the danger become apparent and also about the ways in which missionaries believed that they could change the moral constitution of a country through the training of women. The general focus on females was, it has been argued, an effort to counter the secular influences that elite males received in English-language government schools.[120] Yet, women were not a homogeneous group and as the Liverpool Missionary Conference of 1860, as well as Singh's own experiences demonstrate, missionary ideology and practices were often at odds given the complex situation on the ground.

After Liverpool

Although Behari Lal Singh's presence at Liverpool was unique, his work as a New Christian in education was not. At Liverpool, he was able to share his knowledge as well as expectations for mission schooling. Back in India after his 1859–61 trip to Britain, he put some of these hopes into practice. He was 'providentially brought into communication' with some friends of the English Presbyterian Church in the indigo and silk districts of Rajshahye, Bengal (current Rajshahi in Bangladesh), which had a mixed Hindu and Muslim population.[121] The Muslim response to missionary ideas of female education was less recorded by missionaries as the initial focus in Bengal was on Hindus, as also demonstrated in the discussions at Liverpool.[122] These districts of Rajshahye were considered isolated, with no established Christian churches, and therefore in need.[123] In the late 1850s, Singh had made a missionary journey there reporting that there were some one and a half million people living in Rajshahi, with not one single Christian missionary.[124] In 1862, he was seconded by the Free Church of Scotland to the English Presbyterian Mission to establish a mission in Rajshahi.[125] Singh was aware of the importance of his position as a Native Missionary, a term he used to refer to himself. 'I need not tell you', he wrote in March 1862, 'that I occupy at present a most responsible and arduous and I may add a most anxious position in the indigo district without a single friend to sympathize in my worth.'[126] In the same year, he and his wife, an orphan raised by the English General Baptist Dr Amos Sutton, established a mission in the town of Rampore Bauleah (also known as Rampur Boalia, now Rajshahi) in the Rajshahi district, some 300 kilometres north of Calcutta. Arriving in late March 1862, they established a vernacular school for both boys and girls. Both Behari Lal Singh and his wife had been well educated for these positions, as he had spent more than ten years at Dr Duff's Training Institute in Calcutta and she was educated at a boarding school in America.[127] They opened the school on 1 April 1862 with ten pupils in the presence of the parents and guardians, in order to explain the educational concept to them.[128] Schools were already in existence in the town; however, Singh dismissed them as being rudimentary and 'humble in their character', with those who taught there being demeaned as 'mere pretenders to learning'.[129]

The first report of the school already boasted seven local teachers and scripture readers, plus Singh and his wife as the superintendent of the female school. It also noted the willingness of the parents, many of them Muslims, to send their children to school, with Singh stating that: 'No restraint whatever was laid on the Christian character of the instruction which these children receive.'[130] Some two weeks after the boys' school had been established,

Singh reported to the committee that a 'few villages have promised to confide their daughters to Mrs. Singh: but the difficulties connected with female education are so great, that we must not be hasty and over sanguine'.[131] His own gender would have also provided barriers to the elite and their daughters. According to Singh, problems associated with female education included the unwillingness of the fathers to allow their daughters to be taught, for according to him, fathers considered the 'ignorance and seclusion [of the daughters to be] essentially necessary to the honour of [the] family'.[132] This was a sentiment that he espoused in numerous texts, repeating the claim that fathers stood in the way of the moral elevation of their daughters.[133] Reiterating the claims of other contemporaneous texts for a British reading public, Singh highlighted how women were oppressed by culture, religion and family, and the higher the caste the more suppressed the women were.[134] Rather than focusing on the wealthy, who were already secluded, Singh saw the training poor of women to be the avenue to take first, as they were more accessible than the 'top 10,000' elites, who had access to whatever education they wished for. However, the focus on orphaned and lower class girls also allowed him to progress with teaching without having to change, in his words, 'the whole texture of Beengalee society'.[135] The lower class, mostly Muslim, girls in the vernacular school were taught to read and write Bengali, 'with moral and religious lectures on the evils of telling lies, using bad language, and also how to worship God and the true way of Salvation'.[136] Female education was thus not a means of liberating lower class women from gendered roles to allow them full access to colonial society, but a way for these women to support men in their Christian beliefs. Thus, rather than 'saving brown women from brown men', as Gayatri Chakravorty Spivak's broader discussion on English moral reform in British India noted, female Christian education could be aptly described as saving brown women *for* brown men.[137] Unlike Banerjea, who wrote in his prize-winning essay of the value in educating upper class females in the privacy of the zenana, Singh overlooked this group.[138] His focus on poor women was based on the consideration that the 'opulent and influential can educate themselves, without the aid of Government or Missionary Society, but the masses cannot elevate themselves without the countenance and pecuniary assistance of the Christian philanthropists'.[139] It was amongst this large group of people that Singh hoped to 'rescue ... from the evils of ignorance and superstition'.[140] In doing so, he inverted the focus on elite women, which was a common Anglo-American interest and one which helped in recruiting British and American women to the mission.[141] Singh, as a New Christian, had only a pool of local teachers to draw on, with the first European missionary, Dr Donald Morrison, only arriving three years after Singh's death with Singh's wife taking on responsibility for those three years. Singh's focus on lower-caste women was calculated, for although he did not have access to the rich and influential, he assumed that success amongst the lower classes would raise the interest of higher classes, who, ideally, would seek out missionary teachers to educate their wives and daughters.[142] According to Singh's writings, by 1871 the tactic was successful as the higher classes were impressed by the education of lower class girls and were looking themselves towards missionaries for education.[143]

When reading Singh's writings, one could be excused for thinking that Christian missionaries brought female education to Bengal, as he almost completely excluded reference to non-Christian schools. His book on the *History of Female Education in Calcutta*, for example, focused on Christian education, despite the breadth of the title.[144] When he referred to non-Christian education, it was generally 'tradition' education from an ancient past and as an indication that as it had been possible in the past for Indians to educate their females, it could also be so again the future.[145] Such sentiment was also evident in Priscilla Chapman's 1839 *Hindoo Female Education*, which was a call for a British Christian public to support female education in Bengal.[146] As David Savage has argued, this book was an indication of the 'fully articulated ideology of female education' circulating about colonial India in missionary circles in the 1830s and 1840s which expressed ideals of gender relations adapted to the Indian colonial setting.[147] It was not only British Christians who looked to a distant Hindu past in order to extract an ideal of female education: it was a position taken by Hindu reformers such as Rammohan Roy.[148] Within Bengal in the mid-nineteenth century, the focus upon education, and particularly on female education, both preceded Christian missionary interest as well as developed in parallel to it as a means of 'Bengal's renaissance' and ultimately resistance to British rule.[149] With the establishment of the English-language Hindu College in 1817 a new emerging colonial Bengali elite arose known as the Young Bengal movement that radically rejected traditional Hindu thought. Missionaries such as Alexander Duff were critical of the institution from which the movement arose, claiming that it taught European science and literature without religion creating a mass of 'infidels or sceptics of the most perfect kind, believing in nothing, believing not even in the existence of a Deity, and glorying in their unbelief'.[150] As we read above, such sentiments were reiterated in various forms in relation to secular teaching, particularly after the Indian Uprising of 1857.

Both Christian missionary and Hindu reform movements considered education vital, but had different expectations as to what education should entail. The Young Bengal movement demanded free and compulsory education for all. Women were also included in this call for universal educa-tion, and, if Singh is to be believed, it was partly due to Duff's debating with the young men of the Hindu College that opened their minds to the benefits of female education.[151] The Young Bengal movement was critical of Christianity, as well as Hindu reform movements, such as the Brahmo Sabha, an organisation founded by Raja Ram Mohan [Rammohan] Roy in 1828.[152] Known as the 'Maker of Modern India',[153] Rammohan Roy pushed for the emancipation of women through education as part of his radical reform movement. Education for the masses was part of his radical idea of emancipating penalised classes through social reform. He also pushed the radical ideas of liberal religion – that is, religion extracted from the shackles of superstition and mechanical rituals, as well as a universal theistic progress, or, in the words of David Kopf, 'the notion that the perfectibility of mankind could be achieved by joining social reform to rational religion'.[154] Rammohan Roy's ideas were disseminated through the Brahmo Sabha, an organisation for religious reform, which he had established in 1828. His ideas found resonance beyond India in the Unitarian movements in England and America, with financial and intellectual support for Rammohan Roy's work flowing in from overseas.[155] Indeed, the global networks of Brahmo Sabah (Brahmo Samaj) and the Unitarian movements influenced each other. The Hindu woman was for Rammohan Roy the Unitarian's proletariat, in need of education in order that the social reform could change the structure of society. In this sense, Rammohan Roy was more of a humanitarian wishing to change social structures rather than a philanthropist wishing to affect individual moral development. With such radical reform ideas in mind, Rammohan Roy had initially encouraged upper-caste Bengalis to educate their daughters in missionary schools; however, there was a backlash amongst the group as the content of the schooling was deemed too full of Christian religion.[156] At his death in 1833 in London, the movement that he had founded continued in various incarnations, with the name being changed to Brahmo Samaj (society) in 1843 and a splinter group the Adi (original) Brahmo Samaj formed in 1866. By the early 1870s, Keshab Chandra Sen, a Brahmo Samaj member closely connected to the Unitarians established schools for mass education, including for women.[157] However, by this time, there was a divide amongst Brahmo men as to the nature of education for women: should it be based on lessons for domestic enlightenment, or should it be of a radical emancipatory nature that would reconfigure Indian society as a whole?[158] Rammohan Roy had during his life advocated for the latter, but Keshab opted for the former, maintaining the status quo within society through providing limited education. The debate between the two poles was carried out in Bengali and English-language newspapers, as well as missionary periodicals, making it a public matter for a variety of audiences.[159] Keshab's standing was similar to many Christian missionary organisations in their wish to keep women, in India and elsewhere, in their places in the home, whilst providing them with Christian moral teachings for them to facilitate their roles as mothers and wives.

In the logic of Christian missionaries, a woman ideally would spread the Christian word as a wife or a mother, and for that she needed to be a pupil at a Christian school. Orphans were a source of recruits for the schools in Bengal, and also those run by Singh and his wife. In his booklet on the *History of Female Education in Calcutta*, Singh noted three sources of female pupils: one source was famine; another rescued children kidnapped by the *Meria Poojah*, destined to be sacrificed to the earth goddess; and a third was girls rescued from prostitution.[160] In all of these rescue scenarios, the perceived benevolence of Christian education overcomes the horror of Indian society. The famine of 1866 greatly affected the region of Orissa and the south-west districts of Bengal, with the mission establishing an orphanage to care for six boys and seven girls reported to have lost their parents to the famine.[161] Orphans in the institute were kept to the age of sixteen in the case of girls and seventeen in the case of boys. They were 'trained to resemble the mass of their fellows, in food, dress, and style of living'.[162] The education of girls was deliberately kept lower than boys to ensure that they would have good chances of marrying, demonstrating the willingness of Singh and the broader mission setting not to provide radical emancipatory education that could facilitate social reform. Moreover, both boys and girls were provided with education perceived to suit their stations in life, and also to ensure that they would not be discontent with their lot in life.[163] Those who demonstrated potential were taught English, as this was becoming the language of commercial and governmental transactions and the mission wished to provide their orphans with an educational advantage. For Singh, as for many other missionaries of the time, the boarding schools were spaces in which girls could be excluded from the perceived negative effects of 'heathen' life, and were the most successful sites of conversion.[164]

Mirroring the discussions of Liverpool, the pupils at the orphanage were kept separated from the 'heathen' influences surrounding them, with the intention of teaching them industrial subjects in order that they themselves could earn their own livelihood after they left the institution.[165] Mrs Singh herself was described of as an orphan at the soirée at Livepool. The story told was that the English General Baptist Rev. Amos Sutton took in an orphaned Brahmin girl in 1829. The girl's father, Punda Narain, is said to have gone missing on a pilgrimage, it was speculated that he had died from cholera, with his wife also dying from the disease.[166] Death also surrounded Sutton, who lost his first English wife, Charlotte, after childbirth in 1825. He remarried the widowed American Baptist, Elizabeth Hubbard Colman Sutton, in June 1826. As they had no children, they adopted the orphaned girl. Elizabeth was herself involved in female teaching in Bengal, founding female schools in Calcutta and subsequently asylums for orphan children in Cuttack, Orissa.[167] It was also in Orissa that this orphaned girl, the future Mrs Behari Lal Singh, taught in girls' schools as an assistant teacher, after having been educated at a boarding school in America.[168] She, like many other female Christian converts, was upheld as an example of the uplifting benefits of Christian education. However, she herself is not provided with a first name in the texts written about her, resulting in the erasure of her person(ality) from the historical record. Singh's imprint from the historical record also stopped abruptly. In 1871, his health had once again deteriorated. Suffering from 'clergyman's bleeding sore throat and fever', he was once again sent to England for the benefits of sea air and a 'better' climate.[169] He died in December 1873, in India.

Conclusion

As the discussions at the Liverpool Missionary Conference of 1860 demonstrated, the mid-nineteenth century saw a new period in mission schooling. Liverpool was a moment of reflection rather than action. The initial optimism of the 1830s had somewhat cooled, as people were not flocking to Christianity as was hoped, nor had any groups reached the third stage of mission, the reproductive stage. Behari Lal Singh's presence at Liverpool was an indication that local people took a vested interest in Christian education, but he was a single exception at this meeting, reflecting the dominance of the 'not yet' mentality within nineteenth century missionary settings. As the debates at Liverpool demonstrated, Christian teaching was thought to be the best means to 'reach' vulnerable non-Europeans, such as orphans, children and women. In fashioning the 'heathen other' to a Christian subject, new moral, social and gender roles were imparted, with missionaries continuing to legitimise their presence in colonials settings through their educational work. The impact of discussions at missionary conferences, in analogy to those from educational conferences, are hard to discern and often have to be inferred.[170] Yet the constant reference to the schooling of the 'rising generation' as a topic of debate throughout the century demonstrates the earnest desire to exchange ideas and offer recommendations as to the best way to recruit, maintain and train people into missionary schooling in order to facilitate the Christianisation of British colonies.

Discussions at Liverpool on education noted the urgency of female education. The focus on female education in missionary fields reflected broader debates on the role of women in British society, as well as the general assumption that females were the moral compass of society. The events surrounding the Indian Uprising of 1857 made missionaries more firm in their belief that secular education led to discontent and revolts, and further underscored their belief that they were the most apt people to provide education, and particularly Christian education, for non-European subjects in the British Empire. Through following the work and writings of Behari Lal Singh, who was both a delegate at the conference as well as an educational practitioner in Bengal subsequent to the conference, the chapter has highlighted the interactions between metropole ideologies as well as social reform movements in Bengal at the time. Importantly, the writings of Behari Lal Singh demonstrate that local people also contribute to the creation of mission modernity in their positing of women as the centre point of domestic Christianity. The next chapter will examine the life trajectories of New Christians in Sri Lanka and missionary focus upon morality, rather than academic aptitude, in the selection of local teachers. Morality, as a focus of missionary modernity, was deemed both an essential quality of the teacher as well as an essential part of the curriculum. However, as the following chapter will argue, in the complex educational landscape of Sri Lanka and India in the second half of the nineteenth century, modernity brought with it secularisation and subsequently tension between missionary and government bodies, as well as local people.

Notes

1 University of London (UL), School of Oriental and African Studies Archive (SOAS), © United Reformed Church, Presbyterian Church of England Foreign Missions Committee Archives (PCE), Foreign Mission Committee (FMC), 8 – Bangladesh/East Pakistan/01 – Correspondence, minutes and reports/01 – Early Correspondence and Papers/Item 1, W.S. Mackay to Mr. [Hugh] Matherson, 8 August 1859.

2 UL, SOAS, © United Reformed Church, PCE/FEM/8/03/04- Newspaper clippings, [Death notice] 'Behari Lal Singh (Communicated)', [no date, no publication].

3 UL, SOAS, © United Reformed Church, PCE/FMC/8/02 – Individual files/08 – Rev. Behari Lal Singh/Item 8, [Anonymous], *Behari Lal Singh* (Ranken & Co. London, 1874), p. 3.

4 UL, SOAS, © United Reformed Church, PCE/FMC/8/01/01/Item 1 W.S. Mackay to Mr. Matherson, 8 August 1859; UL, SOAS, © United Reformed Church, PCE/FMC/8/02/08/Item 8, [Anonymous], *Behari Lal Singh* (Ranken & Co. London, 1874), 3; Other than contemporaneous material, there has been no sustained biography of Behari Lal Singh. Andrew Walls wrote a short piece drawing from printed sources. See: Andrew F. Walls, 'Distinguished visitors: Tiyo Soga and Behari Lal Singh in Europe and at home', in Judith Becker and

Brian Stanley (eds), *Europe as the Other: External perspectives on European Christianity* (Göttingen: Vandenhoeck & Ruprecht, 2014), pp. 243–254.

5 The Secretaries to the Conference, *Conference on missions held in 1860 at Liverpool: Including the papers read, the deliberations, and the conclusions reached; with a comprehensive index shewing the various matters brought under review* (London: Strangeways & Walden, 1860); Walls, 'Distinguished visitors'.

6 UL, SOAS, © United Reformed Church, PCE/FMC/8/03 – Miscellaneous and Printed Materials/02 – Various Pamphlets/Item 2, Behari Lal Singh, *The history of Native female education in Calcutta*, 3rd edition (London: George Henry, 1874), note to the second edition.

7 Secretaries, *Conference on missions held in 1860 at Liverpool* (London: Strangeways & Walden, 1860), p. 26.

8 Joseph Mullens, 'Appendix I. Previous conferences on missions', in Secretaries, *Conference on missions held in 1860 at Liverpool*, p. 374.

9 Secretaries, *Conference on missions held in 1860 at Liverpool*, p. 72.

10 Written applications were accepted for the tickets. See: *Liverpool Mercury etc.*, 20 March 1860, Issue 3775: front page.

11 Andrew Porter, *Religion versus empire? British Protestant missionaries and overseas expansion, 1700–1914* (Manchester: Manchester University Press, 2004), p. 189.

12 William Richey Hogg, *Ecumenical foundations: A history of the International Missionary Council and its nineteenth-century background* (New York: Harper & Brothers, 1952), pp. 17–18; see: *Proceedings of the South India missionary conference held at Ootacamund, April 19th–May 5th, 1858* (Madras: SPCK, 1858).

13 Hogg, *Ecumenical foundations*, p. 32.

14 Ibid., p. 21.

15 Ibid., p. 50.

16 Ibid., p. 39; Secretaries, *Conference on missions held in 1860 at Liverpool*, pp. 1–3; 'Preface', *Periodical Accounts*, 24 (1861), ix–x.

17 'ART. I. Conference on missions held in 1860 at Liverpool, including the papers read, the deliberations, and the conclusions reached: with a comprehensive index, showing the various matters brought under review', *The Christian Remembrancer*, 44:118 (1862), 258.

18 Ibid., 252–272.

19 Ibid.

20 Secretaries, *Conference on missions held in 1860 at Liverpool*, pp. 95–96.

21 This delegate was the Rev. T.L. Badham, Joint Secretary of the Moravian Missionary Society. Tellingly, the Moravians did not have a large presence in India at the time; Secretaries, *Conference on missions held in 1860 at Liverpool*, p. 149.

22 These included missionaries who had had experience in the West Indies, such as the Rev. P.H. Cornford, a former Baptist missionary in Jamaica, Rev. T.L. Badham, Secretary of the Moravian Mission, and former missionary in the West

Indies and Rev. Hope M. Waddel, former missionary in the West Indies of the United Presbyterian Church.

23 Olive Anderson, 'The growth of Christian militarism in mid-Victorian Britain', *The English Historical Review*, 86:338 (1971), 49.

24 Alexander Duff, *The Church of Scotland's India mission: or a brief exposition of the principles on which that mission has been conducted in Calcutta, being the substance of an address delivered before the General Assembly of the Church, on Monday, 25th May 1835* (Edinburgh: John Waugh, 1835), p. 18.

25 C.B. Leupolt, *Recollections of an Indian missionary* (London: Society for Promoting Christian Knowledge, 1863), p. 44.

26 Tim Allender, *Learning femininity in colonial India, 1820–1932* (Manchester: Manchester University Press, 2016), p. 66.

27 See: M.A. Laird, *Missionaries and education in Bengal, 1793–1837* (Oxford: Clarendon Press, 1972), pp. 63–100, 120–128.

28 Porter, *Religion versus empire?*, p. 68.

29 Ibid., p. 74.

30 Joseph Hardwick, 'Anglican Church expansion and the recruitment of colonial clergy for New South Wales and the Cape Colony, c. 1790–1850', *Journal of Imperial & Commonwealth History*, 37:3 (2009), 365, doi: 10.1080/03086530903157565.

31 Henry Rosher James, *Education and statesmanship in India, 1797–1910* (London and New York: Longmans, Green, 1911), p. 77.

32 Secretaries, *Conference on missions held in 1860 at Liverpool*, p. 115.

33 Ibid., p. 181.

34 Ibid., p. 122.

35 World Missionary Conference (WMC), *Report of Commission III. Education in relation to the Christianisation of national life. With supplement: Presentation and discussion of the report in the conference on 17th June 1910 together with the discussion on Christian literature* (Edinburgh and London, New York, Chicago and Toronto: Oliphant, Anderson & Ferrier, Fleming H. Revell Company, 1910), pp. 370–371.

36 UL, SOAS, © United Reformed Church, PCE/FMC/8/03/01 – Reports/Item 1, *First Indian report of the Bauleah Mission in conjunction with the Presbyterian Church of England* (Serampore, India: Serampore Press: 1863), p. 6.

37 Secretaries, *Conference on missions held in 1860 at Liverpool*, p. 114.

38 Ibid., p. 181.

39 Ibid., p. 111.

40 Ibid.

41 Ibid., p. 118.

42 Ibid., p. 121.

43 Ibid., p. 123.

44 Ibid., p. 118.

45 At this conference CMS, Free Church of Scotland, BMS, LMS, Church of Scotland and WMMS missionaries attended. 'Bengal, Calcutta', *Papers relative to*

the Wesleyan Missions and the State of the Heathen countries (London: James Nichols, December 1868), p. 4.

46 Such ideas are exemplarily expressed in: Immanuel Kant, 'Beantwortung der Frage: Was ist Aufklärung?', *Berlinische Monatsschrift*, 12 (1784), 481–494.

47 David Kopf, *The Brahmo Samaj and the shaping of the modern Indian mind* (Princeton, NJ: Princeton University Press, 1979), doi: 10.2307/j.ctt13x0tkz.

48 Secretaries, *Conference on missions held in 1860 at Liverpool*, p. 120.

49 Ibid., p. 112.

50 Michel Foucault, *Discipline and punish: The birth of the prison*, trans. Alan Sheridan (London: Penguin Books, 1977).

51 See, for example, Robert W. Strayer, 'The making of mission schools in Kenya: A microcosmic perspective', *Comparative Education Review*, 1:3 (1973), 316. Laird, *Missionaries and Education in Bengal*, esp. chapter 2.

52 In non-literate societies, such as those of the First Nations in Canada, knowledge was transmitted inter-generationally through what historian James Miller has called the three L's: Looking, listening and learning. See: James R. Miller, *Shingwauk's vision: A history of native residential schools* (Toronto: University of Toronto Press, 2009), p. 16.

53 Secretaries, *Conference on missions held in 1860 at Liverpool*, p. 119.

54 WMC, *Report of Commission III*, p. 191.

55 Secretaries, *Conference on missions held in 1860 at Liverpool*, p. 123.

56 Ibid., p. 124.

57 The delegate was Mr Elphinstone in the Third Session of the Conference. See ibid., p. 136.

58 William Campbell speaking during the Third Session of the Conference. See ibid., p. 137.

59 William Howitt, *Colonization and Christianity: A popular history of the treatment of the Natives by the Europeans in all their colonies* (London: Longman & Co., 1838). See also: *The Eclectic Review*, 4 (December 1838), 657.

60 Stephen Evans, 'Macaulay's minute revisited: Colonial language policy in nineteenth-century India', *Journal of Multilingual and Multicultural Development*, 23:4 (2002), 260–281; 'Lord Macaulay's minute. 2nd February, 1835', in Nassau Lees (ed.), *Indian Musalmáns: Being three letters reprinted from the 'Times' … With an appendix containing Lord Macaulay's minutes* (London: Williams and Norgate, 1871), pp. 87–104; John Marriot and Bhaskar Mukhopadhyay (eds), *Britain in India, 1765–1905* (London: Pickering & Chatto, 2006), pp. 142–160; Catherine Hall, 'Making colonial subjects: Education in the age of empire', *History of Education*, 37:6 (2008), 783, doi: 10.1080/00467600802106206.

61 See: Godfrey N. Brown, 'British educational policy in West and Central Africa', *The Journal of Modern African Studies*, 2:3 (1964), 365.

62 C.F. Andrews, *The renaissance in India, its missionary aspect* (London: Church Missionary Society, 1912), p. 35.

63 Henry Rosher James, *Education and statesmanship in India, 1797–1910* (London and New York: Longmans, Green, 1911), pp. 32–34.

64 UL, SOAS, © United Reformed Church, PCE/FMC/9/03/01/*Second Indian report of the Bauleah Mission in conjunction with the Presbyterian Church of England* (Baptist Mission Press: Calcutta, 1864), p. 12.

65 Secretaries, *Conference on missions held in 1860 at Liverpool*, p. 124.

66 Ibid., p. 125.

67 Brian Stanley, 'The Church of the three selves: A perspective from the World Missionary Conference, Edinburgh, 1910', *The Journal of Imperial and Commonwealth History*, 36:3 (2008), 167–169, doi: 10.1080/03086530802318524.

68 Dipesh Chakrabarty, *Provincializing Europe. Postcolonial Thought and Historical Difference*, reissue (Princeton, NJ: Princeton University Press, 2000).

69 See: John Lawson and Harold Silver, *A social history of education in England* (London and New York: Routledge, 2007); Ivor Morrish, *Education since 1800* (London and New York: Routledge, 2007); W.B. Stephens, *Education in Britain 1750–1914* (Basingstoke and London: Macmillan Press, 1998).

70 Secretaries, *Conference on missions held in 1860 at Liverpool*, p. 113.

71 See, for example, Carol Devens, '"If we get the girls, we get the race": Missionary education of Native American girls', *Journal of World History*, 3:2 (1992), 219–237; see also: Fiona Paisley, 'Childhood and race: Growing up in the empire', in Philippa Levine (ed.), *Gender and empire* (Oxford: Oxford University Press, 2004), pp. 240–259. See also other contributions in: Philippa Levine (ed.), *Gender and empire* (Oxford: Oxford University Press, 2004); Alison Norman, 'Race, gender and colonialism: Public life among the Six Nations of Grand River, 1899–1939' (University of Toronto, PhD Dissertation, 2010), esp. chapter 2.

72 J. Donald Wilson, '"No blanket to be worn in school": The education of Indians in nineteenth-century Ontario', in Jean Barman, Yvonne Hébert and Don McCaskill (eds), *Indian education in Canada* (Vancouver: University of British Columbia Press, 1986), p. 68.

73 Secretaries, *Conference on missions held in 1860 at Liverpool*, p. 150.

74 Ibid., p. 113.

75 See, for example, an overview in: Stephen J. Minton (ed.), *Residential schools and indigenous peoples: From genocide via education to the possibilities for processes of truth, restitution, reconciliation, and reclamation* (London: Routledge, 2019).

76 Secretaries, *Conference on missions held in 1860 at Liverpool*, p. 113.

77 Ibid., p. 115.

78 Porter, *Religion versus empire?*, p. 165.

79 See: *Proceedings of the South India missionary conference held at Ootacamund, April 19th–May 5th, 1858* (Madras: SPCK, 1858), p. 161.

80 Ibid.

81 HC Deb, 'Committee', 3 August 1869, vol. 198 cc1161.

82 See: Church Missionary Society, *Grants-in-aid to mission schools*, Occasional Papers on India, No. 6 (London: Church Missionary House, 1859).

83 Secretaries, *Conference on missions held in 1860 at Liverpool*, pp. 150–151.

84 The topic was so important that at the third missionary soirée a session was devoted to female education in India entitled 'Female education in the East'. See ibid., pp. 273–274.

85 Benoy Bhusan Roy and Pranati Ray, *Zenana mission: The role of Christian missionaries for the education of women in the 19th century Bengal* (Delhi: Indian Society for Promoting Christian Knowledge, 1998), p. 191.

86 Jeffrey Cox, *The British missionary enterprise since 1700* (New York and London: Routledge, 2008), p. 217.

87 Secretaries, *Conference on missions held in 1860 at Liverpool*, p. 112.

88 Padma Anagol, 'Indian Christian women, c. 1850–c.1920', in Clare Midgley (ed.), *Gender and imperialism* (Manchester: Manchester University Press, 1998), p. 81.

89 Secretaries, *Conference on missions held in 1860 at Liverpool*, p. 111.

90 Leupolt, *Recollections of an Indian missionary*, p. 47.

91 'Miscellany. Liverpool missionary conference', *Missionary Magazine* (published by the American Baptist Missionary Union), 40 (1860), 181.

92 Secretaries, *Conference on missions held in 1860 at Liverpool*, p. 111.

93 UL, SOAS, © United Reformed Church, PCE/FMC/8/03/01, *Fifth Indian report of the Bauleah Mission in conjunction with the Presbyterian Church of England for 1866–67* (Calcutta: Baptist Mission Press, 1868), p. 11.

94 For an overview see: Norman Etherington, 'Education and medicine', in Norman Etheringon (ed.), *Missions and empire* (Oxford: Oxford University Press, 2005), pp. 261–284.

95 UL, SOAS, © United Reformed Church, PCE/FMC/8/03/02/Item 2, Behari Lal Singh, *Female education*, p. 61.

96 UL, SOAS, © United Reformed Church, PCE/FMC/8/03/02/Item 1, Behari Lal Singh, *Our orphan home* (London: W. Spearing, 1874), p. 15; HC PP 1836 (538) 'Report from the Select Committee on Aborigines (British Settlements) Together with the minutes of evidence, appendix and index', Johan Tzatzoe, 22 June 1836 [4688], p. 573.

97 For an overview of female missionary work see: Regina Ganter and Patricia Grimshaw, 'Introduction: Reading the Lives of White Mission Women', *Journal of Australian Studies*, 39:1 (2015), 1–6.

98 Secretaries, *Conference on missions Held in 1860 at Liverpool*, p. 112.

99 UL, SOAS, © United Reformed Church, PCE/FMC/8/03/01, *Fifth Indian report of the Bauleah Mission*, p. 11.

100 Antoinette M. Burton, 'The white woman's burden: British feminists and the Indian woman, 1865–1915', *Women's Studies International Forum*, 13 (1990), 295–308. See also: Sutapa Dutta, *British women missionaries in Bengal, 1793–1861* (London: Anthem Press, 2017), online ISBN 9781783087273 via Cambridge Core.

101 See, for example, Katherine Ellinghaus, *Taking assimilation to heart: Marriages of white women and indigenous men in the United States and Australia, 1887–1937* (Lincoln, NE: University of Nebraska Press, 2006); Joanna Cruickshank, '"A most lowering thing for a lady": Aspiring to respectable whiteness on Ramahyuck mission', in Claire McLisky and Jane Carey (eds), *Creating white Australia* (Sydney: Sydney University Press, 2009), pp. 80–96: Angus McLaren, 'Abortion in England, 1890–1914', *Victorian Studies*, 20 (1977), 379–400; Gordon Sayre, 'Native American sexuality in the eyes of the beholders, 1553–1710', in Merril D. Smith (ed.), *Sex and sexuality in early America* (New York, 1998), pp. 35–54.

102 David Savage examines these three texts in detail. See: David W. Savage, 'Missionaries and the development of a colonial ideology of female education in India', *Gender & History*, 9 (1997), 205, doi: 10.1111/1468–0424.00055.

103 Burton, 'The white woman's burden', p. 295, p. 303.

104 Clare Midgley, 'Mary Carpenter and the Brahmo Samaj of India: A transnational perspective on social reform in the age of empire', *Women's History Review*, 22:3 (2013), 363–385, doi: 10.1080/09612025.2012.726121.

105 'ART. VI.-1. The daughters of India: Their social condition, religion, literature, obligations, and prospects', *London Review* (April 1861), 153.

106 Midgley, 'Mary Carpenter and the Brahmo Samaj of India'.

107 'Heathen female education. No. II', *Evangelical Magazine and Missionary Chronicle*, 15 (1837), 145; see also: Savage, 'Missionaries and the development of a colonial ideology'.

108 University of Birmingham Library, Misc Z4/1 'Circulars re: closing of the Society for Promoting Female Education 1 in China, India, and the East (or Female Education Society)', Empire Online, www.empire.amdigital.co.uk/ [last accessed 16 February 2016].

109 Elizabeth E. Prevost, *The communion of women. Missions and gender in colonial Africa and the British metropole* (Oxford: Oxford University Press, 2010), p. 3.

110 Cox, *The British missionary enterprise*, p. 217.

111 Secretaries, *Conference on missions held in 1860 at Liverpool*, p. 274.

112 Judith Rowbotham, '"Hear an Indian sister's plea": Reporting the work of 19th-century British female missionaries', *Women's Studies International Forum*, 21:3 (1 June 1998), 251, doi: 10.1016/S0277–5395(98)00022–3.

113 Secretaries, *Conference on missions held in 1860 at Liverpool*, p. 274.

114 Ibid., p. 323. See also: Rowan Strong, 'A vision of an Anglican imperialism: The annual sermons of the Society for the Propagation of the Gospel in Foreign Parts 1701–1714', *Journal of Religious History*, 30 (2006), 175–198, doi: 10.1111/j.1467–9809.2006.00447.x. For an analysis of the 'motherly' image of Queen Victoria in British India see: Miles Taylor, *Empress: Queen Victoria and India* (New Haven, CT: Yale University Press, 2018).

115 Secretaries, *Conference on missions held in 1860 at Liverpool*, p. 274.

116 Ibid., pp. 150–151.

117 Ibid., pp. 205–206, 230.

118 Clare Midgley, *Feminism and empire. Women activists in Imperial Britain, 1790–1865* (London and New York: Routledge, 2007), pp. 65–91. The foundational feminist postcolonial critique to this practice is to be found in: Gayatri Chakravorty Spivak, 'Can the subaltern speak?' in C. Nelson and L. Grossbergs (eds), *Marxism and the interpretation of culture* (Basingstoke: Macmillan Education, 1988), pp. 271–313. This is not to suggest that missionary groups were successful in this cause. Sati was abolished in 1829. For discussions on Sati and the social reform behind it see: Andrea Major, *Sovereignty and social reform in India: British colonialism and the campaign against Sati, 1830–1860* (London: Routledge, 2010).

119 See, for example, Rowbotham, 'Hear an Indian sister's plea'; Burton, 'The white woman's burden'; Elizabeth Prevost, 'Assessing women, gender, and empire in Britain's nineteenth-century Protestant missionary movement', *History Compass*, 7:3 (2009), 765–799, doi: 10.1111/j.1478–0542.2009.00593.x; Jane Haggis, '"A heart that has felt the love of God and longs for others to know it": Conventions of gender, tensions of self and constructions of difference in offering to be a lady missionary', *Women's History Review*, 7 (1998), 171–193, doi: 10.1080/09612029800200170.

120 Savage, 'Missionaries and the development of a colonial ideology', p. 211.

121 UL, SOAS, © United Reformed Church, PCE/FMC/8/02/08/Item 16, *Behari Lal Singh*, p. 3.

122 For reference to the Muslim situation see: Muhammad Mohar Ali, 'The Bengali reaction to Christian missionary activities, 1833–1857', PhD dissertation (London: University of London, School of Oriental and African Studies, 1963), pp. 16–17, available from ProQuest Dissertations & Theses A&I; ProQuest Dissertations & Theses Global (2184778950).

123 UL, SOAS, © United Reformed Church, PCE/FMC/8/03/01, *First Indian report of the Bauleah Mission*, p. 4.

124 Anon, *Leading incidents connected with a missionary tour in the Gangetic Districts of Bengal: Undertaken by Behari Lal Singh & friends, chiefly with a view to distribute the Scriptures* (Calcutta: Baptist Mission Press, 1853).

125 The English Presbyterian Mission was established in 1844 as part of the Presbyterian Church in England, through their Foreign Missions Committee (FMC). They had a focus on China.

126 UL, SOAS, © United Reformed Church, PCE/FMC/8/02/08/Item 1, Behari Lal Singh to Dear Sir [PCE], Rampone Bauleah, 29 March 1862.

127 Secretaries, *Conference on missions held in 1860 at Liverpool*, p. 184; UL, SOAS, © United Reformed Church, PCE/FMC/8/03/04 – Newspaper clippings, [no source, no date after 1874], 'Behari lal Singh'. Note: there are no details of her name or of what school she was sent to.

128 UL, SOAS, © United Reformed Church, PCE/FMC/8/02/08/Item 1, Behari Lal Singh to Mr Dear Sir, Rampore Bauleah, 29 March 1862; UL, SOAS, © United Reformed Church, PCE/FMC/8/03/01, *First Indian report of the Bauleah Mission*, p. 4.

129 UL, SOAS, © United Reformed Church, PCE/FMC/8/02/08/Item 3, 'Appeal on behalf of the Bengal Mission of the English Presbyterian Church by Rev. Behari Lal Singh'.

130 UL, SOAS, © United Reformed Church, PCE/FMC/8/03/01, *First Indian report of the Bauleah Mission*, pp. 2–3.

131 Ibid., p. 4.

132 UL, SOAS, © United Reformed Church, PCE/FMC/8/03/01, *Fifth Indian report of the Bauleah Mission*, p. 11.

133 UL, SOAS, © United Reformed Church, PCE/FMC/8/03/02/Item 2: Behari Lal Singh, *Female education*, note to the second edition.

134 Savage, 'Missionaries and the development of a colonial ideology'. See also: Priscilla Chapman, *Hindoo female education* (London: R.B. Seeley and W. Burnside, 1839).

135 UL, SOAS, © United Reformed Church, PCE/FMC/8/03/02/Item 2: Behari Lal Singh, *Female education*, p. 50.

136 UL, SOAS, © United Reformed Church, PCE/FMC/8/03/01, *First Indian report of the Bauleah Mission*, p. 5.

137 Spivak, 'Can the subaltern speak?'; Partha Chatterjee, 'Reflections on "Can the subaltern speak?" Subaltern studies after Spivak', in Rosalind C. Morris (ed.), *Can the subaltern speak? Reflections on the history of an idea* (New York: Columbia University Press, 2010), pp. 81–86.

138 Savage, 'Missionaries and the development of a colonial ideology', p. 212.

139 UL, SOAS, © United Reformed Church, PCE/FMC/8/03/01, *Fifth Indian report of the Bauleah Mission*, p. 11.

140 Ibid., p. 10.

141 Savage, 'Missionaries and the development of a colonial ideology'; Antoinette Burton, 'Contesting the zenana: The mission to make "Lady Doctors for India", 1874–1885', *Journal of British Studies*, 35:3 (1996), 368–397; Cox, *The British missionary enterprise*.

142 UL, SOAS, © United Reformed Church, PCE/FMC/8/03/01, *Fifth Indian report of the Bauleah Mission*, p. 10.

143 UL, SOAS, © United Reformed Church, PCE/FMC/8/03/01, *Eighth Indian report of the Bauleah Mission in connection with the Presbyterian Church in England, in 1870–1871* (Calcutta: Baptist Mission Press, 1871), p. 10.

144 UL, SOAS, © United Reformed Church, PCE/FMC/8/03/02/Item 2, Behari Lal Singh, *Female education*.

145 Ibid., p. 11.

146 Chapman, *Hindoo female education*.

147 Savage, 'Missionaries and the development of a colonial ideology'.

148 Kopf, *The Brahmo Samaj*, p. 11.

149 Anil Seal, *The emergence of Indian nationalism: Competition and collaboration in the later nineteenth century* (Cambridge: Cambridge University Press, 1968), 194, doi: 10.1017/CBO9780511563409.

150 Alexander Duff, *The Church of Scotland's India mission: Or a brief exposition of the principles on which that mission has been conducted in Calcutta, being*

the substance of an address delivered before the General Assembly of the Church, on Monday, 25th May 1835 (Edinburgh: John Waugh, 1835), pp. 10–11.

151 UL, SOAS, © United Reformed Church, PCE/FMC/8/03/02/Item 2, Behari Lal Singh, *Female education*, p. 55.

152 Ali, 'The Bengali reaction'.

153 Brian A Hatcher, 'Remembering Rammohan: An essay on the (re-) emergence of modern Hinduism', *History of Religions*, 46:1 (2006), 50–80, doi: 10.1086/507928.

154 See: Kopf, *The Brahmo Samaj*, p. 3; see also: Brian A Hatcher, *Hinduism before reform* (Cambridge, MA and London: Harvard University Press, 2020).

155 Kopf, *The Brahmo Samaj*.

156 Savage, 'Missionaries and the development of a colonial ideology', p. 203.

157 For more on Keshab see: John Stevens, *Keshab: Bengal's forgotten prophet* (published to Oxford Scholarship Online, 2019), doi: 10.1093/oso/9780190901752.001.0001.

158 Kopf, *The Brahmo Samaj*, p. 34.

159 In Bengal, a very lively, and often anti-missionary, press landscape evolved. Debates about the issue of female education were published in the English-language *Hindu Patriot*, and republished in the German *Evangelisches Missions-Magazin* (EMM). See, for example, 'Missions-Zeitung. Indien im Jahr 1860', *EMM*, 5 (1861), 242–248.

160 UL, SOAS, © United Reformed Church, PCE/FMC/8/03/02/Item 2: Behari Lal Singh, *Female education*, p. 33.

161 UL, SOAS, © United Reformed Church, PCE/FMC/8/03/02, Item 1: Behari Lal Singh, *Our orphan home*.

162 UL, SOAS, © United Reformed Church, PCE/FMC/8/03/01, *Eighth Indian report of the Bauleah Mission*, p. 4.

163 Ibid., p. 4; UL, SOAS, © United Reformed Church, PCE/FMC/8/03/02/Item 2: Behari Lal Singh, *Female education*, pp. 34–35.

164 UL, SOAS, © United Reformed Church, PCE/FMC/8/03/02/Item 2: Behari Lal Singh, *Female education*, p. 49.

165 UL, SOAS, © United Reformed Church, PCE/FMC/8/03/01, *Fifth Indian report of the Bauleah Mission*, p. 13.

166 Conference, *Conference on missions*, pp. 180–184.

167 John Gregory Pike, *Memoir of Mrs. Charlotte Sutton: A missionary to Orissa, East Indies* (Boston: Gould, Kendall & Lincoln, 1835); 'After labor, rest', *Baptist Missionary Magazine* (Boston), 56 (1876), 155. See also: *Baptist Missionary Magazine* (American Baptist Foreign Mission Society), LVI (May 1876), 155–156; UL, SOAS, © United Reformed Church, PCE/FMC/8/03/02/Item 2: Behari Lal Singh, *Female education*, p. 15.

168 Secretaries, *Conference on missions held in 1860 at Liverpool*, p. 184.

169 UL, SOAS, © United Reformed Church, PCE/FMC/8/01/01/File 1/Item 6, EC Gensley to B.L. Singh, 16 March 1871; UL, SOSA, © United Reformed Church, PCE/FMC/8/03/01/*The Ninth Indian report*, p. 4.

170 Peter Kallaway, 'Conference litmus: The development of a conference and policy culture in the interwar period with special reference to the New Education
Fellowship and British colonial education in Southern Africa', in Kim Tolley
(ed.), *Transformations in schooling: Historical and comparative perspectives*
(New York: Palgrave Macmillan, 2007), p. 144.

4

Sustaining and secularising mission schools

In 1842, eighteen young Sri Lankan males wrote essays at the Cotta (Christian) Institution (now known as Sri Jayawardenepura Maha Vidyalaya), a training institute for male Christian youth to become future mission agents run by the CMS. The CMS had arrived in Sri Lanka in 1818 and established the institute in 1822 at Cotta (Kotte, or Kôtte, now Sri Jayewardenepura), outside of Colombo, Ceylon (present-day Sri Lanka).[1] The topics the youth wrote on were all religious and included ones that drew on the Bible as well as Church of England doctrine. Samuel wrote on Church doctrine penning an essay entitled 'How can you prove that men can not go to heaven on account of their own good works?' Robert Harling Richardson wrote on 'Mention some of the chief convents in the history of Abraham?' W.B. Ratruayeka wrote on the topic 'If we wish to understand the true way of salvation, what should we do?' Franeiseus De Mel wrote on 'What is prayer?' David wrote on comparative religion in his essay on 'Mention some of the chief points of difference between Christianity and Budism [sic]'.[2] He argued that 'although both religions do teach morality, but as to all points of faith they are diametrically opposed to each other', focusing particularly on the issues of monotheism and idolatry.[3] The names on these essays represent a cross section of nineteenth-century Sri Lanka with the males having English, Anglicised Sri Lankan, Portuguese or Sinhalese names.[4] The topic of the essays reflected the focus of the Cotta Institution on forming a new generation of Sri Lankans who were indoctrinated in Christian history and doctrines and could express them in eloquent English in well-formed writing. In 1842, the school was open only to Christian boys, with the first-person prose in some of these essays suggesting that some of the boys had an affinity with their subject matter.

In the same year that the youth wrote their essays, 1842, Henry Venn, the CMS's Clerical Secretary wrote to the Rev. J.F. Haslam in Sri Lanka. Haslam, the principal of the CMS Cotta Institution, was one of just sixteen British men sent by the CMS from its founding in 1799 to 1841 that had had a university education.[5] In his letter, Venn lauded the Cotta Institution as 'one of the brightest spots of the Christianising work' and wished to receive the regulations of the school so that they could be used 'as a guide in similar Institutions' beyond Ceylon.[6] The Cotta Institution had already borne fruit for the Ceylon mission, and as the essays demonstrate, there was further potential. Moreover, in 1842 the Central School Commission in Ceylon decided to provide conditional grants-in-aid to mission schools, with this scheme expanding annually for the benefit of Christian schools.[7] In his letter 1842, Venn lamented that at Cambridge, where he had been a tutor and the university where Haslam had studied, 'the spirituality, what in former years happily pervaded academical [sic] studies' had been 'entirely' lost.[8] Venn urged Haslam to pray 'for your pupils & with your pupils: This alone will prevent the secularizing effects of secular studies & enable us to study to the glory of God'.[9]

Venn's letter to Haslam reflected the concern of many people within missionary societies in the nineteenth century, that the students would not gain the full potential of a Christian education if only secular subjects were taught. Moreover, it also pointed to the concern that circulated within missionary circles that graduates of such schools might be lost to the Christianising project and take up positions in government or commerce. In Ceylon, as in the many other parts of the British Empire, local people were desired as teachers in mission schools because of their cultural sensitivities and language skills, and furthermore cost less to employ that Europeans. They were also deemed to be better able to tolerate local climates. There was also, as the LMS's Dr John Philip had noted from his two-year journey around Britain in the 1830s, not a large enough initial supply of capable young British men suitable for the job or knowledgeable about the local situations willing to come forward.[10] Yet, the employment of local people nevertheless engendered anxieties regarding their moral standing.

In the introductory stage of missions, European missionaries could closely supervise local workers, including teachers, particularly if the schools were aimed at an 'elevated' form of education in English. However, when the mission started to spread beyond the immediate physical sphere of European missionary influence, constant supervision through European missionaries was impractical. The movement from introductory to permanent and, finally, reproductive stages of mission also necessitated that local people took over roles in the mission church slowly morphing it into a Native Church that was self-supporting, self-governing, self-extending, to use the terminology of CMS secretary, Henry Venn, the 'three-selves' ideal.[11] Often the permanent stage was one in which schools for the 'masses' were established. This led to a significant increase in the number of local teachers employed, and often to a move to teach in the vernacular, with the acknowledgement that not all graduates of these schools would go on to 'elevated' education. The local teachers who ran these schools were not a homogeneous group, with the thousands of people with this title over the nineteenth century coming from different cultural, linguistic, geographical, religious, gender, 'racial', social, generational and political backgrounds. At times, many of these differences were evident in the same school, creating their own tensions as well as synchronicities.

Despite the numbers of local teachers working in Christian missions, this heterogeneous group has been often overlooked as scholars have more frequently focused on local Christian elites, who were more often ordained ministers, and thus more often to be found in a church rather than in a schoolroom.[12] As I have argued elsewhere, teaching was just one of a variety of jobs that local people could hold on Christian missions, alongside assisting, preaching, helping and other, non-religious work.[13] Only a few studies have placed local teachers in the centre of analysis, partly as source material is often scarce.[14] In the initial stages of mission, the boundaries between roles that New Christians undertook were often blurred, so that the label 'teacher' might mean more than instructing pupils within a (semi-) formalised situation. It could, for example, mean an auxiliary role as volunteer catechist. Through the subsequent stages of mission, roles of local assistants often became more defined, with teaching being a critical role in the handing down of normalised knowledge to the next generation of Christians.

This chapter extends from the previous focus on female education in missionary discourse, and the role of Behari Lal Singh as one local New Christian in the establishment of schools for female orphans in Bengal, to examine more generally the role of morality for missionary schooling, and, as an extension, missionary modernity, in terms of traits of the teachers and the content of the curriculum. Starting with CMS in Sri Lanka, the chapter will explore the establishment of schools within the heterogeneous cultural, social and religious landscape of Sri Lanka and examine some autobiographical writings of converts in Ceylon to explore what role Christian schooling played in influencing their life choices. Sri Lanka is a complex site where religious identities, castes and political identities were in constant flux.[15] By taking Sri Lanka as the centre of the analysis I acknowledge Nira Wickramasinghe's critique of essentialism, which she suggests some colonial historians undertake in their cases studies, assuming that their pronouncements of one space are universal for all.[16] Her critique is levelled at concepts of colonial governmentality and the construction of a political, rather than social, group. The sources used here do not shed light on individuals' access to civil government representation or of the facilitation of a colonial governmentality, but rather on the creation of a missionary modernity, in which individuals are defined in relation to the church, through church governmentality in terms of religious status, and are under church surveillance and control.[17] Here I acknowledge that 'modernity' itself is often an ideological, rather than an analytical, category.[18] The chapter argues that in the framework of missionary modernity, morality, rather than academic aptitude, was the foremost quality that missionaries desired in their teachers. Yet for local people, the reasons to become teachers were complex and not just an expression of faith.

Missionary modernity assumed that the Christian religion would be the guiding principle in all aspects of 'modern' life. In the mid-nineteenth century, as Venn's letter to Haslam in 1842 indicates, missionary groups were already concerned that secular studies would led to 'secularizing effects'. As we read in the previous chapter, Protestant missionary groups increasingly focused upon female education as a means to remain relevant, by broadening the population to whom they offered Christian schooling. Progressively over the nineteenth century, colonial governments themselves encroached into the content of missionary schooling through dictating what was to be taught in return for government funding. As we read in Chapter 2, there had already been a subtle shift in government terminology from 'religious and moral education' in relation to the Negro Education Grant to that of 'religious instruction and education' in the Select Committee (Aborigines Committee). A further and more formalised split occurred between secular and religious subjects from the mid-nineteenth century, as colonial governments increasingly dictated what was to be taught in grant-in-aid schools. I argue that through dictating content and regulating inspections governments contributed to the secularisation of mission schools. I demonstrate this shift through examining the reactions in both Ceylon (Sri Lanka) and India to government interference in mission school curricula. As such, the chapter examines debates around curriculum to elucidate another moment when mission societies responded to changing colonial and global circumstances, using their arguments for Christian education as a means to prove and maintain their legitimacy and worth in a modernising and secularising world. The chapter argues that even under a liberal religious equality model within a government system, as was practised in Sri Lanka, mission schools were progressively secularised over the century, partly due to the forces from outside and the demands of 'modernisation'. In doing so, the chapter provides a framework in which to conceptualise government funding as a form of secularisation of mission schools.

Sri Lanka, religious schools and colonial government

The CMS first established their mission in Sri Lanka, then known as Ceylon in 1818 with four missionaries: Joseph Knight, Samuel Lambrick, Robert

Mayor and Benjamin Ward.[19] By the time these four CMS men arrived, the island inhabitants had been under various forms of European rule or administration since the Portuguese had first landed around 1500. Under the Portuguese, local Theravada Sinhalese Buddhist and Tamil Hindus and Muslims were exposed to Catholicism, temples destroyed and a strategy for conversation to Catholicism put in place.[20] From the early 1600s, the Dutch in the form of the *Verenigde Oost-Indische Compagnie* (VOC, Dutch East India Company) arrived in Ceylon at the behest of the kingdom of Kandy to help resist Portuguese persecution, bringing with them Calvinism and the Dutch Reformed Church. With the expulsion of the Portuguese by VOC by 1656, the Dutch supplanted Roman Catholicism with the Dutch Reformed Church, persecuting Catholics and requiring children to go to schools where the Protestant religion was taught.[21] As Bente de Leeds has argued, the VOC focused upon the Protestant education of children in order to create a certain form of colonial subject amenable to Dutch rule.[22] Nominally, all Sinhalese and Tamils under the VOC administration became Christian, with membership of the Reformed Church a prerequisite for higher offices.[23] With the defeat of the Dutch in Europe, the British seized Dutch colonies, including Ceylon, with British soldiers occupying coastal areas from 1796. In 1802, the Netherlands ceded Dutch Ceylon to the British. Just over a decade later in 1815, the British defeated the kingdom of Kandy, deposing King Sri Vikrama Rajasinhathe and exiling him and his wives to Vellore, in British India.[24] With the dethroning of Vikrama, the British took control of the whole island as a Crown colony governed by colonial authorities in London through the local governor in Colombo. The inhabitants become British subjects. Unlike the Portuguese, who had used the Catholic Church as an arm of their rule, or the VOC, which was initially very intolerant of other forms of Christianity and supressed Theravada Buddhism and Hindu Saivism, the British administration was theoretically religiously neutral. Or, in the aggrandising words of Eugene Stock, the *fin de siècle* historian of the CMS, the British 'restored religious liberty'.[25] The British government demonstrated their allegiances through still dissuading the presence of Catholic missionaries and encouraged the work of Protestant and Church of England missionaries over 'foreign' missions. With the restoration of religious liberty many of the island's inhabitants returned to Theravada Buddhism and Hindu Saivism.

When the CMS missionaries arrived in 1818, there was a heterogeneous religious environment in which traditional religions were regaining adherents, and in which British missionary societies were trying to gain hold, particularly of schooling. There were also still pockets of Catholics, a reflection of the Portuguese influence on the island. Unlike in British India, there was no East India Company in Sri Lanka to 'exclude or expel missionaries'.[26] There were already missionaries from the LMS (from 1805 until 1819), the BMS (from 1812), the WMMS (from 1813) and the American Boards of Commissioners for Foreign Mission (from 1812), who had all enjoyed the support of the Governor, Sir Robert Brownrigg.[27] These missionaries built on the Christian influences of the Dutch and Portuguese, spreading across the island, initially on the coast, and as the influence of the British colonial government increased, into the hill country and across the whole island. The educational system that had been established by the VOC was still in existence with some of these schools supported by the new colonial government. Robert Mayor, one of the first CMS missionaries, was dismissive of many of these schools stating that they were 'in a very bad state for want of proper masters and regular inspectors'.[28] He cited an example of a village school some six miles from Galle, where none of the forty-two boys could tell him their Christian name, only a couple could read and the catechism was unknown by most. Mayor saw the need for improvement of the situation of the school through increasing the salary of the schoolmasters.[29]

From the beginning of the British administration in Sri Lanka, schooling was an important topic for the CMS, as it was in all other colonial spaces. Sir Alexander Johnston, the Chief Justice of Ceylon, encouraged the CMS, and took a plan with him for schools to present to the CMS when he travelled to London in 1817.[30] He would later become a Vice-President of the CMS.[31] In this initial entry of the CMS into Sri Lanka, Alexander Johnston had suggested a plan that the CMS, as part of the Established Church, should take on the supervision of four proposed fee-paying schools at Colombo, Galle, Jaffnapalam and Princamale, under the protection of the British government. Moreover, each of these stations would have sub-stations for the children of emancipated slaves as well as children of the lower classes. Already within this plan was a division into social classes, reflecting some of the caste and class differences evident in nineteenth-century Sri Lanka. The graduates of these schools, it was assumed, would 'be apprenticed to some useful trade, or be trained up so as to qualify them to be sent as catechists, school masters &c into the interior [Kingdom of Kandy] for the instruction of their country men'.[32] Within the plan Johnston proposed, a point was made that principal stations should be run by a committee consisting of the supervising missionary 'and two members of the most respectable persons under the denomination of Burghers [Euroasians], and of those of the natives higher casts residing at the place and to be chosen annually'.[33] The inclusion of local people demonstrates a broader awareness on the part of missionary groups of the need to engage the support of local elites in building up Christian educational institutions, particularly in locations in which formalised education was already part of the fabric of society.

The Buddhist temples and monastic colleges, called *Pirivena* in Sri Lanka, had been traditionally supported though royal patronage. They provided predominantly religious education with secular subjects also taught. However, by the time the CMS reached Sri Lanka these Buddhist educational structures had been diminished through the nascent domination of successive colonial regimes and Christian mission schools were the predominant form of education available for Buddhist, as well as Hindu families.[34] The CMS in London were led by Johnston's recommendations in terms of locations and disseminated the plan amongst the friends of the society.[35] Once he returned to Ceylon, Johnston continued to support the CMS, as too did the Governor, Sir Robert Brownrigg.[36] The support of the British colonial government also ensured that Christian mission schools maintained their predominant place in the educational market until the increase in Buddhist schools during the Buddhist revival at the end of the nineteenth century.[37]

Government schools during British rule in Sri Lanka were under the supervision of colonial clergy from the Church of England. In the early 1830s, the Colebrooke–Cameron Commission (from 1831 to 1832 headed by William Colebrooke, mostly a Whig liberal, and C.H. Cameron) focused on reforming government, the economy and the judiciary and also schooling.[38] David Scott has called these reforms the 'formation of Sri Lanka's modernity', as they make an important break with the past providing new ideas of political representation, 'modern' social institutions and supporting the capitalist plantation economy.[39] Under the Portuguese and the Dutch colonial administration, much of the Indigenous administrative system had been maintained, facilitating indirect rule.[40] With the Colebrooke–Cameron reforms, sweeping changes were made. The Legislative Council, for example, included political representation of Sri Lankans by Sri Lankans, an innovative move for a Crown Colony.[41] Scott calls these reforms 'far-reaching and comprehensive: they led to the unification of the administration of the island, the establishment of executive and legislative councils, judicial reform, the development of capitalist agriculture, and of modern means of communication, education, and the press'.[42]

In relation to education, Ranjit Ruberu notes that the recommendations of the Colebrooke–Cameron Commission in Sri Lanka in 1833 had directed government policy to place the responsibility for vernacular education with missionary organisations, with government schools primarily giving instruction in English and government vernacular schools closing down.[43] Many CMS vernacular schools of the time taught reading and writing in Tamil or Singhalese, plus Bible verses. The Colebrooke–Cameron Report stated that the government schools maintained by the British government were 'extremely defective and inefficient', with schools mostly teaching to write and read in the local language.[44] The government schoolmasters were not required to have English. Those in the north were furthermore reported as being 'totally inefficient and neglectful of their duties'.[45] The report suggested that a reform of the government schools was needed under a direction of a commission, including Christian and government leaders. It also recommended closing government schools in areas where mission schools teaching English had been established, for although: 'English missionaries have not very generally appreciated the importance of diffusing a knowledge of the English language through the medium of their schools, but I entertain no doubt that they will co-operate in this object.'[46] The focus on English language government schools in Sri Lanka has been framed by some scholars as a means to make 'the Ceylonese loyal subjects and to tie them closer to the British government'.[47] Yet, from the mid-nineteenth century, the teaching of English was considered to contribute to the perceived denationalising of local people, and to political discord. At the Liverpool Missionary Conference on 1860, the term 'denationalising' referred to the concern that local people had risen above their station in life, and consequently had become less useful to the mission as they could not communicate with their fellow countrymen and women in the same 'simple habits and the national feelings and sympathies'.[48] Moreover, it was considered to lead to political discontent amongst locals, leading in some case to outright insurgence. This tendency towards denationalisation was considered preventable if the predominant focus within teaching institutions was placed on the vernacular.[49]

Around the time of the Colebrooke–Cameron Report in the 1830s, the CMS had expanded its initial four stations: Cotta (near Colombo), Kandy (in the Hill Country), Nellore (in the Tamil district of the Jaffna Peninsula) and Baddagama (in the southern Singhalese country). In 1835, it had eight missionaries, four catechists and seventy-eight other assistants, including probationary catechists, local schoolmasters and a European Layman, who ran the printing and bookbinding establishments at Cotta. The CMS mission also included fifty-three schools with 1,226 boys and 251 girls. In addition there were seventy-one Seminarists and Institution Youth.[50] With so many schools, the CMS looked for more people to teach and needed to train more men to be schoolteachers and catechists. At the beginnings of the CMS work in Sri Lanka, there were few Christians deemed suitable to be teachers in the CMS schools (indeed in schools of any denomination), so Buddhists were recruited as teachers. At a CMS school in Kandy, established in 1819 by Lambrick, a Buddhist was employed as a teacher, which provided Lambrick the opportunity to speak to him about Christian religion, in the hope of converting him.[51] Although non-Christians were used, Christian teachers were preferred. The most important qualities that missionaries looked for in their potential teachers were Christian piety, morality and zeal. In essence, piety was a measure of personal religiosity, morality a measure of good conduct, and zeal a measure of active engagement at spreading the Christian message. These qualities were seen as important in teachers so that they could engage in developing the 'character' of their pupils, and ultimately help in their conversion to Christianity. The ideal teacher, suggested a member of the interdenominational missionary conference in Lahore in 1862–63, was of sound religious and moral character as 'no amount of intellect, education, or mere amiability, will supply the place of godliness'.[52] Such sentiments were common in missionary writings that prioritised religious aptitude over scholarly ability.

The CMS missionaries in Sri Lanka may have had the support of the government; however, there were other hindrances to their schooling ambitions, including the encroachment of other missionary groups into schooling as well as the lackadaisical reaction of local people to Christian schools. The tensions between the different denominations over the conversion of local groups were already evident in a letter that Joseph Knight sent back to the CMS in London in 1818, and they would continue over the century. In this 1818 letter, Knight stated that the Wesleyans had stayed amongst the European population, and had had little success with the locals. The Americans, he noted, had gone into the villages and were quite successful. Yet he had not made up his mind on whether to go to a village or not, but would travel to Jaffna (formally a kingdom) to the home town of the first convert of the Indian mission, a Sri Lankan boy called Christian David, who had been ordained at Calcutta.[53] Knight was dismissive of the local populations, finding them disinterested in schooling. He wrote:

> So insensible are the natives in general of the advantages of instruction, that it is with the greatest difficulty that even the richest of them can be induced to part with one dollar per month to other missionaries, for the instruction of their own children. Very unlikely then would such persons be to contribute generally for the establishing of schools, and the support of Christianity.[54]

This trope of local people being ambivalent towards education was ubiquitous in missionary writings and was found in various geographical, denominational and temporal spaces. The LMS missionary Rev. J.C. Thompson in Southern India, for example, bemoaned in 1837 that:

> Education is not valued, and even where no opposition exists, every trifle is used by parents and children as a pretext for non-attendance, so that only a person of some influence among them is able to secure their attendance in any moderate degree, and that with many a painful rebuff.[55]

Placing the blame on both parents and their children for not valuing education was a common trope. Parental attitudes towards schooling were often in flux. In her study of Congolese reactions to mission schools, Barbara Yates has argued that three stages could generally be discerned as reactions to mission schools moved from initial indifference to curiosity and, finally, to widespread acceptance.[56] The gradual acceptance and ultimately positive attitudes towards schools, she argues, were also connected to a variety of political, social and economic factors including 'the mystical aura surrounding books and western learning', the disintegration of traditional societies and an increasing awareness of the connection between education and individual economic benefit.[57] Yates' stages are not applicable universally, but reflect her reading of a particular historical situation. Indeed the sequence of her stages has been critiqued, with scholars providing counter examples where African chiefs actively wished for the establishment of mission schools for their people, with children wishing to attend, but parents preferring their children to engage in agricultural work.[58] In the Kandy region of Sri Lanka, counter examples can also be given of local people approaching the CMS to establish mission schools and providing the funds as well as stipulating the conditions for an English-language school for the 'pure Kandian'.[59] Yet an important point that Yates' work makes is that non-European parents' attitudes and interests towards schooling changed dependent upon multiple intrinsic and extrinsic factors, and not always in accord with local elites or children. Moreover, as other studies into missionary schooling have concluded, there is a paucity of information stemming from parents themselves as to their intent behind sending their children to school.[60]

In Sri Lanka, as in many other colonial spaces, the most promising of missionary scholars were initially sent to Europe or to North America by various missionary bodies to be trained as teachers or as missionaries.[61] Frederic David, son of Christian David, one of the first local preachers in Sri Lanka, was sent to England under the protection of the CMS in 1815.[62] Later in the century, Christian local women from various locations with potential were also send abroad – for example, Behari Lal Singh's wife was trained in America before becoming a teacher in Bengal, and there are a few examples of females from West African elite families being sent to England for a Christian education.[63] As David Killingray has noted, by the early-nineteenth century there was already a tradition of missionary groups sending young West Africans to Britain for education.[64] Yet, the high costs, including that of local lives, did not always justify the results. Shipwrecks, illness and death were not uncommon.[65] It was not only missionary societies that acknowledged these costs: government reports in Sri Lanka in the 1830s, such as the Colebrooke–Cameron Report, suggested that the sending of young Sinhalese men to Europe to educate them in English universities was not cost effective compared to the Christian seminaries established in Ceylon.[66]

It was not only the training of local people that was an issue for mission-ary societies: there were also many issues with the training of European missionaries, with training often beginning very ad hoc and, as the following chapter will demonstrate, only formulising and professionalising over the course of the century. The CMS, for example, was first established in April 1799, but it took a quarter of a century for a training institute, the Church Missionary Institution at Islington, to be established for outgoing mission-aries. Prior to this, individuals had been trained in private homes. The stan-dardisation and institutionalisation of teaching and teacher training was a slow process both in Europe as well as in the colonies. Many missionary societies were acutely aware of the need to train local people to become preaches and teachers, not least because it was often initially difficult for societies to find willing Europeans. Already in 1827, the CMS established the African Institution at Fourah Bay in their first mission field of Sierra Leone. One of the first pupils of this missionary training institution, which would subsequently become Fourah Bay College and then the future Univer-sity of Fourah Bay, was Samuel Adjai Crowther, a Yoruba from Western Nigeria. As one of the most widely known African Christians of the nine-teenth century, Crowther's biography is well known, in contrast to many other teachers in mission schools of the nineteenth century.[67] His biography records the importance of Christian schools in his trajectory from rescued slave, to mission school pupil, to baptised Christian, to college student, to teacher, to clergyman, to missionary, then founder of a new mission and then first African bishop.[68]

Training schools in both Europe and in British colonies were considered by both missionary groups as well as governments as being an important aspect for providing more teachers for schools.[69] Indeed, as we read in Chapter 1 in the context of the Negro Education Grant in the West Indies, training schools (also known as Normal Schools) were established as part of the Grant. George Grey noted the importance of training teaching from the local population, stating that:

> Even if a sufficient member of such teachers were to be found in this country [England] (which is far from being the case) they would hardly be induced to go to the Colonies without such Salaries as could not easily be afforded, whilst the state of Society in the West Indies renders it in vain to seek in that Society, at once and without due preparation, for the requisite competency. Under these circumstances, the most economical, as well as the most effectual mode of proceeding will be at once to establish Normal Schools.[70]

In his correspondence with the Treasury, Grey stated that candidates for these schools were to be 'recommended by the respective Societies, or their Agents in the Colonies'[71] and that instructors were to be of high moral character.[72] The Methodists, Baptists, Presbyterians, Anglicans and Moravians also established Normal Schools on various Caribbean islands.[73] Yet, even with Normal Training schools or Christian Institutes, the moral suitability of a graduate was not guaranteed. At the South India Missionary Conference held at Ootacamund in 1858 a CMS missionary, the Rev. E. Sargent, noted that: 'We have of course, neither in this nor in any country, such a form of moral machinery that needs only the placing of an individual of unknown character at one end, to bring him out at the other, an accomplished Christian teacher...'[74] Although moral machinery in terms of reliable instruments or institutions for the moulding of Christian teachers did not exist, training schools were the best substitute that missionary groups had. The Rev. Daniel Jayesingha [also written Jayasingha], a local Sri Lankan CMS missionary made this point clear in his criticism of the CMS in the late 1870s for not having the foresight to provide more training facilities for schoolmasters in Sri Lanka. He disparagingly remarked that:

> For want of men trained for the work, the missionaries were obliged to appoint men inefficient for the work; and when they were found unfit, they were obliged to discontinue their services, and to appoint other men in their place, which provoked them so much that they became opposes and enemies to the cause of the Gospel, and the name of Christ is despised in the eyes of the heathens.[75]

Jayesinghe, himself a 'Native Agent', believed, like many other missionaries of his time, that training institutes were the most suitable way to ensure the spiritual and academic quality of the graduate. Indeed, around the same time there was discussion in Anglican periodicals in Sri Lanka that teachers should have at least passed standard four of the curriculum to ensure a quality education for potential future adherents.[76] Moreover, through drawing on their own graduates, the CMS could mitigate the complication of disgruntled employees turning against them. One of the CMS schools which produced 'Native Agents' was the Cotta Institution. Some of the graduates of this institute left behind writings that provide information as to the reasons why they were educated there.

Autobiographical notes from local teachers

The position of 'Native Agent' was embraced by non-European teachers, as well as 'Native Evangelists' for various reasons. Within the mission hierarchy, teachers had positions of responsibility, yet were lower than ordained local Ministers were. They were in positions of trust with the knowledge that they imparted able to shape and inspire the rising generation. However, teachers, similar to local catechists, were under the surveillance and control of Western missionaries and local ministers. Norman Etherington has argued that local teachers in mission schools were not given autonomy in their work until well into the twentieth century, whereas local evangelists obtained autonomy earlier.[77] Yet this did not circumvent people who had been taught at mission schools from establishing their own schools outside of the structure of a particular society.[78] There are a myriad of reasons as to why non-Europeans became teachers in mission schools, but they are often difficult to locate as missionary archives do not always have writings from local teachers. In the CMS archive in Birmingham, we have access to at least some voices in the form of autobiographical notes from Sri Lankan men wishing to become ordained, many of whom were teachers, as well as other notes that shed light on the reasons people became teachers. Although there are limitations with these sources in terms of gender bias as well as the fact that these men were within the CMS system, they can shed light on why these men became teachers, even if it was a stepping-stone to something else. Some, like B.P. Weerasinghe at the Cotta Institution in the 1860s, became teachers as they were devout Christians and had strong faith.[79] The option of a stable, albeit meagre, income may have been an impetus for some to turn to teaching. This was the reason given for the unnamed orphaned graduate of a Sri Lankan CMS school in 1877 to accept a small salary after years of 'struggling with disease and poverty'.[80] Some, like Baptist Karunaratne, were trained from a young age within missionary structures. Karunaratne was from an early age under the supervision of his uncle, a schoolteacher of the CMS in Beddagama (near Cotta).[81] Others may have enjoyed the social status and standing within their communities that went with teaching. However, the Rev. Daniel Jayesinghe in Sri Lanka suggested that government positions provided more dignity and payment than a position in a mission school ever could.[82] In the examples from Sinhalese men applying to the CMS, many used teaching as a stepping-stone to becoming catechists towards their aim of becoming ordained ministers. Becoming a teacher in a Christian school was also a way for people to acquire knowledge and for some teachers it was a means to subvert Western knowledge, and to instil their pupils with a sense of pride in their Indigenous culture.[83] These are just some of the many reasons why local people become teachers at mission schools, with not all teachers themselves converts, as the example of the Buddhist at Lambrick's school at Kandy demonstrates. Missionary groups preferred converted people as teachers rather than 'native heathen teachers', who were considered by some individual missionaries to be 'a positive evil'.[84] Indeed some missionaries thought it better not to hold schools at all than to have 'heathens' teaching.[85] As the biographical notes from Christian Singhalese converts in the mid-nineteenth century demonstrate, teachers were some of the first waves of converts to the mission.

The autobiographical note of an unnamed man writing to the CMS to support his ordination, demonstrates the 'ideal' conversion to Christianity that Christian boarding schools engendered. He was born into a non-Christian family and his exclusion from the influences of his Buddhist family at a boarding school helped him make the first steps towards his conversion to Christianity. He was born in 1816, with his father sending him to the English boarding school at Nellore, 'no doubt', he noted, 'with a secular object in view'.[86] He described his attraction to Christianity and his willingness to be converted. The Rev. M. Adly sent him to the Christian Institution at Cotta to finish his education, and at the age of around 20, he was accepted as a Church member. He decided to give himself to the mission rather than, in his words, to 'enjoy the riches of this transitory world'. As an English teacher in the Nellore Boarding school for four years, he believed he had had the opportunity to made a Christian impression on the youth. In 1840, he married the Christian daughter of a catechist of the CMS mission, and subsequently had 11 children with her. In the year after his marriage, he was appointed a probationary catechist. He then was called by the CMS missionary Rev. J. Johnston 'to help him'. After working amongst 'heathens' he wished to be ordained.

This unnamed man's autobiographical note follows the same trajectory as the majority of notes from 'heathen' or nominal Christian progressing to believer through the influence of Christian education and ministers, and, finally, to wishing to be ordained themselves. For European missionaries as well, schools, and particularly Sunday Schools, were training grounds for a life within the church, with pupils moving to monitors, to teachers and from there to missionaries.[87] Schooling and teaching were decisive steps on the way towards conversion to Protestant Christianity and taking up a life of employment with the CMS. H. Kannager, for example, described his upbringing as heathen, although he was baptised into the Protestant church early in life. As a 'nominal' Christian – one who did not really believe in Christianity – Kannager was in his own words 'a most awful caviller with my teacher against the Christian religion', engaging in debates about the comparative benefits of Christianity verses Buddhism.[88] Through the influence of ordained men, including the local minister Cornelius Jayesingha (ordained by the Bishop Spencer of Madras in 1839), Kannager was brought closer to Christianity and wished to be ordained. Jayesingha also influenced the Christian trajectory of Johannis Perera Kolpegay, who was baptised as an infant by him. Kolpegay's father was a Christian schoolmaster, which suggests that Kolpegay had a Christian upbringing. As a youth, Kolpegay went to a CMS school, at which Jayesingha often taught religion. Subsequently Jayesingha sent Kolpegay to the Cotta Institution for 'training native Catechists'. He was affected by the teachings of Rev. Daniel de Silva, who himself was ordained in the late 1860s, and had a conversion moment.[89] Kolpegay subsequently was employed by Jayesingha as a catechist.

Silvester Mendis wrote his biographical note in Sinhalese in 1868, a reflection perhaps of his lower educational profile and resulting low proficiency in English. His note demonstrates the dynamic nature of religious adherence as well as the movement to different places because of schooling or work, ensuring a dynamic exchange of ideas throughout areas of Sri Lanka. Mendis was born in 1828 into a Buddhist family, who desired him to dedicate his life to Buddha, yet he was baptised a Roman Catholic. He went to a vernacular (Sinhalese) school, then progressed to a government school, where his faith in Christianity increased. Being too poor to pay for further instruction, he left the school and worked as a carpenter.[90] With some friends, he worked in his village as a voluntary teacher in order to hold prayer meetings. He subsequently moved to Kandy for work and came into contact with Mr Higgins, who, after some time, gave him a position as an itinerate catechist. In his autobiography, which was translated into English, Mendis referred to his continuing desire to be a Christian minister despite the hindrances that his life put in his way.

Other autobiographical notes presented the nominal Christian upbringing that the youth had had as being placed into question when in contact with Christian European teachers in the mission schools. B P. Weerasinghe [Bartholomew Peris Wirasinha] was brought up 'nominally' Christian, being baptised into the CMS and going to a CMS vernacular school at Nugagodda [Nugegoda] until he was 11, then transferring to the Cotta English School, until he was 16. Weerasinghe had a conversion moment, in which he was reading John 14:6 (Jesus saith unto him, I am the way, the truth, and the life: no man cometh unto the Father, but by me[91]), which led him to question the truths of Buddhism. He was confirmed, was made a master of the Cotta English School, then subsequently became a catechist. He desired to become an ordained minister in early 1868.[92] As an ordained minister, one of his duties was to give weekly catechistical lectures at the boys school at Katukele, ensuring that his connection to teaching continued in his role as a minister.[93]

H. Kananger's parents were also Buddhist. His introduction to Christianity came through the teacher at the local government school in Bentotte (Bentota), who was a Christian graduate of the Cotta Institution.[94] Similar to the life story of Kannager [Kannangara], Kananger said that he was outspoken when the tutor at the school tried to impart Christian message. He later was employed under a CMS minister at Baddagama in the school, and converted to Christianity. He believed ordination was a 'post of dignity and of much respectability on the light of God'.[95] Hendrick De Silva's autobiographical note follows a similar trajectory. He stated that he was born in 1828, and baptised, but stayed indifferent to Christianity during his early education at a local village school, then at a school in the larger centre of Galle. He subsequently went to the Cotta Institution, during a period where the Rev. Mr Haslam was still principal (before his death in 1850). In his own words, 'a decisive change was brought about – which I attribute to the divine blessing accompanying the invaluable instructions given me by my much esteemed and truly pious tutor Mr Haslam'.[96] He explained his desire to become an ordained missionary as an inner calling, and a desire to be more 'useful to my fellow sinners'.[97] De Silva was one of four Singhalese ordained in 1867–69, the others being Daniel Jayasinha [*sic*], Bartholomew Peris Wirasinha and Henry Gunasekara (son of Abraham Gunasekara).[98]

Within the autobiographical notes, the role of Christian women as wives of catechists and as teachers is evident. In his autobiographical note, another unnamed man preparing to be ordained noted that he was baptised into the Church of England as an infant, went to a mission day school, then to the mixed day school, sent to the Baddagama Seminary for three years, then to the Cotta Institution for four further years of instruction. During this time, he became a confirmed member of the church. After completing his studies at Cotta, he became a teacher in the English day school attached to the mission compound for a year. Subsequently he became a probationary catechist, and then a full catechist of the Kalapaloowawa District, building up the congregation from Sunday services in the boys' school room to such an extent that a piece of land was donated by local chief men and a small chapel erected. He married a Christian women, who had also been educated at the Cotta girls' school, and she established a girls' school in the district. Some of the pupils reportedly themselves became schoolmistresses employed by the CMS. When they subsequently moved, first to the Borella district and then to the Katukella and Gattambe districts near Kandy, she continued her work in female education.[99] Often girls education was limited to reading, arithmetic and Scripture.[100] The autobiography points to the importance of education in his trajectory towards ordination, as well as the axillary work of his wife in female education. The fact that he was a teacher in an English school also suggests that there were larger numbers of local people engaged in these positions than are often recorded in official histories of mission schools.

The autobiographies also highlight the desire of Buddhist parents to obtain education for their sons. In Simon Dias' paper, he describes his Buddhist parents' desire for him to be educated, and how they engaged a teacher for home visits before he was old enough to go to school. He was sent to a Christian school, and learnt some aspects of Christianity and reading and writing. Dias writes of his indecisiveness as to whether he would become a Catholic or a Protestant, and his own views on Christianity. He eventually became a scripture reader for the CMS, being paid 15 shillings a month. The CMS found a potential wife for him, but he left the CMS because 'a connexion with that family was bad' and all his family were opposed to the union. He subsequently returned to the CMS as an itinerant catechist under Mr Coles at Ranegalle in 1872 and married Salina Botaja in 1873. In March of the same year they had a son.[101] G.A.W. Liyanage was also born of Buddhist parents and was taught to read and write in both the temples as well as the mission schools. Whilst he was at school, the district missionary, Mr Parsons, made enquiries of having a messenger, with Liyanage being recommended by his teacher. After a couple years of continuing his schooling and working as a messenger, he was appointed to the position of School master.[102] When Parsons left for England, the Rev. A. Gunasakera gave Liyanage the duties of preaching twice a day to the 'heathen'. He then became the manager of the mission's property, whilst still maintaining his role as school master. When an opening occurred at the Office of Marriage Register he was torn between this secular role, which his family supported, and the Church. He chose to apply to become an ordained minister of the church.

These biographical notes, written by hand by the applicants, provide details into the life trajectories of men who wished to become ordained Christian ministers and the role that Christian teachers played in these trajectories. Their descriptions are limited to following a chronological pattern from 'heathen' or 'nominal' Christian to a zealous Christian in order to convince the readers of the application that the men were ready to be ordained. They follow in some ways the trajectories of European missionaries in that, initially, piety rather than formal training was the primary determining factor of European missionary suitability.[103] Although these sources from the pens of Sri Lankan men provide some insight into their lives, they like many missionary sources are to be read with caution. As Hugh Morrison has argued, the extant writings of Indigenous teachers and mission workers in other contexts tend to create 'a group portrait that is limited by source parameters and a lack of deep biographical detail, contextually bounded, and "tainted" by both European mediation and by missionary idiosyncrasies or predilections'.[104] This is not to say that the autobiographical data of potential ministers does not provide illuminating information; however, it does remind us that the voices of the 'normal' teachers are often lost to history, and only the voices of 'elite', or 'elevated', scholars are maintained. For the 21 local catechists in 1857 in Sri Lanka, there were 72 local teachers, demonstrating the comparative magnitude of lost voices.[105]

As the biographical notes of potential local CMS ministers in Sri Lanka suggest, the pupils of the Cotta Institution were hand-picked from CMS feeder schools to be sent to the Institution. That is, they were screened prior to attending the school in a primary act of control and surveillance. Yet, in his history of the CMS, Eugene Stock referred to the Cotta Institution as a failure. Of the 130 graduates until 1851, 48 had become agents of the mission, with only 23 still serving in 1851. Stock suggested an overhaul was needed for the costs did not justify the results. He noted that 'the better the education, the more did the students, after getting all its advantages at the Society's expense, shirk Mission employment and drift away to more lucrative occupations; besides which, a promising scholar did not always develop into a fervent "fisher of men"'.[106] The lack of zeal amongst mission school pupils was something that missionary groups often complained about, and was nothing specific to Sri Lanka. Missionaries at a conference in Ootacamund, India in 1858 recommended that a system of boarding schools be established where 'boys are received at a tender age, and their minds cultivated by European supervision and instruction'.[107] However, as we have previously read, even boarding schools could not affect everyone in ways which missionaries desired, with a warning in Ootacamund that: 'No doubt, many of these lads will eventually prove unfit for the work of Christian teachers, and we must prepare ourselves for much disappointment on this score.'[108] Pupils of mission schools were categorised into three groups: a select few who hungered for the Christian message that they received in the school; a group that was attentive to the lessons, yet was affected only in the mind and not in the heart; and a majority who only attended classes when required – for example, for examinations. The pessimism attached to the aptitude of local people to become Christian teachers or Christian helpers was a manifest part of essentialist missionary beliefs which increased over the century, and according to which missionaries generally blamed local people for failing to live up to their expectations.

The problems that missionary groups had with attracting teachers were also pragmatic. Many missionary societies struggled with the inordinate cost of employing people and therefore offered only low wages for teachers compared to wages offered by the government. Within South Africa, for example, the differentiation of payment for teachers of various classes of schools saw by the end of the nineteenth century African teachers at mission schools in the Cape being paid a fifth of what first-class aided public schoolteachers received.[109] Such differences in salaries for local workers, including teachers and catechists, compared to other professions was often a point of discussion in mission churches around the colonial world, with Sri Lanka being no exception. As we read in the previous chapter, at the Liverpool Conference on Missions held in 1860, Behari Lal Singh had advocated for the payment of local people to be Christian teachers and helpers. He himself had chosen to work for the Free Church of Scotland as a missionary for a tenth of the income that he had received as a government teacher.[110] As a seconded missionary to the English Presbyterian Mission in Rampore Bauleah (Rampur Boalia) in the Rajshahi district of Bengal, he reiterated this stance, noting that New Christians connected with a Christian mission increased their expectations for their material standing. He argued that in order to recruit and maintain well qualified New Christians to teach in mission schools then they needed to be adequately remunerated, as:

> They have acquired various wants and habits, and rather resemble Europeans than the mass of their countrymen, in food, dress, manners, and style of living. Their expenditure is correspondingly increased. They find various openings in the Government service, in the educational, mercantile, or railway lines where they can obtain much larger pay than they can get as Christian teachers or professors. If it be most desirable to engage agents of this class, who, from their superior training, are peculiarly qualified to command the respect of the rationalistic intuitionalists, pantheists or materialists who have sprung up since the introduction of European infidel literature into this country, and secure a ready attention to the proclamation of the gospel; we must be prepared to provide them with adequate remuneration, not that they should have the same salary as their European colleagues; for that would be impracticable. English gentlemen require more in this country than natives.[111]

At Liverpool, the Rev. J. Walton, a Wesleyan missionary at Jaffna, Ceylon, was less magnanimous in his comments. The salary question had caused, he noted, 'much embarrassment in Ceylon'. He framed his comments with the acknowledgment that the position of the missionary was to be temporary, a nod towards the progressive three stages of native churches, where after the initial stage the local churches became permanent and then self-propagating. He decried the tendency that within churches 'a race of hybrids, dressing like Europeans, detached from their own countrymen, and needing an income which the native churches will, of themselves, be unable to furnish for a long time to come'.[112] The anxiety that Walton expressed about a 'race of hybrids' was felt in other parts of society in Ceylon, but also in other parts of the colonised and Christianised world, where a new middle class had emerged, taking on British habits and language. Walton's thoughts reflected anxiety about denationalisation of locals and their inability to be 'controlled' or led to be similar to, but not the same as, Europeans. This colonial anxiety has been examined by scholars such as Dipesh Chakrabarty in his analysis of historicism. For him, historicism 'posited historical time as a measure of the cultural distance (at least in institutional development) that was assumed to exist between the West and the non-West' and provided legitimisation for colonialism.[113] It also was a way of suggesting that colonial subjects were 'not yet' ready to fully participate in political modernity, or in the particular forms of colonial modernity.[114] Or, I would argue, in missionary modernity, a form of modernity in which the driving rationale is religious rather than political. Missionary modernity took on many of the liberal ideas of the age; it rejected 'heathen' superstition for Christian faith, controlled people through church order and discipline and provided the framework to say 'not yet' to non- or new Christians. One of the measures used to determine Protestant religious progress was Christian morality.

Missionary modernity could also use protest forms of political modernity, such as petitions. In writing about petitions in colonial Sri Lanka, Nira Wickramasinghe has discerned that petitions were used as political instruments in the Dutch colonial period for people outside of the field of governmentality used by people who had no civil rights. She argues that they used petitions to express their demands, and when these were not met, they rebelled.[115] Such petitions, Wickramasinghe argues, were maintained under British rule and can be 'understood as a democratic instrument and as a form of political action'.[116] Yet, within the context of a petition to a missionary society, such as the petitions that were sent around the time of the Ceylon Controversy of 1876–1880, in which the CMS clashed with the Church of England over ideals and practices, petitions were also used to engaged with church rather than secular politics. [117] Wickramasinghe notes that political petitions 'did not encourage the formation of political institutions that represented rather than simply listened to grievances of the people'.[118] However, the petitions of Sri Lankans to the CMS did not rule out the possibility of a split from the society and the establishment of a local church – notwithstanding the unclear relationship with the Anglican church – and thus, potentially provided the religious petitioners with more agency than political ones.

It is not the intention here to examine the dogmatic aspects of the controversy, but rather to examine what role local Christians, and particularly local teachers, took in the controversy. One of the issues which had inflamed the tension between the CMS and the Bishop centred on the Tamil Coolie Mission, which had been established in the 1850s amongst indentured labourers from British India brought over to work on plantations.[119] The issue at stake was the supervision of un-ordained men acting as catechists or scripture readers. The Bishop lay claim to controlling them if no ordained missionary was in charge of the Mission station. The CMS contested this point.[120] As the Bishop refused to ordain local men, the CMS missionaries saw this as an obstacle, or a 'not yet' moment, to the growth of the congregations.[121] The broader point at hand was the structure of a unified Diocese under which Europeans and local people were equally represented at the Church of England Conferences or Synods in Ceylon, or whether these two groups would continue to be separated. The Bishop took the former position, with the CMS missionaries in Ceylon taking the latter, noting that nothing should be able to get in the way of building a Native Church – nor were they willing to give up the independence that they had enjoyed in running the mission.[122]

Members of the Tamil Coolie mission petitioned the CMS in England to send out a Missionary Bishop to Ceylon.[123] Of the purported 1,000 individuals belonging to the Tamil Coolie Mission, some 553 people signed the petition, including Tamils as well as Europeans. As most of the signatories were labourers on the tea estates, the names of the estates rather than the occupations were mostly given. A small number of people were obviously unable to write and signed an X next to their names, while most of the names were written in Tamil script. A number of catechists and teachers also signed the petition. At the time the petition was sent to London in 1876, the Tamil Coolie Mission had two Native ministers, 32 catechists and 60 schoolmasters who had been conducting religious service amongst the Christian Tamils as well as to the 'heathens on the Estates'.[124] They had established some of their own missionary societies and congregations and, like the Tamil Christians in Jaffna, were also against the High Church practices of the incumbent Bishop of Colombo, fearing that this would be a 'stumbling block to feeble Christians' as well as being too close to the doctrines of the Roman Catholic Church. They also showed unity with the 12 CMS missionaries whose licences had been revoked by the Bishop, stating that 'it would not be agreeable to us to remain'.[125] A further petition signed in Colombo in October 1876 by 819 Tamil Christians contained similar concerns and requests.

Local Christians in Jaffna were also concerned that if the CMS missionaries conceded to the Bishop, it would 'alter the Character of the Native Church' and undo much good work. In an 1876 letter, local members of the CMS at Jaffna wrote a petition to the CMS secretaries in London that stating that they would rather remain true to the Gospel than some form of Church government, and thus threatening to create a schism. They requested a missionary Bishop to be sent to Ceylon. Of the 93 signatories, over a third gave their position as a teacher, with four more belonging to the local Seminary.[126] The large number of teachers points to both their high social standing in questions of church politics, as well as perhaps the threats that they felt themselves under as teachers of CMS schools if the Native mission was to be subsumed into the Church of England in Ceylon.

Ultimately, the Ceylon Controversy was settled without a schism. Nevertheless, Sri Lankans connected with the CMS used democratic instruments as a form of political action to affect change in religious matters that were part of a broader missionary modernity. This missionary modernity also influenced discussions about wages to be paid for local agents, and particularly the regulations and control mechanisms to be put in place as part of a missionary governmentality. In 1868, the Rev. Jones and Richard Dowbiggin informed the CMS conference in Sri Lanka, that: 'Few if any of our agents ever seem satisfied with the amount allotted to them.'[127] One of the problems they noted was that salaries had been discretionary rather than standardised. The solution presented was to categorise catechists in terms of spiritual quality, and to be examined in academic learning of 'certain subjects approved by the conference', such as The Holy Scriptures, Evidences, General Theology, Formularies Prayer Book, Outlines of History (including History of Ceylon), Arithmetic and Buddhism. A requisite number of marks needed to be obtained to pass. The difference between classes was academic as both classes were expected to be morally sound. The memorandum set out clear sums of payment based on location, the annual incremental increases, stipulations as to percentages of monthly payments that individuals had to set aside for disabled catechists and widows, and supplementary sums for married men. It even stipulated that the potential wife of the local agent must be vetted by the missionary, and that she should be able to teach in the girls' school, before the catechist was allowed to marry. The memorandum was to be disseminated amongst all current catechists and provided to all the youth entering the training seminary. These regulatory and standardising measures were evidence of an increased missionary governmentality, in which the measures were transparent to all, yet at the same time the standardisation and generalisation of the rules allowed for assessment and comparison of the intellectual and moral standards of mission agents. Under the logic of missionary modernity, it was the spiritual quality that was privileged over the intellectual achievements for advancement within the church hierarchy.

Government involvement in mission schools

In 1877, a discussion was raised in the Ceylon *Diocesan Gazette* as to the nature of school inspections in Church of England schools. The article began by suggesting that a plan had long been needed for the inspection of Anglican schools, for:

> It is difficult for either teacher or children to estimate at the right importance the religious lesson, when, after being expressly ignored by the Government Inspector, it is in no way publically recognised by the Church: and the secular result is the only one by which the value of the teaching given is estimated.[128]

The visibility and accountability of mission school inspections and examinations were considered an important role in Anglican, as with many Protestant, mission schools. In nineteenth-century pedagogical texts, inspections and examinations were two discrete, yet entwined concepts, as evinced by Daniel Fearon, an assistant-commissioner of the Endowed Schools in Britain, who wrote in 1876 that:

> By 'inspection' is meant the process of seeing a school at work in the course of its ordinary routine; noting how it is constructed, warmed, drained, ventilated, furnished, and supplied with apparatus and other materials; how its journals, registers, and other records are kept; what is the course of education, physical and intellectual, which it supplies to its scholars; whether it is conducted on the most approved methods for economizing time and labour; what is the order and discipline; what the relations of the scholars, to their teachers and to one another; how the teachers give their lessons, and how in other respects they are qualified to perform, and do perform their duties. By 'examination' is meant the process of testing, by written and oral questioning of the scholars, whether the results of the instruction given in the school are satisfactory.[129]

In Fearon's classification, inspections focused upon the materiality of schools and the conditions under which knowledge was transmitted. Examinations, on the other hand, assessed the ability to recall knowledge. For Fearon, inspections and examinations were intimately connected, with inspections to precede examinations in temporal terms, but not in importance. His booklet was published in a period during which a system of payment-by-results was in place (through the Revised Code of 1862, UK), and although he noted that the provision of grants was tied only to the results of examinations and not inspections, the latter was nevertheless useful in gaining insight into the broader educational environment. As examinations became more formalised they became more standardised and generalised, allowing for assessment and comparison of the standards of pupils across various schools, and ultimately leading to the 'normalisation' of knowledge. According to Michel Foucault: 'The examination combines the techniques of an observing hierarchy and those of a normalizing judgement. It is a normalizing gaze, a surveillance that makes it possible to qualify, to classify and to punish.'[130] The examination process intimately links knowledge and power. Here it is argued that in accepting grants-in-aid, mission schools opened themselves up to secularisation through government inspection and examination, with colonial governments increasingly setting the agenda for examinations that prioritised secular, rather than religious, subjects. In arguing that mission schools were secularised, I draw on Mark Chaves' concept of 'structural secularisation', which is understood as 'the declining scope of religious authority', and not the decline of religion per se. This term considers the capacity for religious proponents to maintain authority in light of other ideological, material or political alternatives. That is, governments were not necessarily suggesting that their citizens turn away from their adherence to denominational religion in their private lives; rather, they wished to mitigate some of the power that churches held over aspects of structures and institutions that the government itself wished to have ultimate influence over. In terms of missionary schooling this was manifest through avenues such as government funding, the introduction of secular curricula or government inspection and control over teaching personnel with the introduction of minimal qualifications.

Grants-in-aid

Grants-in-aid for mission schools were applied broadly across the British imperial world. In many instances these grants were conditional upon the provision of a set curriculum, including reading, writing, arithmetic, English and geography, often with the Irish National Readers used as the textbooks. These textbooks perpetuated ideas of racial hierarchies, as well as a unified British Empire.[131] Grants were also conditional upon inspections by government officials.[132] Government funds were often raised for the grant-in-aid system through local taxes. For example, in India revenue was raised for the system through the opium trade, creating tension and division between missionary groups.[133] In the Cape of Good Hope in the 1860s, money from the Slave Compensation Fund was used by the Superintendent-General of Education to supply 'mission schools established chiefly for the education of the poor' with funds for the 'payment and training of pupil-teachers'.[134] Within the same set of regulations from the Cape Colony provision was given to supply mission schools with grants, exclusively for the (part) payment of teachers, demonstrating the shift evident in government policies since the introduction of the Negro Education Grant where the payment of Dissenting teachers was contested. In India, the grants-in-aid system stipulated that teachers of all religions, even Muslims and Hindus, could be paid from the funds, with similar stipulations in other colonies. The religious beliefs of teachers in government-supported grants-in-aid schools was of limited interest to governments, although this remained a point of anxiety for missionary groups.

Conditional grants, such as grants-in-aid, were an institutionalised means to support public–private partnerships in education throughout the colonies. Conditional grants provided substantial, but by no means comprehensive, funds to realise a public service. In the nineteenth century, grants-in-aid were utilised in many public–private enterprises in the colonies including for public worship houses, public works, museums, parks and gardens, libraries, cemeteries and agricultural societies.[135] Originally devised in Britain, grants-in-aid for non-government schools were subsequently exported to the colonies. In the Cape Colony, the Superintendent-General of Education, Dr James Rose-Innes, established a grant-in-aid system from 1843 for first- and second-class schools with a further categorisation into Division A, B and C schools. Categorised under Division C, mission schools received less funding than established schools (Division A).[136] In India, grants-in-aid were adopted under Wood's Educational Despatch of 1854 as a means to engage the local community in universal education, though providing funding to any group regardless of religious persuasion as long as religion was not taught in the schools. Or, in the words of the Duke of Argyll in a House of Lords debate in 1859, grants-in-aid were 'the least aggressive in form of any [system] that could be devised, for it had at least the appearance of co-operation on part of the Natives'.[137] The heterogeneous religious landscape within Britain and the colonies called for a solution in which the majority of religious players would not be discouraged. The grants-in-aid scheme was a pragmatic solution that aimed to minimise governmental costs. Or, in the words of the Duke of Argyll, 'it was the principle which afforded the best and easiest solution of the difficulties in respect of religion which beset all schemes of education in both [England and India]'.[138] The intention behind the Indian grants-in-aid were to encourage local engagement in education with the aim of reducing direct government intervention for local management.[139]

The British state slowly extended control over their own schools during the course of the nineteenth century. From the 1840s an inspected curriculum was introduced, with the Revised Code of 1862 focusing upon the three Rs of reading, writing and arithmetic. The 1870s saw the introduction of a nationwide system, with compulsory attendance introduced in 1880.[140] Such developments in Britain were mirrored by colonial governments at various times and speeds, with government influence also dependent upon the type of school. As described in Chapter 1, in the nineteenth century, four models of government schools were touted for the colonies: a pure Church of England model; a liberal religious equality model within a government system; a primarily government model with additional religious components; and a purely secular government model. In the purely secular government model, as enacted in India, aided schools were to be secular. The funds were not to go to supporting religious education, although religious instruction was tolerated.[141] In other places, such as Sri Lanka and the Cape of Good Hope, where a liberal religious equality model within a government system existed, schools were permitted to provide religious training as part of the normal school hours.[142] The conscience clause in Sri Lanka placed the responsibility on parents to withdraw their children if they did not wish them to participate in religious instruction. This need for consent theoretically provided parents a say in the education of their children within religious epistemology. However, until 1939 there was no obligation of mission schools to ask parents whether they objected.[143]

In Sri Lanka, the non-interference, indeed interdependence of government and missionary societies, was greeted by Protestant missionary societies. At the Liverpool conference on mission, the delegates had heartily cheered at the statement that in the government schools in Ceylon, the Bible was introduced from the beginning (of British rule).[144] Using common missionary hyperbole, the Rev. J. Walton, a missionary in the Tamil territory of Jaffna, claimed that he had 'never head of a single instance of a boy not coming to school during the first hours when the Bible was read. They know (for Hindoo boys are very sharp) that it is the most important lesson of the day, and it is never missed.'[145] Ceylon was presented as an example where mission schooling had received the support of the government from the beginning, and thus where the Christian religion was taking hold. Walton provided as support to this claim a story that when a new school was established by locals in protest to the mission school having mixed-caste classes, that parents insisted that the Bible should be part of the school curriculum.[146] The importance of his story was that the Bible was deemed to equate to English education, and thus to the potential for social progress within the British colonial apparatus.

The situation in Sri Lanka was, nevertheless, more complex than Walton portrayed with various religious groups vying for government support. The liberal religious equality model within a government system as practised in Sri Lanka allowed mission schools of all religions, denominations and confessions to apply. However, around the 1860s the Catholic missionary Father Charles Bonjean of Bollawate was vocal in his disapproval of the way in which government grants-in-aid for religious schools were granted. Over a series of fourteen articles in the *Examiner* newspaper from December 1860 to February 1861, Bonjean stated his thoughts about the government system of grants-in-aid and the associated need to provide a secular curriculum.[147] He was not against the need to provide secular education – indeed he argued that within Catholic educational institutions religion and science had been simultaneously taught for hundreds of years – but against the system because he judged 'the present system to be fraught with momentous evils to the faith of the catholic youth' as it eroded the Catholic nature of this education.[148] In Sri Lanka, the Central School commission required grants-in-aid schools to use books published by the Commissioners of National Education in Ireland including Watt's *Scripture History* and Tyler's *Elements of General History*.[149] This curriculum was considered by Bonjean to be detrimental to Catholicism as all doctrine had been erased and was prejudice against Catholics. Furthermore, he saw the grants-in-aid system as disadvantageous to Catholics as it did not offer a representational system of religious schooling based upon taxation.[150]

Bonjean particularly disapproval of two petitions presented by Protestant groups to the Legislative Council in Sri Lanka in December 1859 and August 1860. The petitions called for no government restrictions to be made to the time or manner of Christian teaching performed in the schools receiving government grants-in-aid or to the appointment or dismissal of teachers. The petition suggested that appointments and dismissal of teachers should be undertaken by the individual school boards. A further proposal that established schools should be free of competition from other groups, was deemed by Bonjean as an infringement of the civil rights and 'religious toleration, freedom of conscience and equality of rights'.[151] Bonjean gave the number of Catholics in Sri Lanka as 'at least' 150,000 and those of 'Protestants of all sects at most' 10,000, and argued with these numbers that the Catholic voice should not be overlooked, particularly since the inhabitants of the Crown colony paid taxes that went to fund the educational system.[152] His broader argument was that the Protestants wished to have the monopoly of education through government grants-in-aid schools. Bonjean argued against the mixed and common system (or a liberal religious equality model within a government system) and argued for a separate and denominational system (akin to the Irish system).[153] In a convoluted argument, he suggested that parents consciously objecting to religious teachings would be doubly burdened through having to pay taxes, which flowed into grants-in-aid schools, as well as paying a price for private education, as the government would not establish multiple grants-in-aid schools in the same locality.[154] His broader implicit argument was that the Catholics were treated unfavourably within a liberal religious equality model within a government system. Indeed, from the beginnings of British government support of mission schools in the colonies, such as we read in Chapter 1 in relation to the Negro Education Grant, measures had been undertaken to negate Catholic influence. What the petitions to the Legislative Council further demonstrate is not only the way in which Protestants used government institutions to push their claim for privileged treatment, but also that in petitioning to government, Protestants turned to secular, rather than religious, authorities to decide on the content and structure of their schools.

More broadly, the policy of providing grants-in-aid to mission schools with secular instruction was contested from Catholic and some Protestant groups in the British colonial world.[155] A common criticism over the long nineteenth century was that missionaries would forgo their duties to provide religious education in order to provide curricula that policy dictated as well as to prepare for government inspections and examinations.[156] As one missionary in Southern Africa at the beginning for the twentieth century pointedly noted: 'When the Government gives grants, then the government inspector comes, and very soon the schoolmaster works for the inspector and not for religion.'[157] The government inspections could also hinder the progress of the schools. For example, in Sri Lanka, the local minister in Kandy complained that the 'new government inspector's method of examination was such that the school failed to obtain any grant this year'.[158] The school had suffered from a large turnover of teachers early in 1876, resulting in a significant loss of students. Although the teaching staff again became stable, the boys at school were beginners not able to be presented for examination for the next inspection, ensuring that no government funding would be forthcoming in the following year.

Despite such dangers, the grants-in-aid programme was taken up by many missionary bodies as a means to supplement funding to their schools, to provide access to the government educational system and to provide legitimacy for their own schools. Many missionary bodies accepted both government funding and consequently unavoidable interference, because it obviated the otherwise onerous need for their schools to be fully self-funding. By the World Missionary Conference in Edinburgh in 1910 (examined in detail in the next chapter), the commissioners on Christian education in their report praised secular governments for their work in external inspections of schools. 'In many cases', noted the report in relation to India, 'it is confessed that, without Government inspection and regulations, mission schools would have been content to drift along with antiquated methods, low standards, and easy-going ways'.[159] Inspections from external bodies were seen as 'an education necessity', with '[s]upervision and inspection by Government a source of stability'.[160] Inspections potentially restricted local agency because missionaries could not adapt curricula to local wishes without facing the prospect of losing funding. Thus, in order for missionaries to move towards compliance with government regulations – and towards secular curricula – they inhibited their ability to negotiate and comply with local desires.

Not all missionary groups unequivocally accepted government grants. Baptist and Congregational missions refused to engage in the grants-in-aid policy in India due to their voluntary principles, and therefore had to rely upon funds from their British supporters.[161] Similarly in the West Indies in the 1830s, Baptists refused to take grants from the local Legislature, also relying upon funds from their supporters.[162] In British India, Basel missionaries accepted government funding, but were particularly dismissive that 'heathen' teachers were to be employed to teach 'worldly' subjects, leading them to suggest that the outlook for the schools was bleak.[163] Even those missionary societies which willingly accepted government funding often had cause to complain as conditional requirements were increasingly placed upon curricula. Norman Etherington has described government funding of mission schools in southern Africa as a 'poisoned chalice' as the government tried to reform them towards industrial schools and to weaken missionary influence.[164] One of the major concerns that missionary groups had was the secularisation of curricula, which had potential to diminish missionary influence as well as to undermine the rationale behind establishing mission schools.

Government inspections were not only a means to examine and control the content of the curricula, but they were also a means to regulate and control the work of teachers. Teachers in the initial local permanent stages of missions were likely to be European. As increasingly more local teachers were employed they too were subject to government inspection. One measure of secular control over teachers was the system of payment by results, which, as the name suggests, afforded teachers payment above and beyond their salary, based upon the examination results of pupils. In England this system was introduced under the Revised Code of 1862. Unsurprisingly, the system was also taken up in many places in the British Empire including Ireland, India and colonies in southern Africa, Australia and the West Indies.[165] In Britain as well as in the colonies the system was criticised by religious groups who were concerned that the focus upon results would leave less time in the curriculum for religious studies.[166] This was similar to complaints that missionary bodies expressed in relation to grants-in-aid, for the focus on government inspections and examinations was deemed to leave missionary teachers with little time to teach religion, thus effectively directing their work towards purely secular subjects.[167] Missionary bodies commonly complained that focusing upon results was detrimental to general learning as focus was placed upon the parroting of knowledge rather than the instruction of the whole individual as a member of society.[168] The focus upon payment by results as a means to remunerate teachers made adhering to official curricula of utmost importance, and demonstrates the use of examination systems to regulate educational outcomes. Missionary bodies were aware of the need to have good quality teachers at their school, but not always able to obtain suitably capable teachers.

Secular education in government schools allowed pupils to receive the language training they desired without necessarily overt religious education. Government schools had competitive fees, higher-paid teachers, higher prestige and, in places such as India, gave holidays on all the feast days, allowing pupils to engage in their own religious festivals.[169] These were all aspects of government involvement with which mission schools had to find ways to engage, or to counter. Wood's Despatch stipulated that colleges receiving grants-in-aid should not be required to charge rates as high as government colleges, which early twentieth century commentators considered to be a reason for the multiplication of inefficient and under-equipped private colleges.[170] The competition from government schools also forced mission schools to adapt their curricula within colleges to reflect the wishes of the pupils, many of whom aspired to sit for university entrance examinations. This required missionary groups, such as the WMMS, to broaden their curricula. Whereas the Bible had been the primary book for the learning of the English language, it was relegated to a separate subject as curricula took on a more secular appearance to meet the needs of preparing pupils for university entrance examinations.[171] Christian religious studies were also relegated to a separate subject, or effectively deleted from curricula to allow more time for secular subjects. The desire for English as a language of instruction was also linked to secular aspirations to become clerks in government positions. Such positions were undesired by the British, or needed bilingual skills.[172] Yet, even English education was not always enough for potential careers in the British colonial apparatus. At Trinity College in Kandy, Sri Lanka, in 1877 a prize day was held for the 160 boys on the books. The principal, the Rev. R. Collins, noted his surprise at the number of names on the roll given that 'it was a riddle which he could not guess how it came to pass that not many more than 100 ever come to School'.[173] He further noted that there were very few openings for young men in Ceylon and that 'scarcely any of them read, wrote, or studied with any other aim than the Police Court', urging the boys to look beyond government work to become traders and manufactures.[174] Collins' concern spoke to broader missionary concerns about the ability of missionary societies to make 'useful' members of society out of the pupils, and not just to be a training ground for future government employees.

The provision of secular education was initially seen by some missionary groups, such as the WMMS, as not necessarily being in competition with religious education, but rather as another means to the common end of debasing 'heathen' beliefs. In 1853 the Wesleyan missionary Edward Robinson, stationed in North Ceylon, where the large proportion of the population were Tamil, noted to great applause at the Annual meeting of the WMMS that even the 'secular education that we impart is directly destructive to heathenism'.[175] This sentiment was mirrored in other contexts, with, for example, the teaching of secular geography designed to undermine Hindu scriptural beliefs in India.[176] Hayden Bellenoit has argued that in the period leading up to the Indian Uprising, 'Christianity, western scholarship and European civilisation were all intertwined' and that in the period between the 1830s and 1860s 'education was a means whereby Christian values and examples could be secretly invoked'.[177] He suggests that indirect teaching of Christianity through English literature was 'a clear example of insidious Christianisation' as the pupils reading William Cowper, Alexander Pope and John Milton were, according to a contemporaneous inspector of Bengali schools, learning to appreciate Christian values yet 'without any warning whatsoever'.[178] Such concerns highlight the difficulties of categorising prose, poetry or literature as either secular or religious given that the morals of Britain were Christian, and separating morality from Christianity was a difficult if not futile task. At the Liverpool Missionary Conference of 1860 similar concerns about secular subjects seeping into curricula were raised. The Rev. Thomas Gardiner, a Free Church missionary in Calcutta, noted in relation to reading lists, that it was indeed 'a grave question to be considered, whether, as missionaries, they were justified in putting themselves in the position of being bound to take lists of works which upon the whole might not be what they themselves would have chosen'.[179] With such musings he pointed to some of the compromises that missionary groups had to contemplate if they wished to take on government funding. As Tim Allender has argued, the conflicts between missionary groups and government over the teaching of secular curricula were sometimes so great that missionaries at times withdrew from their commitment to education rather than accept government funding.[180] Such difficulties reached beyond India to other spaces, and demonstrate that principles were often more important for missionaries than obtaining government funding for their educational work.

After the Indian Uprising, government secular education continued to be seen by some missionary groups as being supportive of and not destructive to missionary aims. The Rev. Ebenezer Jenkins, a missionary in Madras, India, told the annual WMMS meeting in 1864 that secular scientific government schooling in India was 'the star that ushers in the dawn' of a new age in which the 'religions of India are doomed to extinction'.[181] Secular education was deemed to enlighten people and to make them rational beings free both of superstitions and of 'heathen' religions. These views were perpetuated throughout the 1860s, with the annual conference in 1868 hearing that, 'Christian Education is giving right views of God's purposes of mercy to our fallen humanity; while secular education, as carried out by the Government, is undermining the whole fabric of Hinduism'.[182] Through means such as secular education, the dissemination of British literature in government schools and the introduction of 'fair' government, the British government in India was seen to be acting as 'unconscious missionaries'[183] providing Indians with alternative corpora of knowledge that had the potential to destabilise Indian epistemic systems.

However, this view was not held by all. Missionary groups prior to the Indian Uprising had already decried the proliferation of secular Western education in India. The CMS missionary C.B. Leupolt, for example, suggested some fifteen years before the uprising that secular education was dangerous to the British rule over India as the 'Government are nourishing vipers in their bosom, and if they should one day be stung by them, they must not be surprised.'[184] Yet a secular curriculum was maintained after the Indian Uprising and the implementation of Wood's Despatch. In 1864, LMS missionaries disparagingly complained of what they saw as the deficiency of a purely secular system, which 'sharpened the mind' but failed to 'touch the heart'.[185] Secular education was important, they maintained, but it must be in combination with religious education. The secularisation of Indian schools was seen to have debased traditional religiosity and created a moral crisis as no alternative moral system was provided in secular schools.[186] Even the WMMS, which had embraced government schools as helping to destabilise 'heathen' knowledge systems, changed its tune as the competition between mission and government schools increased. By 1869, a WMMS missionary in Bangalore noted the difficulties that English language mission schools faced against increasing competition from secular government schools. The mission schools were forced to adapt their curricula in order to entice pupils to remain with them throughout their preparation for university entrance examinations, for if they did not provide preparation for these exams they feared losing their brightest pupils, and therefore their potential influence over the higher classes in India.[187] The WMMS in Bangalore were not alone in their anxiety towards shifting their curricula to encompass secular demands, with the interdenominational General Missionary Conference at Allahabad in 1872–73 expressing similar concerns in terms of the need for missionary High Schools to teach towards the entrance examinations for universities, at the expense of religious subjects.[188] These musings led the participants to question whether they should 'continue the unequal competition with Government in secular education for diminishing spiritual results?'[189] Here the question was between striving for a share of educating the intellectual elite in the hope of alumni maintaining close connection with the mission as they obtained influential positions within government and society – yet with a distinct possibility that these same alumni might become bitter opponents of the mission – or of placing efforts into educating the masses, and thereby freeing the curricula from the restrictive requirements for university examinations. By the end of the 1860s, the previous positive sentiments that missionaries had espoused about secular education dimmed. Secular education, which had only recently been praised for the destabilising effect it had had upon the 'whole fabric of Hinduism', was decried, as it 'does not make them in the least susceptible to Christian influences', but sceptical of all religions.[190] As mission schools were the means by which missionary groups tried to reach the higher classes of Hindu society, it was seen to be imperative to provide education of a level on par with that of government schools, for in the latter it was assumed that Hinduism would be destroyed only by turning the pupil into an atheist.[191] Missionary education, even with a somewhat secularised curriculum, was advanced as the antidote to such irreligious thinking.

Even in Sri Lanka, where Protestant missionaries were treated favourably, some were also expressing their anxieties about the secular influence that governments were exerting over mission schools. A pertinent example is found in the Wesleyan *Missionary Notices* of 1874 in which the Rev. Edmund Rigg in Ceylon notes with pride that the Educational Report of 1872 reported that the Jaffna Central School for Tamil boys obtained higher grades in both English and the vernacular than any other aided school in Ceylon. Rigg expressed his conviction that education was a means to an end, and not an end in itself, with the ultimate aim of schooling being the Christianisation of the pupils. He expressed his anxiety at the secularisation of mission schools through government inspections, or in his words: 'And yet I feel that these Government examinations for grants have a tendency towards secularising all education.'[192] The Jaffna Central School was an elite school associated with the Madras University from 1869, leading perhaps to some concern that recalling facts, rather than Christian morality, had become the driving focus behind the school.

From the 1870s in Sri Lanka, the Catholics found common grievances with Buddhists as both groups considered themselves as being supressed by Protestants.[193] This was part of a broader ongoing belief that Bonjean had expressed in the 1860s that claimed that colonial government ill treated non-Protestants. By the 1880s, the CMS missionaries were not only concerned about Catholic competition, nor schisms within their own church but also increasing Buddhist influence. In this decade, a Buddhist revival occurred in Ceylon, partly due to the establishment of the Theosophical Society in New York by Madame Blavatsky and Colonial Olcott, and their lecture tour of Sri Lanka in the same year.[194] One of the resulting impacts was the establishment of Buddhist schools modelled on Western Christian schools, with some 300 schools established over the next three decades.[195] Despite the tensions between the CMS and the Bishop, Protestant and Catholics, Protestants and Buddhists and the pressures of a secular education, Protestant missionaries maintained control over much of the vernacular and increasingly the English language education in Sri Lanka. Schooling remained for the CMS a site in which they wished to maintain influence over content, both in terms of pupils and, where possible, teachers. As a report from the Kanian Itinerary had noted in 1873: 'But schools must be maintained in an efficient state as nurseries of the Churches for a church without a school is like a community without children; both most soon become extinct.'[196] Maintaining a group of local teachers was one way to ensure that this would not occur, as too was maintaining the belief already expressed in 1834 by Jabez Bunting that education without religion would fail to be of benefit to either the pupil, the church or the state.[197]

Conclusion

The expansion of the British colonial empire over the nineteenth century encouraged an increase in the number of mission schools, particularly in places where the government provided grants-in-aid. Consequently, missionary societies needed to engage more teachers, with support for local teachers coming from local Christians, such as Jan Tzatzoe and Behari Lal Singh. Local people were desired because of their cultural sensitivities and language skills, and furthermore they cost less to employ than Europeans, and were seen to be better able to tolerate local climates. Yet, the employment of local people nevertheless engendered anxieties regarding their moral standing. Through focusing on the CMS work in Sri Lanka and examining some autobiographical writings of converts, this chapter has argued that in the logic of missionary modernity, morality, rather than academic aptitude, was the foremost quality that missionaries desired in their teachers. Yet for local people, the reasons to become teachers were complex and not just an expression of faith.

The Negro Education Grant of the 1830s and 1840s had not allowed for government involvement in the provision of religious and moral education; however, in different parts of the Empire it became increasingly common for schools receiving government funding through grants-in-aid to be inspected by government representatives, and to be obliged to implement a standard, non-denominational curriculum (mostly following the Irish National System). As the examples from both British India and Sri Lanka demonstrate, there were various reactions to government involvement, with many missionaries in India complaining that a secular curriculum left no room for religion and created irreligious denationalised pupils who were a threat to British rule. Even in Sri Lanka, where the government was overwhelmingly supportive of Protestant schools, grants-in-aid created tensions between Catholics and Protestants, with some Protestants also considering that government examinations in the higher levels of schools reduced the religious content, and thus had the potential to debase society. Missionaries nevertheless argued that their form of schooling was superior as it imparted the highest moral lessons needed for people drawn into a modernising world. In juxtaposing the situation in Ceylon with India, the chapter has argued that mission schools in India felt compelled to omit religious teaching from curricula in order to satisfy the wishes of potential pupils for education of sufficient quality to facilitate passing entrance examinations into university. Some missionary groups themselves may have secularised the curricula; however, there were more subtle ways in which schools became secularised, such as through inspections and examinations, as well as the increased governmental ability to regulate and determine the structure and content of mission schools. The secularisation of mission schools, as we shall read in the next chapter, remained a major concern for missionary groups at the start of the twentieth century, as it placed in question their ability to maintain relevance in a secularising and modernising world.

Notes

1 Here I use the terms Ceylon as well as Sri Lanka interchangeably.
2 University of Birmingham (UB), Cadbury Research Library Special Collections (Cadbury), Church Mission Society Archive (CMS)/B Foreign (later Overseas) Division/OMS Overseas (Missions) Series 1803–1934/C CE O (Original papers incoming Ceylon Mission) 20, Papers relating to education/1/1–18, Essays by boys at Cotta Christian Institution 1842.
3 CMS/B/OMS/C CE O20/1/8, David, Cotta, 20 September 1842.
4 The use of Portuguese names amongst the Sri Lankans was not necessarily a sign of mixed heritage, but rather of cultural mimetism. See: Nira Wickramasinghe, *Sri Lanka in the modern age. A history* (Oxford: Oxford University Press, 2014), pp. 23–24.
5 Eugene Stock, *The history of the Church Missionary Society: Its environment, its men and its work*, vol. 1 (London: Church Missionary Society, 1890), p. 264.
6 CMS/ACC – Church Missionary Society unofficial papers, Accession 362: Papers of Rev John Fearby Haslam (1838–1849) [362], F- Family Papers 3/2, Henry Venn, Church Missionary House to Rev Mr. F. Haslam (Cotta), 1842 [rest of date is missing].
7 Ranjit Ruberu, 'Missionary education in Ceylon', in Brian Holmes (ed.), *Educational policy and the mission schools: Case studies from the British Empire*, 2nd edition (London and New York: Routledge & Kegan Paul, 2007), pp. 85–86.
8 CMS/ACC 362, F3/2, Henry Venn, Church Missionary House to Rev Mr. F. Haslam (Cotta), 1842 [rest of date is missing].
9 Ibid.
10 Tim Keegan, *Dr Philip's empire: One man's struggle for justice in nineteenth-century South Africa* (Cape Town: Zebra Press, 2016), p. 235.
11 Brian Stanley, 'The church of the three selves: A perspective from the World Missionary Conference, Edinburgh, 1910', *The Journal of Imperial and Commonwealth History*, 36:3 (2008), 435–451.
12 See, for example, Edward Andrews, *Native apostles: Black and Indian missionaries in the British Atlantic World* (Cambridge, MA and London: Harvard University Press, 2013); Roger S. Levine, *A living man from Africa: Jan Tzatzoe,*

Xhosa chief and missionary, and the making of nineteenth-century South Africa (e-book: Yale University Press, 2000); Peggy Brock, 'New Christians as evangelists', in Norman Etherington (ed.), *Missions and empire* (Oxford and New York: Oxford University Press, 2005), pp. 132–152; Martin Fuchs, Antje Linkenbach and Wolfgang Reinhard (eds), *Individualisierung durch Christliche mission?* (Wiesbaden: Harrossowitz, 2015).

13 Felicity Jensz, 'Non-European teachers in mission schools: Introduction', *Itinerario*, 40:3 (2016), 389–403.

14 Ibid.; Richard Hölzl, 'Educating missions: Teachers and catechists in Southern Tanganyika, 1890s and 1940s', *Itinerario*, 40:3 (2016), 405–428; Jan Hüsgen, 'The recruitment, training and conflicts surrounding "Native teachers" in the Moravian mission in the Danish West Indies in the nineteenth century', *Itinerario*, 40:3 (2016), 451–465; Hugh Morrison, 'Negotiated and mediated lives: Bolivian teachers, New Zealand missionaries and the Bolivian Indian mission, 1908–1932', *Itinerario*, 40:3 (2016), 429–449.

15 Wickramasinghe, *Sri Lanka*, esp. chapter 2.

16 Nira Wickramasinghe, 'Colonial governmentality: Critical notes from a perspective of South Asian studies', *Comparativ: Zeitschrift für Globalgeschichte und Vergleichende Gesellschaftsforschung*, 21:1 (2011), 32–40, here 35.

17 On Foucault's concept of governmentality see the useful study of Graham Burchell, Colin Gordon and Peter Miller (eds), *The Foucault effect: Studies in governmentality with two lectures by and an interview with Michel Foucault* (Chicago: University of Chicago Press, 1991).

18 For a short overview in a missionary context see: Charles Piot, 'Of hybridity, modernity, and their malcontents', *Interventions: International Journal of Postcolonial Studies*, 3:1 (2001), 85–91. https://doi.org/10.1080/136980100 20027047.

19 Here the terms Ceylon and Sri Lanka will be used interchangeably to indicate the historical space of British colonial Sri Lanka. For overviews on the history of Sri Lanka see: John Clifford Holt (ed.), *The Sri Lanka reader: History, culture, politics* (Durham, NC: Duke University Press, 2011); Sujit Sivasundaram, *Islanded: Britain, Sri Lanka and the bounds of an Indian Ocean colony* (Chicago: University of Chicago Press, 2013); Wickramasinghe, *Sri Lanka*.

20 Wickramasinghe, *Sri Lanka*, p. 23.

21 K. Paranavitana, 'Suppression of Buddhism and aspects of Indigenous culture under the Portuguese and the Dutch', *Journal of the Royal Asiatic Society of Sri Lanka*, 49, new series (2004), 1–14.

22 Bente de Leede, 'Children between company and church: Subject-making in Dutch colonial Sri Lanka, c. 1650–1790', *BMGN – Low Countries Historical Review*, 135:3–4 (2020), 106–132, doi: 10.18352/bmgn-lchr.10880.

23 Paranavitana, 'Suppression of Buddhism'; Ruberu, 'Missionary education in Ceylon'.

24 For an account of his dethroning see: Robert Aldrich *Banished potentates: Dethroning and exiling Indigenous monarchs under British and French colonial rule, 1815–1955* (Manchester: Manchester University Press, 2018).

25 Stock, *The history of the Church Missionary Society*, vol. 1, p. 216.

26 Ibid.

27 Ruberu, 'Missionary education in Ceylon'. See also: Richard Lovett, *The history of the London Missionary Society, 1795–1895*, vol. 1 (London: H. Frowde, 1899), pp. 20–21.

28 CMS/CE/E1/38, Rev Robert Mayor to the CMS Sec, Point de Galle, 6 October 1818.

29 Ibid.

30 CMS/C CE/E1/23, Rev. James M.S. Glenic to the Sec, Point de Galle Ceylon, 27 October 1817.

31 Stock, *The history of the Church Missionary Society*, vol. 1, p. 119.

32 CMS/B/OMS/C CE/E1/22. Sketch of a plan for establishing free schools under the supervision of the Church Missionary Society of London in the Island of Ceylon, 4 June 1817.

33 Ibid.

34 Ruberu, 'Missionary education in Ceylon'.

35 CMS/B/OMS/C CE/E1/25, Josiah Pratt to Rev. Mr. Twisterton, 24 November 1817.

36 Stock, *The history of the Church Missionary Society*, vol. 1, p. 216.

37 Ruberu, 'Missionary education in Ceylon'. See also: Roland Wenzlhuemer, *From coffee to tea cultivation in Ceylon, 1880–1900: An economic and social history* (Brill, e-book, 2008), p. 271.

38 Wickramasinghe, *Sri Lanka*, pp. 30–31.

39 David Scott, *Refashioning futures: Criticism after postcoloniality* (Princeton, NJ: Princeton University Press, 1999), p. 42.

40 Wickramasinghe, *Sri Lanka*, chapter 1.

41 Ibid., pp. 43, 54.

42 Ibid., p. 79. Scott, *Refashioning futures*, p. 42.

43 Ruberu, 'Missionary education in Ceylon', p. 94, p. 99.

44 HC PP (274) Ceylon. Reports of Lieutenant-General Colebrooke and Charles Hay Cameron, Esq. (1831–1832), p. 31.

45 Ibid.

46 Ibid., p. 32.

47 Almut Steinbach, 'Imperial language policy in the nineteenth century: A study on the spread of English under early British rule in Ceylon and the Protected Malay States', *Comparativ: Zeitschrift Für Globalgeschichte und Vergleichende Gesellschaftsforschung*, 22:1 (2012), 33–48.

48 The Secretaries to the Conference, *Conference on missions held in 1860 at Liverpool: Including the papers read, the deliberations, and the conclusions reached; with a comprehensive index shewing the various matters brought under review* (London: Strangeways & Walden, 1860), p. 122.

49 Ibid., p. 123.

50 CMS/B/OMS/C CE/O 23/1, Brief Statement of the Ceylon Mission of the Church Missionary Society.

51 CMS/B/OMS/C CE/E1/55, Rev S. Lambrik to the Sec. 8 July 1819.

52 *Report of the Punjab Missionary Conference held at Lahore in December and January, 1862–63, Including the essays read, and the discussions which followed them* ..., xix, 398 (no place: no publisher, 1863), p. 32.

53 CMS/B/OMS/C CE/E1/39, Rev Joseph Knight to the CMS Sec, 21 October 1818. See also: Stock, *The history of the Church Missionary Society*, vol. 1, p. 191, p. 300.

54 CMS/B/OMS/C CE/E1/39, Rev. Joseph Knight to the CMS Sec, 21 October 1818.

55 'Heathen female education. No. II', *Evangelical Magazine*, 10 (1837), 145.

56 Barbara A. Yates, 'African reactions to education: The Congolese case', *Comparative Education Review*, 15:2 (1971), 158–171.

57 Ibid., p. 161.

58 For example, Terrence Ranger has details more proactive interest from African chiefs for education. See: Terence Ranger, 'African attempts to control education in East and Central Africa 1900–1939', *Past & Present*, 32 (1965), 57–85.

59 CMS/B/OMS/C CE O24/8, J. A. Cunerwilli to Rev. C.C. Fenn, Kandy, 13 August 1855.

60 Helen May, Baljit Kaur and Larry Pochner, *Empire, education, and Indigenous childhoods: Nineteenth-century missionary infant schools in three British colonies* (Farnham: Ashgate, 2014), p. 19.

61 Before the CMS arrived in Sri Lanka two Sinhalese youth, Petrus Hermannus Geradus Phillips and John Gerad Pevera Appohamy, were selected by the Chief Justice, the Hon. Sir Alexander Johnston, to be educated by the CMS in England. See: 'Protestant missionary stations and missionaries throughout the world', *Missionary Register* (January 1816), 1–9. For other examples see: Kokou Azamede, 'Ewe-Christen zwischen Württemberg und westafrikanischen Missionsstationen (1884–1939)', in Rebekka Habermas and Richard Hölzl (eds), *Mission global: Eine Verflechtungsgeschichte seit dem 19. Jahrhundert* (Köln, Weimar and Wien: Böhlau, 2014), pp. 177–198; 'Western Africa', *Missionary Register* (January 1842), 24.

62 CMS/B/OMS/C CE/E1/1, Colonial Chaplain (Twisleton) to CMS Secretary (Pratt), Colombo, 3 April 1815.

63 David Killingray, 'Godly examples and Christian agents: Training African Missionary workers in British institutions in the nineteenth century', in Judith Becker and Brian Stanley (eds), *Europe as the Other. External perspectives on European Christianity* (Göttingen: Vandenhoeck & Ruprecht, 2014), pp. 165–195.

64 Ibid.

65 Petrus Hermannus Geradus Phillips and John Gerad Pevera Appohamy were assumed to have perished in a ship wrecked off the coast of Cape of Good Hope. See: 'Protestant missionary stations and missionaries throughout the world', *Missionary Register* (January 1816), 5. Death was the fate of two Tahitians that the LMS sent to England to be taught at the Moravian school in Yorkshire in the early 1800s. See: William Thorp et al., *Four sermons, at the*

tenth General Meeting of the London Missionary Society, May 9, 10,11, 1804 by the Rev. William Thorp, London; Rev. James Bennet, Romsey; Rev. David Dickson, Edinburgh; Rev. Thomas Scott, Aston-Sandford. Also, the report of the Directors, and a list of the subscribers (London: T. Williams, 1804), p. 5.

66 HC PP (274) Ceylon, p. 31.

67 See, for example, Jesse Page, *The black bishop: Samuel Adjai Crowther* (London: Hodder and Stoughton, 1908); Andrew F. Walls. 'The legacy of Samuel Ajayi Crowther', *International Bulletin of Missionary Research*, 16:1 (1992), 15–21, doi: *10.1177/239693939201600104*.

68 Samuel Crowther trained in England at the Parochial School in Islington, and when he returned to Sierra Leone was appointed to the position of schoolmaster by the Colonial government. Page, *The black bishop*, p. 34.

69 Other influential missionary training schools for local people included Lovedale in southern Africa. See, for example, Stephen Volz, 'The rise and fall of the Moffat Institution: Mission education in a colonial borderland', *South African Historical Journal*, 66:3 (2014), 470–485; James Stewart, *Lovedale, South Africa: Illustrated by fifty views from photographs* (Edinburgh and Glasgow: Andrew Elliot and David Bryce and Son, 1894).

70 TNA, CO 318 Colonial Office and Predecessors: West Indies Original Correspondence/122 West India Miscellaneous 1835, vol. 3, Negro Education, Grey to Treasury, Downing Street, 21 July 1835, p. 559.

71 Ibid.

72 TNA, CO 318/118 West India Miscellaneous 1834, vol. 1, Public Office, John Dyer (Secretary, Baptist Missionary Society) to Johan Lefevre, Esq. Under Secretary of State to the Colonies, 8 April 1834, pp. 399–402.

73 Shirley C. Gordon, *A century of West Indian education: A source book* (Bristol: Longmans, 1963), pp. 169–170.

74 South India Missionary Conference, *Proceedings of the South India Missionary Conference held at Ootacamung, April 19th–May 5th, 1858* (Madras: SPCK, 1858). p. 161.

75 CMS/B/OMS/C CE M17 [Mission books incoming] (1877–78), Ceylon, 1877–78, No. 4, Rev. Jayesinghe (Native).

76 CMS/B/OMS/C CE O19/3, *The Ceylon Diocesan Gazette*, 2:3, 3 November 1877, p. 35.

77 Norman Etherington, 'Education and medicine', in Norman Etheringon (ed.), *Missions and empire* (Oxford: Oxford University Press, 2005), p. 261.

78 Hölzl, 'Educating missions'.

79 CMS/B/OMS/C CE O22/1/3A, B.P. Weerasinghe 1868. For the issue of conversion and local people, of which there has been an enduring debate see: Judith Becker, *Conversio im Wandel. Basler Missionare zwischen Europa und Südindien und die Ausbildung einer Kontaktreligiosität, 1834–1860* (Göttingen: Vandenhoeck & Ruprecht, 2015); Robert Hefner (ed.), *Conversion to Christianity: Historical and anthropological perspectives on a great transformation* (Berkeley: University of California Press, 1993); Peter van der Veer,

Conversion to modernities: The globalization of Christianity (New York and London: Routledge, 1996); Richard V. Peace, 'Conflicting understandings of Christian conversion: A missiological challenge', *International Bulletin of Missionary Research*, 28:1 (2004), 8–13; Fuchs, Linkenbach and Reinhard, *Individualisierung durch Christliche Mission?*

80 CMS/B/OMS/C CE M17 (1877–78), Ceylon, 1877–78, No. 29, Rev. J. Allcock.

81 CMS/B/OMS/C CE O22 File on Local Workers. 1/5A Baptist Karunaratne 1874.

82 CMS/B/OMS/C CE M17 (1877–78), Ceylon, 1876–77, No. 11, Rev. D. Jayesinghe (Native).

83 Examples of this were evident in the Indian Service of the United States. See: C.D. Cahill, *Federal fathers & mothers: A social history of the United States Indian Service, 1869–1933* (Chapel Hill: University of North Carolina Press, 2011), p. 104.

84 Secretaries, *Conference on missions held in 1860 at Liverpool*, p. 142.

85 Ibid., p. 143.

86 CMS/B/OMS/C CE O22/1/1 Unnamed.

87 This was the experience of the LMS's Rev. Pritchard of the South Seas. See: 'The Exeter Hall meeting', *The Missionary Repository for Youth and Sunday School Missionary Magazine*, 4 (1842), 72.

88 CMS/B/OMS/C CE O22/1/2A H. Kannanger [Kannangara] 1866.

89 CMS/B/OMS/C CE O22/1/5B Johannis Perera Kalpege [Kolpegay] 1874; Stock, *The history of the Church Missionary Society*, vol. 2, p. 289.

90 CMS/B/OMS/C CE O22/1/3D Silvester Mendis 1868.

91 KJB John 14:6.

92 CMS/B/OMS/C CE O22/1/3A, B.P. Weerasinghe 1868.

93 CMS/B/OMS/C CE M17 (1877–78), Ceylon, 1876–77, No. 247, Rev. B.P. Weerasinghe.

94 CMS/B/OMS/C CE O22/1/3B, H. Kananger 1868.

95 Ibid.

96 CMS/B/OMS/C CE O22/1/3C, H. de Silva 1866.

97 Ibid.

98 Stock, *The history of the Church Missionary Society*, vol. 2, p. 289.

99 CMS/B/OMS/C CE O22, 1/4 No name [educated at Baddegama, worked at Baddegama, Borella and Kandy 1860], 1868.

100 CMS/B/OMS/C CE M17 (1877–78), Ceylon, 1876–77, No. 13, Rev. John Peter (Native).

101 CMS/B/OMS/C CE O22/1/5F, S. Dias' paper 1874.

102 CMS/B/OMS/C CE O22/1/5G, A.W. Liyanage's paper 1874.

103 See, for example, Peter Hinchliff, 'The selection and training of missionaries in the early nineteenth century', in G.J. Cuming (ed.), *The mission of the Church and the propagation of the faith* (Cambridge: Cambridge University Press, 1970), pp. 131–135; John Pritchard, *Methodists and their missionary societies 1760–1900* (Farnham: Ashgate, 2013), p. 215. See also: Alison Hodge, 'The training of

missionaries for Africa: The Church Missionary Society's training college at Islington, 1900–1915', *Journal of Religion in Africa*, 4:2 (1971), 81–96.

104 Morrison, 'Negotiated and mediated lives', p. 439. The reference to 'tainted' comes from: Doug Munro and Andrew Thornley, 'Pacific Islander pastors and missionaries: Some historiographical and analytical issues', *Pacific Studies*, 23:3/4 (2000), 1–31.

105 CMS/B/OMS/C CE O25 Miscellaneous papers, /3. Names of missionaries & other labourers Ceylon Mission [1857].

106 Stock, *The history of the Church Missionary Society*, vol. 2, p. 282.

107 *Proceedings of the South India Missionary Conference held at Ootacamung*, p. 161.

108 Ibid.

109 Linda Chisholm, *Teacher preparation in South Africa: History, policy and future directions* (Bingley, UK: Emerald Publishing, 2019), p. 36.

110 University of London (UL), School of Oriental and African Studies Archive (SOAS), © United Reformed Church, Presbyterian Church of England Foreign Missions Committee Archives (PCE), Foreign Mission Committee (FMC), 8 – Bangladesh/East Pakistan/01 – Correspondence, minutes and reports/01 – Early Correspondence and Papers/Item 1, W.S. Mackay to Mr. [Hugh] Matherson, 8 August 1859.

111 UL, SOAS, © United Reformed Church, PCE/FMC/8/03/01, *Eighth Indian report of the Bauleah Mission in connection with the Presbyterian Church in England, in 1870–1871* (Calcutta: Baptist Mission Press, 1871), p. 7.

112 Secretaries, *Conference on missions held in 1860 at Liverpool*, p. 224.

113 Dipesh Chakrabarty, *Provincializing Europe: Postcolonial thought and historical differences* (Princeton, NJ: Princeton University Press, 2000), p. 7.

114 Ibid. See also: David Scott, 'Colonial governmentality', *Social Text*, 43 (1995), 191–220.

115 Wickramasinghe, 'Colonial governmentality', p. 38.

116 Ibid.

117 For more on the Ceylon Controversy see: Stock, *The history of the Church Missionary Society*, vol. 3, pp. 203–216. See also: CMS/B/OMS/C CE/M17 (1877–78).

118 Wickramasinghe, 'Colonial governmentality'.

119 For more on the indentured labourers see: Wickramasinghe, *Sri Lanka*, p. 18.

120 CMS/B/OMS/C CE O19/1, To the Right Reverend the Lord Metropolitan Bishop for the Diocese of Colombo. 24 July 1876.

121 CMS/B/OMS/C CE O23/13 Report of the Kandyan Itinerancy for the year ending 30 September 1879.

122 See the various files in: CMS/B/OMS/C CE O19/5 and CMS/B/OMS/C CE O19/6.

123 CMS/B/OMS/C CE O19/11, Petition to Committee of the Church Missionary Society in England [20 October 1876].

124 Ibid.

125 Ibid.

126 CMS/B/OMS/C CE O19/10, Petition to the members of the Committee of the Church Missionary Society (London), Jaffna, 9 August 1876 (Printed with the *Ceylon Messenger* Nr. 5).

127 CMS/B/OMS/C CE O22/2/6 Memorandum on salaries of catechists, by Rev. J.I. Jones and Richard T. Dowbiggin 1868.

128 CMS/B/OMS/C CE O19/3, *The Ceylon Diocesan Gazette*, 2:3 (Saturday 3 November 1877), p. 35.

129 D.R. Fearon, *School inspection*, 2nd edition (London: Macmillan and Co., 1876), p. 2.

130 Michel Foucault, *Discipline and punish: The birth of the prison*, trans. Alan Sheridan (London: Penguin Books, 1977), p. 184.

131 John Coolahan, 'Imperialism and the Irish national school system', in J.A. Mangan (ed.), *'Benefits bestowed'? Education and British imperialism* (Manchester: Manchester University Press, 1988), pp. 76–93; Robert J. Graham, 'The Irish Readers revisited: The power of the text(book)', *Canadian Journal of Education/Revue Canadienne de l'éducation*, 14:4 (1989), 414–426, doi: 10.2307/1495424; Patrick Walsh, 'Education and the 'universalist' idiom of empire: Irish National School books in Ireland and Ontario', *History of Education*, 37:5 (2008), 645–660, doi: 10.1080/00467600701504964.

132 *Grants-in-Aid to Mission Schools*, Occasional papers on India, 6 (London: Church Missionary House, 1859); Cape of Good Hope [Cape Colony] Gazette [G] 97–1904 'Education Act of 1865. Regulations promulgated under same, together with additional related legislation and all regulations that have appeared in reference to education since the passing of Act No. 13 of 1865' (Cape Town, Government Printer 1904).

133 John Pritchard, *Methodists and their missionary societies 1760–1900* (Farnham: Ashgate, 2013), p. 112.

134 Cape Colony, G 97–1904, 'Education Act of 1865', p. 2.

135 See, for example, *Victorian Government Gazette*, 44 (Friday, 3 April 1833), p. 803; *Victorian Government Gazette*, 10 (22 January 1861), p. 127; *Victorian Government Gazette*, 64 (29 June 1883), p. 1526; *Victorian Government Gazette*, 9 (30 January 1880), p. 253; 'State-aid to religion', *The Sydney Morning Herald* (12 June 1862), p. 5; 'The Grants in Aid', *South Australian Register* (5 October 1868), p. 2.

136 Chisholm, *Teacher preparation in South Africa*, pp. 33–34.

137 HL Deb, 15 April 1859, vol. 153, cc1778–93, 1780, 'Address for returns'.

138 Ibid.

139 Henry Rosher James, *Education and statesmanship in India, 1797–1910* (London and New York: Longmans, Green, 1911), p. 48.

140 Stephen Colclough and David Vincent, 'Reading', in David McKitterick (ed.), *The Cambridge history of the book in Britain*, vol. VI: 1830–1914 (Cambridge and New York: Cambridge University Press, 2009), pp. 281–323.

141 Andrew Porter, *Religion versus empire? British Protestant missionaries and overseas expansion, 1700–1914* (Manchester: Manchester University Press, 2004), p. 173.
142 Cape Colony G 97–1904 'Education Act of 1865', pp. 4–5, p. 7.
143 Ruberu, 'Missionary education in Ceylon', p. 102.
144 Secretaries, *Conference on missions held in 1860 at Liverpool*, p. 138.
145 Ibid.
146 Ibid., pp. 138–139.
147 CMS/B/OMS/C CE/O26, Newspaper cuttings of a series of fourteen letters by Ch. Bonjean to the *Examiner* (December 1860–February 1861).
148 CMS/B/OMS/C CE/O26, Newspaper cutting (*Examiner*). Letter 1. Ch. Bonjean to Editor, 13 December 1860.
149 CMS/B/OMS/C CE/O26, Newspaper cutting (*Examiner*). Letter 12. Ch. Bonjean to Editor, 24 January 1861.
150 CMS/B/OMS/C CE/O26, Newspaper cutting (*Examiner*). Letter 10. Ch. Bonjean to Editor, 19 January 1861.
151 CMS/B/OMS/C CE/O26, Newspaper cutting (*Examiner*). Letter 2. Ch. Bonjean to Editor, 19 December 1860.
152 Ibid.
153 CMS/B/OMS/C CE/O26, Newspaper cutting (*Examiner*). Letter 3. Ch. Bonjean to Editor, 26 December 1860; Letter 9. Ch. Bonjean to Editor, 18 January 1861.
154 CMS/B/OMS/C CE/O26, Newspaper cutting (*Examiner*). Letter 3. Ch. Bonjean to Editor, 26 December 1860.
155 See, for example, Hayden J.A. Bellenoit, *Missionary education and empire in late colonial India, 1860–1920* (London: Pickering & Chatto, 2007); 'Grants-in-aid to mission schools', *Occasional papers on India*, 6 (London: Church Missionary House, 1859); HL Deb, vol. 153, cc1778–93, 15 April 1859, 'Address for returns',
156 World Missionary Conference (WMC), *Report of Commission III. Education in relation to the Christianisation of national life. With supplement: Presentation and discussion of the report in the conference on 17th June 1910 together with the discussion on Christian literature* (Edinburgh and London, New York, Chicago and Toronto: Oliphant, Anderson & Ferrier, Fleming H. Revell Company, 1910), p. 61.
157 WMC, *Report of Commission III*, p. 198.
158 CMS/B/OMS/C CE M17 (1877–78), Ceylon, 1876–77, No. 13, Rev. John Peter (Native).
159 WMC, *Report of Commission III*, pp. 33–34.
160 Ibid.
161 David W. Savage, 'Evangelical educational policy in Britain and India 1857–60', *The Journal of Imperial and Commonwealth History*, 22:3 (1994), 432–461.
162 Carl Campbell, 'Social and economic obstacles to the development of popular education in post-emancipation Jamaica, 1834–1865' (University of the West Indies, Department of History, n.d. 196?), pp. 29–30.

163 'Die Nilagiri (Die Gründung der Basler Mission auf den Bergen) Die Früchte des Glaubens und der Geduld', *Evangelisches Missions Magazin*, 5 (1861), 236–237.

164 Norman Etherington, 'Missionaries, Africans and the state in the development of education in Colonial Natal, 1836–1910', in Patricia Grimshaw and Andrew May (eds), *Missionaries, Indigenous peoples and cultural exchange* (Brighton, Portland and Toronto: Sussex Academic Press, 2010), p. 133.

165 For example, the payment by results system was established in the Colony of Victoria in 1872 under section of 17 of *The Education Act 1872* (36 Vic. c. 447). See also: Anthony Welch, 'Mammon, markets, and managerialism – Asia-Pacific perspectives on contemporary educational reforms', in Robert Cowen and Andreas M. Kazamias (eds), *International handbook of comparative education* (Dordrecht, Heidelberg, London and New York: Springer, 2009), pp. 590–593. See also: Richard Johnson, 'Educational policy and social control in early Victorian England', *Past & Present*, 49:1 (1970), 96–119; George F. Madaus, Joseph Ryan, Thomas Kellaghan and Peter Airasian, 'Payment by results: An analysis of a nineteenth century performance-contracting programme', *The Irish Journal of Education/Iris Eireannach an Oideachais*, 21:2 (1987), 80–91; Shirley C. Gordon, *A century of West Indian education: A source book* (Bristol: Longmans, 1963), p. 82.

166 Mary Clare Martin, 'Church, school and locality: Revisiting the historiography of "state" and "religious" educational infrastructures in England and Wales 1780–1870', *Paedagogica Historica*, 49:1 (3012), 78.

167 WMC, *Report of Commission III*, p. 61.

168 Ibid.

169 'India', *Wesleyan Missionary Notices*, 4th Series, 1 (June 1869), 119.

170 James, *Education and Statesmanship in India*, p. 50.

171 'India', *Wesleyan Missionary Notices*, 4th Series, 1 (June 1869), 119. See also: Bellenoit, *Missionary education and empire in late colonial India*, pp. 93–98.

172 Bellenoit, *Missionary education and empire in late colonial India*, p. 1.

173 CMS/B/OMS/C CE O19/3, *The Ceylon Diocesan Gazette*, 2:3 (Saturday 3 November 1877), p. 37.

174 Ibid.

175 'Anniversary of the Wesleyan-Methodist Missionary Society', *Wesleyan Missionary Notices*, New Series, 6 (June and July, 1853), p. 102.

176 M.A. Laird, *Missionaries and education in Bengal, 1793–1837* (Oxford: Clarendon Press, 1972), p. 86. See also: Sanjay Seth, *Subject lessons: The Western education of colonial India* (Durham, NC: Duke University Press, 2007), pp. 49–50; Tim Allender, *Ruling through education: The politics of schooling in the colonial Punjab* (New Delhi: New Dawn Press, 2006), pp. 98–103.

177 Bellenoit, *Missionary education and empire in late colonial India*, p. 25.

178 Bellenoit unfortunately does not provide information as to when this incident was assumed to have occurred and thus it is difficult to place it within the historical framework. Ibid., p. 26.

179 Secretaries, *Conference on missions held in 1860 at Liverpool*, p. 146.

180 Tim Allender, 'Anglican evangelism in North India and the Punjabi missionary classroom: The failure to educate the "masses", 1860–77', *History of Education*, 32:3 (2003), 273–288, doi: 10.1080/00467600304142.

181 'Anniversary of the Wesleyan-Methodist Missionary Society', *Wesleyan Missionary Notices*, 3rd series, 15 (25 May 1864), 100–102. For further discussion on missionary acceptance of secular learning as a means to Christianise see, for example, Seth, *Subject lessons*, pp. 47–56.

182 'Anniversary of the Wesleyan-Methodist Missionary Society', *Wesleyan Missionary Notices*, 3rd series, 15 (25 May 1864), p. 91.

183 Ibid., p. 111.

184 C.B. Leupolt, *Recollections of an Indian missionary*, New Edition (London: Society for Promoting Christian Knowledge, 1863), p. iii.

185 'India', *Missionary Magazine and Chronicle*, 28 (June 1864), 178.

186 Seth, *Subject lessons*, pp. 47–78.

187 'India', *Wesleyan Missionary Notices*, 4th series, 1 (June 1869), 119. For contemporaneous debates about the determinant effects of cramming for exams see, for example, Seth, *Subject lessons*, pp. 22–26.

188 'The General Missionary Conference at Allahabad', *The Wesleyan-Methodist Magazine* 20 (July 1874), 626–634.

189 Ibid., 628.

190 'India', *Wesleyan Missionary Notices*, 4th series, 1 (June 1869), p. 120.

191 'India', *Wesleyan Missionary Notices*, 4th series, 1 (April 1869), p. 59.

192 'Ceylon', *Wesleyan Missionary Notices*, 4th series, 6 (February 1874), p. 36.

193 Tessa Bartholomeusz, 'Catholics, Buddhists, and the Church of England: The 1883 Sri Lankan riots', *Buddhist-Christian Studies*, 15 (1995), 89–103.

194 Ibid., 95. See also: James Martin Pebbles, *Buddhism and Christianity face to face: Or an oral discussion between the Rev. Migettuwatte, a Buddhist Priest, and Rev. D. Sliva, an English Clergyman. Held at Pantura, Ceylon. With an introduction and annotations* (Boston: Colby and Rich, 1878); Cornelia Haas, 'From theosophy to Buddhism' in Martin Fuchs, Antje Linkenback and Wolfgang Reinhard (eds), *Individualisierung durch christiliche Mission* (Wiesbaden: Harrossowitz, 2015), pp. 504–515.

195 Wickramasinghe, *Sri Lanka*, p. 80.

196 CMS/B/OMS/C CE O23/12, Report of the Kanian Itinerary for the year ending September 30 1873.

197 TNA, CO 318/118 West India Miscellaneous 1834, vol. 1, Public Office, Jabez Bunting (Wesleyan Mission House) to John Lefevre (Colonial Office), 16 April 1834, p. 406.

5

Missionary lessons for secular states: the Edinburgh World Missionary Conference, 1910

In September 1909, Professor Ernest D. Burton of the University of Chicago wrote to Professor Edward Caldwell Moore of Harvard University in relation to the upcoming World Missionary Conference to be held in Edinburgh, Scotland, in July 1910. He was rather perplexed that: 'my name had been printed in the announcement of the Committee (incorrectly by the way my middle initial being D. not F.). It is still impossible for me to decide whether I can be in Edinburgh.'[1] He ultimately received permission from his university to participate in the conference. He had an important function as the Secretary of the North American commissioners for Commission III on *Education in Relation to the Christianisation of National Life,* and was largely responsible for the final written report.[2] Moore himself was the Vice-Chairperson under the Chairperson, the Bishop of Birmingham, the Right Rev. C. Gore. The report of Commission III is an important snapshot of missionary activities at the start of the twentieth century, at a time during which missionary groups were reconsidering their strategies for working in non-European societies. The 470 pages of Commission III's report reveal that mission education was facing mounting pressures from various sides. The three major pressures perceived to affect mission schools were, in no particular order, the spread of Islam, the increasing instigation of national educational systems, which in turn side-lined missionary efforts, and, finally, the increase in nationalist sentiments often expressed through anti-Western, anti-missionary stances. The report from Commission III encapsulated the growing anxiety that missionary bodies were unable to effectively compete against mounting religious, political and nationalist pressure.

The Edinburgh conference of July 1910 was held only a few short years before the world was to be plunged into a war that redrew geographic, political and religious boundaries. This conference occurred during the period of New Imperialism, where much of the non-European world had come under Imperial rule of countries in Europe and of the United States. For missionary societies, it was a time of anticipated ecumenical work as well as concern for the increased presence of Islam in Northern Africa and the secularisation of many 'modernising' countries in Asia. Approximately 1,200 Protestant and Anglican members of missionary societies came together over ten days for the conference to discuss broad issues affecting Christian missions around the globe. The centenary of the World Missionary Conference at Edinburgh in 2010 prompted theologians and church historians to examine the legacies of the conference and the role the conference placed for the establishment of the World Council of Churches.[3] Within the history of education, Peter Kallaway has argued that Edinburgh facilitated a missionary educational network which itself marked the beginning of closer cooperation between missionary and educational networks, and with missionary groups realising the need for professionalisation in order to 'maintain their influence in a changing world'.[4] The report from Commission III has, however, been only cursorily examined by historians.[5] The eminent mission historian Brain Stanley devoted a chapter to it in his book on the 1910 conference, concluding that the report was a missed opportunity to suggest strategies for education that would have supported the development of national churches.[6] Another scholar who has written on the report is the late theologian Ogbu Kalu who rightly criticised the conference for its blatant under-representation of African voices to determine both the problems and solutions for education within Africa.[7] Both Stanley and Kalu focus upon the religious ramifications of the missed opportunities at Edinburgh, whereas here the report will be examined as an historical document that reveals contemporary tensions between religion and politics in the provision of education across the non-Western world.

The title of the report, *Education in Relation to the Christianisation of National Life*, evinced a focus upon 'education [...] as an instrument for raising native Christian Churches'[8] rather than on education in general. For colonial governments, missionary schooling had traditionally provided a cheap means of schooling the masses. Yet by the beginning of the new century, many colonial governments had taken a more active role in education, reflected in increased institutionalisation and regulation of schooling. Government involvement offered both opportunities as well as limitations for missionary education.[9] With such issues in mind, the report on education at Edinburgh was self-critical of missionary educational work, noted failings and negative consequences of previous work and called for a 'reconsideration of the educational methods and ideals of missionaries'.[10]

Missionary groups were both contributors to the process of modernisation (having ushered in the process of individualisation in many places and the broadening of perspectives[11]) as well as critics of the materialism and secularism that it entailed. Edinburgh was a moment of soul searching and of comparing various situations in order to find options that did not compromise the three essential functions of missionary education. The crisis of identity evident at and prior to Edinburgh led missionary groups to re-position themselves as experts and professionals best placed to be the providers of moral authority within a modernising world. As one contemporaneous assessment written shortly after the conference ended noted, missionary education 'occupies a place of primary importance in the estimate of those who lead the Christian enterprise in all the world. It always has done so; through the rationale of its importance was not always fully realised.'[12] The discussions at Edinburgh and the establishment of a separate commission helped propel missionary education onto a broader stage together with governments and other educational committees that helped define the shape of educational policy in much of the colonial world from the 1920s.

This chapter begins by placing the report of Commission III in the broader context of the Edinburgh conference. It will then focus on three issues highlighted in Commission III's report: the relationship between missions and governments in relation to mission schools; the changing gendered focus of missionary education towards adaptive learning in various contexts; and, finally, the concerns of how mission education had led to denationalised locals who could undermine both missionary as well as political modernity. The discussions surrounding these issues reveal the tensions and collaborations between governments and missionary groups in relation to the education of non-Europeans, as well as uncovering conflicting notions of progress and modernisation. The final report from Commission III was self-critical at the lack of success that missionary organisations had had in the three-pronged aims of being evangelistic, edificatory and leavening, and contained a profound sense of disappointment at the ineffectiveness of missionary schooling. The chapter argues that such negative reports encouraged missionary groups to reconsider their educational work and their collaborations with governments.

Commission III: 'Education in relation to the Christianisation of national life'

By the time of the 1910 World Missionary Conference in Edinburgh there had been prolonged contact between missionary groups and locals in almost all parts of the globe, and the importance of schooling was undeniable as a means of evangelising, but also as a means of improving the moral tone of societies. Yet, as Burton noted in his correspondence with Moore in 1909:

> There is serious danger that either under the impression that missionary schools are better than they really are, or under the influence of the equally

misleading notion that their intellectual defects are compensated for by their better moral tone, Christian schools shall soon fall into disrepute in all these countries [India, China and Japan]. This is indeed an underestimate of the case – they have already fallen into disrepute, and are in danger of becoming contemptible.[13]

Burton was concerned that a school that only focused upon religion would not be not up to the academic standards of the day. Indeed, he also argued that: 'I have been led gravely to doubt the vision at least under most conditions, of making the study of the Bible, or of the Christian religion as such, compulsory', with this practice being particularly dubious in schools that charged less tuition than government schools.[14] His concerns were on the quality of mission schools, as well as the unclear loyalties of the pupils at these schools. Other contemporaneous commentators also focused on the perceived inability of pupils at mission schools to stand up to the negative influences of modernisation, particularly in relation to the secular influences that modernity brought.[15]

When the commission was established for the Commission III for Edinburgh, it contained twenty members, who were European and Euro-Americans, all of whom had professional experience as educators.[16] No non-Western Christians were part of the Commission. Three women were members of the Commission, one of whom was a North American (Grace Hodge of the Teacher's College of Columbia University). No active missionaries were on the Commission; rather, they contributed through responding to survey questions grouped into 14 broad topics. This was a change from missionary conferences in the nineteenth century, which had provided an opportunity for practising missionaries to relay their experiences and to exchange ideas. The commissioners based their report and conclusions upon over 200 responses from missionaries across the globe. The topics included: the purpose of missionary education; the main results; changes needing to be undertaken; the role of government; the state of synthesis of European and local epistemologies in the classroom; the use of English; the state of female education; industrial training; the continuing influence on ex-pupils; Sunday Schools; the uses of Christian literature; ecclesiastical work; missionary training; and potential growth. The report was qualitative, rather than quantitative, with the commissioners emphasising the 'unoriginal' nature of their conclusions as they drew from the evidence presented and did not endeavour to be innovative or original. Seven of the members of Commission III were North American, and it was this fraction that was responsible for the inclusion of the fourth aim for mission education, that being 'the philanthropic desire to promote the general welfare of the people'.[17] Indeed, the report itself was compromised to satisfy the various opinions that helped shape it and the

tensions that existed between the British and North American commissioners, including tensions over the use of the word 'heathen'.[18] The majority of
the commissioners at Edinburgh were Anglophones, and within this group
the majority worked in the British Empire. As such, the experiences from
these geographical spaces influenced the focus of the report. The inclusion of
so many North Americans working in the British colonial world also highlighted the opening up of mission fields over the previous century to non-
British missionary societies.

Unlike the missionary conference in 1860 where speakers discussed their
personal views, the 1910 World Missionary Conference was built on the
prior establishment of committees commissioned to report upon specific
topics, of which Commission III was one of eight. Other commissions
discussed issues such as: The Church in the Mission Field (Commission II),
The Preparation of Missionaries (Commission V) and Missions and Governments (Commission VII). Prior to the 1910 Conference the eight
commissions were established to draft reports on issues central to the future
of Christian missions, which were commented on by various experts. The
final reports were to be ready for the press by the end of March 1910, in
order that they could be read prior to the conference.[19] The final report, with
the discussion, were subsequently printed and sold to missionaries, ministers
and interested laypeople.[20]

The systematic collection of material from missionaries around the world
for the resultant eight reports contributed to the newly developing discipline
of missionary science, known as missiology.[21] The 1910 conference provided
authority to the work of missionaries as professionals, and drew upon the
mood of willingness amongst various missionary societies to engage in
ecumenical work that had been developed over the previous century. The
tone of the conference also followed the self-critical precedent set in previous conferences, most notably at the Centenary Mission Conference held in
London in 1888.[22] The progression towards professionalism was evident
within Commission III's report on *Education in Relation to the
Christianisation of National Life*, particularly in relation to teacher training.[23] The need to professionalise missionary work can itself be seen as a
response by missionary groups to retain their influence amongst governments. As secular governments began to aggressively provide welfare
services, the provision of which had previously been almost completely in
the hands of churches and religious groups, and to establish national education boards, missionary groups needed to exert their authority in order to
maintain their legitimacy. Moreover, the conference occurred at a time when
missionary groups were refashioning themselves as 'experts' and were
moving more into the administration of school systems in an effort to assert
their presence in an area that they had previously dominated. In the decades

following the conference, missionary education networks and secular education networks would draw closer to each other in their similar trajectories to professionalise, internationalise and standardise educational outcomes.[24] Sue Krige has documented this change in the context of South Africa, arguing that at the beginning of the twentieth century as the content and control of schools became secularised, missionaries portrayed themselves as being expert advisers to the Education department in order to regain control over their schools.[25] Such re-positioning meant that missionary influence became institutionalised.

The report of Commission III was predominantly structured around geographical areas, and considered many areas beyond the reach of the British Empire, including the 'missionary lands' of Japan and China. The former British settler colonies, subsequent dominions, Australia, Canada and New Zealand, were not included, despite the heavy – and subsequently very problematic – involvement of missionaries in the education of Indigenous peoples, for these countries were considered predominantly Christianised and outside of the scope of the commission.[26] The other contemporaneous British dominion, the Union of South Africa, was considered within the report, despite it having receiving its self-governing dominion status in May 1910. Countries that were predominately Catholic were also not included, due to the belief that it was best for Protestants not to be in open competition with Catholic mission groups. Only in a few cases were the experiences of mission schools deemed sufficiently analogous to be treated collectively. India, China, Japan, Africa and the 'Mohammedan Lands of the Near East' were dealt with as discrete regions (and other lands generally neglected). The topics of literature, the training of teachers, the relation of Christian truth to Indigenous Thought and Feeling (synthesis of epistemologies) and Industrial training were deemed of sufficient commonality to be discussed in general, rather than regional, terms. The broader geographical context at Edinburgh in comparison to the missionary conference held in Liverpool half a century earlier reflected the broadening of imperial and Protestant missionary spheres of influence. With the intensified colonisation of Africa during the period of New Imperialism in the late-nineteenth century, missionaries had also directed more attention there, although Protestant missionary attempts, including missionary schooling, had been undertaken since the early eighteenth century. As Ogbu Kalu has argued, the report presented a distorted image of education in Africa due to the uneven distribution of the correspondence, with much from South Africa and none from parts of Nigeria.[27] Although the Commission was aware of the limitations of the report in terms of the omission of material from Catholic missions, as well as regional biases to the detriment of other spaces, the conference was nevertheless able to gain the support of the breadth of the Church of England, an unparalleled achievement in the history of missionary conferences.[28]

The concerns raised in Edinburgh in relation to missionary education included equitable gender access to schooling, concern about competition with government schools, the dangers of secular and modern life and the kinds of education that needed to be provided in mission fields so that independent, self-governing churches could be established. Moreover, there was a common belief that European missionaries themselves needed to be trained in the newest educational methods in order to provide the best learning environment for non-Europeans. This was the focus of Commission V, *The Preparation of Missionaries*. Indeed, Jane Leeke Lathan, a member of Commission III, had spent six months in India at the behest of Commission V to survey the state of training of female missionaries.[29] Commission V also employed members of its commission to visit missionary colleges in England to report on the state of these institutions, with the Rev. Herbert Kelly arguing that the 'virtual monopoly enjoyed by University theology has been also disastrous', as it was focused on the intellectual aspect of missionary training and not on the spiritual side.[30] In the discussions at Edinburgh, Professor M.E. Sadler of the University of Manchester, member of Commission III and author of the draft report on Africa, reproached educational scientists in Europe for not taking enough account of the educational work of missionaries.[31] Sadler, extolled by contemporaries as 'probably one of the highest educational authorities living',[32] argued that mission education could contribute greatly to resolving the crisis of education in the West, where education was becoming increasingly organised and dependent upon government funding. He saw an inherent danger in such developments as the hyper-intellectual milieu of European education could lead to moral scepticism. He rhetorically asked how one could 'knit together the intellectual side of education with the emotional and spiritual'.[33] His questions were evident in discussions surrounding missionary education, leading contemporary commentators to highlight the connection between missionary education and the reciprocal effects for the crises of modern, secular education.[34] Such questions, as this book has argued, were evident throughout the nineteenth century, as missionary groups consistently shaped their educational offerings to maintained their legitimacy in a modernising and secularising world amidst countervailing criticism from varied sources.

The report of Commission III was extremely self-reflective and critical of previous missionary work in education. It sought to refashion educational procedures as a response to the crisis of identity – but importantly it did not question the three functions of missionary education, although it did question their relative importance. Critical expression of missionary education had been expressed at previous conferences – for example, discussions

at Missionary Conference in Calcutta in 1868 noted that the state of education of the masses of India after 100 years of British presence was deplorable.[35] However, the criticism at Edinburgh was reflected inwards. Kalu
writes positively of this self-critical stance, seeing it as having provided an
opportunity to 'nudge missionary practices in new directions'.[36] This
self-criticism can also be read to reflect anxiety on behalf of missionary societies that they were facing unprecedented competition from nationalist
movements, from Islam, from the increased focus that national governments
were placing on education, consequently devaluing missionary efforts.
Missionaries at Edinburgh in 1910 were setting their sights on the Muslim
communities of North Africa, with potential evangelical work there being a
major topic of discussion.[37] Commission VII (*Missions and Governments*)
held British colonial policy to be unfairly skewed towards Islamic regions.[38]
This was seen to be unacceptable for a Christian Empire. To overcome the
three-pronged pressure felt from Islam, governments and nationalist
movements, Commission III called for greater collaboration between missionary groups, advocated that missionaries work within government
frameworks and stressed the need for professionally trained educators. The
paucity of collaborations was seen to have contributed to the lack of missionary footing in many regions. A united front was called for in order to
present a unified front to foreign governments, many of whom were sceptical of the influences of Christian missionaries. Yet throughout the colonial
world there was also a very real tension between retaining influence with
governments and retaining influence with local peoples.[39] Drawing upon
vast historical knowledge and experience, Commission III's report repeatedly
emphasised the need to engage local people in curricula that were suitable
to the local conditions, and to engage them in schooling the rising generation. Missionaries could not, however, overlook the stipulations and
requirements of governments, especially in those spaces where Christianity
could easily be marginalised. The report reflected the needs of missionary
groups within the sphere of education to accede to the pressures of functional
differentiation within modernising societies through professionalising themselves in order to maintain, or to obtain, legitimacy.

Commission III was not interested in the general state of education in the
countries under examination. Such broader concerns would become more
evident from the 1930s when the interconnections between missionary
groups and professional educationalists became thicker through international
educational networks that brought professional educationalists and
missionary networks in closer connection.[40] Commission III instead
concentrated upon education 'as an instrument for raising native Christian
Churches, which', according to the report, 'shall be in the fullest sense
national, and capable of a growing independence of foreign influence and

support'.[41] The report focused upon three aims of missionary education that could be generalised over time and space: *evangelistic, edificatory* and *leavening*.[42] As we have previously read, these aims respectively referred to the spreading of the gospel amongst both children and their communities; the training and supply of Native leaders for Indigenous churches; and disseminating Christian morals and teachings throughout local communities, without focusing upon conversion per se – an aim that Brian Stanley has claimed reflected a 'diffusionist view'.[43] These aims complemented those of Henry Venn of the CMS, who propagated the three-selves ideal of self-supporting, self-governing and self-extending Indigenous churches, as a progressive step away from missionary involvement towards local control. In order to achieve this end, mission schools needed to train the rising generation of Christian leaders. The report was interested in more than 'just' the making of an elite, it was interested in providing suggestions that would see the integration of mission schools into local communities that would value the skills that such schooling provided. Although the accent varied over spatial and temporal realms, the edificatory function was seen as the most important in the raising up of Indigenous churches towards independence and self-governance. In this regard, the report prioritised higher education over primary or elementary education. It also conveyed an anxiety that the Christian churches had not undertaken enough work to ensure that Christian education would be nationalised, leaving it open to being deemed foreign and thus rejected in light of growing nationalist movements across the colonial and postcolonial world.

Commission II (*The Church in the Mission Field*) also reported disappointing progress in training a rising generation of Christian leaders, with much of the disappointment related to the complete lack of Native forms of churches having been established. Although there were a number of Chinese churches that followed the three-self ideal, there remained multitudes of churches – for example, in India – that were still reliant upon funding from Western mission bodies. In searching for an explanation, the Commission drew upon contemporaneous racial ideals of Indians as 'gentle and submissive' and Chinese as more suited to individual leadership.[44] Commission II furthermore voiced their concern that the remuneration for Native workers, including male and female schoolteachers, lay well below what one would be expected to obtain in secular employment, with some Native helpers earning only a quarter to a third of what secular jobs on average offered. This, as we read in the previous chapters, Behari Lal Singh had expressed similar sentiments at the Liverpool Missionary Conference some fifty years earlier. At Edinburgh, as Brian Stanley has argued, Commission II concluded that the inferior remuneration of Native assistants was causally correlated with their insufficient education.[45] Such sentiments were another instance of the 'not yet' mentality that was rife in missionary education in the nineteenth century, as well as an indication of the difficulties that missionary groups faced in trying to establish mission schools modelled on British notions of Christianity to people not interested in Christianity.

Rather than being purely congratulatory in tone, Commission III's report clearly noted the 'weaknesses and perils' of Christian education.[46] Six weaknesses that were explicitly stated were: a tendency to denationalise converts; low pedagogical standards in schools; competition from government schools; limited attention given to the training of local leaders; insignificant teacher training amongst Western missionaries; and a lack of collaboration amongst missionary groups. These issues, complex and intertwined as they were, were evident, as this book has argued throughout the history the missionary education in the nineteenth century. At Edinburgh, they provided further impetus to 'reconsider the educational methods and ideals of missionaries' as another response to shifting expectations of modernising societies.[47] The fundamental ideal of missionary education as a form of moral improvement was, however, not placed into question. The ensuing reconsideration was framed as a need to focus upon 'education as an instrument for raising Native Christian churches, which shall be in the fullest sense national, and capable of a growing independence of foreign influence and support'.[48] One reason to reconsider missionary practices was political. There was an explicit concern within the report that growing national conscience might link anti-British sentiment with anti-missionary sentiment.[49] Decades of close work with governments left missionary groups hardly distinguishable from governments for many colonised peoples. Missionary methods had contributed to the alienation of converts from national life through a focus upon English and educational methods that had little relevance to local life. This was something to be attended to through changing pedagogy as well as through engaging locals as teachers. The commissioners urged for a reversal of contemporaneous practices that privileged the imparting of ideas and rote learning, and suggested tailoring missionary education to local needs and social environments. As stated, rather than considering this aspect of the report in detail, the focus here is upon the relationship between missionary groups and governments, which has been considered a uniquely important feature of the conference.[50] This relationship was manifest in a dedicated commission to this topic (Commission VII: *Missions and Governments*), yet has not been examined in relation to Commission III. As we shall read below, there was an inherent tension in the report between the churches and governments, with the supporting role of governments acknowledged, and simultaneously an urgent need expressed for missionary groups to work together to combat the aggressive spread of government schools as well as to disentangle the Christian message from Western governmental imperialism in order to allow Christianity to integrate itself in national life.

Hierarchies and national systems

The regional foci of Commission III reflected those of Commission VII (*Missions and Governments*). This latter report concluded that 'the differences in government with which the commission is concerned are seldom political or constitutional, but arise from the nature of the religion and the stage of civilisation of the countries concerned'.[51] Commission VII divided mission lands into five groups of perceived increasing levels of civilisation: '(a) those of low civilisation, but independent; (b) those of higher civilisation, and independent; (c) those of low civilisation, under Christian rule or influence; (d) those of higher civilisation, under Christian rule or influence; (e) those of the highest international rank'.[52] Japan was categorised in the last group (e). Commentators were perplexed at the challenges to Christian moral superiority that came from Japan. There, it was noted, a widespread criticism existed in relation to the 'the idea that Christianity was too individualistic on one side, and too cosmopolitan on the other', with this criticism being directed at the Japanese family.[53] The first group was not considered by the Commission, as it was thought that the 'absolutely independent savage chief' as representative of this group, had 'disappeared'.[54] Of the three remaining groups, China and Persia were regarded as belonging to group (b), the African Protectorates group (c) and India group (d), 'those of higher civilisation, under Christian rule or influence'. Within Commission III's report, these blatantly racist, hierarchical notions of civilisation were incorporated, with both reports consequently reinforcing the idea that Christianity alone manifests the highest moral tone of all religions. To contextualise how Commission III depicted Africa and India – two sites of intense effort in missionary schooling – it is necessary to understand attitudes between governments and missionaries in relation to mission education in China and Japan.

Commission III argued that Christian education in Japan faced three challenges. One was the fact that Japan was 'one of the great Powers of the world' in which Christian missionaries had little leverage.[55] Indeed, Commission VII reported that in Japan Christian mission groups had 'few direct dealings with the civil authorities'.[56] Second, the coherent Japanese national educational system, backed by 'the great resources of the Imperial, prefectural, and local Governments', left little room for missionary influence or participation.[57] And third, Japan was highly patriotic, ensuring that any foreign influences that tried to control or dominate the Japanese were resented.[58] The combination of these issues prompted contemporary commentators to deem the situation in Japan as 'of very great difficulty and urgency'.[59] Commission III lamented that Christian schooling had difficulties competing with a strong cohesive national body that had established its own educational system and cultivated a robust national identity.[60] The specific deliberations of Commission III on education recommended that Japan needed high quality schooling so as not to '[cheapen] Christianity in popular estimation'.[61] Missionaries were considered in danger of becoming intellectually irrelevant in Japan as the 'leadership of Christian thought has passed to the Japanese'.[62] Missionary societies were also irrelevant in terms of education as they could not compete with the financial resources of the government. They were only infrequently able to fulfil the government requirements for certification, and thus were seldom incorporated into the national education system. In short, Japan was seen to be too economically and politically powerful to have any need for outside influence in schooling and thus the Commission suggested a focus upon the two weaker parts of the educational system, kindergarten and the establishment of a Christian university, in which leaders of the local church could be trained.

China was seen as independent, and only slightly lower on the scale of civilisation than Japan. It was further seen as a country in which opportunities were currently being opened up to missionaries as the government was reorganising their system of education as one of the many means of realigning national and foreign politics in order for China to assume a greater part on the international stage.[63] Commission VII reported that in China an intellectual toleration of missionary work existed amidst a more general suspicion of Western religions as agents of foreign powers, resulting in tolerance, without overt support.[64] Yet missionaries were also keenly aware and cautious of the developing national sentiment that opposed all things non-Chinese.[65] It has been suggested that the strong ties some missionaries had to the international press made the Chinese government cautious of how they responded to missionaries lest a negative image of China be propagated throughout the world.[66] The recent Boxer War of 1900–01 had engendered caution on all sides.[67] Commission III saw the opportunity for missionary societies to engage in education as a means to create 'a new civilisation... and in many respects a new ethic'.[68] In this sense missionary education was seen to enact a leavening function in its Christian response to 'helping China at the critical hour to achieve the highest possible type of national life'.[69] The competition with government schools was portrayed as advantageous as it forced mission schools to be more 'efficient' and furthermore led the Commission to advocate for educational professionals in mission schools in China.[70] Yet other commentators saw this competition as a crisis, which diminished the influence of Christian missionaries every day.[71] Concrete suggestions at Edinburgh included the establishment of collaborative interdenominational higher educational institutions, and for the placing of Christian Chinese as teachers within the newly developing government elementary school system to fulfil the leavening aim. The focus upon higher education continued into the twentieth century, as Albert Wu has demonstrated, and remained a battleground of conflicting ideologies struggling for control over the religious and moral education of Chinese youth, and, as an extension, China's future.[72] In short, as China was perceived as not as economically capable as Japan, the Commission saw a niche for Western missionaries and Chinese Christians to supplement the government system, which was perceived of as welcoming of additional support.

Commission VII presented British India as a location of high civilisation, under Christian rule or influence. It commented that the majority of Indians had lost political sovereignty, and that caution was therefore necessary in proselytising the Christian message as this could upset the relative stability that existed whilst religious freedoms had remained intact.[73] This was a clear reference to the Indian Uprising of 1857 and the ensuing British policy of religious neutrality. In order not to create a Christian Indian who was outside of her or his society it was suggested that vernacular languages be used in schools and that Indians would be brought into leadership roles in education, as well as in the Indigenous churches – once again rekindling the debates of the Anglo-Orientalists from the early nineteenth century. Debates surrounding the denationalisation of non-European Christians led to broader questions of cultural adaptation. There was a sense through many of the reports from Edinburgh that the cultural contexts in which missionaries worked needed to be taken into much greater account than had traditionally been the case, with the Report of Commission V (*The Preparation of Missionaries*) reiterating the need for professionally trained Western teachers who were culturally sensitive to the groups that they were to work amongst.[74] This included the need to learn local languages, histories, cultures and religious and philosophical traditions.[75] Commission III also pushed for greater professional training for educational missionaries, with 'nothing short of the best' being desirable in the training of Western missionaries.[76] As the previous chapters have demonstrated, such discussions were not new; however, by 1910 they had obtained a new urgency.

Competition between government and mission schools led to Commission III advocating for increased professionalisation in local teaching staff. Burton in his correspondence with Moor in the year prior to the conference had argued that:

In most of the countries which I have visited I have been led to believe that this time for the treatment of education as a mere adjunct to evangelization is past. In the beginning this policy was naturally, if not necessarily, adopted, with the consequence that often education was entrusted to men and women who came to the mission field full of zeal to engage in evangelical work, but with no fitness or taste for educational work, and that the strictly intellectual efficiency of education was regarded as of small consequence compared with the results in conversion and spiritual education. Today, however, if educational work is to be undertaken by foreigners in India, China or Japan, it is imperatively necessary that the work shall be fully up to standard from the point of view of educational efficiency as this term is usually understood. In fact Christian schools ought to be the best in the country from this point of view, and add thereto a moral and religious effectiveness which their rivals do not possess.[77]

Burton had travelled extensively some years before through the 'Far East' as part of a tour financed by the Baptist John D. Rockefeller to examine the lands for possibilities for philanthropic work as well as for American missionaries in China.[78] He was therefore well acquainted with the situation and the need to offer the best possible education in lands that had strong government education systems. Discussing the situation in India, Commission III noted that the number of Christian schools was relatively low, with the majority of schools classified as private schools that did not receive support through grants-in-aid, and thus did not need to conform to government standards.[79] Nevertheless missionaries could not afford to let governments push them away from their work, nor could they afford to be overwhelmed by a need to pander purely to the governmental demands, lest they would have no energy left to pursue the religious aims of mission schools.[80]

Freedom of action: mission schools in African protectorates

Commission VII reported that missions working in countries in group (c) – that is, the African protectorates – could 'fairly expect, as a general policy, not only freedom of action, but even the countenance and encouragement of the civil power on the ground of the proved value of the missionary enterprise to civilisation, peace, and humanity'.[81] This was a sentiment which was seconded by Commission III, which stated that 'at the present time, there is a fruitful interchange of experience between Government officials and the missionary educators'.[82] Particularly in the Southern African colonies that would become the Union of South Africa in May 1910, there had been some significant collaboration with government. In 1908, a Select Committee of the Cape House of Assembly had been constituted to deal with the subject of 'Native education'.[83] As a result of this committee, a conference of government and mission representatives was held in early 1910 to discuss reform in the education of locals in South Africa. The Rev. James Henderson had presented evidence at the 1908 Select Committee. As a proven expert, he provided critical feedback for the draft report of Commission III, and particularly Sadler's draft section on Africa. In his written comments on the draft report, Henderson stated that 'nothing is now to be gained by reflections upon the old system which is thus passing away'.[84] He looked towards future possibilities under the newly formed Union of South Africa, rather than to a colonial past in which, to quote Henderson, 'What [the "African"] has received is, as a rule, but a travesty of education.'[85]

The report of Commission III noted that where missionaries were allowed to act free from government regulations, Christianity was seen to be a uniting force, ensuring that both 'Civilisation and religion' were seen as almost indistinguishable from one another.[86] The mutual benefit of religion and politics in this instance was deemed unquestionable, with any failings reflecting governing parties having not placed sufficient proper emphasis upon the welfare of the people they ruled. Practically this meant for sub-Saharan Africa that missionaries enjoyed expansive freedom over educational enterprises until the early twentieth century. Commission III felt free to criticise governments – for example, through declaring that education in South Africa had 'in the past, followed too closely the lines laid down by Colonial Governments for the inspection of European pupils'.[87] A continued focus upon curricula for White pupils, rather than an adaptive curricula for Africans, was seen not to accommodate African needs. Henderson, however, had disagreed with this statement in his criticisms of the draft report, suggesting that a proposal for two steams of education would be 'particularly dangerous at the present time when native affairs are in the melting pot consequent upon the Union of the South African States and there is danger of a policy reactionary in respect to book education and probably also in the direction of regular trades'.[88] He hoped that the government and missionary bodies could draft a plan that would include much flexibility for all people, regardless of colour. The report of Commission III included reference to the Cape Colony conference, but generalised the findings and did not present the optimism of Henderson.[89]

The African Protectorates faced their own unique challenges, due to modernisation, economic, growth, White colonial interests, an increased influence of Islam and changing marriage patterns. Such challenges rendered a need to reconceptualise the education provided to Africans, including to women. Unlike the situation in India, where mission schools were in competition with government schools, mission schools in Southern Africa were generally supported by the government as a tool of social control and regulation, particularly from the 1870s in places such as the Cape Colony where a 'mineral revolution' increased labour needs.[90] However, by the time of Edinburgh, many British colonial governments in sub-Saharan Africa were increasingly dictating curricula in return for funding, as they too had vested interests in 'improving' and controlling their local societies.[91] Increased government involvement was seen to be a 'chief cause of mischief' in the provision of non-relevant education to Africans.[92] Commission III's report decried the 'bookish' schooling that Africans were receiving under government frameworks as the wrong type of education.[93] Even for Protestant missionaries, who focused upon teaching people to read, too much focus upon 'bookish' schooling could be problematic. The Rev. W.T. Balmer of Freetown in Sierra Leone, for example, considered that 'book-knowledge' made (implicitly male) pupils discontent with manual labour, leading them to seek new opportunities in townships, and resulted in them falling into trouble as they were not able to withstand moral temptations.[94] The paradox of missionary intellectual education was that it 'raised' expectations without being able to 'save' individuals from the temptations found outside of known social situations. Too much emphasis upon 'bookish' learning without complementary industrial training was said to 'spoil' the African, with excessive focus upon the latter only deemed not to 'develop the whole man'.[95] Such concepts reflect those that were circulating in missionary conferences throughout the nineteenth century, and other missionary texts, drawing upon older notions of a complete education needing to simultaneously develop the heart, head and body. At turn of the twentieth century, missionaries were under increasing pressure to ensure that the education of the heart (that is, moral or religious education) maintained its position within this triad. Missionary schooling was presented as imperative to the modernisation of Africa, ensuring that missionaries maintained their privileged position as providers of Western education.

Within the Southern African context, government officials as well as missionaries were frustrated at the perceived slow moral progress of Africans. For both missionary groups and governments, the instilling of a sense of individualism in Africans was deemed important, for individual salvation, economic freedom and the breaking down of 'tribalism', which itself was depicted as 'heathen' and 'savage'.[96] Although the weighting of these aspects were different within missionary and colonial modernity, they contributed to both the moral legitimation of colonial and missionary expansion. In a broader context, the individual nature of Christianity and missionary education was considered to lead to the breaking down of family, social and national bonds either through instilling epistemic rifts between children and parents, or physically removing children from families in order to educate them in mission schools.[97] Christian missions contributed to the individualisation of many societies and through doing so contributed, whether intentionally or not, to an aspect of their modernisation.[98] In Southern Africa, although individuality was not necessarily the initial aim of missionaries, the economic and political situation led to missionaries focusing on the conversion of single, isolated individuals, which underscored governmental plans to loosen 'tribal' authority.

The situation in Africa was so varied and complex that Commission III could only offer a few conclusions that could be applied to the whole of the continent. In Natal, the provision of industrial training was costly and thus this form of training was not implemented uniformly.[99] In South Africa, Henderson had argued prior to the conference that there should not be a tiered system, under the threat of political unrest. The Commission concluded that there was a need for more adaptive education – that is, industrial and agricultural education. It also considered that more attention was needed to the training of girls and women, the appointment of inspectors and follow-up care for scholars who had left mission schools and colleges.[100] No Africans were permitted to speak at the Conference; rather, they were spoken for.[101] The solutions touted were ones in which the collaborative efforts of missionary groups and governments were seen to benefit the Africans who would otherwise be 'ruinously injured' by commercial enterprises.[102] The paternalistic tone evident in debates over religious and moral education in the West Indies in the 1830s as discussed in Chapter 1 was thus heard again in relation to the future of Africans three quarters of a century later. In both spaces the concerns of White settlers also contributed to the debates, with anxieties voiced in parts of Africa as to the competition White artisans would receive from trained Africans.[103] As Rebecca Swartz has demonstrated, these concerns of White settlers were already evident in the early nineteenth century.[104] Given such competing agendas, the final report of Commission III positioned missionary education more broadly as the only system under which all demands might be met, for by focusing upon moral and religious elements, missionary education was best placed to contribute to the 'world's thought and life'.[105] These ideological musings were not meant to be reflected in definite conclusions for practical implementation in sub-Saharan African schools. That was left to later commissions and educational bodies, such as the USA-based Phelps-Stokes Commission in the 1920s. This committee had a strong missionary focus, with many of the commissioners being experienced missionaries. The commission provided policy for the British Colonial Office for educational reform in British Eastern and Western Africa, and thus legitimised missionary voices as educational experts in government circles. The Phelps-Stokes Commission came to many of the same conclusions that the Commission III did in terms of the need for Africans to focus upon 'adaptive' education, industrial skills and education for the leavening of society.[106] Commission III from Edinburgh had a more self-reflective aim in that it wished to 'stimulate thought and to provide a basis for discussion'.[107] Yet already at Edinburgh the germination of an idea for African education was being hatched. The report made repeated reference to the model example of the Hampton Institute in Virginia, an Industrial training institute for African-American and Native American Indians. Its director, Dr Thomas Jesse Jones, would subsequently devise an important plan for African education in the 1920s in his work on the Phelps-Stokes Commission.[108] Jones was a correspondent for Commission III. Sadler himself had toured the institute in 1901, facilitating its citation as a model institution for Africans in Commission III's report.[109] Such international connections underscore the entangled histories of missionary education in a global setting and also the ability of missionary groups and individuals to position themselves as experts to the government on the educational needs of Africans, and effectively as (censoring) conduits for the ideas of Africans.

Adaptive learning

The Report of Commission III labelled mission schools as contributing to the production of lazy and conceited people by providing Africans with the same education as European children, rather than taking local conditions into consideration.[110] Similar concerns had been expressed at other missionary conferences, such as the 1904 General Missionary Conference held in South Africa, as well as in broader colonial debates as to the level of missionary education that should be offered to Black pupils.[111] The missionary concern of creating lazy, dependent Christians was also voiced at Edinburgh in relation to India, reflecting common missionary concerns that locals would abuse missionary benevolence as a form of social security. A lazy Christian was considered a false Christian.[112] The onus on the 'dignity of labour' and the moral value of work was apparent through a shift from 'bookish' learning to adaptive education and the focus upon providing people with training to support themselves. From the 1830s, legislation in Britain had enmeshed the concepts of work and dignity through the Poor Laws. The idea of work equating with dignity permeated colonial administrations and humanitarian notions of social improvement, ideologically connecting non-Europeans with Western concepts of poverty. The concept of education in the African Protectorates was broadened to include low-level manual training as a form of moral education. The discussions at Edinburgh on the appropriate level of training for Africans were based on racial hierarchies which portrayed Africans as intellectually less capable than Europeans or indeed Indians, and thus more suited to manual labour, particularly agricultural labour. As Andrew Paterson has noted, at the turn of the century the majority of Africans in the Cape Colony remained unschooled. Attendance nevertheless increased as academic and industrial education came to be considered an 'alternative source of economic security in a time of land dispossession'.[113] The education provided to African children was generally not aimed at providing them with skills to engage in a trade, but rather to teach them the 'dignity of labour' applicable to manual labour. In the period prior to Edinburgh, increased amounts of industrial training for White students were provided, while opportunities available to African students were reduced.[114]

Commission III's report particularly emphasised adapting industrial teaching to local conditions, providing skills for individuals to become self-supporting and instilling dignity into labour.[115] Yet, as Henderson in his comments prior to the conference, noted: 'The position appears to be this, that industrial work is still lacking in dignity in the eyes of the Natives.'[116] Henderson was talking from a particular position, that of the principal of the Lovedale Missionary Institute, in which African and European youth of both sexes could receive a liberal Christian education. He continued:

> There are pupils that come to Lovedale belonging to families of very high social standing among their own people who had previously never put their hand to any kind of work and whose relatives would be shocked to find them performing the tasks and taking the industrial training which the Institution insists upon.[117]

Henderson's comments spoke to the heterogeneous economic standing of Africans, along with different understandings of dignity. Yet in the final report, it was stated that Henderson writing from Lovedale:

> urges that more should be done for industrial training. The pressure, the cramming for examinations, is squeezing industrial work out of the curriculum. Hardly anything, he thinks, is more urgent than the consideration of measures which will arrest the deepening poverty and misery of the natives. But lack of means is a hindrance: and the training of natives to trades is apt to be regarded with jealousy by European artisans.[118]

This non-differentiated comment reflected both the editing process of the report to present a particular agenda as much as it did the creation of external forces that could be seen to hinder mission work – in this case European tradespeople. It also homogenised Africans as requiring working-class education, and in doing so diminished evidence of Africans of high social status.

Commission III generally recommended that in relation to the whole of Africa more attention be given to 'industrial and agricultural education, adapted to the needs of the native races'.[119] Given the varied conditions in different parts of Africa, no specific suggestions of subjects were provided;

rather, reference was made to the Hampton Normal and Agricultural Institute and the Tuskegee Normal and Industrial Institute, both in the USA. The report made frequent reference to these two institutions, both primarily for African-Americans, as models of industrial and adaptive education – that is, education tailored by educators for the perceived needs of the local population focusing on practical rather than academic offerings – suitable to be adapted for the situation in the African Protectorates.[120] In the decades after Edinburgh, these two American institutions received greater recognition as models for adapting education for perceived African needs,[121] with the idea of adaptive education further underscored in the 1920s through work of the Phelps-Stokes Commission and the growth in support for adaptive education in segregated learning environments.[122]

Although Africa was considered by the commission at Edinburgh as having been too complex for a simple reading of the state of education due to differences in government policies, peoples and histories, as well as the ability to provide missionary schooling within modernising societies, the 'problem' of female education as a whole was considered sufficiently simple and common to all female Africans. In describing the 'position of native women in Africa', the report echoed sentiments reminiscent of descriptions of Indian women at the 1860 Liverpool Missionary Conference, as discussed in Chapter 3, in calling women, amongst other terms, immoral, unclean, ignorant and wasteful, all reinforcing conceptions of helpless and needy Africans. It was, as the Commission III report stated, parroting rhetoric directed at Indian women from the early nineteenth century, 'from this position of degradation that the missionary workers in Africa would save her'.[123] Pointedly, the trope of the degraded non-European in need of 'raising' through missionary education that had circulated at the middle of the century was still circulating in 1910, but the ethnicity of the women had changed from Indian to African. Polygamy, the Edinburgh report argued, contributed to this degradation, rendering woman 'vastly inferior to man, whereas the Christian ideal would raise her to the position of man's helpmate'.[124] Christianity had forced a social change in marital customs to conform to ideas of morality evident in missionary modernity. Polygamy was undermined by intolerant missionary practices. Many churches would not let a polygamous man become a Christian, or would force him to release all but one wife before converting. Once converted, African men could only have one wife. Taking another wife commonly led to excommunication.[125] The report was aware that in restricting polygamous marriage, women would need to find avenues for securing financial independence, such as through domestic service, teaching or nursing. Industrial training thus contained a two-fold aim of training women to be good housewives in their roles as mothers and wives and of changing social structures for those excluded from this 'chief profession' to be able to be financially independent of men in modernising societies. Through independent financial earnings women were seen to be 'raised' in their societal position, with this financial security effectively hindering marriage at an early age. Moreover, work was considered to ward off idleness and thus to prevent moral relapse. Although the primary purpose of all female education in Africa was to 'raise up a Christian ideal in the home',[126] the discussions surrounding female adaptive education suggest that an African woman's role was also as a labourer, with adapted industrial education helping her to emancipate herself from traditional society and from traditional marriage patterns. Adaptive education was suggested at Edinburgh to provide women with skills to work outside the home and to provide them the moral codes to remain Christian in a modernising world. This was a different form of adaptive education than that actually introduced by British colonial governments following the Phelps-Stokes Commission of the late 1920s, which sought to use traditionalism as a fortification against colonial modernity and its perceived moral dangers through keeping females in local settings. In both concepts, the inherent tension of education for females was the question as to whether their role in a modernising society was as bastions of family life or as integrated members of a skilled workforce. The conflicting ideas between African women as independent economic agents or members of community labour which Elizabeth Prevost has located in the 1930s were thus already apparent in missionary ideas of female adaptive education around 1910.[127]

African women were also being trained to be teachers in mission schools. In the draft of the report a sentence suggested one 'characteristic of the native women' as 'a love of ease that shirks responsibility – so that responsible posts are impossible at present'.[128] Henderson disagreed with this sentiment in his comments prior to the conference, stating instead that:

> I have heard it repeatedly said by the missionary superintendents of schools of much experience that their best teachers are women and it is admitted by native teachers themselves that it is the women teachers that put forth the greatest and most earnest endeavour after leaving the Institution to develop their efficiency and carry into effect the principles of education that they have been taught while in training. The difficulty is that circumstances make it unsuitable in many cases for native girls to take over charge of a school alone in a village where there is no European missionary.[129]

His comment presented South African women as fully capable of the intellectual and moral challenges of teaching, indeed as more capable than African men. However, the printed report presented a different slant on his text, quoting him as allegedly stating: 'Native girls are being trained as teachers at a number of institutions and become in many cases highly efficient. But the posts that they can occupy are limited, and the dangers and temptations to which they are exposed very serious.'[130] Following the pattern relating to Henderson's comments on dignity of labour, the text from the letter is much more open and positive than the final redacted text. A particular image of Africans, and of African women, was presented in the final report, which artificially reflected European and North American generalised expectations of African people rather than a more complex reality.

Unlike the trope of the 'degraded' Indian woman against which British women rallied, the 'degraded' African woman as a foil with which to compare British women did not feature as prominently in contemporaneous British feminist writings. The majority of British female missionaries were stationed in India, not Africa, and consequently more was written and known about the situation in India than Africa.[131] In the 1830s, the quest to quash *sati* was a cause that had banded together British women. Although individual women championed various causes on behalf of sub-Saharan women, it was not until the late 1920s that a similar rallying point emerged around African women's bodies, as epitomised in the 'female circumcision controversy' or in the debates around *lobola* (a form of bride wealth).[132] Even in humanitarian networks, the plights of Africans did not receive much public attention after the Select Committee Report on Aborigines in British Settlements in the late 1830s, which was discussed in Chapter 2. It was not until after the 1920s that the predicament of sub-Saharan Africans was brought to light through philanthropist activities such as the Phelps-Stokes Commissions on the educational needs of Africans. Yet, as Elizabeth Prevost has argued, the encounters between British missionaries and African women in the nineteenth century were complex sites of identity formations, which contributed to the interrogation of prevailing gender norms.[133] Her work underscores the broader argument that there was a discursive divide between the metropole and the mission field, a divide that allowed for the privileging of metropolitan voices in metropolitan spaces. This is also evident in analysing missionary conference reports, which provide an authoritative view on contemporaneous missionary education, although simultaneously filtering, summarising and marginalising voices and actual practices from the mission 'field'. Thus although gender was still a category which was discussed, it was complicated by issues of race, government involvement and local Christian structures.

Missionary lessons for hyper-intellectual Western moral sceptics

By the start of the twentieth century, missionary education in Africa, as well as in China and India, was considered a means to stabilise the population with Christian morals during the periods of modernisation.[134] Yet, the foregoing initial concerns of Henderson notwithstanding, Commission III considered African women too lazy to be of great use to the mission as teachers, and their usefulness was limited to girls' schools. The great fear of missionaries that ran through the report's sections on Africa was that women were idle, and would thus fall into moral danger, just like African men would fall into moral danger if they left their homelands and moved into cities. As Africans were cast as morally immature, the moral and religious influences of missionaries were seen to be paramount to 'saving' Africans. At Edinburgh, a global survey of education work had convinced those involved of the continued need for missionary educators as a group distinct from professional (secular) educators to provide a strong moral and religious basis throughout the non-European world, particularly in light of modernisation and the effects of European colonial expansion. Without Christian moral underpinnings within education, missionaries believed that a moral crisis would abound in society, and they drew upon the lessons of India to underscore this point.

At the turn of the twentieth century, several Indian Chambers of Commerce argued that government schools in India were 'notorious nurseries of sedition' as the secular school system had 'no moral influence'.[135] According to Eugene Stock, the *fin-de-siècle* historian of the CMS, the 'Educational Problem' in India was so bad that numerous political, commercial and religious groups had lamented the provision of English education devoid of religion. Stock quoted William Duff as prophesising that knowledge without a religious component would lead to the creation of 'restless agitators'.[136] As this book has demonstrated, this sentiment was ubiquitous in missionary writings and discourses, which placed missionary schooling as imperative for the moral stability of the British Empire from post-emancipation West Indies societies, to settler colonial societies, to post Uprising India, to the colonial modernity of Sri Lanka and to the perceived secular modernity of the early twentieth century. Missionaries considered themselves to be the best providers of education to non-Europeans as they instilled a moral code, which would idyllically prevent local people from political or social dissent. The 'Educational Problem' was more pronounced in India, given the government's focus upon secular education and their unwillingness to include religion in the curriculum so as not to aggravate religious sensibilities. For missionaries the situation in India was a warning as how bad things could get if religion was completely left out of the curricula and if the government school system was purely secular.

The major concern that Commission III raised in relation to India was the creation of denationalised locals – that is, people who had taken on the

Christian message but as a result had lost connection to their own cultural identities, languages and social structures. In the words of Commission III's report at Edinburgh, denationalisation was a peril of missionary education as it 'alienates them from the life and sympathies of their fellow country-men [*sic*], so as to make it possible to suggest that Christianity is a foreign influence, tending to alienate its converts from the national life'.[137] The denationalisation of converts was not a new topic as it had been discussed also at Liverpool. Yet at Liverpool denationalising was not yet connected to strong anti-British sentiments or to a strong anti-Christian movement, but rather to a concern that denationalised Indians would be uprooted from their cultural setting.[138] By the start of the twentieth century, Christian education was considered to paradoxically contribute to both the denationalisation of locals as well as the creation of nationalists. The period was characterised by a 'new political consciousness'.[139] Although not explicitly stated in the Edinburgh reports, the growing national consciousness in India was epitomised through the modern nationalist movement. The establishment of the Indian National Congress in 1885 fuelled missionary fears that 'anti-British feeling, in undiscerning minds, becomes anti-Christian feeling'.[140] The nationalist movement was predominantly secular and instigated from educated urban Indian professionals, who had been inspired by Western liberal education. Within Britain, public attention had been given to the 'Indian Unrest' in the columns of *The Times* in 1910, with its correspondent Valentine Chirol linking secular education in India, bereft of all moral and religious content, with political unrest.[141] Although 'unrest' was a term associated with the 'Indian Renaissance' of the time, other commentators considered the Renaissance to be 'a New Birth', a time of awakened political awareness that would not necessarily overthrown British Imperialism.[142] C.F. Andrews in his 1912 book, *The renaissance in India, its missionary aspect* claimed that this Renaissance was advanced through English Literature and Western Science.[143] Coinciding with this, he noted, was a religious Reformation in which new sects and religious groups sprung up and older religious traditions were questioned, including those of Buddhism and Hinduism.

Associated problems in India were seen to manifest in the emerging nationalist movements, which rejected everything foreign. In the words of the report, 'the new political consciousness, as has been shown, is almost inevitably anti-British and pro-Indian or pro-Hindu, and in Ceylon pro-Buddhist', with anti-British feeling equating to anti-Christian feeling.[144] Such national sentiments had been increasing since the late 1880s.[145] There were, however, groups that had existed earlier that had pushed back at traditional religious movements and created a new interpretation of religion inspired by Western philosophy such as the Young Bengals from the late

1820s. Amil Seal has argued that the formation of such groups was not iso-lated to the missionary context; rather, Western education in India facili-tated the emergence of national political organisations which laid the foundation of Indian nationalism.[146] Charles Reed has categorised Seal as an imperial apologist, suggesting instead that British ideas about nationhood and modernity were reappropriated by local people, so that Indian nation-alism was no so much an accidental consequence of British imperial culture, but rather a reframing and active engagement with these ideas within spe-cific Indian contexts.[147] These debates indicate various ways in which mis-sionary schooling was a source of information and ideologies that could contribute to the formation of alternative forms of nationalism and moder-nity. The interaction with missionary modernity spurred religious revivals in other spaces, such as Sri Lanka, with religious revivals evident in Buddhist, Hindu and Muslim communities at the end of the century. Buddhists in par-ticular established more schools in competition with Protestant mission schools. In other locations such as sub-Saharan Africa, reactions to Chris-tian missionaries had spurred on nationalistic churches, such as the reli-giously inspired political movement called 'the Order of Ethiopia' (commonly called 'the Ethiopian movement'). This movement arose in the late nine-teenth century with the radical separatism of this African church movement engendering anxiety amongst Established Churches that the Christian mes-sage would be co-opted for radical political means.[148] Stemming from within the Anglican Church of South Africa, by 1910 it was seen as in competition with missionary moral influence and a force of social destruction and antag-onism towards governments across southern Africa as it advocated 'Africa for Africans'.[149] Ethiopianism was not the form of Indigenous churches that missionaries had envisaged, nor desired, and it caused a crisis for missionary groups. However, as Henderson noted in his comments to the draft report, there was a 'general feeling' amongst missionaries in South Africa that 'a good deal too much had been made of Ethiopianism and that there was a tendency to take it much too seriously'.[150]

In the context of India, modern education was equated with secular English-language and advanced knowledge and enlightened thought.[151] Yet for many commentators, modern secular education brought its own issues. Behari Lal Singh had articulated these thoughts in the 1870s when reporting that the pupils at the orphanage were not encouraged to adopt foreign man-ners stating that:

No one can entertain towards the British Government and the British People sentiments of greater loyalty and respect than I do, but I am patriotic enough none the less to observe with regret that imitation and copying of European method and manner which is at the present day so prevalent in Bengal. It is not

only unbecoming and unpatriotic to be thus prominently ashamed of one's
nationality, but, as I have already said, it seriously hinders a man's power to
benefit his less enlightened fellow-country-men.[152]

Commission III noted that missionaries feared that Christian Indians who
had been educated in Western ways would be rejected by nationalistic
movements just as Christianity and Christian schools would be rejected.
Contemporaneous commentators, including members of the Indian
government, provided similar assessments that it was not education itself
which led to the unrest in India; rather, disaffection had a political root
which was exacerbated by ineffective education. Moreover, blame was
placed for the growing political unrest on an unregulated press.[153] Already
in the early 1870s, Behari Lal Singh had noted that there had been an
increase in European infidel literature in India, which had led to an increase
in 'rationalistic intuitionalists, pantheists or materialists'.[154] Secular education without moral undertones was deemed dangerous. However, religious
diversity hindered the offering of a common moral theology. Within India
the Hunter Commission of 1882 reported that the movement to produce a
Moral Textbook 'based on principles of theology common to all religions'
was put aside as the government did not think it probable that one textbook
'of morality sufficiently colourless to be accepted by Christians,
Mohammedans, and Hindoos, would do much to remedy the defects, or
supply the shortcoming of a secular education'.[155]

Rather than question the role of liberal education in the rise of such
national movements, Commission III at Edinburgh considered the solution
to political agitation in India to be the provision of more religious and
secular education at all levels.[156] In typical missionary style, the message
itself was not questioned; rather, it was concluded that: 'ignorance, not
education, is the cause of the religious prejudice that mingles with the
political movement; that more and not less education, both secular and religious, both higher and lower, is required'.[157] Christian education itself,
according to the tenet of the report, was not the problem; the problem was
that not enough attention had been given to local needs or to engaging local
people as teachers. Thus, the report suggested an increased focus upon
establishing and maintaining Christian higher educational institutions to
train leaders of the new societies.[158]

Government policy in India was unpopular with many missionaries, for
in their opinion the pressures of studying for university examinations forced
religion out of the curricula of high level schools for males, leaving
missionaries to complain that secular education led to a morally debased
society and to a moral crisis.[159] Education for females in India had been
provided for many decades so that in some provinces almost all females

received education, albeit of lower primary level than that provided for males.[160] Few females extended their schooling past the primary stage, with Commission III reporting little demand for it in India.[161] Missionaries reported that cultural expectations in India limited women's access to education, as women with too much literary education were deemed to be negligent housewives, unfit for gender-specific duties and thus detrimental to household happiness.[162] Education for the majority of non-Christian females was limited to lower-primary – that is, learning to read and write in the vernacular, to do easy sums and to do a little needlework.[163] Only a small minority of female Indians, mostly Christianised, had access to higher education. Many Hindu girls married young and were only allowed to continue attending mission schools with their husbands' permission, which was seldom granted.[164] Unlike the situation in sub-Saharan Africa, where the introduction of Christianity had forced a social change in marital customs particularly in relation to polygamy, missionaries were not willing to force change in the age of marriage for girls in India. Rather than change these cultural practices, it was considered 'better to reach a lower aim than to aim higher and fail altogether'.[165] After over a century of trying, many Protestant missionary groups were aware of the impossibility of changing cultural structures within India, and thus lowered their expectations for non-Christian women for the immediate future in the hope that social reform would occur at a later date at the behest of locals. The difference in the discourse at Edinburgh between a continued focus on moral education to maintain social order in India and suggestions for industrial education to emancipate females from traditional roles in Africa can be read in terms of the dual role of Christianity and individualism circulating in the early twentieth century.[166]

Social reform was not considered desirable for everyone. According to the Commissioners at Edinburgh, there was a pervasive dread amongst Indian society that 'the general education of women means a social revolution, the extent of which cannot be foreseen'.[167] It was feared that if women were provided with too much education they would become 'either self-assertive or one-sidedly intellectual'.[168] Both scenarios caused anxiety, for if women were to break out of their previous submissive roles as good wives and nurturing mothers, Western missionary education would be condemned for this transition along with the ensuing social unrest. From its position as a group of experts on colonial education, Commission III stressed that Indian society was not yet ready for women to be educated to levels natural to British or American women, for this would only bring discontent and social unrest.[169] Similar ideas were circulating in the mission field at the time.[170] Although Commission III's report on education made no clear connections to the changing role of women in Britain, allusions were made

to the social turmoil that might arise if women were allowed too much freedom in education. Women in the Edwardian era were becoming increasingly
politicised, evident, for example, in the suffragette movement, and in the
higher rate of abortions, reflecting changing sexual politics.[171] There is no
clear indication in the report as to what extent British anxiety for suffrag-
ettes fed into this fear of female emancipation in India. It is nevertheless
clear that women such as Sophia Duleep Singh were important suffragette
figures known in both locations.[172] Given both British women's feelings of
responsibility towards Indian women and missionary concerns about secular education, it is not surprising that the report noted anxiety about the role
of women in potential Indian social uprisings due to secular education. Such
opinions, couched in terms of expert knowledge and assumed universal sisterhood and humanitarian values, reflected contemporaneous beliefs in British, and broader Western, moral superiority along with the growing anxiety
that Britain's tenuous hold on imperial power might collapse.[173]

Rather than contribute to a political revolution, the Report of Commission III overwhelmingly recommended missionary societies to limit their
educational offerings to females to rudimentary schooling in order to
conform to cultural expectations, and only cautiously expand into higher
education for females. Through 'aiming low' the Commissioners also
avoided the delicate situation through which Indian women with literary
education were seen to neglect their household duties, or worse, to be to
morally suspect, as a literary education was traditionally associated with
forms of prostitution.[174] Such fears for the morality of women reflected
broader debates around the roles of sex, sexuality, gender and intimacy as
sites of close colonial surveillance and anxiety.[175] Although the goal of
equitable gender access to schooling was not in doubt, the education of
women was always considered categorically different to that of men. The
image of Indian females within international missionary reports shifted
between Liverpool and Edinburgh from 'degraded' women shackled by their
religion and in need of Christian moral education to women who needed to
be contained within families and not educated about social expectations lest
they contribute to social unrest. Within missionary modernity, the main
place of women remained within the confines of the family. Yet just a couple
of years later, in 1912, Charles Andrews in his book, *The renaissance in
India*, would argue that:

> The last few years have witnessed, however, a change of attitude in the matter
> of women's education which is nothing less than revolutionary. The younger
> generation of India's women have now set their hearts on being educated, and
> in the long run they will win their way through all opposition. Then, and then
> alone, will the National Movement be established on a firm basis.[176]

According to him, the highest qualified and most spiritual women were needed to be sent out to meet India's claim on England and the increased demand for female education.[177]

In his analysis of the report of Commission III, Brian Stanley has noted that the relationship between the twin goals of educating local national leaders ('not exotic to their own cultures') and that of 'the diffusion of Christian moral principles throughout society' were often not distinct.[178] He notes that particularly in the sections on Africa focus was placed more on the second aim than the first, with the report advocating the raising of African women from their 'supposed "ignorance" and "degradation"' through making them good mothers and housewives in order to subvert concept of 'heathenism'.[179] An alternative interpretation of this, as with many other aspects of the report, is that missionary groups feared that previous methods had the potential to alienate them from the local populous as these methods were too easily dismissed as foreign or exotic. In the growing nationalistic environment in which missions were operating, a change in course was needed to ensure that Christianity would become so deeply embedded within familial, social, societal and governmental structures that it could not be rooted out when anti-European feelings erupted.

Evident through the report was a tension between colonial and missionary modernity. Nira Wickramasinghe draws on the work of David Scott to suggest that modernity, in the context of Sri Lanka, is characterised by shaping colonial subjects into political actors, and through governmental reforms introducing political representation, modern social institutions and capitalist plantation economies.[180] Yet for missionary organisations, modernity was more about breaking free of 'heathen' superstitions, perceived repressive social and familial structures and 'awakening' individuals to a Christian god. For missionary societies, modernity was couched more in philanthropic than humanitarian aims – that is, it was more about helping the individual rather than changing the structure of society. Conversely, colonial modernity followed more the logic of humanitarian aims of changing societal structures through government reforms. Modernising societies could thus be perceived as 'succeeding' or 'failing' depending upon the terms of reference used. For many missionary groups, as evident in Edinburgh, colonial modernity had failed as it had not provided a solid moral footing for people 'progressing' into a modern world.

The report did not attempt to provide universal models for effective education. Rather, as the title of the report emphasised, 'education' was 'considered as an instrument for raising native Christian Churches, which shall be in the fullest sense national, and capable of a growing independence of foreign influence and support'.[181] Given the diversity of the situations and the variance of local responses, not much more could have been achieved.

The report explicitly noted the concern that government efforts were overshadowing missionary efforts, especially since missionary societies often competed against one another rather than acting in unison.[182] Education can be used as a political tool to shape civil and national identities, and the relationship between missions and governments in the provision of education was an important determinant of how much influence missionaries could expect to have. The report was very short in its conclusions regarding cooperation with governments, suggesting only that it was difficult to compete with governments in terms of higher education, although cooperation was desired so long as it did not compromise Christian principles. A specific proposal of this section was that Christian hostels should be established where feasible so that students at higher education institutes could have personal Christian support when undertaking their studies. Once again, the conclusions of the report focused upon the raising of local leaders through higher education institutes, and neglected to provide conclusions regarding elementary school work, which represented the overwhelming majority of all missionary educational work.

Conclusion

The World Missionary Conference of 1910 revealed a crisis of identity for missionary societies in their provision of education. No longer could they see themselves as the providers of education towards modernity. Indeed, the multiple forms of modernity that missionaries were faced with prevented a uniform approach; however, it was evident that previous strategies needed to be revised. The report made clear that missionaries had, for example, no place in the construction of a modern Japanese society, a situation that was foreboding. Western education propagated in Japan without reference to Christianity, with Commission V fearing that this situation 'must come to be the case in India and China, most probably in Turkey, and in time perhaps throughout Africa'.[183] Commission V predicted that 'children of far more than half of the human race may within the next generation be educated without any reference to those spiritual truths which are the only real and permanent support of social order and personal morality'.[184] The establishment of secular schooling systems all over the world was causing great anxiety amongst missionary groups for the morality of humanity, particularly given their belief in the moral deterioration of non-Christian peoples exposed to the destructive aspects of Western civilisation and the associated break-down of traditional moral and social codes.[185] Within Commission III's report, the evidence from China indicated that educational systems could be constructed without input from missionaries, providing concerns for the future of Africa. There a very heterogeneous educational landscape was present, with government policy often able to severely impinge upon missionary endeavours.[186] In response, missionary educators had refashioned themselves at the end of the nineteenth century and into the twentieth century into educational experts, providing advice to governmental committees to ensure their ongoing investment in educational enterprises. There was a tension present in the report of Commission III between pandering to governmental wants and local needs. Previous policies of adopting British educational standards were harshly criticised as these were deemed irrelevant to local lives, and moreover raised people above their perceived position or denationalised them so that they no longer had a valid place within local societies. This latter concern especially fed into broader concerns for the fragility of missionary education in locations such as India, where nationalism was increasingly prevalent, or in Africa, where independent churches were growing and the effects of the Ethiopian movement were felt. The modern concept of nation states was seen to threaten Christian education in its current form. Christian schools were considered a foreign influence, rather than institutions that were deeply embedded in local lives, societies and politics and adapted to the local setting. Western civilisation, and by implication Western education, was seen to corrupt and lead to moral miasma if provided without a Christian moral component. The evidence compiled within the report suggested that missionary education was not achieving the goals to which it aspired. The solution was not to give up, but to find ways to reinstate missionary education as imperative to the morality of the British Empire. Within the colonies this included contemplations on how to establish and maintain Indigenous churches, particularly through training a strong leadership in mission schools. In a further gesture of self-reflection, missionary schooling was seen at Edinburgh as an antidote to rising hyper-intellectualism within Europe itself.[187] The lessons learnt in the global Christian classroom of building schooling on a firm foundation of moral and religious instruction were held up as an effective means to counter the 'moral scepticism' of modern Europeans. The decades after Edinburgh saw closer cooperation between missionary and educational networks, with missionary groups realising the need for professionalisation and presenting themselves as colonial experts in order to 'maintain their influence in a changing world'.[188] Yet, as we have read, Edinburgh was just one of many moments throughout the long nineteenth century in which missionary groups sought to combat their marginalising in modernising societies through asserting their claim to offering a better form of modernity accessible through Christian schooling. Missionary groups thereby continued to argue for their legitimacy and worth in a modernising and secularising world framed by British imperialism.

Notes

1 Columbia University (New York) (CU), Burke Library (BL) Missionary Research Library (MRL) Section 12, World Missionary Conference Records, 1883–2010, Box 19, Series 1, Commission 3, letter by Professor Ernest Burton to Professor Edward Caldwell Moore, 14 September 1909.

2 For more on Burton see: Felicity Jensz, 'The 1910 Edinburgh World Missionary Conference and comparative colonial education', *History of Education*, 47:3 (2018), 339–414, doi: 10.1080/0046760X.2018.1425741. For the report see: World Missionary Conference (WMC), *Report of Commission III. Education in relation to the Christianisation of national life. With supplement: Presentation and discussion of the report in the conference on 17th June 1910 together with the discussion on Christian literature* (Edinburgh and London, New York, Chicago and Toronto: Oliphant, Anderson & Ferrier, Fleming H. Revell Company, 1910).

3 See, for example, Anon, 'Documentation. Towards common witness to Christ today: Mission and visible unity of the Church study paper on theme 8 of the Edinburgh 2010 study process submitted by the Commission on World Mission and Evangelism, World Council of Churches', *International Review of Mission*, 99 (2010), 86–158, doi: 10.1111/j.1758–6631. 2010.00038.x; see also: Klaus Koschorke, 'Die Weltmissionskonferenz Edinburgh 1910 und die Globalisierung des Christentums', *Pastoraltheologie*, 100 (2011), 215–226. Two of the legacies of the 1910 World Missionary Conference in Edinburgh included the establishment of a Continuation committee as well as the establishment of the journal *International Review of Missions*. See: Brian Stanley, 'Edinburgh 1910 and the genesis of the IRM', *International Review of Mission*, 100:2 (2011), 149–159, doi: 10.1111/j.1758–6631.2011.00064.x; see also: Timothy Yates, 'Mission conferences', in Jonathan J. Bonk (ed.), *The Routledge encyclopaedia of missions and missionaries* (New York and London: Routledge, 2010), p. 257.

4 Peter Kallaway, 'Conference litmus: The development of a conference and policy culture in the interwar period with special reference to the New Education Fellowship and British colonial education in Southern Africa', in Kim Tolley (ed.), *Transformations in schooling: Historical and comparative perspectives* (New York: Palgrave Macmillan, 2007), p. 139.

5 In the edited volume on the history and legacy of the Edinburgh Conference there are two articles on Commission III: Ogbu U. Kalu, 'To hang a ladder in the air: An African assessment', in David A. Kerr and Kenneth R. Ross (eds), *Missions then and now* (Oxford: Regnum Books International, 2009), pp. 91–104; M.P. Joseph, 'Missionary education: An ambiguous legacy', in David A. Kerr and Kenneth R. Ross (eds), *Missions then and now* (Oxford: Regnum Books International, 2009), pp. 105–120.

6 Brian Stanley, *The World Missionary Conference, Edinburgh 1910* (Grand Rapids, MI: William B. Eerdmans Publishing Company, 2009), p. 201.

7 Ogbu U. Kalu, 'To hang a ladder in the air: Talking about African education in Edinburgh in 1910', in Chima J. Korieh and Raphael Chijioke Njoku (eds), *Missions, states, and European expansion in Africa* (New York and London: Routledge, 2007), pp. 101–126.

8 WMC, *Report of Commission III*, p. 8.

9 Jensz, 'The 1910 Edinburgh World Missionary Conference'.

10 WMC, *Report of Commission III*, p. 8.

11 See, for example, the contributions in: Martin Fuchs, Antje Linkenbach and Wolfgang Reinhard (eds), *Individualisierung durch Christliche Mission?* (Wiesbaden: Harrossowitz, 2015).

12 W.H.T. Gairdner, *Echoes from Edinburgh 1910: An account and interpretation of the World Missionary Conference* (New York: Layman's Missionary Movement, 1910), p. 115.

13 CU, BL, MRL, Section 12, Box 19, Series 1, Commission 3, letter by Professor Ernest Burton to Professor Edward Caldwell Moore, 14 September 1909.

14 Ibid.

15 Jensz, 'The 1910 Edinburgh World Missionary Conference'.

16 Kalu, 'To hang a ladder in the air' (2007), p. 108.

17 WMC, *Report of Commission III*, p. 369; see also: Stanley, *The World Missionary Conference*, p. 173.

18 Kalu, 'To hang a ladder in the air' (2007), p. 109; Stanley, *The World Missionary Conference*, pp. 170–171.

19 University of York (UY), Papers of the Society of the Sacred Mission (PSSM), Herbert Kelly Papers (HK)/Correspondence[C]/L/469, World Missionary Conference (1910) List of Subjects to be dealt with by Commissions (Private and Confidential).

20 All of the reports from 1910 can be found on the 'Edinburgh 1910 Conference' website: www.edinburgh2010.org/en/resources/1910-conference.html [last accessed 4 October 2020].

21 Stanley, 'Edinburgh 1910 and the genesis of the IRM'; see also: Yates, 'Mission conferences', p. 257.

22 Steven Maughan, '"Mighty England do good": The major English denominations and organisation for the support of foreign missions in the nineteenth century', in Robert A. Bickers and Rosemary Seton (eds), *Missionary encounters: Sources and issues* (Richmond: Curzon Press, 1996), p. 13.

23 WMC, *Report of Commission III*.

24 Kallaway, 'Conference litmus', pp. 123–149; Eckhardt Fuchs, 'Educational sciences, morality and politics: International educational congresses in the early twentieth century', *Paedagogica Historica*, 40:5/6 (2004), 757–784, doi: 10.1080/0030923042000293751.

25 Sue Krige, '"Trustees and agents of the state"? Missions and the formation of policy towards African education, 1910–1920', *South African Historical Journal*, 40 (1999), 81.

26 For the Canadian experience see, for example, the final reports of the Truth and Reconciliation Commission of Canada, at: https://nctr.ca/reports2.php.

27 Kalu, 'To hang a ladder in the air' (2007), p. 108.

28 William Richey Hogg, *Ecumenical foundations: A history of the International Missionary Council and its nineteenth-century background* (New York: Harper & Brothers, 1952). pp. 110–111.

29 Stanley, *The World Missionary Conference*, p. 168.

30 See, for example, UY, PSSM, HK/C/L/469, Reports of Visits to Missionary Colleges. See: World Missionary Conference (WMC), *Report of Commission V. The preparation of missionaries. With supplement: Presentation and discussion of the report in the conference on 22nd June 1910 together with the discussion on Christian literature* (Edinburgh and London, New York, Chicago and Toronto: Oliphant, Anderson & Ferrier, Fleming H. Revell Company, 1910), p. 244.

31 WMC, *Report of Commission III*, pp. 423–424; CU, BL, MRL, Section 12, Box 19, Series 1, Commission 3, Folder 4, Comments and criticisms of proposed Report of Commission III by the Rev. James Henderson D.D., Principal (United Free Church of Scotland) Lovedale, Cape Colony, South Africa. Letter from James Henderson (Lovedale, South Africa) to Rev. John H. Oldham (Edinburgh), 16 February 1910.

32 Gairdner, *Echoes from Edinburgh*, p. 118.

33 WMC, *Report of Commission III*, p. 424.

34 Gairdner, *Echoes from Edinburgh*, pp. 119–120.

35 At this conference CMS, Free Church of Scotland, BMS, LMS, Church of Scotland and WMMS missionaries attended. 'Bengal, Calcutta', in *Papers relative to the Wesleyan Missions and the state of the heathen countries* (London: James Nichols, December 1868), p. 4.

36 Kalu, 'To hang a ladder in the air' (2007), p. 110.

37 John H. Ritson, 'The growth of missionary co-operation since 1910', *International Review of Mission*, 8:1 (1919), 54, doi: 10.1111/j.1758–6631.1919. tb01598.x. See also: Gairdner, *Echoes from Edinburgh*, pp. 123–124.

38 World Missionary Conference (WMC), 1910, *Report of Commission VII. Missions and governments. With supplement: Presentation and discussion of the report in the conference on 20th June 1910* (Edinburgh, London, New York, Chicago and Toronto: Oliphant, Anderson & Ferrier, and Fleming H. Revell Company, 1910), p. 113. See also: Andrew F. Walls, 'Africa as the theatre of Christian engagement with Islam in the nineteenth century', in David Maxwell (ed.), with Ingrid Lawrie, *Christianity and the African imagination: Essays in honour of Adrian Hasting* (Leiden, Boston and Köln: Brill, 2002), p. 59.

39 Kallaway, 'Conference litmus', p. 140.

40 Ibid., pp. 123–149.

41 WMC, *Report of Commission III*, p. 8.

42 A fourth function was that of philanthropic desire to promote general welfare, but this was contested. WMC, *Report of Commission III*, p. 369.

43 WMC, *Report of Commission III*, pp. 369–370; Stanley, *The World Missionary Conference*, p. 191.

44 Brian Stanley, 'The church of the three selves: A perspective from the World Missionary Conference, Edinburgh, 1910', *The Journal of Imperial and Commonwealth History*, 36:3 (2008), 445, doi: 10.1080/030865308023 18524.

45 Ibid., 438–441.

46 WMC, *Report of Commission III*, p. 6.

47 Ibid., p. 8.

48 Ibid., p. 8.

49 Ibid., p. 31.

50 Richard Pierard, 'The World Missionary Conference, Edinburgh 1910: Its shortcomings and historical significance', in Ulrich van der Heyden and Andreas Feldtkeller (eds), *Missionsgeschichte als Geschichte der Globalisierung von Wissen* (Stuttgart: Franz Steiner Verlag, 2012), p. 301.

51 WMC, *Report of Commission VII*, p. 88.

52 Ibid.

53 *Pan-Anglican Congress 1908, Volume III Section B. Christian truth and other intellectual forces. Speeches and discussions together with the papers published for the consideration of the congress* (London, 1908), p. 47.

54 WMC, *Report of Commission VII*, p. 88

55 WMC, *Report of Commission III*, p. 122.

56 WMC, *Report of Commission VII*, p. 5.

57 WMC, *Report of Commission III*, p. 122.

58 Ibid.

59 Gairdner, *Echoes from Edinburgh*, p. 126.

60 For an overview of some of the debates and influences on Japanese education at the turn of the century see, for example, Mark Lincicome, *Imperial subjects as global citizens: Nationalism, internationalism, and education in Japan* (Lanham, MD: Lexington Books, 2009).

61 WMC, *Report of Commission III*, p. 130.

62 Ibid., p. 136.

63 Ibid., p. 111.

64 WMC, *Report of Commission VII*, p. 89.

65 WMC, *Report of Commission III*, p. 84.

66 Jürgen Osterhammel, *Die Verwandlung der Welt: Eine Geschichte des 19. Jahrhunderts*. Jubiläumsedition (München: C.H. Beck, 2015), p. 1267.

67 See, for example, Thoralf Klein, 'Protestant missionary periodicals debate the Boxer War, 1900–1901', in Felicity Jensz and Hanna Acke (eds), *Missions and media: The politics of missionary periodicals in the long nineteenth century* (Stuttgart: Franz Steiner, 2013), pp. 187–204.

68 WMC, *Report of Commission III*, p. 114.

69 Ibid.

70 Ibid., p. 90.
71 Gairdner, *Echoes from Edinburgh*, p. 130.
72 Albert Wu, 'Catholic universities as missionary spaces: Wilhelm Schmidt, Chen Yuan, and the Catholic University in Beijing', *Österreichische Zeitschrift für Geschichtswissenschaften*, 24:2 (2013), 92–112.
73 WMC, *Report of Commission VII*, p. 91.
74 WMC, *Report of Commission V*, pp. 127–128.
75 Ibid., p. 128.
76 WMC, *Report of Commission III*, p. 330.
77 CU, BL, MRL, Section 12, Box 19, Series 1, Commission 3, letter by Professor Ernest Burton to Professor Edward Caldwell Moore, 14 September 1909.
78 Jensz, 'The 1910 Edinburgh World Missionary Conference'.
79 WMC, *Report of Commission III*, pp. 11–14.
80 Ibid., p. 35.
81 WMC, *Report of Commission VII*, p. 90.
82 WMC, *Report of Commission III*, p. 168.
83 Cape of Good Hope [A 1- '08] *Report of the Select Committee on Native Education* (Cape Town: Cape Times Limited Government Printers, 1908).
84 CU, BL, MRL, Section 12, Box 19, Series 1, Commission 3, Folder 4, Comments and Criticisms of Proposed Report of Commission III by the Rev. James Henderson D.D., Principal (United Free Church of Scotland) Lovedale, Cape Colony, South Africa. Letter from James Henderson (Lovedale, South Africa) to Rev. John H. Oldham (Edinburgh), 16 February 1910. For more on Henderson see: Paul Rich, 'The appeals of Tuskegee: James Henderson, Lovedale, and the fortunes of South African liberalism, 1906–1930', *The International Journal of African Historical Studies*, 20:2 (1987), 271–292, doi: 10.2307/219843.
85 CU, BL, MRL, Section 12, Box 19, Series 1, Commission 3, Folder 4, Comments and Criticisms, Letter from Henderson, p. 24.
86 WMC, *Report of Commission VII*, p. 90.
87 WMC, *Report of Commission III*, p. 167.
88 CU, BL, MRL, Section 12, Box 19, Series 1, Commission 3, Folder 4, Comments and Criticisms, Letter from Henderson, p. 24.
89 WMC, *Report of Commission III*, p. 179.
90 D.M. Schreuder, 'The cultural factor in Victorian imperialism: A case-study of the British "civilising mission"', *The Journal of Imperial and Commonwealth History*, 4 (1976), 283–317, doi: 10.1080/03086537608582465.
91 Andrew Paterson, '"The gospel of work does not save souls": Conceptions of industrial and agricultural education for Africans in the Cape Colony, 1890–1930', *History of Education Quarterly*, 45 (2005), 377–404, doi: 10.1111/j.1748-5959.2005.tb00040.x.
92 WMC, *Report of Commission III*, p. 167.
93 Ibid., p. 169.
94 Ibid., p. 191. Such arguments would be echoed throughout the twentieth century. For a South African example pertaining to Bantu Education; see: Linda

Chisholm, *Teacher preparation in South Africa: History, policy and future directions* (Bingley, UK: Emerald Publishing, 2019), esp. chapter 5.

95 Gairdner, *Echoes from Edinburgh*, p. 125.

96 Schreuder, 'The cultural factor in Victorian imperialism', p. 292.

97 Segregation was the method preferred in many settler colonies such as Canada. See, for example, James R. Miller, *Shingwauk's vision: A history of Native residential schools* (Toronto: University of Toronto Press, 2009).

98 See: Norman Etherington, 'Individualization in Southeast Africa: Missions and the colonial state', in Martin Fuchs et al. (eds), *Individualisierung durch Christliche Mission?* (Wiesbaden: Harrossowitz, 2015), pp. 582–598.

99 Chisholm, *Teacher preparation in South Africa*, p. 43.

100 WMC, *Report of Commission III*, p. 213.

101 Kalu, 'To hang a ladder in the air' (2007).

102 WMC, *Report of Commission III*, p. 170.

103 Ibid., p. 171.

104 Rebecca Swartz, *Education and empire: Children, race and humanitarianism in the British settler colonies, 1833–1880* (Cham: Palgrave Macmillan, 2019).

105 WMC, *Report of Commission III*, p. 369.

106 On the Phelps-Stokes Commission and their visitations in West, South, Central and East Africa between 1920–1924 see, for example, Stephen J. Ball, 'Imperialism, social control and the colonial curriculum in Africa', *Journal of Curriculum Studies*, 15:3 (1983), 237–263, doi: 10.1080/0022027830150302; Edward H. Berman, 'American influence on African education: The role of the Phelps-Stokes Fund's Education Commissions', *Comparative Education Review* 15:2 (1971), 132–145; George E. Urch, 'Education and colonialism in Kenya', *History of Education Quarterly*, 11:3 (1971), 249–264, doi: 10.2307/367292; Eric S. Yellin, 'The (White) search for (Black) order: The Phelps-Stokes Fund's first twenty years, 1911–1931', *The Historian*, 652 (2002), 319–352. There is a vast amount of literature on the development of commissions in the development of sub-Saharan African educational policies. It is beyond the scope of this work to provide an exhaustive listing. For some overviews see the contributions in: *International handbook of comparative education* edited by Robert Cowen and Andreas M. Kazamias (Dordrecht, Heidelberg, London and New York: Springer, 2009); see also: Lord Hailey, *An African survey: A study of problems arising in Africa south of the Sahara* (Oxford: Oxford University Press, 1938); Aaron Windel, 'British colonial education in Africa: Policy and practice in the era of trusteeship', *History Compass*, 7:1 (2009), 1–21, doi: 10.1111/j.1478–0542.2008.00560.x; Clive Whitehead, 'The historiography of British imperial education policy, Part II: Africa and the rest of the colonial empire', *History of Education*, 34:4 (2005), 441–454, doi: 10.1080/00467600500138147.

107 WMC, *Report of Commission III*, p. 4.

108 Kalu, 'To hang a ladder in the air' (2007), p. 108; Godfrey N. Brown, 'British educational policy in West and Central Africa', *The Journal of Modern African Studies*, 2:3 (1964), 366.

109 Kenneth King, 'Africa and the southern states of the USA: Notes on J.H. Oldham and American Negro education for Africans', *Journal of African History*, 10:4 (1969), 660.

110 WMC, *Report of Commission III*, p. 169. A similar conclusion is made in Kalu, 'To hang a ladder in the air' (2009), p. 100.

111 Paterson, '"The gospel of work"', 395–396.

112 WMC, *Report of Commission III*, p. 187.

113 Paterson, '"The gospel of work"', p. 382.

114 Ibid., p. 387.

115 WMC, *Report of Commission III*, p. 277.

116 CU, BL, MRL, Section 12, Box 19, Series 1, Commission 3, Folder 4, Comments and Criticisms, Letter from Henderson, p. 4.

117 Ibid.

118 WMC, *Report of Commission III*, pp. 273–274.

119 Ibid., p. 213.

120 Ibid.

121 See, for example, Gita Steiner-Khamsi and Hubert O. Quist, 'The politics of educational borrowing: Reopening the case of Achimota in British Ghana', *Comparative Education Review*, 44 (2000), 272–299, doi: 10.1086/447615.

122 Udo Bude, 'The adaptation concept in British colonial education', *Comparative Education*, 19 (1983), 341–355.

123 WMC, *Report of Commission III*, p. 210.

124 Ibid.

125 See, for example, 'Introduction', *Periodical Accounts*, 1 (1790), 5–16, 13–14.

126 WMC, *Report of Commission III*, p. 211.

127 Elizabeth E. Prevost, 'Troubled traditions: Female adaptive education in British colonial Africa', *The Journal of Imperial and Commonwealth History*, 45 (2017), 475–505, doi: 10.1080/03086534.2017.1332134.

128 CU, BL, MRL, Section 12, Box 19, Series 1, Commission 3, Folder 4, Comments and Criticisms, Letter from Henderson, p. 14.

129 Ibid.

130 WMC, *Report of Commission III*, p. 313.

131 Judith Rowbotham, '"Hear an Indian sister's plea": Reporting the work of 19th-century British female missionaries', *Women's Studies International Forum*, 21:3 (1998), 251, doi: 10.1016/S0277–5395(98)00022–3.

132 Elizabeth Prevost, 'On feminists, functionalists, and friends: Lobola and the gender politics of imperial trusteeship in interwar Britain', *The Journal of Modern History*, 89 (2017), 562–600, doi: 10.1086/693002; Lynn M. Thomas, '"Imperial concerns and women's affairs": State efforts to regulate clitoridectomy and eradicate abortion in Meru, Kenya, c. 1910–1950', *The Journal of African History*, 39 (1998), 121–145, doi: 00218537, 14695138; Antoinette Burton, 'States of injury: Josephine Butler on slavery, citizenship, and the Boer War', *Social Politics: International Studies in Gender, State & Society*, 5 (1998), 338–361, doi: 10.1093/sp/5.3.338.

133 Elizabeth Prevost, *The communion of women: Missions and gender in colonial Africa and the British metropole* (Oxford: Oxford University Press, 2010).

134 Jensz, 'The 1910 Edinburgh World Missionary Conference'.

135 Eugene Stock, *The history of the Church Missionary Society: Supplementary volume* (London: Church Missionary Society, 1916).

136 Ibid., p. 6.

137 Ibid.

138 The Secretaries to the Conference, *Conference on missions held in 1860 at Liverpool: Including the papers read, the deliberations, and the conclusions reached; with a comprehensive index shewing the various matters brought under review* (London: Strangeways & Walden, 1860), pp. 122–123.

139 WMC, *Report of Commission III*, p. 31.

140 Ibid.

141 Henry Rosher James, *Education and statesmanship in India, 1797–1910* (London and New York: Longmans, Green, 1911), pp. 4 and 74.

142 Stock, *The history of the Church Missionary Society: Supplementary volume*, p. 143.

143 C.F. Andrews, *The renaissance in India, its missionary aspect* (London: Church Missionary Society, 1912), p. 10

144 WMC, *Report of Commission III*, p. 31.

145 Kalu, 'To hang a ladder in the air' (2007), pp. 113–114.

146 See: Anil Seal, *The emergence of Indian nationalism: Competition and collaboration in the later nineteenth century* (Cambridge: Cambridge University Press, 1968).

147 Charles V. Reed, *Royal tourist, colonial subject and the making of a British world, 1860–1911* (Manchester: Manchester University Press, 2016), p. 154 fn 4.

148 WMC, *Report of Commission III*, pp. 171 and 192–195. The Ethiopianism movement was purportedly enthusiastically embraced by many African intelligentsia including many at Lovedale, an institution of the Free Church of Scotland. See, for example, Greg Cuthbertson, '"Cave of Adullam": Missionary reaction to Ethiopianism at Lovedale, 1898–1902', *Missionalia*, 19:1 (1991), 57–64. Missionaries at Lovedale disagreed that the movement was so influential; see: CU, BL, MRL, Section 12, Box 19, Series 1, Commission 3, Folder 4, Comments and Criticisms, Letter from Henderson, p. 24. For a brief overview of the movement(s), in somewhat outdated terminology see: George Shepperson, 'Ethiopianism and African nationalism', *Phylon*, 14:1 (1953), 9–18.

149 WMC, *Report of Commission III*, pp. 193–194. See also: Norman Etherington, 'Indivdualization in Southeast Africa: Missions and the colonial state', in Martin Fuchs et al. (eds), *Individualisierung durch Christliche Mission?* (Wiesbaden: Harrossowitz, 2015), pp. 591–596.

150 CU, BL, MRL, Section 12, Box 19, Series 1, Commission 3, Folder 4, Comments and Criticisms, Letter from Henderson, p. 24.

151 James, *Education and statesmanship in India*, pp. 29–30.

152 University of London (UL), School of Oriental and African Studies Archive (SOAS), © United Reformed Church, PEC/FMC Series 1, Box 59, file 2, Behari Lal Singh, *Our orphan home* (London: W. Spearing, 1874), pp. 21–22.

153 James, *Education and statesmanship in India*, pp. 132, 134–135.

154 UL, SOAS, © United Reformed Church, PCE/FMC Series 1, Box 59, File 1, *The eighth Indian report of the Bauleah Mission in connection with the Presbyterian Church in England, in 1870–1871* (Baptist Mission Press: Calcutta, 1871), p. 7.

155 UL, SOAS, © United Reformed Church, PCE/FMC Series 1, Box 59, File 2. *Minute on the resolution of the Indian Government on the report of the Education Commission of the General Council of Education in India* (Edinburgh: Lorimer & Gilles, 1885).

156 WMC, *Report of Commission III*, p. 32.

157 Ibid.

158 Stanley, *The World Missionary Conference*, p. 195.

159 Sanjay Seth, *Subject lessons: The Western education of colonial India* (Durham, NC: Duke University Press, 2007), pp. 47–48. See also: Tim Allender, *Ruling through education: The politics of schooling in the colonial Punjab* (New Delhi: New Dawn Press, 2006). Hayden J.A. Bellenoit, *Missionary education and empire in late colonial India, 1860–1920* (London: Pickering & Chatto, 2007).

160 WMC, *Report of Commission III*, p. 43.

161 Ibid., p. 44. See also: Tim Allender, *Learning femininity in colonial India, 1820–1932* (Manchester: Manchester University Press, 2016).

162 WMC, *Report of Commission III*, p. 43.

163 Ibid.

164 Benoy Bhusan Roy and Pranati Ray, *Zenana mission: The role of Christian missionaries for the education of women in the 19th century Bengal* (Delhi: Indian Society for Promoting Christian Knowledge, 1998), p. 191.

165 WMC, *Report of Commission III*, p. 51.

166 See the discussion on Protestant missions and individualisation in: Martin Fuchs, Antje Linkenbach and Wolfgang Reinhard (eds), *Individualisierung durch christliche Mission?* (Wiesbaden: Harrossowitz, 2015).

167 James, *Education and statesmanship in India*, p. 44.

168 Ibid., p. 47.

169 Ibid., p. 59.

170 Leslie A. Flemming, 'A new humanity: American missionaries' ideals for women in North India, 1870–1930', in Nupur Chaudhuri and Margaret Strobel (eds), *Western women and imperialism: Complicity and resistance* (Bloomington and Indianapolis: Indiana University Press, 1992), pp. 191–206.

171 Angus McLaren, 'Abortion in England, 1890–1914', *Victorian Studies*, 20:4 (1977), 379–400.

172 See, for example, Anita Anand, *Sophia: Princess, suffragette, revolutionary* (London: Bloomsbury Publishing, 2015).

173 Antoinette M. Burton, 'The white woman's burden: British feminists and the Indian woman, 1865–1915', *Women's Studies International Forum*, 13:4 (1990), 299, doi: 10.1016/0277–5395(90)90027-U.

174 WMC, *Report of Commission III*, p. 43. See also: 'ART. VI.-1. The daughters of India: Their social condition, religion, literature, obligations, and prospects', *London Review* (April 1861), 154–155.

175 See, for, example, Tony Ballantyne and Antoinette Burton, *Moving subjects: Gender, mobility, and intimacy in an age of global empire* (Urbana and Chicago: University of Illinois Press, 2009); Ann L. Stoler, "Making empire respectable: The politics of race and sexual morality in 20th-century colonial cultures', *American Ethnologist*, 16:4 (1989), 634–660; Elisa Camiscioli, 'Women, gender, intimacy, and empire', *Journal of Women's History*, 25 (2013), 138–148, 10.1353/jowh.2013.0056.

176 Andrews, *The renaissance in India*, pp. 24–25.

177 Ibid., p. 58.

178 Stanley, *The World Missionary Conference, Edinburgh 1910*, p. 187.

179 Ibid.

180 Nira Wickramasinghe, 'Colonial governmentality: Critical notes from a perspective of South Asian studies', *Comparativ: Zeitschrift für Globalgeschichte und Vergleichende Gesellschaftsforschung*, 21:1 (2011), 32–40; David Scott, 'Colonial governmentality', *Social Text*, 43 (1995), 191–220.

181 WMC, *Report of Commission III*, p. 8.

182 Ibid., pp. 6–8.

183 WMC, *Report of Commission V*, p. 7.

184 Ibid.

185 Ibid., pp. 7, 9–10.

186 The evidence from the French colony of Madagascar underscores this point by demonstrating the strict conditions that the government placed on missionary education including inspections and examinations. More detrimental to missionary schools was the government requirement that all scholars of higher education (including normal, medical, law and industrial schools) had to have at least two years of governmental schooling to attend. Simultaneously, the government opened up more schools that were purely secular, and, even anti-religious. See: WMC, *Report of Commission III*, pp. 201–202.

187 WMC, *Report of Commission III*, p. 424.

188 Jensz, 'The 1910 Edinburgh World Missionary Conference'; Kallaway, 'Conference litmus', p. 139.

Conclusion

The idea that missionary schooling was a necessary tool to introduce non-Europeans to missionary modernity within British colonial settings proved to be remarkably robust over the nineteenth century. In this logic, missionary societies were the most suited to provide schooling as they were the only ones with the ability to provide religious and moral instruction infused across all aspects of the curricula and thereby help colonised societies to fulfil their potential. There remained constant optimism attached to the belief that missionary schooling was beneficial in spite of changes in stages of mission, government involvement, curricula, increasing examinations and fluctuating non-European engagement. Even at the World Missionary Conference in Edinburgh in 1910, where a sense of disappointment was expressed at missionary schooling having not attained its goals, a fundamental belief in the necessity of missionary schooling held fast conceding only that its form needed to be reconsidered in response to the various threats that it was up against, including the spread of Islam, the increasing nationalisation of educational systems and burgeoning nationalist sentiments. It was considered important for missionary schooling to continue and strive to further its hold despite these pressures. Moreover, missionary education with its focus upon mind, body and soul was considered to provide an antidote to Western secular education that produced hyper-intellectual Western moral sceptics. Practitioners in the mission field had fought to maintain the place of religion in mission schools believing that civilisation without Christianisation was 'a mere matter of clothes and whitewash'.[1] Experts who congregated at Edinburgh used the lessons from the mission field to conceptually reassert the place of religion in the metropole.

This book has examined competing expectations held over the long nineteenth century for the schooling of non-Europeans in the British Empire by evangelical missionary societies, various governments and non-European groups as a means to participate in or reject certain ideas about 'modernity' within the colonial context. It has considered the debates surrounding the provision of missionary schooling in British governmental settings, in international interdenominational missionary conferences, in the writings of local non-European missionaries and in contemporaneous local debates on the value and function of missionary schooling. The debates around schooling highlight broader tensions surrounding expectations for non-Europeans within modernising societies. Moreover, they demonstrate how British missionary groups sought to combat their marginalisation in the nineteenth century during a period of secularisation by dynamically positioning themselves as the most apt providers of education to non-Europeans within the British colonies. Schooling, as an aspect of missionary modernity, was an important site where changing ideas of gender, class, morality, legitimacy and adaptability were played out. Missionary schooling was a complex, heterogeneous and messy affair with the terms used to describe it shifting and transforming in response to external pressure as well as to fit changing ideals held by missionary groups. Despite temporal, spatial and cultural variations, there remained a belief in the essential need for mission schools, with this belief itself contributing to the homogenisation of the ideal of missionary schooling, creating a circular argument that has remained difficult to question. One of the aims of this book has been to chart the ways in which ideals of missionary schooling reflected various influences in the British Empire, as a means to consider the broader relationship between missionary modernity and colonial modernity with its secularising effects.

Missionary schools as a political tool

The distinction made in this book between colonial modernity and missionary modernity underscores the point that – despite the continued assertion of some scholars – missionary groups cannot be equated exclusively with empire.[2] They worked both within and beyond the limits of colonial settings and contributed to knowledge of the boundaries of the British Empire, seeing themselves often as the moral counterweight to the negative effects of colonisation and civilisation. They were often the first groups to provide education, and in places such as sub-Saharan Africa were the major providers of education well into the twentieth century. Missionary groups held a belief that progress equated with the moral and religious 'improvement' of non-Europeans and worked tirelessly to realise such progress through providing religious instruction. Moral progress was seen as a prerequisite for assimilation into colonial structures, with religious moral teachings assumed to enable non-Europeans to resist the temptations of modern society. For various governments of British colonial spaces, morally upstanding subjects were also desirable so that society could be regulated and controlled without recourse to expensive police systems or extensive legal systems. Indeed, non-Europeans needed to be Christian in order to swear on the Bible and to give evidence in courts of law, thus necessitating their conversion to Christianity. The emancipation of slaves in the British Empire provided an opportunity for missionary groups to collaborate with the imperial government in supplying schooling. Missionary groups placed themselves as the sole groups qualified to provide the moral and religious training needed in post-emancipation societies. Within government debates the centrality of Christian religion was not questioned; rather, these debates were centred upon the question as to who should provide moral and religious schooling, effectively abdicating responsibility for constructing civic and religious identity. These were not just empty debates, but had ramifications for the standing of Nonconformist groups in Britain, with government funding providing legitimation for these groups in their quest for funding and support from home audiences.

The collaborations between governments and missionary bodies in providing education appear at first glance to be symbiotic; however, there were tensions that did not always make these relationships smooth. Government intervention was contested, ignored and responded to through acts of professionalisation and collaboration, resulting in highly ambiguous relationships between missionary groups and governments. The weak secularisation forces evident in the early nineteenth century slowly gave way to more stringent means of separating church and religion from government roles. Government grants meant conditions, inspections and control. In collaborating with governments to provide education, missionaries were drawn into local and colonial government systems, and in many cases into secular educational systems. These conditions brought with them the need for commonality and standardisation which characterised the latter stages of missionary education, just as adaptation and individualisation had characterised the earlier stages. Through collaborating with governments, missionary schooling was secularised in terms of curricula as well as through the effects of inspections, both areas in which missionary groups relinquished control to governments in exchange for economic support. The reactions of missionary groups and individuals to government regulation, control, inspection and examination were highly diverse as exemplified in this study through the consideration of the varied reactions of different missionaries from the same society under the same political entity in the same geographical location. Government control could be seen as a means to improve the quality of schools with many missionaries actively wishing for government control through inspection, while holding fast to ideals of non-interference in the teaching of religion and morals.

Mission schools were used as political tools in many spaces, pertinently in settler colonies such as Canada and Australia where the control over Indigenous peoples was more invasive than in places where the majority of the population were non-European, or in India, where government support for schools was nominally secular. Missionary schooling could be used as a means to exclude Indigenous people from the broader populations until they had obtained skills considered sufficient for them to assimilate into broader society, as was the case in Canada, particularly through the residential schools system. For missionary groups, schools were spaces in which the individual could be shaped into a model Christian, with this philanthropic endeavour contributing to the 'raising' of individuals, families and communities. Yet schools were more than that. Schooling was a means to discipline the body, mind and soul of non-European pupils, contributing to humanitarian understandings of social order. It was also a means to normalise knowledge and to shape non-Europeans into industrious, diligent Christian members of colonial societies, allowing them to participate in colonial modernity. Schooling 'civilised' people was simultaneously considered a sign of a civilised people. Yet, as was evident throughout the century, these ideals were often not achieved, with local people behaving contrary to missionary expectations and following their own agendas.

Missionary education as a religious ideal

Religion was an important aspect of the British Empire; however, as David Bebbington noted in 2003, it is often relegated to the margins of analysis.[3] In spite of increased scholarly interest since that time, religion still remains understudied in considerations of Empire.[4] As this study has aptly demonstrated, missionary groups are an important lens to examine tensions that arose between religion and politics in relation to moral reform and philanthropic drive in the colonies. Missionaries worked within empire, yet the beliefs and aims of missionaries and colonial administrators never completely overlapped: tensions, gaps and jagged edges meant that ideologies did not, or could not, be smoothly joined. Missionaries were more often focused upon the philanthropic aims of schooling in terms of providing individuals with the skills considered necessary to survive in a modernising world, particularly in terms of moral self-control. The philanthropic aim complemented, yet was also distinct from, humanitarian notions that wished to change systems that negatively impacted upon individuals, such as with the system of slavery. Together humanitarians and missionaries provided information on the state of non-Europeans in British colonies, and in doing so constantly reminded the metropole of its moral obligation to its denizens. For many missionaries this moral obligation included schooling to allow non-Europeans to engage fully with the Christian message through reading.

The educational work of Nonconformist missionaries in the colonies affected their standing in the metropole, as revealed by the preceding discussions of the introduction of the Negro Education Grant in the West Indies in the 1830s. Nonconformists positioned themselves as potential partners for the imperial government in the provision of schooling to emancipated slaves and in doing so gained legitimacy for their work, which could be used as a 'powerful plea' amongst supporters in Britain. Relationships between government and missionary bodies, especially Nonconformists, needed to be negotiated to ensure the effective provision of schooling and the effective maintenance of political power. Although they were natural allies, not all missionaries worked with governments, not all did so harmoniously, nor did all accept the conditions attached to government funds. For those groups which did accept funds, some saw it as a 'poisoned chalice' while others complained about the secularisation of their work. As this study has demonstrated, discussions surrounding the schooling of local people reflected broader debates as to the role of religion in the formation of the modern political subject, and also, implicitly, the place of religion within modernising Western societies.

Networks of knowledge

Missionary schooling was a global endeavour which connected the pupil under instruction into broader global networks through the circulation of knowledge. This book has considered the global networks of knowledge circulating around and connecting mission schools across the globe. The exposure of non-Europeans to normalised Western knowledge ruptured local epistemologies and provided alternative views that were assumed to be superior for the creation of moral, modern subjects. Enlightenment-inspired ideas of reason and individual conscience were espoused as setting the 'heathen' free from superstition, yet were deemed valid only if embedded within Protestant Christian frameworks. Missionaries could not, however, control the way in which the knowledge that they disseminated through schooling was circulated, changed and adapted, which led to much anxiety, but no solutions other than to increase the supervision of pupils. Although the transmission of knowledge was never a one-way process, there was little scope for non-Europeans to contribute to global networks of knowledge; rather, information about and extending from them was invariably filtered through religious and imperial lenses.

Knowledge of missionary schooling also circulated through missionary conferences, providing individuals and societies access to information of potential aid in devising, establishing and maintaining current and future mission schools. The denominational and increasingly interdenominational international networks created and extended at these conferences provided a valuable means of connecting, consolidating and crystallising knowledge about the education of non-European peoples. The heterogeneous nature of schooling became ordered, measured and conceptually controlled through the provision of recommendations for future work. Once again there were only limited opportunities for non-Europeans to be involved in these networks, as reflected in the low numbers of non-European delegates at such meetings into the twentieth century. The dissemination and presentation of knowledge about mission schools to home audiences was also carefully monitored, edited and controlled. Those snippets of information that reached European audiences reflected the centrality of schooling in evangelising non-European peoples, and the beliefs in the transformative power of Western knowledge. Reports on the progress of schools or examination results also contributed to images of advancement of the 'rising generation'.

Regional and federal governments required missionary groups to provide information about the state of their schools as a condition of grants, or sent government inspectors to collect such information. This information mostly remained within these colonial or national settings, unable to reverberate out to international realms, unlike the information that was provided at missionary conferences or through missionary periodicals. Interconnections between missionary groups and professional educationalists only became more evident after the 1930s through international educational networks that brought professional educationalists and missionary networks in closer contact.[5] As this study has argued, missionary groups professionalised themselves from the late nineteenth century in order to secure their position as experts in education. This trend to professionalisation was evident at the World Missionary Conference in Edinburgh in 1910 where knowledge networks had brought together masses of information from missionary groups in diverse parts of the globe. The collation, analysis and synthesis of this information enabled specific and general suggestions to be made as to the future direction of the educational work of missionaries. Missionaries were urged to adapt their educational offerings in response to pressures from a modernising world. The report of Commission III on education also conveyed an anxiety that the Christian churches had not undertaken enough work to ensure that Christian education would be nationalised, leaving it open to being deemed foreign and thus rejected in light of growing nationalist movements across the colonial and postcolonial world.

The dynamics of missionary schooling

One of the themes of this book has been the dynamics of missionary schooling. Missionaries believed in the progression of mission through the three stages of introductory/initial, permanent and reproductive in which the ultimate goal of native churches was realised. Throughout these stages non-Europeans were expected to be raised ever further as individuals, communities and societies towards Western expectations of a particular form of modernity: missionary modernity. People were to break free from the superstitions that fettered them to 'heathen' cultures through the lessons that Christian schooling provided them. The preparation of Native teachers was seen as essential to the permanent stage of mission; however, local teachers were often considered lacking and the aim of native churches remained elusive. In the early stage of mission, adaptation and individualisation of educational offerings were important, whereas commonality and standardisation were important aspects of the later stages. The three major aims of missionary schooling – evangelistic, edificatory and leavening – were considered to be in a dynamic interrelationship, positively reverberating in individuals, communities and societies. Local people were not passive recipients of missionary education; their resistance to, resilience against and engagement with various forms of knowledge transfer and production affected what and how missionaries taught. Voices of local teachers, such as Behari Lal Singh, could bring to a British and global audience broader concerns that local teachers in the schools had, including low remuneration, which itself was a reflection of more complex issues including low valuation of local workers, chronic shortages of funds and the difficulties in providing higher educational standards. In progressing through various stages, mission schools also dynamically responded to the political and social environment and to external expectations placed upon curricula. As this book has argued, schools became more formalised, disciplined and standardised in response to increased government intervention and progressively so as external controls such as examinations were introduced. Subsequently there was increasingly less room for the wants or needs of non-Europeans to be incorporated into curricula. By the World Missionary Conference of Edinburgh in 1910 the normalisation and standardisation of Western knowledge in mission schools was seen to be counterproductive to the goal of 'Christianisation of National Life'. A solution touted was that curricula should be adapted to local needs. Such considerations demonstrate that Western education was not seen to be a uniform solution to the perceived needs of non-Europeans. It took time, however, for this conclusion to be reached, and even then, it was without significant representation of or considerations from non-Europeans.

Governments also affected the dynamics of missionary schooling through their support or through providing competition to mission schools. Government grants were often connected to conditions that secularised mission schools in terms of both curricula and structures. Schools were not the only place where religious ideas could be disseminated, yet the knowledge that was transmitted in schools was considered crucial to the identity formation of pupils through shaping the body, mind and soul to reflect Christian ideals. The ideology behind the provision of missionary schooling was never going to be realised in the messy, ever-changing realities of the colonial world. The aspirations that missionaries held for religious schooling did not always overlap with those of their pupils, and the forces of government impinged in many places on the ability to provide liberal and comprehensive religious education. Despite changes in forms and functions of mission schools, the ideology that held Christian religious instruction as essential to the formation of a model modern moral subject was never placed in question. The robustness of this idea and the hope that perseverance would lead to the 'Christianisation of National Life' reverberated in the metropole and continues in many religious circles well into the twenty-first century.

Notes

1 James Stewart, *Lovedale, South Africa: Illustrated by fifty views from photographs* (Edinburgh and Glasgow: Andrew Elliot and David Bryce and Son, 1894), p. 4.
2 For example, in a recent study on infant schools in the early nineteenth century missionaries were equated with the British Empire, this is despite the historiographical tradition established by Andrew Porter. See: Sarah de Leeuw and Margo Greenwood, 'Foreword. History lessons: What *empire, education, and Indigenous childhoods* teaches us', in Helen May, Baljit Kaur and Larry Pochner, *Empire, education, and Indigenous childhoods: Nineteenth-century missionary infant schools in three British colonies* (Farnham: Ashgate, 2014), p. xix; Andrew Porter, *Religion versus empire? British Protestant missionaries and overseas expansion, 1700–1914* (Manchester: Manchester University Press, 2004).
3 See: David W. Bebbington, 'Atonement, sin and empire, 1888–1914', in Andrew Porter (ed.), *The imperial horizon of British Protestant missions 1880–1914* (Grand Rapids, MI: William B. Eerdmans, 2003), p. 14. See also: Peter Kallaway, 'Education, health and social welfare in the late colonial context: The International Missionary Council and educational transition in the interwar years with

specific reference to colonial Africa', *History of Education*, 38:2 (2009), 217–246, doi: 10.1080/00467600801969786.

4 See, for example, Hilary M. Carey, *God's empire: Religion and colonialism in the British world, c. 1801–1908* (Cambridge: Cambridge University Press, 2011).

5 Peter Kallaway, 'Conference litmus: The development of a conference and policy culture in the interwar period with special reference to the New Education Fellowship and British colonial education in Southern Africa', in Kim Tolley (ed.), *Transformations in schooling: Historical and comparative perspectives* (New York: Palgrave Macmillan, 2007), pp. 123–149.

Select bibliography

Archives

The United Kingdom

The National Archives (TNA), UK
Colonial Office (CO) 318 Colonial Office and Predecessors: West Indies Original
Correspondence
115 West India Miscellaneous 1833, vol. 2, Miscellaneous A to Z
117 West India Miscellaneous 1833, vol. 4, Slavery Abolition, Part 2
118 West India Miscellaneous 1834, vol. 1, Public Office
122 West India Miscellaneous 1835, vol. 3, Negro Education
131 West India Miscellaneous 1837, vol. 4, Negro Education Religious Societies
University of Birmingham, Cadbury Research Library Special Collections, Church
Mission Society Archive (CMS)
ACC – Church Missionary Society Unofficial Papers
Accession 362: Papers of Rev John Fearby Haslam (1838–1849)
F- Family Papers
B – Foreign (later Overseas) Division, OMS – Overseas (Missions) Series
1803–1934, CE – Ceylon mission
C CE O19 Ceylon controversy papers, 1875–1880
C CE O20 Paper relating to education, 1833–1876
C CE O22 Papers relating to catechists, 1832–1876
C CE O23 Miscellaneous reports, 1831–1879
C CE O24 Miscellaneous letters written direct to headquarters, 1821–1878
C CE O25 Miscellaneous papers
C CE O26 Miscellaneous printed papers. 1826–1865
C CE E1 Letters and papers: 3 April 1815–17 February 1820
C CE M17 (1877–1878), Mission Books [incoming]
G – General Secretary's Department, AC – Administration, Correspondence
19 Letter books of Dandeson Coates' private and confidential correspondence
1824–1847, two volumes
University of Cambridge Library, Cambridge, UK
Society for Promoting Christian Knowledge Archive (SPCK Archive)
Manuscript A33/4, Special Committee Minutes, 1713–30
Manuscript (MS) B1, Society's Reports, 1704–1714
University of London (UL), School of Oriental and African Studies Archive (SOAS),
UK

Microfilm M6293 (Reel 1), The London Secretaries' Association minutes, 1819–1848

© United Reformed Church, Presbyterian Church of England Foreign Missions Committee Archives (PCE), Foreign Mission Committee (FMC)

8 – Bangladesh/East Pakistan

/01 – Correspondence, minutes and reports

/01 – Early Correspondence and Papers/

/02 – Individual files

/08 – Rev. Behari Lal Singh

/03 – Miscellaneous and Printed Materials

Council for World Mission Archive (CWMA)/London Missionary Society (LMS)/ South Africa incoming correspondence/

Box 16A/1838

Box 21/1845

University of York (UY)

Papers of the Society of the Sacred Mission (PSSM), Herbert Kelly Papers (HK)

The United States of America

Columbia University (New York) (CU), Burke Library (BL) Missionary Research Library (MRL)

Section 12, World Missionary Conference Records, 1883–2010

Box 19, Series 1, Commission 3

Printed reports (non-governmental)

Aborigines Protection Society

Report of the Parliamentary Select Committee on Aboriginal Tribes (British Settlements). Reprinted, with comments, by the 'Aborigines Protection Society' (London: William Ball, Aldine Chambers, Paternoster Row, and Hatchard & Son, Piccadilly, 1837).

Liverpool Missionary Conference, 1860

The Secretaries to the Conference, *Conference on missions held in 1860 at Liverpool: Including the papers read, the deliberations, and the conclusions reached; with a comprehensive index shewing the various matters brought under review* (London: Strangeways and Walden, 1860).

World Missionary Conference, 1910, Edinburgh

Report of Commission III. Education in relation to the Christianisation of national life. With supplement: Presentation and discussion of the report in the conference on 17th June 1910 together with the discussion on Christian literature (Edinburgh and London, New York, Chicago and Toronto: Oliphant, Anderson & Ferrier, Fleming H. Revell Company, 1910).

Report of Commission V. The preparation of missionaries. With supplement: Presentation and discussion of the report in the conference on 22nd June 1910 (Edinburgh and London, New York, Chicago and Toronto: Oliphant, Anderson & Ferrier, Fleming H. Revell Company, 1910).

Report of Commission VII. Missions and governments. With supplement: Presentation and discussion of the report in the conference on 20th June 1910 (Edinburgh and London, New York, Chicago and Toronto: Oliphant, Anderson & Ferrier, Fleming H. Revell Company, 1910).

Printed reports (governmental)

UK Parliament, Commons and Lords Hansards 1803–2005 (London, England) [available from http://hansard.millbanksystems.com/index.html], House of Commons Debates (HC Deb) (London, England), House of Lords Debates (HL Deb) (London, England), 1833

House of Commons Parliamentary Papers (HC PP) (London, England) 1831–32 (274) 'Ceylon. Reports of Lieutenant-General Colebrooke and Charles Hay Cameron, Esq.'

    1836 (211) 'Negro education. Statement showing the appropriation, in detail, of the sum of £20,000 voted by Parliament in 1835, towards the erection of school-houses in the colonies'

    1836 (538) 'Report from the Select Committee on Aborigines (British Settlements) Together with the Minutes of Evidence, Appendix and Index'

    1837 (425) 'Report from the Select Committee on Aborigines (British Settlements); with the Minutes of Evidence, Appendix and Index'

Periodicals

Baptist Missionary Magazine
The British And Foreign Review; or, European Quarterly Journal (London, England)
Church Missionary Records, Detailing the Proceedings of the Church Missionary Society (London, England)
The Eclectic Review (London, England)
Evangelisches Missions-Magazin (Basel, Switzerland)
Evangelical Magazine and Missionary Chronicle (London, England)
London and Westminster Review (London, England)
London Review (London, England)
The Methodist Magazine (London, England)
Missionary Magazine (Boston, USA)
Missionary Magazine and Chronicle (London, England)
The Missionary Register (London, England)
The Monthly Review (London, England)
Periodical Accounts Relating to The Missions of the Church of the United Brethren, established among the Heathen (London, England)
Quarterly Journal of Education (London, England)
The Wesleyan-Methodist Magazine. Being a continuation of the Arminian or Methodist magazine first published by the Rev. John Wesley (London, England)
The Wesleyan Missionary Notices, Relating Principally to the Foreign Missions under the Direction of The Methodist Conference (London, England)

Printed material

Akenson, Donald H., *The Irish education experiment. The national system of education in the nineteenth century* (London and Toronto: Routledge & Kegan Paul and University of Toronto Press, 1970).

Allender, Tim, *Learning femininity in colonial India, 1820–1932* (Manchester: Manchester University Press, 2016).

Andrews, C.F., *The renaissance in India, its missionary aspect* (London: Church Missionary Society, 1912).

Anagol, Padma, 'Indian Christian women, c. 1850–c.1920', in Clare Midgley (ed.), *Gender and imperialism* (Manchester, Manchester University Press, 1998), pp. 79–103.

Anon, *Leading incidents connected with a missionary tour in the Gangetic Districts of Bengal; Undertaken by Behari Lal Singh & friends, chiefly with a view to distribute the Scriptures* (Calcutta: Baptist Mission Press, 1853).

Azamede, Kokou, 'Ewe-Christen zwischen Württemberg und westafrikanischen Missionsstationen (1884–1939)', in Rebekka Habermas and Richard Hölzl (eds), *Mission Global: Eine Verflechtungsgeschichte seit dem 19. Jahrhundert* (Köln, Weimar, Wien: Böhlau Verlag, 2014), pp. 177–198.

Bacchus, M. Kazim, *Education as and for legitimacy: Developments in West Indian education between 1846–1895* (Waterloo, Ontario: Wilfrid Laurier University Press, 1994).

Ball, Stephen J., 'Imperialism, social control and the colonial curriculum in Africa', *Journal of Curriculum Studies*, 15:3 (1983), 237–263, doi: 10.1080/0022027830150302.

Ballantyne, Tony, *Webs of empire, locating New Zealand's colonial past* (Vancouver and Toronto: UBC Press, 2012).

Ballantyne, Tony and Antoinette Burton, *Moving subjects: Gender, mobility, and intimacy in an age of global empire* (Urbana and Chicago: University of Illinois Press, 2009).

Barnard, John, 'The survival and loss rates of psalms, ABCs, psalters and primers from the stationers stock, 1660–1700', *The Library*, s6–21:2 (1999), 148–150, doi: 10.1093/library/s6–21.2.148.

Barnett, Michael, *Empire of humanity: A history of humanitarianism* (Ithaca, NY: Cornell University Press, 2011).

Barry, Amanda, '"Equal to children of European origin": Educability and the civilising mission in early colonial Australia', *History Australia* 5:2 (2008), 41.1–41.16, doi: 10.2104/ha080041.

Bartholomeusz, Tessa, 'Catholics, Buddhists, and the Church of England: The 1883 Sri Lankan riots', *Buddhist-Christian Studies*, 15 (1995), 89–103, doi: 10.2307/1390037.

Bayly, C.A., 'The second British Empire', in Robin W. Winks and Alaine Low (eds), *The Oxford history of the British Empire*, vol. 5, *Historiography* (Oxford: Oxford University Press, 1999), pp. 54–72.

Bebbington, D.W., *Evangelicalism in modern Britain: A history from the 1730s to the 1980s* (London: Unwin Hyman, 1989).

Bell, Andrew, *An experiment in education, made at the male asylum at Egmore, Near Madras: Suggesting a system by which a school or family may teach itself under the superintendence of the master or parent* (London: Cadell and Davies, 1797).

Bellenoit, Hayden J.A., *Missionary education and empire in late colonial India, 1860–1920* (London: Pickering & Chatto, 2007).

Bennet, William, *The excellence of Christian morality: A sermon, preached before the Society in Scotland for Propagating Christian Knowledge, at the anniversary meeting, Thursday, 6th June 1799* (Edinburgh: J. Richie, 1800).

Berman, Edward H., 'American influence on African education: The role of the Phelps-Stokes Fund's Education Commissions', *Comparative Education Review*, 15:2 (1971), 132–145.

Bickers, Robert and Rosemary Seton (eds), *Missionary encounters: Sources and issues* (Richmond: Curzon Press, 1996).

Blackstock, Michael, 'The Aborigines Report (1837), A case study in the slow change of colonial social relations', *The Canadian Journal of Native Studies*, XX:1 (2000), 67–94.

Blouet, Olwyn M., 'Slavery and freedom in the British West Indies, 1823–33: The role of education', *History of Education Quarterly*, 30:4 (1990), 625–643, doi: 10.2307/368950.

Brock, Peggy, 'New Christians as evangelists', in Norman Etherington (ed.), *Missions and empire* (Oxford/New York: Oxford University Press, 2005), pp. 132–152.

Brown, Godfrey N., 'British educational policy in West and Central Africa', *The Journal of Modern African Studies*, 2:3 (1964), 365–377.

Bude, Udo, 'The adaptation concept in British colonial education', *Comparative Education*, 19:3 (1983), 341–355.

Burchell, Graham, Colin Gordon and Peter Miller (eds), *The Foucault effect: Studies in governmentality with two lectures by and an interview with Michel Foucault* (Chicago: University of Chicago Press, 1991).

Burnard, Trevor, 'British West Indies and Bermuda', in Robert L. Paquette and Mark M. Smith (eds), *The Oxford handbook of slavery in the Americas* (Oxford: Oxford University Press, 2010), pp. 134–153.

Burton, Antoinette M., 'The white woman's burden: British feminists and the Indian woman, 1865–1915', *Women's Studies International Forum*, 13:4 (1990), 295–308, doi: 10.1016/0277-5395(90)90027-U.

Buxton, Thomas Fowell, *Memoirs of Sir Thomas Fowell Buxton, Baronet* (ed. Charles Buxton) (London: John Murray, 1848).

Camiscioli, Elisa, 'Women, gender, intimacy, and empire', *Journal of Women's History*, 25 (2013), 138–148, doi: 10.1353/jowh.2013.0056.

Campbell, Carl, 'Towards an imperial policy for the education of Negroes in the West Indies after emancipation', *The Jamaican Historical Review*, 7 (1967), 68–104.

Carey, Hilary M. *God's empire: Religion and colonialism in the British World, c. 1801–1908* (Cambridge: Cambridge University Press, 2011).

Chakrabarty, Dipesh. *Provincializing Europe: Postcolonial thought and historical differences* (Princeton, NJ: Princeton University Press, 2000).

Chapman, Priscilla, *Hindoo female education* (London: R.B. Seeley and W. Burnside, 1839).

Chatterjee, Partha, 'Reflections on "Can the subaltern speak?" Subaltern studies after Spivak', in Rosalind C. Morris (ed.), *Can the subaltern speak? Reflections on the history of an idea* (New York: Columbia University Press, 2010), pp. 81–86.

Chaves, Mark, 'Secularization as disciplining religious authority', *Social Forces*, 72:3 (1994), 749–774, doi: 10.2307/2579779.

Clark, J.C.D., 'Secularization and modernization: The failure of a "grand narrative"', *The Historical Journal*, 55:1 (2012), 161–194, doi: 10.2307/41349650.

Coates, Daniel, John Beecham and William Ellis, *Christianity and the means of civilization: Shown in the evidence given before a Committee of the House of Commons, on Aborigines, by D. Coates, Esq., Rev. John Beecham, and Rev. William Ellis. Secretaries of the Church Missionary Society, the Wesleyan Missionary Society, and London Missionary Society. To which is added selections from the evidence of other witnesses bearing on the same subject* (London: R.B. Seeley and W. Burnside, L. and G. Seeley, and T. Mason, 1837).

Coolahan, John, 'Imperialism and the Irish national school system', in J.A. Mangan (ed.), *'Benefits bestowed'? Education and British imperialism* (Manchester: Manchester University Press, 1988), pp. 76–93.

Copland, Ian, 'Christianity as an arm of empire: The ambiguous case of India under the Company, c. 1813–1858', *The Historical Journal*, 49:4 (2006), 1025–1054, doi: 10.1017/S0018246X06005723.

Cowherd, R.G., 'The politics of English dissent, 1832–1848', *Church History*, 23:2 (1954), 136–143, doi: 10.2307/3161486.

Cox, Jeffrey, *The British missionary enterprise since 1700* (New York and London: Routledge, 2008).

Duff, Alexander, *The Church of Scotland's India mission; or a brief exposition of the principles on which that mission has been conducted in Calcutta, being the substance of an address delivered before the General Assembly of the Church, on Monday, 25th May 1835* (Edinburgh: John Waugh, 1835).

Dutta, Sutapa, *British women missionaries in Bengal, 1793–1861* (London: Anthem Press, 2017), online ISBN 9781783087273 via Cambridge Core.

Edmonds, Penelope, 'Travelling "under concern": Quakers James Backhouse and George Washington Walker tour the antipodean colonies, 1832–41', *The Journal of Imperial and Commonwealth History*, 40:5 (2012), 769–788, doi: 10.1080/03086534.2012.730830.

Edmonds, Penelope and Laidlaw, Zoë, '"The British government is now awaking": How humanitarian Quakers repackaged and circulated the 1837 Select Committee Report on Aborigines', in Samuel Furphy and Amanda Nettelbeck (eds), *Aboriginal protection and its intermediaries in Britain's antipodean colonies* (New York: Routledge, 2020), pp. 38–57.

Egger, Christine and Martina Gugglberger, 'Missionsräume/Missionary spaces', *Österreichische Zeitschrift für Geschichtswissenschaften*, 24:2 (2013).

Eisenstadt, S.N. 'Multiple modernities', *Daedalus*, 129:1 (2000), 1–29.

Elbourne, Elizabeth, *Blood ground: Colonialism, missions, and the contest for Christianity in the Cape Colony and Britain 1799–1853* (Montreal and Ontario: McGill-Queen's University Press, 2002).

Etherington, Norman, 'Education and medicine', in Norman Etherington (ed.), *Missions and Empire* (Oxford: Oxford University Press, 2005), pp. 261–284.

Evans, Stephen, 'Macaulay's minute revisited: Colonial language policy in nineteenth-century India', *Journal of Multilingual and Multicultural Development*, 23:4 (2002), 260–281.

Fearon, D.R., *School inspection*, 2nd edition (London: Macmillan and Co., 1876).

Findlay G.G. and W.W. Holdsworth, *The history of the Wesleyan Methodist Missionary Society, in five volumes* (London: The Epworth Press, 1921).

Foucault, Michel, *Discipline and punish: The birth of the prison*, trans. Alan Sheridan (London: Penguin Books, 1977).

Fuchs, Martin, Antje Linkenbach and Wolfgang Reinhard (eds), *Individualisierung durch Christliche Mission?* (Wiesbaden: Harrossowitz, 2015).

Gairdner, W.H.T., *Echoes from Edinburgh 1910: An account and interpretation of the World Missionary Conference* (New York: Layman's Missionary Movement, 1910).

Goodman, Joyce, Gary McCulloch and William Richardson, '"Empires overseas" and "Empires at home": Postcolonial and transnational perspectives on social change in the history of education', *Paedagogica Historica*, 45:6 (2009), 695–706, doi: 10.1080/00309230903384619.

Gordon, Shirley C., 'The Negro Education Grant 1835–1845: Its application in Jamaica', *British Journal of Educational Studies*, 6:2 (1958), 140–150.

Green, William A., *British slave emancipation: The sugar colonies and the great experiment, 1830–1865* (Oxford: Clarendon Press, 1976).

Grimshaw, Patricia and Andrew May (eds), *Missionaries, Indigenous peoples and cultural exchange* (Brighton, Portland and Toronto: Sussex Academic Press, 2010).

Gross, Izhak, 'The abolition of negro slavery and British parliamentary politics 1832–3', *The Historical Journal*, 23:1 (1980), 63–85.

Habermas, Rebekka and Richard Hölzl (eds), *Mission Global. Eine Verflechtungsgeschichte seit dem 19. Jahrhundert* (Köln, Weimar, Wien: Böhlau. 2014).

Hailey, Lord, *An African survey: A study of problems arising in Africa south of the Sahara* (Oxford: Oxford University Press, 1938).

Hall, Catherine, *Civilising subjects: Metropole and colony in the English imagination 1830–1867* (Cambridge: Polity, 2002).

Hatcher, Brian A, *Hinduism before reform* (Cambridge, MA and London: Harvard University Press, 2020).

Heartfield, James, *The Aborigines' Protection Society, humanitarian imperialism in Australia, New Zealand, Fiji, Canada, South Africa, and the Congo, 1836–1909* (London: Hurst & Company, 2011).

Hefner, Robert (ed.), *Conversion to Christianity: Historical and anthropological perspectives on a great transformation* (Berkeley: University of California Press, 1993).

Hodge, Alison, 'The training of missionaries for Africa: The Church Missionary Society's training college at Islington, 1900–1915', *Journal of Religion in Africa*, 4:2 (1971), 81–96.

Hogg, William Richey, *Ecumenical foundations: A history of the International Missionary Council and its nineteenth-century background* (New York: Harper & Brothers, 1952).

Holmes, Brian (ed.), *Educational policy and the mission schools. Case studies from the British Empire*, 2nd edition (London: Routledge & Kegan Paul, 2007).

Howitt, William, *Colonization and Christianity: A popular history of the treatment of the Natives by the Europeans in all their colonies* (London: Longman & Co., 1838).

Hunt, Alan, *Governing morals: A social history of moral regulation* (Cambridge: Cambridge University Press, 1999).

James, Henry Rosher, *Education and statesmanship in India, 1797–1910* (London and New York: Longmans, Green, 1911).

Jensz, Felicity, 'Non-European teachers in mission schools: Introduction', *Itinerario*, 40:3 (2016), 389–403, doi: 10.1017/S0165115316000620.

Jensz, Felicity and Hanna Acke (eds), *Missions and media. The politics of missionary periodicals in the long nineteenth century* (Stuttgart: Franz Steiner Verlag, 2013).

Johnson, Richard, 'Educational policy and social control in early Victorian England', *Past & Present*, 49:1 (1970), 96–119, doi: 10.1093/past/49.1.96.

Joseph, M.P., 'Missionary education: An ambiguous legacy', in David A. Kerr and Kenneth R. Ross (eds), *Missions then and now* (Oxford: Regnum Books International, 2009), pp. 105–120.

Kallaway, Peter, 'Conference litmus: The development of a conference and policy culture in the interwar period with special reference to the New Education Fellowship and British colonial education in Southern Africa', in Kim Tolley (ed.), *Transformations in schooling: Historical and comparative perspectives* (New York: Palgrave Macmillan, 2007), pp. 123–149.

Kallaway, Peter and Rebecca Swartz (eds), Special section: 'Imperial, global and local in histories of colonial education', *History of Education*, 47:3 (2018), 362–431.

Kalu, Ogbu, 'To hang a ladder in the air: Talking about African education in Edinburgh in 1910', in Chima J. Korieh and Raphael Chijioke Njoku (eds), *Missions, states, and European expansion in Africa* (New York and London: Routledge, 2007), pp. 101–126.

Kamphuis, Kirsten and Elise van Nederveen Meerkerk, 'Education, labour, and discipline: New perspectives on imperial practices and Indigenous children in colonial Asia', *International Review of Social History*, 65:1 (2020), 1–14, doi: 10.1017/S0020859019000750.

Kay-Shuttleworth, James, *Recent measures for the promotion of education in England* (London: Ridgeway, 1839).

Keegan, Tim, *Dr Philip's empire: One man's struggle for justice in nineteenth-century South Africa* (Cape Town: Zebra Press, 2016).

King, Kenneth, 'Africa and the southern states of the USA: Notes on J.H. Oldham and American Negro education for Africans', *Journal of African History*, 10:4 (1969), 659–677.

Kopf, David. *The Brahmo Samaj and the shaping of the modern Indian mind* (Princeton, NJ: Princeton University Press, 1979), doi: 10.2307/j.ctt13x0tkz.

Krige, Sue, '"Trustees and agents of the state"? Missions and the formation of policy towards African education, 1910–1920', *South African Historical Journal*, 40 (1999), 74–94.

Laidlaw, Zoë, '"Aunt Anna's report": The Buxton women and the Aborigines Select Committee, 1835–37', *The Journal of Imperial and Commonwealth History*, 32:2 (2004), 1–28, doi: 10.1080/03086530410001700381.

de Leede, Bente, 'Children between company and church: Subject-making in Dutch colonial Sri Lanka, c. 1650–1790', *BMGN – Low Countries Historical Review*, 135:3–4 (2020), 106–132, doi: 10.18352/bmgn-lchr.10880.

Lester, Alan, 'Humanism, race and the colonial frontier', *Transactions of the Institute of British Geographers*, 37:1 (2011), 132–148, doi: 10.1111/j.1475-5661.2011.00450.x.

Lester, Alan and Dussart, Fae, *Colonization and the origins of humanitarian governance: Protecting Aborigines across the nineteenth-century British Empire* (Cambridge: Cambridge University Press, 2014).

Leupolt, C.B., *Recollections of an Indian missionary*, new edition (London: Society for Promoting Christian Knowledge, 1863).

Levine, Philippa, *Gender and empire* (Oxford: Oxford University Press, 2004).

Levine, Roger S., *A living man from Africa: Jan Tzatzoe, Xhosa chief and missionary, and the making of nineteenth-century South Africa* (New Haven, CT: Yale University Press, 2011).

Lovett, Richard. *The history of the London Missionary Society, 1795–1895*, vol. 1 (London: H. Frowde, 1899).

Machin, G.I.T., 'Resistance to repeal of the Test and Corporation Acts, 1828', *The Historical Journal*, 22:1 (1979), 115–137.

Mangan, J.A. (ed.), *'Benefits bestowed'?: Education and British imperialism* (Manchester: Manchester University Press, 1988).

Martin, Mary Clare, 'Church, school and locality: Revisiting the historiography of "state" and "religious" educational infrastructures in England and Wales, 1780–1870', *Paedagogica Historica*, 49:1 (2013), 70–81, doi: 10.1080/00309230.2012.744070.

Marriot, John and Bhaskar Mukhopadhyay (eds), *Britain in India, 1765–1905* (London: Pickering & Chatto, 2006).

Maughan, Steven S., *Mighty England do good: Culture, faith, empire, and world in the foreign missions of the Church of England, 1850–1915* (Grand Rapids, MI: William B. Eerdmans Publishing Company, 2014).

May, Helen, Baljit Kaur and Larry Pochner, *Empire, education, and Indigenous childhoods: Nineteenth-century missionary infant schools in three British colonies* (Farnham: Ashgate, 2014).

McLeod, Hugh, 'Separation of church and state: An elusive (illusive?) ideal', in Karl Gabriel, Christel Gärtner and Detlef Pollack (eds), *Umstrittene Säkularisierung: Soziologische und Historische Analysen zur Differenzierung von Religion und Politik*, 2nd edition (Berlin: Berlin University Press, 2014), pp. 460–480.

McLisky, Claire, '"Due observance of justice, and the protection of their rights": Philanthropy, humanitarianism and moral purpose in the Aborigines Protection Society circa 1837 and its portrayal in Australian historiography, 1833–2003', *Limina: A Journal of Historical and Cultural Studies*, 11 (2005), 57–66.

Midgley, Clare, 'Mary Carpenter and the Brahmo Samaj of India: A transnational perspective on social reform in the age of empire', *Women's History Review*, 22:3 (2013), 363–385, doi: 10.1080/09612025.2012.726121.

Minton, Stephen J. (ed.), *Residential schools and Indigenous peoples: From genocide via education to the possibilities for processes of truth, restitution, reconciliation, and reclamation* (London: Routledge, 2019).

Möller, Esther and Johannes Wischmeyer (eds), *Transnationale Bildungsräume: Wissenstransfers im Schnittfeld von Kultur, Politik und Religion* (Göttingen: Vandenhoeck & Ruprecht, 2013).

Morris, Rosalind C. (ed.), *Can the subaltern speak? Reflections on the history of an idea* (New York: Columbia University Press, 2010).

Motte, Standish, *Outline of a system of legislation, for securing protection to the Aboriginal inhabitants of all countries colonized by Great Britain; extending to them political and social rights, ameliorating their condition, and promoting their civilization. Drawn up at the request of the committee of 'The Aborigines Protection Society,' for the purposes of being laid before the Government* (London: John Murray, Albermarle Street; Saunders and Otley, Conduit Street; Hatchard and Son, Piccadilly; Smith, Elder, and co, Cornhill, G. Fry, Bishopgate Street, Without; and W. Houlston, 35, High Holborn, 1840).

Munro, Doug and Andrew Thornley, 'Pacific Islander pastors and missionaries: Some historiographical and analytical issues', *Pacific Studies*, 23:3/4 (2000), 1–31.

Murphy, James, *Church, state and schools in Britain, 1800–1970* (London and New York: Routledge, 2007).

Novoa, Antonio, 'Empires overseas and empires at home', *Paedagogica Historica*, 45:6 (2009), 817–821, doi: 10.1080/00309230903370972.

Nyamnjoh, Francis B., '"Potted plants in greenhouses": A critical reflection on the resilience of colonial education in Africa', *Journal of Asian and African Studies*, 47:2 (2012), 129–154, doi: 10.1177/0021909611417240.

Page, Jesse, *The black bishop: Samuel Adjai Crowther* (London: Hodder and Stoughton, 1908).

Paisley, Fiona, 'Childhood and race: Growing up in the empire', in Philippa Levine (ed.), *Gender and empire* (Oxford: Oxford University Press, 2004), pp. 240–259.

Paranavitana, K., 'Suppression of Buddhism and aspects of Indigenous culture under the Portuguese and the Dutch', *Journal of the Royal Asiatic Society of Sri Lanka*, 49, new series (2004), 1–14.

Paterson, Andrew, '"The gospel of work does not save souls": Conceptions of industrial and agricultural education for Africans in the Cape Colony, 1890–1930', *History of Education Quarterly*, 45 (2005), 377–404, doi: 10.1111/j.1748-5959.2005.tb00040.x.

Paz, Denis, *Popular anti-Catholicism in mid-Victorian England* (Stanford, CA: Stanford University Press, 1992).

Pebbles, James Martin, *Buddhism and Christianity face to face; or an oral discussion between the Rev. Migettuwatte, a Buddhist Priest, and Rev. D. Sliva, an English Clergyman. Held at Pantura, Ceylon. With an introduction and annotations* (Boston: Colby and Rich, 1878).

Philip, John, *Researches in South Africa volume 1: Illustrating the civil, moral, and religious condition of the Native tribes: Including journals of the author's travels in the interior, together with detailed accounts of the progress of the Christian missions, exhibiting the influence of Christianity in promoting civilization* (London: James Duncan, 1838).

Pierard, Richard, 'The World Missionary Conference, Edinburgh 1910: Its shortcomings and historical significance', in Ulrich van der Heyden and Andreas Feldtkeller (eds), *Missionsgeschichte als Geschichte der Globalisierung von Wissen* (Stuttgart: Franz Steiner Verlag, 2012), pp. 299–306.

Piggin Stuart and Robert D. Linder, *Fountain of public prosperity: Evangelical Christians in Australian history* (Clayton: Monash University Publishing, 2018).

Pike, John Gregory, *Memoir of Mrs. Charlotte Sutton: A missionary to Orissa, East Indies* (Boston: Gould, Kendall & Lincoln, 1835).

Porter, Andrew, *Religion versus empire? British Protestant missionaries and overseas expansion, 1700–1914* (Manchester: Manchester University Press, 2004).

Prevost, Elizabeth, 'Troubled traditions: Female adaptive education in British colonial Africa', *The Journal of Imperial and Commonwealth History*, 45 (2017), 475–505, doi: 10.1080/03086534.2017.1332134.

Pritchard, John, *Methodists and their missionary societies 1760–1900* (Farnham: Ashgate, 2013).

Ranger, Terence, 'African attempts to control education in East and Central Africa 1900–1939', *Past & Present*, 32:1 (1965), 57–85, doi: 10.1093/past/32.1.57.

Reckord, Mary, 'The Jamaica slave rebellion of 1831', *Past & Present*, 40 (1968), 108–125.

Reed, Charles V., *Royal tourist, colonial subject and the making of a British world, 1860–1911* (Manchester: Manchester University Press, 2016).

Rich, Paul, 'The appeals of Tuskegee: James Henderson, Lovedale, and the fortunes of South African liberalism, 1906–1930', *The International Journal of African Historical Studies*, 20:2 (1987), 271–292, doi: 10.2307/219843.

Ritson, John H., 'The growth of missionary co-operation since 1910', *International Review of Mission*, 8:1 (1919), 53–70, doi: 10.1111/j.1758-6631.1919.tb01598.x.

Rooke, Patricia T., 'A scramble for souls: The impact of the Negro Education Grant on evangelical missionaries in the British West Indies', *History of Education Quarterly*, 21:4 (1981), 429–47.

Rothblatt, Sheldon, *Tradition and change in English liberal education: An essay in history and culture* (London: Faber and Faber, 1976).

Rowbotham, Judith, '"Hear an Indian sister's plea": Reporting the work of 19th-century British female missionaries', *Women's Studies International Forum*, 21:3 (1998), 247–261, doi: 10.1016/S0277-5395(98)00022-3.

Roy, Benoy Bhusan and Pranati Ray, *Zenana mission:. The role of Christian missionaries for the education of women in the 19th century Bengal* (Delhi: Indian Society for Promoting Christian Knowledge, 1998).

Ruberu, Ranjit, 'Missionary education in Ceylon', in Brian Holmes (ed.), *Educational policy and the mission schools: Case studies from the British Empire*, 2nd edition (London and New York: Routledge & Kegan Paul, 2007), pp. 73–114.

Rutz, Michael A., 'The problems of church and state: Dissenting politics and the London Missionary Society in 1830s Britain', *Church and State*, 48 (2006), 379–398.

Savage, David W., 'Missionaries and the development of a colonial ideology of female education in India', *Gender & History*, 9 (1997), 201–221, doi: 10.1111/1468-0424.00055.

Scott, David, 'Colonial governmentality', *Social Text*, 43 (1995), 191–220.

Seal, Anil, *The emergence of Indian nationalism: Competition and collaboration in the later nineteenth century* (Cambridge: Cambridge University Press, 1968).

Sedra, Paul, 'Exposure to the eyes of God: Monitorial schools and Evangelicals in early nineteenth-century England', *Paedagogica Historica*, 47:3 (2011), 263–281, doi: 10.1080/00309231003625562.

Seth, Sanjay, *Subject lessons: The Western education of colonial India* (Durham, NC: Duke University Press, 2007).

Sharkey, Heather J. (ed.), *Cultural conversions: Unexpected consequences of Christian missionary encounters in the Middle East, Africa, and South Asia* (Syracuse, NY: Syracuse University Press, 2013).

Shepperson, George, 'Ethiopianism and African nationalism', *Phylon*, 14:1 (1953), 9–18.

Sivasundaram, Sujit, *Islanded: Britain, Sri Lanka and the bounds of an Indian Ocean colony* (Chicago: University of Chicago Press, 2013).

Spivak, Gayatri Chakravorty, 'Can the subaltern speak?', in C. Nelson and L. Gross-bergs (eds), *Marxism and the interpretation of culture* (Basingstoke: Macmillan Education, 1988), pp. 271–313.

Stanley, Brian, *The World Missionary Conference, Edinburgh 1910* (Grand Rapids, MI: William B. Eerdmans Publishing Company, 2009).

Stephens, W.B., *Education in Britain 1750–1914* (Basingstoke and London: Macmillan Press, 1998).

Stewart, James, *Lovedale, South Africa: Illustrated by fifty views from photographs* (Edinburgh and Glasgow: Andrew Elliot and David Bryce and Son, 1894).

Stock, Eugene, *The history of the Church Missionary Society: Its environment, its men and its work*, vols 1–3 (London: Church Missionary Society, 1899).

Stoler, Ann L., 'Making empire respectable: The politics of race and sexual morality in 20th-century colonial cultures', *American Ethnologist*, 16:4 (1989), 634–660.

Strong, Rowan, 'A vision of an Anglican imperialism: The annual sermons of the Society for the Propagation of the Gospel in Foreign Parts 1701–1714', *Journal of Religious History*, 30 (2006), 175–198, doi: 10.1111/j.1467-9809.2006.00447.x.

Swartz, Rebecca, *Education and empire: Children, race and humanitarianism in the British settler colonies, 1833–1880* (Cham: Palgrave Macmillan, 2019).

Thompson, Todd, 'The Evangelical Alliance, religious liberty, and the evangelical conscience in nineteenth-century Britain', *Journal of Religious History*, 33:1 (2009), 49–65, doi: 10.1111/j.1467-9809.2009.00746.x.

Tschurenev, Jana, 'Diffusing useful knowledge: The monitorial system of education in Madras, London and Bengal, 1789–1840', *Paedagogica Historica*, 44:3 (2008), 245–264, doi: 10.1080/00309230802041526.

Turner, Mary, *Slaves and missionaries: The disintegration of Jamaican slave society, 1787–1834* (Urbana, Chicago and London: University of Illinois Press, 1982).

van der Veer, Peter, *Conversion to modernities: The globalization of Christianity* (New York and London: Routledge, 1996).

Volz, Stephan, 'The rise and fall of the Moffat Institution: Mission education in a colonial borderland', *South African Historical Journal*, 66:3 (2014), 470–485.

Walls, Andrew F., 'Distinguished visitors: Tiyo Soga and Behari Lal Singh in Europe and at home', in Judith Becker and Brian Stanley (eds), *Europe as the Other: External perspectives on European Christianity* (Göttingen: Vandenhoeck & Ruprecht, 2014), pp. 243–254.

Whewell, William, *Of a liberal education in general; and with particular reference to the leading studies of the University of Cambridge* (London: John W. Parker, West Strand, 1845).

Whitehead, Clive, 'The contribution of the Christian missions to British colonial education', *Paedagogica Historica*, 35, sup 1 (1999), 321–337, doi: 10.1080/00309230.1999.11434947.

Wickramasinghe, Nira, 'Colonial governmentality: Critical notes from a perspective of South Asian studies', *Comparativ: Zeitschrift für Globalgeschichte und Vergleichende Gesellschaftsforschung*, 21:1 (2011), 32–40.

Wilberforce, William, *An appeal to the religion, justice, and humanity of the inhabitants of the British Empire, in behalf of the Negro slaves in the West Indies* (London: J. Hatchard and Son, 1823).

Winks, Robin W. (ed.), *Historiography, The Oxford history of the British Empire*, vol. 5 (Oxford: Oxford University Press, 1999).

Wolffe, John, 'Anti-Catholicism and evangelical identity in Britain and the United States, 1830–1860', in Mark A. Noll, David W. Bebbington and George A. Rawlyk (eds), *Evangelicalism: Comparative studies of popular Protestantism in North America, the British Isles, and beyond, 1700–1990* (New York and Oxford: Oxford University Press, 1994), pp. 179–197.

Yates, Barbara A., 'African reactions to education: The Congolese case', *Comparative Education Review*, 15:2 (1971), 158–171.

Yates, Timothy, 'Mission conferences', in Jonathan J. Bonk (ed.), *The Routledge encyclopaedia of missions and missionaries* (New York and London: Routledge, 2010), pp. 256–259.

Websites and online databases/sources

Empire online: www.empire.amdigital.co.uk [last accessed 16 February 2016]

Oxford Dictionary of National Biography (Oxford University Press): www.oxforddnb.com [last accessed October 2020]

The Stanford Encyclopedia of Philosophy (Winter 2010 edition), Edward N. Zalta (ed.), John Hare, 'Religion and Morality': http://plato.stanford.edu/archives/win2010/entries/religion-morality/] [last accessed 28 June 2013]

UK Parliament, Commons and Lord Hansards 1803–2005: http://hansard.millbanksystems.com/index.html [last accessed 24 December 2016]

Index

EU authorised representative for GPSR:
Easy Access System Europe, Mustamäe tee 50,
10621 Tallinn, Estonia
gpsr.requests@easproject.com